Language, Education and Discourse:

Functional Approaches

Open Linguistics Series

Series Editor
Robin Fawcett, University of Wales, Cardiff

This series is 'open' in two senses. First, it provides a forum for works associated with any school of linguistics or with none. Most practising linguists have long since outgrown the unhealthy assumption that theorizing about language should be left to those working in the generativist–formalist paradigm. Today large and increasing numbers of scholars are seeking to understand the nature of language by exploring one or other of various cognitive models of language, or in terms of the communicative use of language, or both. This series is playing a valuable part in re-establishing the traditional 'openness' of the study of language. The series includes many studies that are in, or on the borders of, various functional theories of language, and especially (because it has been the most widely used of these) Systemic Functional Linguistics. The general trend of the series has been towards a functional view of language, but this simply reflects the works that have been offered to date. The series continues to be open to all approaches, including works in the generativist–formalist tradition.

The second way in which the series is 'open' is that it encourages studies that open out 'core' linguistics in various ways: to encompass discourse and the description of natural texts; to explore the relationships between linguistics and its neighbouring disciplines – psychology, sociology, philosophy, cultural and literary studies – and to apply it in fields such as education, language pathology and law.

Recent titles in this series

Classroom Discourse Analysis: A Functional Perspective, Frances Christie
Construing Experience through Meaning: A Language-based Approach to Cognition, M.A.K. Halliday and Christian M.I.M. Matthiessen
Cognition, M.A.K. Halliday and Christian M.I.M. Matthiessen
Culturally Speaking: Managing Rapport through Talk across Cultures, Helen Spencer-Oatey (ed.)
Development of Language, Geoff Williams and Annabelle Lukin (eds)
Educating Eve: The 'Language Instinct' Debate, Geoffrey Sampson
Empirical Linguistics, Geoffrey Sampson
Genre and Institutions: Social Processes in the Workplace and School, Frances Christie and J.R. Martin (eds)
The Intonations Systems of English, Paul Trench
Language, Education and Discourse, Joseph A. Foley (ed.)
Language Policy in Britain and France: The Processes of Policy, Dennis Ager
Multifactorial Analysis in Corpus Linguistics: A Study of Particle Placement, Stefan Thomas Gries
Pedagogy and the Shaping of Consciousness: Linguistic and Social Processes, Frances Christie (ed.)
Register Analysis: Theory and Practice, Mohsen Ghadessy (ed.)
Relations and Functions within and around Language, Peter H. Fries, Michael Cummings, David G. Lockwood and William Spruiell (eds)
Researching Language in Schools and Communities: Functional Linguistic Perspectives, Len Unsworth (ed.)
Summary Justice: Judges Address Juries, Paul Robertshaw
Syntactic Analysis and Description: A Constructional Approach, David G. Lockwood
Words, Meaning and Vocabulary: An Introduction to Modern English Lexicology, Howard Jackson and Etienne Zé Amvela
Working with Discourse: Meaning beyond the Clause, J.R. Martin and David Rose

Language, Education and Discourse:

Functional Approaches

Edited by Joseph A. Foley

Continuum
The Tower Building
11 York Road
London SE1 7NX

15 East 26th Street
New York
NY 10010

First published 2004 by Continuum
This paperback published in 2005

British Library Cataloguing-in-Publication Data
A catalogue record for this book is available from the British Library.

ISBN 0-8264-6187-5 (HB)
0-8264-8801-3 (PB)

Library of Congress Cataloging-in-Publication Data
A catalog record for this book is available from the Library of Congress.

Typeset by BookEns Ltd, Royston, Herts
Printed and bound in Great Britain by MPG Books Ltd, Bodmin, Cornwall

Contents

Tables vii
Figures viii
Contributors x
Acknowledgements xii

1 Introduction 1
Joseph A. Foley

PART ONE: CHILDHOOD AND THE GROWING DEVELOPMENT OF DISCOURSE 17

2 Representing the Child as a Semiotic Being (One Who Means) 19
M.A.K. Halliday

3 Reading Picture Reading: A Study in Ideology and Inference 43
Ruqaiya Hasan

4 Learning Language: Learning Culture in Singapore 76
Linda Thompson

5 A Framework for Tracing the Development of Children's Writing in Primary Schools 97
Joseph A. Foley and Cheryl Lee

6 An Analysis of a Children's History Text 120
Bridget Goom

PART TWO: DISCOURSE IN SECONDARY AND TERTIARY LEVELS OF EDUCATION 143

7 Revisiting Some Old Themes: The Role of Grammar in the Teaching of English 145
Frances Christie

8 What Should We Teach about the Paradoxes of English Nominalization? 174
Carolyn G. Hartnett

9 Discourses in Secondary School Mathematics Classrooms According to Social Class and Gender 191
Kay L. O'Halloran

10 Teaching Radha to (Re-)Write: Authority, Positioning, Discourse 226
Anneliese Kramer-Dahl

11 The Evaluation of Causal Discourse and Language as a Resource for Meaning 255
Bernard Mohan and Tammy Slater

12 Sense and Sensibility: Texturing Evaluation 270
J.R. Martin

13 On the Preferential Co-occurrence of Processes and Circumstantial Adjuncts: Some Corpus Evidence 305
Fiona C. Ball and Gordon Tucker

Index 325

Tables

2.1 Examples of material to semiotic transformations
2.2 Examples of pragmatic and mathetic: Nigel 1.6–1.9
3.1 Semantic distance: different points of view, different significance
5.1 Text types
5.2 MOOD in the Primary 1–6 texts
5.3 Types of Adjuncts in the Primary 1–6 texts
5.4 Categories of the total number of MOOD Adjuncts
5.5 Transitivity in the Primary 1–6 texts
5.6 Circumstances in the Primary 1–6 texts
5.7 An analysis of logical relations in the Primary 1–6 texts
5.8 THEME in the Primary 1–6 texts
8.1 Nominalizations in first paragraphs
8.2 Analysis of two *Science* articles about the same research
9.1 SFL systems according to function and rank
9.2 Exchange Structure
9.3 MOOD Adjuncts
9.4 Tenor relations
9.5 Classification of mathematical register items
9.6 Grammatical metaphor and experiential meaning
9.7 LOGICO-SEMANTIC relations: teacher and student
9.8 Classification and components of Theme selections
11.1 Assumptions of SFL and traditional grammar *Source*: Adapted from Derewianka (1999: 19)
11.2 Language features of the two explanations
12.1 Interpersonal resources across strata
12.2 Types of JUDGEMENT
13.1 Frequency of circumstantial Adjuncts with Material and Mental processes
13.2 Number of Adjunct types co-occurring with each process
13.3a Most frequent Adjunct types (>1 per cent occurrence) co-occurring with Material processes
13.3b Most frequent Adjunct types (>1 per cent occurrence) co-occurring with Mental processes
13.4a Percentage of Adjunct types by subclass co-occurring with Material processes
13.4b Percentage of Adjunct types by subclass co-occurring with Mental processes

Figures

2.1 Moving and meaning
2.2 Stages in Nigel's protolanguage: NL1, 0.9–10½
Source: Halliday 1975
2.3a Nigel's construal of 'difference' at 1.7½–1.9
Source: Phillips 1985.
2.3b Nigel's construal of 'difference' at 1.9–1.10½
Source: Phillips 1985.
2.4a Nigel's first stratification of the content plane: 13 months
2.4b Nigel's first stratification of the content plane: 14 months
4.1 SFL analysis of Clause 1
4.2 Clause 2
4.3 Clause 3
4.4 Clause 4
4.5 Clause 5
4.6 Clause 6
4.7 Clause 7
4.8 Clause 8
4.9 Clause 9
4.10 Clause 10
4.11 A summary of the socio-semiotic perspective
Source: Adapted from Martin (1997).
5.1 The organization of language teaching and learning
Source: Curriculum Planning and Development Division, Ministry of Education (2001: 4–6).
5.2 Four pictures used for a story writing task
5.3 Components of the language network system
9.1 The Curriculum Macrogenre, Lesson Genres and Microgenres
9.2 Lesson 1 as a sequence of Microgenres
9.3 Lesson 2 as a sequence of Microgenres
9.4 Lesson 3 as a sequence of Microgenres
9.5 Section of board text: lesson 3
9.6 Section of board text: lesson 2
9.7 Section of board text: lesson 1
9.8 Semantic orientation of discourses
12.1 JUDGEMENT and APPRECIATION as institutionalized feeling

12.2 Interpersonal discourse semantics in relation tenor
12.3 APPRAISAL systems: ENGAGEMENT, ATTITUDE and GRADUATION
12.4 Appraisal keys for media discourse
12.5 Layers of Theme and New
12.6 Strategies for encoding attitude – inscribe, invite, provoke
12.7 Aboriginal Australians in chains
12.8 The Governor Sir Charles and Lady Gairdner with Abbot Gomez inspecting the children of St Joseph's Orphanage, New Norcia, Western Australia
12.9 Newspaper photograph of six young stolen children waiting to be adopted
12.10 Images, imagery and the construal of evaluation
12.11 Sense and sensibility as complementarities

Contributors

Fiona C. Ball and Gordon Tucker lecture at the Centre for Language and Communication, Cardiff University, UK.

Frances Christie is Emeritus Professor of Language and Literacy Education at the University of Melbourne and Honorary Professor of Education at the University of Sydney, Australia.

Joseph A. Foley is a language specialist with the Southeast Asian Ministers of Education Organization (SEAMEO), Regional Language Centre (RELC) Singapore.

Bridget Goom has been a part-time lecturer and tutor with the Department of English Language and Literature, The National University of Singapore and The Open University, UK.

M.A.K. Halliday is Emeritus Professor of Linguistics at the University of Sydney, Australia.

Carolyn G. Hartnett is Emeritus Professor, College of the Mainland, Texas, USA.

Ruqaiya Hasan is Emeritus Professor of Linguistics at Macquarie University, Sydney, Australia.

Anneliese Kramer-Dahl is an Associate Professor at the National Institute of Education, Singapore.

Cheryl Lee has been a researcher in the Department of English Language and Literature, The National University of Singapore.

J.R. Martin is Associate Professor of Linguistics at the University of Sydney, Australia.

Bernard Mohan is Professor in the Department of Language Education, The University of British Columbia, Canada.

Kay L. O'Halloran is an Assistant Professor with the Department of English Language and Literature, The National University of Singapore.

Tammy Slater is a researcher in the Department of Language Education, The University of British Columbia, Canada.

Linda Thompson is Professor of Education and Director of the Language and Literacy Studies Research and Teaching Group at the University of Manchester, UK.

Acknowledgements

The authors and publishers wish to thank the following for permission to use copyright material. All possible care has been taken to trace ownership of the materials included and to provide full acknowledgement of their use. Where proper acknowledgement has not been made, the authors and publishers invite copyright holders to inform them of the oversight.

Evans Brothers, for extracts from *Christopher Columbus: The Discovery of the New World* by Clint Twist (1993).

Archives and Production, Australian Institute of Aboriginal and Torres Strait Islander Studies, Canberra, for permission to reproduce photographs in the chapter 'Sense and Sensibility: Texturing Evaluation'.

1

Introduction

Joseph A. Foley

> Each one of us has this ability (to use language) and [each one of us] lives by it; but we do not always become aware of it or realise fully the breadth and depth of its possibilities.

Halliday (1971: 10) wrote this in his *Introduction to Language in Use* (Doughty *et al.* 1971) and it has become a recurring concern of language teaching in the classroom ever since. The value of discourse and an awareness of the power of discourse are concepts that have to be taught explicitly in the classroom.

Discourse is defined as 'language as a form of social practice'. We use language in ways that are socially determined (conventional) and that have social effects (language maintains social relationships). Consequently, we cannot separate 'language' and 'society'. However, language is realized through 'text', which is the record of the actual words exchanged, while 'discourse' includes the processes of production and interpretation of the text. Therefore, 'texts' do not have intrinsic meanings: meanings emerge from the way texts are located and used in particular social and interactional contexts. That is to say, from the interpretative strategies and world knowledge that readers bring to them.

Assumptions about language and society are reflected in traditional sociolinguistics. The understanding is that social processes arise from the behaviours of individual people when interacting with each other and pursuing their own strategies and goals.

Fairclough (1989) argues that social structures (such as institutions, social class, gender, ethnicity) constrain the activities of individuals in systematic ways, which tend to serve the interests of dominant groups in society. Consequently, in any discourse, participants are able to take up only certain roles. For example, in classroom discourse, where there is a pupil and a teacher role, the recognizable structures of classroom discourse depend on participants agreeing to play these roles. Thus people reproduce and help maintain social and institutional structures by entering into discourses, which require such structures to be understood. This means that 'power' is diffused throughout our daily social and institutional practices because simply by taking up social roles, we are inducted into particular ways of using language and viewing the world.

In some ways, we are trapped inside the discourses we inhabit in our everyday lives, and the ways we are positioned shape our notions of what counts as 'truth' and 'knowledge' and how we think about our own identity. In a systemic functional model of language which forms the theoretical basis for the studies in this present volume, the language of discourse is seen essentially as a system of choices – in fact a system of multiple systems of choices. The various 'texts' that are involved in this discourse are a result of the linguistic choices that speakers/writers make. Consequently, such choices depend on – are determined by – a multiplicity of factors, factors that make our 'choices' far from independent.

The discourse found in education, particularly in what we read and what we write (literacy), is not something autonomous as it is often presented, but as Street (1994) has argued, it is only 'one subculture's view'. In other words, there are in reality varieties of literacy practices carried out in different domains (see Barton and Ivanic 1991). Literacy is more 'ideological' as language and discourse since it is not a fixed set of skills to be learned, but rather new and different skills, which emerge in new and different roles, contexts and domains of knowledge. Literacy, therefore, placed in the larger framework of discourse, is essentially a social process. While the term 'ideological' is necessary because there are always contests around defining and teaching literacy, with power relations embedded in these contests.

The way in which discourse is looked at in this book means that the social processes of learning and the ideologies involved are imbued with the moral philosophy of a society and the education system. This requires taking account of historical and cross-cultural perspectives in classroom practices and of students' own growing awareness of language activities they are involved in and their ideological meanings. Discourse and awareness of how discourse can be used, therefore, is seen to involve imparting a point of view, a way of life, as well as teaching technical skills.

Teachers, in particular, need to be ideologically aware of how language is being used in education and they also need to focus on changing institutions, so that they can become more responsive to learners. This means being more open to the knowledge and skills pupils bring to their learning and more aware of the new roles they are asking learners to take on, with all the implications that these new roles will have for society.

The International Systemic Functional Congress on 'Linguistics and Education on Entering the Twenty-First Century' held in Singapore in 1999 tried to address some of these problems. Several of the papers presented are published in this volume, other contributions have been added to give a more rounded picture of the development of discourse from early infancy through pre-school, primary and secondary schooling, into tertiary education and beyond.

Part One covers early childhood and the growing development of a language system from the basic semiotic system of the infant. As language develops we see, at the same time, the potential for cognitive development, with inferencing playing a key role from quite an early stage. This is followed by the beginnings of literacy with its ideological content already appearing even in kindergarten. As a child moves through primary school, the child's writing can be traced in a systematic way such that the development can be clearly mapped out with reference to the way writing is being taught. To end this first part of the discussion on 'discourse and education', the ideological content of reading material used in primary schools is examined, in this case with reference to a historical figure, a well-established practice in primary schools.

Part Two looks at discourse in secondary and tertiary levels of education. It poses questions about the role of teaching 'grammar' in the school system and the earlier misconceptions about its importance in developing the discourse of the young learner. Then the various contributions look at what characterizes secondary and tertiary levels of discourses and the critical awareness that is necessary not only in subject areas such as mathematics but also in our own writing as teachers. Finally, the language and discourse in education is examined in terms of how to take account of the sort of refinement brought about by looking closely at areas of the network system of 'choices' available to us, such as 'appraisal' or probabilistic features of grammar that can be revealed through corpus-based studies.

1.1 Part One

The first study in this collection is by M.A.K. Halliday: 'Representing the Child as a Semiotic Being (One Who Means)'. He argues against the too commonly held view that a child's language development is a kind of progressive approximation to a goal that is extrinsically fixed, that each new step towards that goal has to be seen as an imperfect attempt to 'acquire' the mother tongue. At each phase of their semiotic development, children have to create forms of expression. But these are not imitations of adult symbolic forms, as the infant brain is not yet able to interpret adult symbols simply because the infant body is not yet able to produce them.

From very early in its development, the brain of the infant is simultaneously directing the body to move (to control itself and its environment) and directing it to mean (to construe itself and its environment). But all such construal is a social process dependent on social symbols and at this stage control is dependent on body movements, since such symbols have to take on material (perceptible) form. For example, the ability to roll over or later to sit up may appear to be a simple act but is an important stage in the infant's development as it allows the child to see the world from different perspectives.

Protolanguage, the child's first 'verbal' semiotic system, interlocks development of material and semiotic resources by being able to communicate by moving and by oral utterances at the same time. Furthermore, the protolinguistic stage allows children to expand their meaning potential and also realize the limits imposed on this expansion by the nature of the protolanguage itself: since it has no lexicogrammatical system, it cannot function to construct a model of experience or to develop a dynamic of dialogue.

The transition from protolanguage to the mother tongue, which allows this expansion, is the transition from primary to higher order consciousness. The critical factors in this development, as far as the semantic interface is concerned, are memory and consciousness of self. Memory allows the child to generalize common nouns to make referential meaning, while consciousness of self allows a systematic distinction to be made between 'how things are' (declarative statements) and 'how I want it to be' (imperative).

Halliday identifies what he sees as the outstanding problems in trying to represent the child as one who is learning as analogous to the building-up of the physical potential that is taking place in the child's own body. Ultimately, both are aspects of the development of brain power and the interaction that is going on in the brain as it builds up these resources. Future research in this area, Halliday feels, must be directed towards studies of individual brain development on the one hand and large-scale corpus studies of natural data from very small children on the other.

In 'Reading Picture Reading: A Study in Ideology and Inference',

Ruqaiya Hasan presents an investigation based on the data she collected from the longitudinal study into the everyday talk between mothers and children from 1984–88. Specifically this part of the data covers child and teacher discourse in the kindergarten.

Hasan suggests that for human beings to go beyond the information given is something quite natural. In fact there is a good case for maintaining that to understand something is to know what it implies, what can be inferred from it.

The question naturally arises: What is it that favours the selection of one inference rather than another from the 'same' information? Hasan sees information as having two stages: first, the need to recognize information for what it is; and second, how a person's position in society will affect how we perceive and interpret a situation.

In the history of describing 'thinking' in society, generalization, abstraction, problem solving, logical inference, etc. have often been attributed to 'systematic instruction and more complex forms of communication' (Luria 1976). That is to say, it is not a natural mental activity, but in fact learned in the experience of instructional discourse, which is characteristically associated with schooling.

Hasan examines some examples of classroom discourse at the level of the kindergarten to see if there is any indication of the shaping of the foundation of 'thinking' that is normally attributed to schooling. She sees teachers as not (re-)producing knowledge per se, in that the discourse does not represent 'complex forms of communication', but rather as the regulative discourse talked about by Bernstein (1996), which acts on the learning subject in that it first and foremost regulates the mind. That is to say, the teachers in kindergarten are already engaged in shaping the consciousness of the young children who might one day interrogate the existing body of knowledge and eventually participate in the production of knowledge.

However, Hasan also points out that although the teacher's discourse is materially available to all students, it does not mean that they all necessarily engage with the discourse in the same way. There is no doubt that systematic instruction and complex forms of communication involving concepts and their relations have the potential to shape scholarly consciousness, but there are also good reasons to doubt that they actually perform this function for every child in the school. The single most important reason for this is the education system's reluctance to recognize multiple points of view that exist in the classrooms of our pluralistic societies. For the dominating classes, the discourse of control makes principles of power and authority invisible, while information is made explicit.

Hasan's claim is that such discourse is already evident, even in kindergarten, and in order to bring about social change through school instruction, a form of communication has to be devised which will overcome the problem of failure in schools. A starting point is to recognize that in pluralistic societies there are different ways of saying and meaning and that the unilateral interaction so common in our classrooms may not be the only one to develop the 'thinking child'.

In 'Learning Language – Learning Culture in Singapore', Linda Thompson presents an analysis of a short rhyme. *Mr Frog* is extracted from a collection of rhymes written specifically for teaching reading in the National Trade Union Council (NTUC) Childcare Co-operative in Singapore. The author of this collection is an influential pre-school educator and the collection is used as teaching material in kindergartens and child-care centres throughout Singapore.

In Hasan's 1985 study of the nursery rhyme she stated, '[it] is simply learnt in such a diffuse way that . . . it is one of the most invisible acts of learning' (1985: 28). It is this invisibility that makes the nursery rhyme of particular significance.

Thompson examines this 'invisibility' in the discourse by analysing the transitivity and mood systems and placing these in their cultural and situational contexts. From this 'deconstruction' of the discourse, Thompson looks at the ways in which the text functions as a means of transmitting and creating social and cultural values, specifically in relation to the Singapore government's stated national priorities of social coherence and nation-building. She further suggests that rhyme does more than entertain or amuse the child reader, it can also be an agent in transmitting prevalent social values within a particular culture. Unlike nursery rhymes, which are typically recited for entertainment purposes, the *Mr Frog* rhyme has additional social significance because it was written as an 'educational text' to be included in the NTUC childcare curriculum. The rhyme genre socializes the reader into modes of thinking dominant in a literate society, especially within the educational context. Hence it is suggested that the rhyme plays a role in shaping the attitudes, behaviour and thinking of its readers.

While it is true that this study presents an adult reading and view of the text, Thompson raises a number of key questions that are crucial and related to ideology and discourse, even at this early stage of a child's language development:

- What do children understand when they read the *Mr Frog* rhyme?

- How do the adults and parents who read *Mr Frog* with and for children understand the text?
- What grammar of social practice are young Singaporeans internalizing when they read the *Mr Frog* text?

In the next study in this section Joseph Foley and Cheryl Lee present 'A Framework for Tracing the Development of Children's Writing in Primary Schools'. The purpose of such a framework would be to give some indication of how a child's growing control of discourse is developing. As McCarthy and Carter (1994) suggested, the better a text analyst the teacher can be, the better equipped their students are likely to be in using the language appropriately.

The context of this study is again Singapore, where English is the medium of education for most children. The approaches to the teaching of English, which have recently been introduced in Singapore, give this study a wider significance as they are similar to those that have been used in Australia and the United Kingdom. Almost all children in Singapore use more than one language and how much the way of 'writing' in different languages can affect the development of writing in a particular language is a factor that has to be considered. Consequently, this study selected students who were considered to be equally fluent and literate in two languages. Having said this, the main focus was on the students' need to understand how a language system works (regardless of the language) and how language conventions can vary according to purpose, audience, context and culture, and apply this knowledge particularly to their writing in both formal and informal situations.

As Bernstein had already pointed out in 1979, teachers have no systemic means for successful language use but fall back on the same values and negative comments, none of which informs the writers in any precise way about their strengths or weaknesses or offers strategies for improvement. This is what he called the nature of language becoming increasingly invisible.

In order to make the use of language more visible, a framework for tracing the development of children's writing in primary schools is proposed in this study. The analysis is on two levels: the 'macro-level' of the schematic structure of the texts in the data and a micro-analysis using a lexico-grammatical analysis constructed around selected components of the language network system.

In the macro-level the main text-types that were used in the primary schools in Singapore were 'Observation-Comment', 'Recount' and 'Narrative'. The limited number of text-types being taught was a consequence of the way the writing section of the Primary School Leaving Examinations (PSLE) was implemented. Indeed, the resulting data show that the students are very proficient in writing 'stories' at the end of their primary schooling. However, there is little development in the more 'factually' oriented text-types, something which the introduction of the new text-based language syllabus is, hopefully, rectifying.

At the micro-level the interpersonal, ideational and textual metafunctions are all necessary to establish a developmental framework by which to analyse the children's written language. However, to make the framework 'workable', only key components of the language network system were selected. At this level of analysis the data indicated an increase in the use of hypotactic and embedded clauses as the children moved from the early stages of primary schooling to their final year in Primary six (age 12). There are indications that there is an increase in the use of a greater variety of conjunctions and marked themes, which normally signals a more efficient rhetorical organization of the discourse. However, tense agreement and the lack of internal conjunctions with some rather formulaic use of adjuncts did sometimes affect overall coherence.

What this study also shows is that a workable framework can be established for tracing the progression of the pupils' writing through their years in primary school by establishing a portfolio of their writings at each level of their primary schooling. Such a portfolio allows the teacher to analyse the children's texts in more detail and give indicators of where the strengths and weaknesses of the individual child might be found.

Such a detailed 'account' of the child's writing can then be passed on to the secondary school. Given the particular context of Singapore, further studies are necessary to look at the developing written discourse in the other languages that the child commands. Such studies have become even more important because of the introduction of the text-type approach to language teaching which is presently being implemented in the schools.

In the final study in this section, Bridget Goom presents an 'Analysis of a Children's History Text'. She looks at an example of a multisemiotic approach to 'text' and how the discourse is developed by examining how the different semiotic threads relate to each other.

The text is written for 9–13 year olds and the focus of Goom's argument is the importance of developing a multimodal approach to literacy in order that the child understands not just the text in terms of wording but also the visual presentations and the ideas conveyed in these visuals. Using a systemic-functional framework, the study shows how the author of a history 'textbook' for children moves in his discourse from congruent construals to metaphorical ones and consequently making judgements and evaluations that are often implicit. Such judgements and evaluations are derived consciously or otherwise from what are described as the 'grand narratives' of the history writers' and history learners' cultures.

The 'text' is one from a series of children's illustrated (pictures, diagrams, maps, explanatory boxes) history textbooks designed for upper primary schools in the UK. The 'field' is that of school history texts which are recontextualizations from the academic field of history (Bernstein 1996). And as Goom quoting Davies (1996) states, in Western cultures, the academic field of history traditionally sees itself as autonomous and often tied to support the political status quo. The 'tenor' for the modern history text may be less the 'authoritarian-sounding' expert but rather that of the role of demystifier of a historical event or personage, as in the case of the iconic figure presented here, Christopher Columbus.

The 'mode' is not just a written text but one that contains multisemiotic presentations of the historical figure and the circumstances that surrounded his life. How much space the author gives to historical generalizations to make the choice of historical icon more explicit can be largely determined by what point of view the author presents to his readers. Consequently, what the young reader might know or not know is very important.

Goom identifies and discusses three areas of 'what young readers might not know': general (non-historical knowledge), historical knowledge and textual knowledge.

In addition to such background knowledge, there is the young readers' experience in terms of social positioning, as the projection by the writer can very often be that of insider/outsider relationship. In this particular case, the use of 'we' and 'us' presupposes accepting a perspective on the relative importance of Columbus and the 'discovery of America'. The 'we' also includes the supposition that the readers have access to information which is presented as definitive facts rather than a result of long and often acrimonious debates.

Goom underlines in her discussion the visual information in the text, where the writing may carry one set of meanings and the images another. However, what seems to be important in a text like this is the integration between images and written text, which can either give overall coherence or create a lack of coherence. The latter case can be particularly unfortunate in a textbook written for children. Goom also points out such inadequacies in this text where the juxtapositioning of crucial information is often missing, thus affecting the interpretation of the visuals.

Finally, Goom looks at the whole process of the use of 'appraisal' in the text, in particular the often implicit judgements and evaluations so frequently found in history text. Various 'themes' are examined such as 'greed', 'failure' and ignorance' together with the broader theme of the European conquest of America. As she points out, it is noticeable that in the final implied judgement of the writer the 'history of the human race' is 'reduced to 'European history'.

2.2 Part Two

One of the most enduring problems that teachers of English have in schools, particularly in secondary schools, is what we do in terms of teaching 'knowledge about language' where the term refers to any area of overt teaching about language, including grammar. In the first study, 'The Role of Grammar in the Teaching of English', Frances Christie discusses this topic with secondary school teachers in Australia. However, the relevance is really much wider as exemplified by the KAL (Knowledge About Language) Project (Carter 1990) in the United Kingdom. Christie sets the scene of her study by outlining the historical background to what has been the contentious nature of the issues of teaching knowledge about language.

Christie describes here how the project was conceived out of interest in addressing the relevance of overt teaching of functional grammar as a means of enhancing the general literacy proficiency of junior secondary students. First, the intention was, in consultation with the English teachers involved, to identify the kinds of text-types they expected their students to read and write. Second, it was to engage directly with the grammatical features of these text-types with the teachers, so that they might teach these overtly as part of their teaching programmes.

As a more direct outcome of this study, two textbooks were produced with the intention of complementing the teacher-training programmes that had been developed. *Language and Meaning 1* was an introduction to the study of KAL for first-year secondary school students, focusing on verbal and non-verbal means of communication, functions of language, language-learning and language systems.

The second book, *Language and Meaning 2*, although a sequel to the first book, pushed the boundaries further in attempting to make both teachers and students more aware of language and literacy and knowledge about language.

Arguments in favour of explicit teaching of the constituent structures of English are because currently both teachers and students, particularly in junior secondary schools, seem to be so bereft of knowledge in this area. This has created a necessary tension in both the understanding of grammar and the teaching of it, which is to do with reconciling the claims of an understanding of both the constituent structure and the functional use.

However, no matter how much we might debate such matters as what is the best point of departure in teaching different age groups, pedagogical decisions will always be significantly influenced by the historical context in which one works. Different educational ideologies will prevail at different times but the one constant element will always be knowledge of how to use effectively the discourse in society.

It is the explicit teaching of a particular (but important) constituent structure of language that is the subject of the next study by Carolyn Hartnett: 'What Should We Teach about the Paradoxes of English Nominalization?' She summarizes the history of nominalizations in Western science and contrasts it with a brief look at its use in another language, Thai. This is followed by a discussion on the frequency of nominalizations in a wide variety of publications and a discussion on the teaching of nominalizations because of its increasing importance in modern-day discourse.

The sort of nominalizations discussed here are nouns that appear to be made by changing a verb either internally or by adding an ending, such as *-ation*. In Systemic Functional Grammar this type of grammatical metaphor is called verb-change nominalizations. It is an important feature of discourse because it appears in a large range of situations, such as abstractions and generalizations in humanities, to explain or interpret changes in social sciences, to name processes and to classify and measure in the physical sciences. So, for example, Hartnett illustrates what she means by the following sentence: 'Examination of split-brain patients both before and after surgery is another tool for the unmasking of such processes.' Heavily modified nominalizations such as this one reduce clausal complexity but also results in 'packing' more lexical content and thus producing greater lexical density, which can sometimes become problematic for the reader to interpret but which is nevertheless extremely common in modern written discourse and therefore something that students need to be aware of in both their reading and their writing.

Kay O'Halloran's study, 'Discourse in Secondary School Mathematics Classrooms According to Social Class and Gender', looks at three mathematics lessons and their discourse, differentiated on the basis of social class and gender. What O'Halloran found was that lessons with working-class students and private school female students were more oriented towards interpersonal meaning where the tendency is towards a deferential position in power relations at the expense of the mathematical content. In lessons with male students in a private school, the ideational content is foregrounded against interpersonal aspects of language of power dominating relations. With the students in the private school, the analysis of experiential and logical meaning also revealed a greater accord with the formal discourse of mathematics. The greater frequency that was found of non-technical mathematical register and non-generic texts in the lesson with working-class students suggested that scaffolding of mathematical discourse does not occur.

The results of the analysis across the three lessons are then situated in the broader context of Bernstein's sociological theory of pedagogical practices and the relationship between educational achievement, language and social structure. Finally O'Halloran suggests that her analysis indicates that single-sex schools can be instrumental in perpetuating stereotypical gender constructions of masculinity and femininity.

Anneliese Kramer-Dahl explores through the case study 'Teaching Radha to (Re-)Write' the need to assemble a critical writing pedagogy with trainee teachers, especially if they are to be aware of how language is used within their own lives and the lives of others. While various critical literacy curricula have been proposed around reading as a sociocultural practice, as previously indicated with the work of Street (1994), less attention has been given to the phenomenon of writing. Even though a move from critical reading to a critical writing pedagogy involves the application of similar critical literacy principles, most notably repositioning students as researchers of their own literacy practices and problematizing classroom texts, in a critical writing class these critical literacy principles are applied to the students' own written discourse rather than that of others.

Building on Comber's (1994) key critical literacy principles, the students were asked to, first, research their own past classroom practices with regard to writing in relation to the part these practices played in alienating them from writing, and, second, undertake a critical reading of specific instances of their present writing within the context of their present role as trainee teachers. They were also asked to reflect on how their writing was received by their teachers and to explore ways, linguistic and otherwise, of crafting more authoritative positions for themselves within the given pedagogical constraints.

Bernard Mohan and Tammy Slater present 'The Evaluation of Causal Discourse and Language as a Resource for Meaning'. The authors point out that Systemic Functional Linguistics has produced a volume of work that has made significant advances in the analysis and assessment of discourse. Such advances are particularly important for assessing the discourse of learners of English as a second language in tertiary education.

However, the question which is posed in this contribution is whether present evaluation theories and practices do what they are supposed to do or as the authors state, '[illuminate] some of the confusion surrounding the assessment of discourse'. To address this question the authors examine the evaluation of causal explanations, an essential part of academic literacy. The example that was used was an explanation of the water cycle using a diagram. One 'explanation' was written by a secondary school teacher whose first language is English and the second by a university student who speaks English as a second language. Both writers were presented with a visual of the water cycle, a series of events that are linked causally, and their written explanations each construct an account of the water cycle. What Mohan and Slater found was disturbing in both theory and practice such that it seriously questioned the adequacy of present models designed to assess competence in a second language. Assessment was often reduced to what were termed 'competent explanations' without any need to go further. That is to say, that to analyse the discourse of causal explanations seemed unnecessary as long as the writers did not violate the basic rules of the language. In other words, competence did not go beyond rule-based assumptions of language.

However, causal discourse was chosen precisely because of its importance as part of the metalanguage of science and an essential part of scientific literacy. Also, causal explanations are important because they are not limited to science, since they occur across many academic disciplines. If language assessment instruments at university level are not capable of dealing adequately with causal explanations in terms of their underlying discourse apart from surface-level 'grammar', one would have to put into question the value of such assessment procedures specifically in relation to scientific literacy and even academic literacy in general.

The last two studies look at areas of discourse which are attracting more and more attention: appraisal (something already touched upon in Goom's research) and the use of corpora in evolving a more probabilistic approach to discourse patterns.

In 'Sense and Sensibility: Texturing Evaluation', J.R. Martin considers aspects of the role played by evaluation in texturing discourse. Although the analysis of evaluation has tended to be marginalized in linguistics, it plays a powerful role in the organizing of discourse. Such a role becomes more transparent in texts relating to highly charged political issues. In considering the texture of evaluation, Martin claims that we need to consider in a holistic way the role of appraisal, imagery and images since they co-articulate the stance that multimodal texts naturalize for viewers and readers.

However, in order to deal with the texture of evaluation, we need a framework for interpersonal resources in English that moves beyond traditional concerns with speech function and exchange structure. Following Halliday's work on the grammar of MOOD, early work on interpersonal discourse analysis leaned towards the interactive dimension. That is to say, the ways in which one interacts with 'give and demand, goods and services and information'. Later work on more specific areas such as secondary school and workplace discourse revealed a need for this essentially grammatical perspective on interactivity to be complemented with a more lexically based focus on 'personal' meanings. So alongside 'negotiation' were developed systems for evaluating meaning, which are referred to by Martin (1997) and White (2000) as 'appraisal'.

What Martin does in this study is to examine a number of different texts: first, from the 'Stolen Generations' issue in Australia and then from several other texts and uses the resources of 'appraisal' (Attitude, Engagement and Graduation) to show how evaluation takes place in the text from a linguistic point of view. As Martin indicates, this study in the development of our appreciation of discourse and, in particular, the texture of evaluation opens up other 'sites' for examination, such as the role played in negotiating social relations and, perhaps even more important, across modalities: verbiage and imagery.

Finally, in 'On the Preferential Co-occurrence of Processes and Circumstantial Adjuncts: Some Corpus Evidence' Fiona Ball and Gordon Tucker set out to explore any potential preferential co-occurrence patterns in discourse that might throw light on the nature of the relations between 'Processes' and attendant 'Circumstances'. For example, one such broad assumption that might be questioned is the relative freedom of Circumstantial Adjuncts in co-occurrence with Processes, in particular the co-occurrence and its correlation with the semantics of Processes. Corpus-based studies, such as the one described here, are necessary to attain the delicacy of description to which modern large-scale studies of discourse aspire. Without such data, statements on the co-occurrence relations between processes and circumstances would either have to remain at a high level of generality or be purely speculative. The accuracy and delicacy of description of English and any other language is clearly important in both language learning and teaching. As this study shows, the co-occurrence phenomena, in terms of colligation and collocation, are important aspects of the development of linguistic competence for both the native speaker of English and the foreign or second language learner. Perhaps even more importantly, the kinds of significant co-occurrence patterning that corpus investigation reveals go well beyond the general phenomena that tend to suggest a neat grammatical-versus-ungrammatical distinction. If we assume that most patterning in a large corpus, especially when found in significant quantities, is grammatical, then we are dealing with probabilistic grammar, or the probability of certain lexico-grammatical patterns occurring rather than others. This is a finding that could have considerable implications for the study of discourse in general and discourse in education in particular.

References

Barton, D. and R. Ivanic (eds) (1991) *Writing in the Community*. London and Newbury Park, CA: Sage.

Fairclough, N. (1989) *Language and Power*. London: Longman.

Halliday, M.A.K. (1971) Introduction. In R. Doughty, J. Pierce and G. Thornton (eds), *Language in Use*. London: Edward Arnold.

Street, B.V. (1994) Cross-Cultural Perspectives on Literacy. In J. Maybin (ed.), *Language and Literacy in Social Practice*. Clevedon: Multilingual Matters and Open University.

PART ONE

CHILDHOOD AND THE GROWING DEVELOPMENT OF DISCOURSE

2

Representing the Child as a Semiotic Being (One Who Means)

M.A.K. Halliday

When I first worked on children's language development, back in the early 1970s, I used to stress that we should pay children the courtesy of treating them as meaningful beings. Now, I hope, this much can be taken for granted. But taking children's acts of meaning seriously is only the first step, the prerequisite for understanding how language develops. The next step is to put these acts of meaning into focus; and that can be rather complex, since it involves shifting our focus along (at least) two dimensions. First, acts of meaning have value both in themselves and as instances of underlying systems – systems of meaning potential; so we need to focus on the **instance**, and also to focus on the system. Second, acts of meaning constitute both a particular stage in a child's development and part of an ongoing progression through time; we need to focus on the **moment**, and also to focus on what we might call the **momentum**. And it might be added that, as observers, we are at the same time both recording and interpreting. Representing children's language is unavoidably a theoretical activity.

One only has to observe about the first half hour of a newborn infant's life to recognize that here is a social creature, whose personality is formed out of the conjunction of material and semiotic modes of being. Like any other small mammal, of course, the human child is bonded to its mother materially, for food, warmth and loving care; but beyond that the human infant is also bonded semiotically from the start through the exchange of attention. Already in the early 1970s Colwyn Trevarthen had recorded, on film, how within a few days of birth the newborn baby would address its mother and respond to being addressed: when its mother's face came into view, the baby's whole being became animated, with movement of arms, legs and head, and facial gestures of all kinds, to which the mother responded in her turn. When the mother's attention was withdrawn, the baby's movements subsided and its body became listless and inactive. As yet there is no clear distinction in the baby's behaviour between material and semiotic acts. All such bodily activity is, of course, displacement of matter, subject to the laws of physics; but it is also, as Bateson (1975) had observed, a kind of 'proto-conversation' – the sharing of attention between infant and mother is actually an exchange of meaning. If we were using the terms favoured by natural scientists, we would talk about 'matter' and 'information' as the two phenomenal domains which we inhabit (cf. Williams 1992); these are incommensurable – matter *being* measure *in* mass, length etc. and information being in bytes. But 'information' is a misleadingly loaded term and even the assumption that it can be measured (like matter) needs to be questioned. I prefer to talk about 'matter' and 'meaning' – the material and the semiotic. Matter is displaced, meaning is exchanged; I suppose we could use the general term 'movement' for both. My point is that in trying to understand early infancy we are faced with a unity of the material and the semiotic. The human infant cannot yet talk, just as it cannot yet walk; neither its body nor its brain has developed to that degree. But both body and brain are being stretched in anticipation of both these tasks.

Representing the newborn child's protoconversation (or 'protosemiosis') is easy, it just needs a VCR, a video-audio recording of the event. This is because the baby's behaviour is not yet systemic: apart from the rather clear distinction between the two states, addressing and not addressing, which is a choice of on or off, within the 'addressing' behaviour itself there is no systematic variation in meaning. To demonstrate this point, suppose we now leap forward – say three years. At three years old the child is a fluent speaker of at least one human language, maybe two or three and also controls various other semiotic modalities besides: producing and recognizing facial expressions and other patterns of non-verbal bodily behaviour, recognizing three-dimensional representations (pictures and models), and operating with a range of symbolic value systems, some realized through language and others not. Representing the semiotic potential of a three year old is a very different matter.

Let me stick with the three year old for a moment to outline just what such representation entails. First and foremost, of course, it means representing the child's language. This is now, by age three, fully systemic; that is to say, each instance has meaning by virtue of selection – as a choice from a vast network of possibilities, all the things that might have been meant but were not. We would need to represent this network of options. But it is not just a single network, because the child's language is now stratified: it has a grammar and phonology as its core. Each of these has its own systemic potential, and each in turn interfaces with the material world: the grammar impinges on the world of the child's experience and interpersonal relationships, via the interface level of semantics; the phonology impinges on the world of the child's own body (the 'signifying body'; see Thibault 2004), via the interface levels of phonetics and kinetics; and each of these interfaces has, in turn, its own systemic potential. In other words, recognizing what children can do with language – what they can mean – by the age of three years means using some form of representation, such as system networks, to display their powers in semantics, in lexico-grammar, in phonology and in phonetics, as well as, of course, the relations they have established among all these different strata of language. Without this kind of theoretical interpretation, a simple record of children's utterances can give only an impoverished account of their striking ability to mean.

Now we have the theoretical resources for representing this ability to mean, because the language of the three year old, although still fragmentary by comparison with that of adults, already has the formal organization of the adult language system. So we can represent it the way we represent adult languages: using phonetic and phonological notations for the expression strata, structural and/or feature representations for the strata of the 'content'. But what about the stages that are rather earlier in time, intermediate between birth and the advanced age of three? How do we track children's progression after those first semiotic encounters within a few days of being born?

Let us set up a schematic framework for the first half of this period, from birth to 18 months, showing the child's development on both fronts – the material and the semiotic. When we take these together, we find notable parallels between phases of moving and phases of meaning (Figure 2.1).

And this is where we may notice an interesting phenomenon. At each phase of their semiotic development, children have to create forms of expression – 'Signifiers', if you like, although the 'sign' in its strict sense is a feature only of a particular phase. Where do these signifying expressions come from? They are not imitations of adult symbolic forms, because the infant brain is not yet able to interpret adult symbols and the infant body is not yet able to produce them. What happens is that bodily actions (including both movement of the

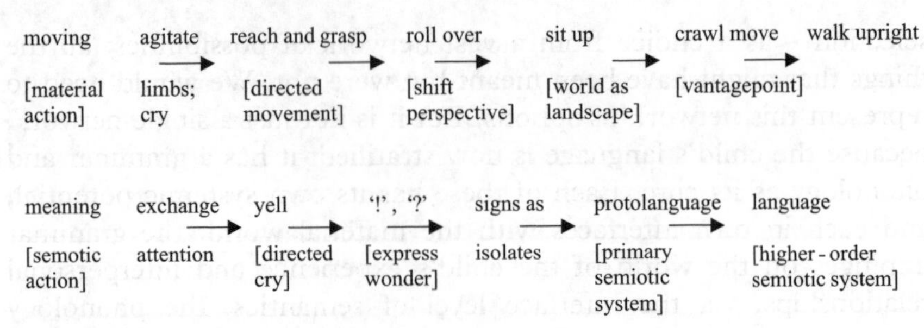

Figure 2.1 Moving and meaning

limbs and the sound-producing movements of the vocal organs) get borrowed, as it were – co-opted into use as symbolic expressions. There is a regular and constant passage from the material to the semiotic, the semiotic powers raiding the material domain for meaning-making resources (rather in the way that, in human societies, cultural practices that start off by being socially functional get co-opted for use in ritual, symbolic contexts).

The first instance of this transference takes place relatively early in infancy, when the cry gets transformed into a yell. A yell is a **directed** cry, a cry that is turned into a message: this semiotic development is analogous to the material development whereby the action of stretching the arms and clasping the fists is gradually transformed into reaching out and grasping – in other words, to action that is directed towards some object in the field of vision. (In the semiotic sphere, of course, 'directed' means directed at a person, or addressed.) But this same process of material to semiotic transformation continues right through into the protolanguage, although, of course, with increasing variation among individual children. Table 2.1 shows some examples from the data.

Possibly the use of intonation (rising and falling pitch) as a primary semiotic resource falls into the same category, although the material origins are not so clear. Traces of this process remain in 'adult' language, such as 'yuk!' derived from the sound of vomiting and 'yum!' from smacking the lips to get the last morsels of a taste.

Table 2.1 Examples of material to semiotic transformations

Form of expression	Material context	Transformed semiotic significance
cry	pain	'do something!'
high-pitched squeak	alarm	'what's going on?'
clasping fist	grasping object	'I want (to hold/be given) that'
sigh	release of tension	'now we're together'
raising and lowering	rhythmic movement	'put music on, sing me a song'
alteration of w/y posture	sucking + vocalization	'I want to be cuddled'

From very early in its development, the brain of the infant is simultaneously directing the body to move (to **control** itself and its environment) and directing it to mean (to **construe** itself and its environment). Of course, the construal takes place within the brain itself, as the infant's primary consciousness develops epigenetically into the higher-order consciousness that is (apparently) uniquely human; but all such construal is a social process, dependent on social symbols – and that takes us back to the body, since such symbols have to take on material (perceptible) form.

When infants learn to roll the body over, to move from prone to supine and then from supine to prone, they now for the first time control their own perspective and can observe the world systematically from these two complementary angles. By this time they have become highly curious, wanting to observe whatever is going on around them. This curiosity may also be transformed into meaning, with some vocal sign such as a squeak, meaning 'what's going on?', again derived, like the yell, from a self-monitored material event, a noise of alarm, and just as they respond to the yell, caregivers typically interpret these squeaks semiotically and respond to them by giving some explanation. But it is at the next stage, when infants learn to sit up, that their view of the world becomes integrated into a coherent landscape, and it is at this stage that they decide (so to speak!) to mean in earnest – to give full value to the semiotic act, as a distinct and self-sufficient form of activity. At first this takes the form of a few isolated simple signs, with meanings such as 'I'm curious: what's happening?', 'I want that', 'I don't want that', 'play with me' and suchlike – although even here we begin to notice different functional orientations, and the isolates are now clearly emerging as signs; that is, as content/expression pairs, such that both the content (the signified) and the expression (the signifier) remain stable over a period of time (even though it may be, in our adult terms, a very short period, sometimes as little as around three to five days).

This relative stability of the sign is a necessary condition for enabling such isolates to develop into a semiotic system, and this is the next phase – that of the protolanguage. The protolanguage is the child's first semiotic system. In terms of 'meaning and moving', the interlocking development of material and semiotic resources, protolanguage is associated with crawling. When infants learn to crawl (that is, to move themselves unaided from place to place), they are able to see the world in three dimensions, shifting the angle of observation at their will, and this gives an added dimension to their perceptions. It is at this phase that they become able to construe their meaning potential into systems, in this way developing their first real language in which meaning is created paradigmatically: each utterance has meaning because it is an instance of a systemic choice. And this is where we need to pause and take stock.

The protolanguage is child tongue, not mother tongue. It is created by the child, in interaction with its caregivers and any other members of its small meaning group (who normally respond to it in their own adult tongue), as a primary semiotic which will eventually lead, via a transitional phase, into the 'mother tongue' of childhood, adolescence and beyond. But it is still itself a primary semiotic (that is, a semiotic of primary consciousness), not a higher-order semiotic as adult languages are; that is to say, it has no lexicogrammar (no structures and no words) in it. Its elements are still simple signs, content/expression pairs. What is new is that these are no longer isolated elements: they enter into systemic contrasts, within a small number of definable functional domains. I was able to identify four such domains to start with: the instrumental, the regulatory, the interactional and the personal (Figure 2.2). I referred to these as 'microfunctions', to contrast with the more abstract functional components of the later, transitional and mother tongue phases of children's speech.

As far as the expression is concerned, children will create their protolinguistic signifiers out of anything that is to hand – or to mouth – provided that they can perform it and that those who exchange meanings with them respond. One source I have already referred to is by borrowing from the material domain. Another source is imitation – which can also be a source of confusion for those involved if it is an imitation of adult speech sounds, because the meaning is not (and cannot be, because the protolanguage is not yet referential) that which the others are disposed to assign to it. Other expressions seem to be just plucked out of the air, so to speak – out of the child's repertory (of sound or gesture) as it happens to be at the time.

It is when we consider the task of 'representing the child', however, that with the protolanguage an entirely new issue arises. Up to this point, the child's behaviour has been pre-systemic: signs have been created instantially, and existed only at the level of performance – they could be recorded, as sounds or gestures, but not theorized in general terms. There was no general principle behind them, no systemic potential – and hence no predictability. The phase of one or two isolated signs is transitional: the time of the protolanguage – and this is what justifies us in referring to it as a form of 'language' – the

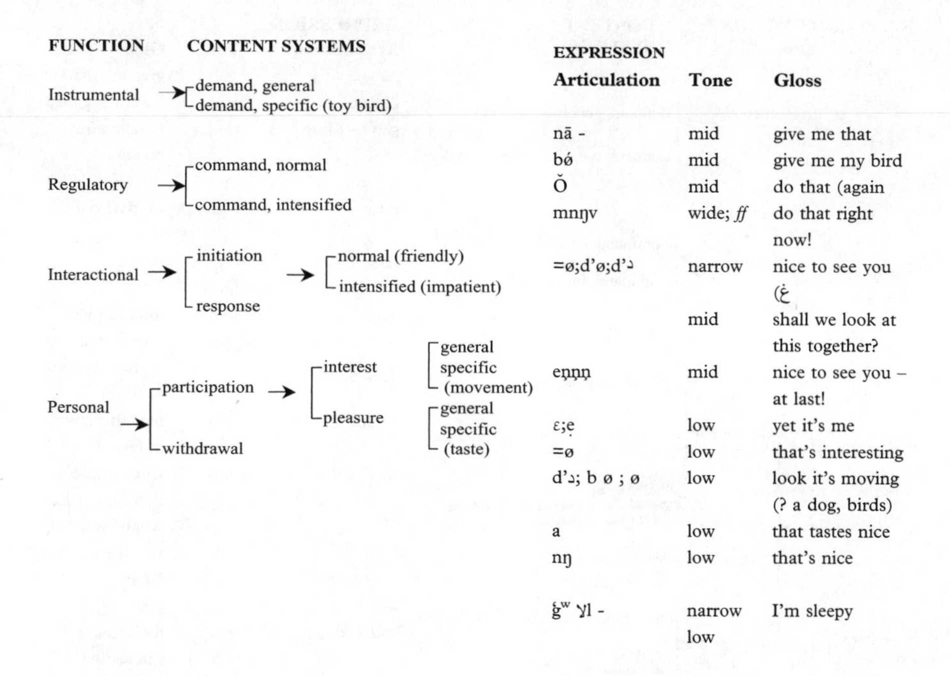

Note: All above on falling tone; mid = mid fall, narrow low = low fall over narrow interval, ἐc. Similarly in Figure 2, except where otherwise shown.

At 0.9, Nigel had two such meanings, both expressed as [Ø] on mid or mid-low falling tone; one interactional, 'let's be together', the other (usually with the wider interval) personal, 'look, its moving'. He also had another three meanings expressed gesturally: two instrumental, 'I want that', grasping object firmly, and 'I don't want that' touching object lightly; and one regulatory, 'do that again', touching person or relevant object firmly (e.g. 'make that jump in the air again'). The gestures disappeared during NL 1–2.

In this and subsequent Figures, favourite items are indicated by *, and rare or doubtful items by?. Where two or three items are related in both meaning and sound these are shown by =, accompanied by an index number where necessary – indicates that the syllable is repeated (-), (-) indicates typical number of optional repetitions.

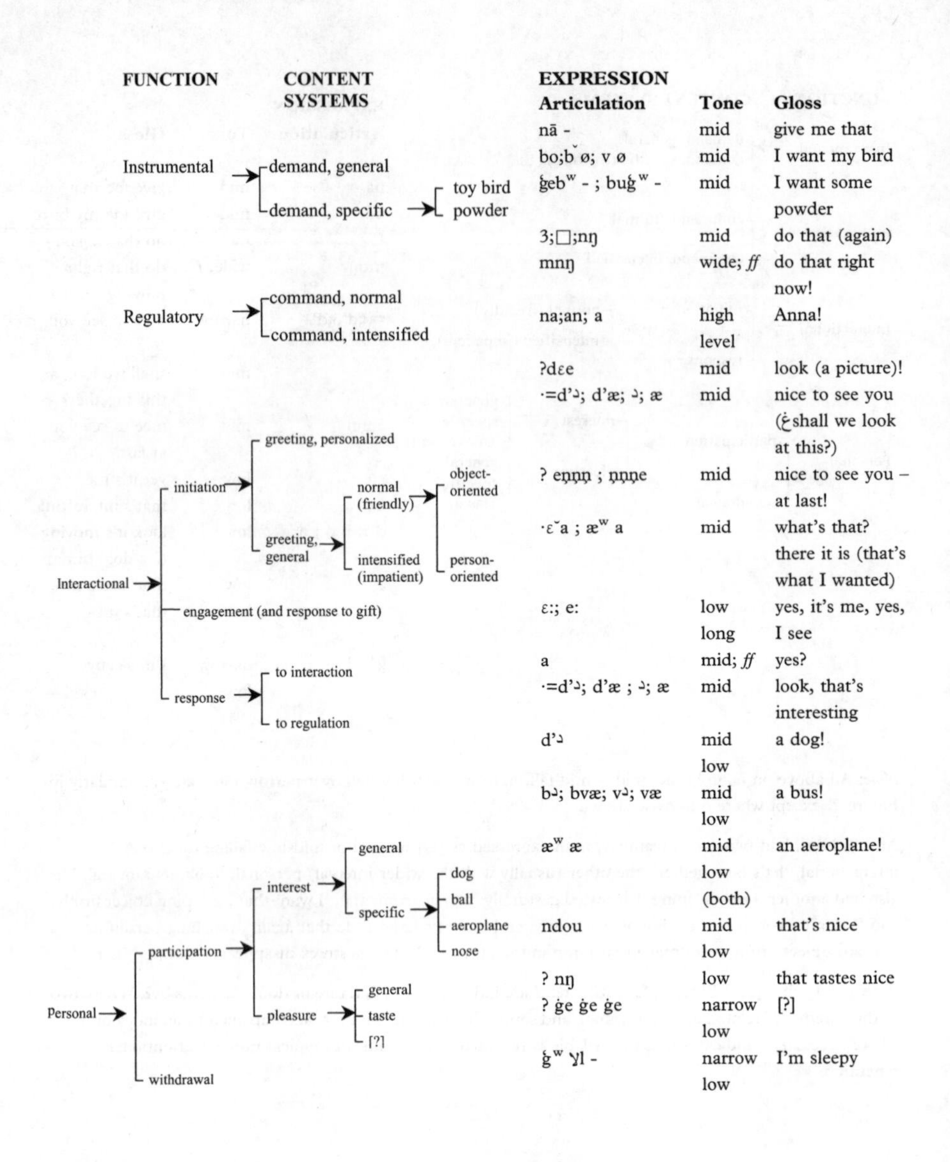
FUNCTION
CONTENT SYSTEMS
EXPRESSION
Articulation
Tone
Gloss
Instrumental
demand, general
demand, specific
toy bird
powder
nā -
mid
give me that
bo;bˇø; v ø
mid
I want my bird
ġebʷ - ; buġʷ -
mid
I want some powder
Regulatory
command, normal
command, intensified
ʒ;□;nŋ
mid
do that (again)
mnŋ
wide; ff
do that right now!
na;an; a
high level
Anna!
Interactional
initiation
greeting, personalized
greeting, general
normal (friendly)
intensified (impatient)
object-oriented
person-oriented
engagement (and response to gift)
response
to interaction
to regulation
ʔdɛe
mid
look (a picture)!
·=d'ɔ; d'æ; ɔ; æ
mid
nice to see you (¿shall we look at this?)
ʔ eŋŋŋ ; ŋŋŋe
mid
nice to see you – at last!
·ɛˇa ; æʷ a
mid
what's that? there it is (that's what I wanted)
ɛ:; e:
low long
yes, it's me, yes, I see
a
mid; ff
yes?
·=d'ɔ; d'æ ; ɔ; æ
mid
look, that's interesting
Personal
participation
interest
general
specific
dog
ball
aeroplane
nose
pleasure
general
taste
[?]
withdrawal
d'ɔ
mid low
a dog!
bɔ; bvæ; vɔ; væ
mid low
a bus!
æʷ æ
mid low (both)
an aeroplane!
ndou
mid low
that's nice
ʔ nŋ
low
that tastes nice
ʔ ġe ġe ġe
narrow low
[?]
ġʷ ɣl -
narrow low
I'm sleepy

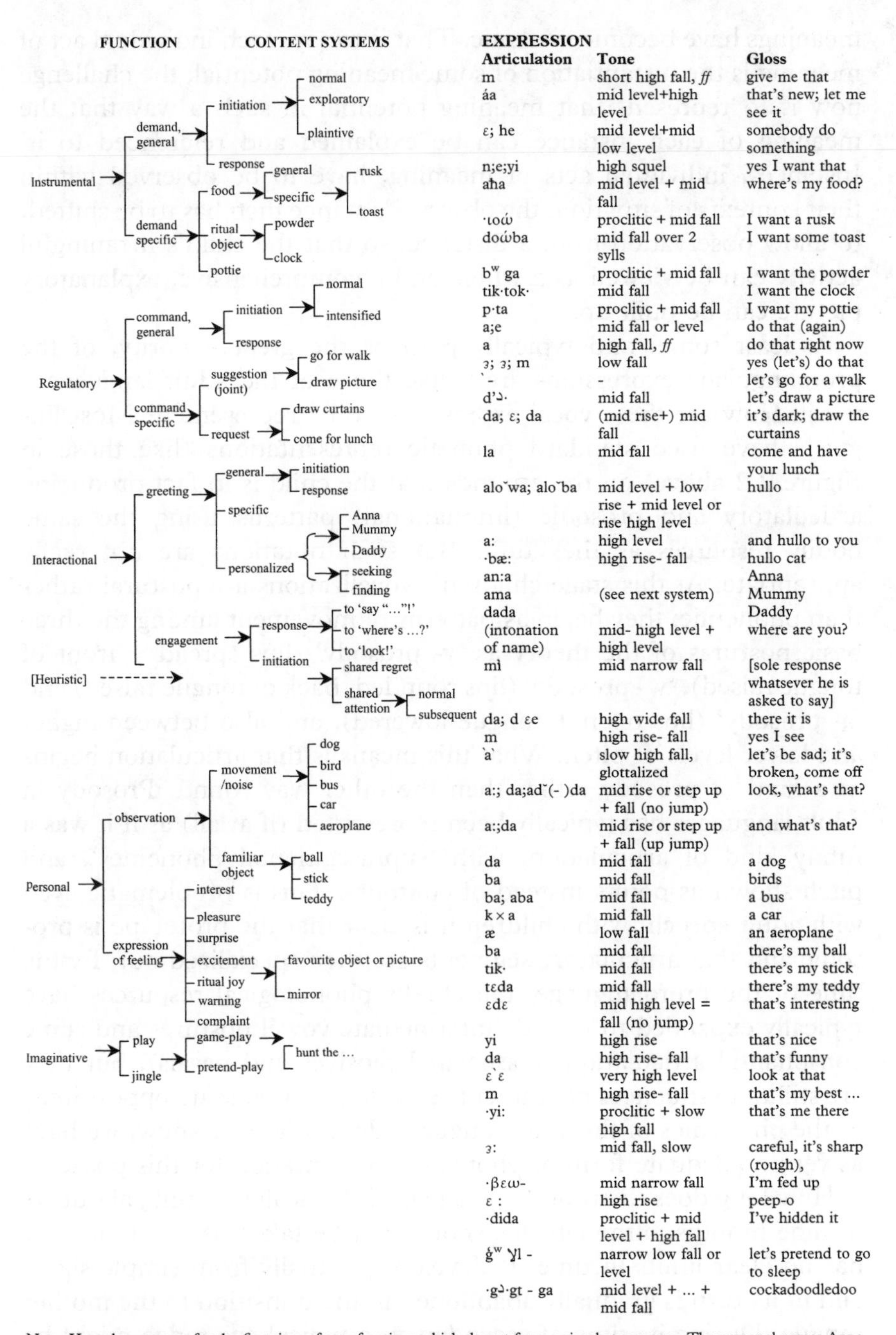

Note: Here there occurs for the first time of set of options which do not form a simple taxonomy. The personal names Anna, Daddy, Mummy combine either with stepping up high level tone, meaning 'where are you', or with mid fall plus low level tone, meaning 'hullo, there you are!' This involves a level of coding intermediate between content and expression.

Figure 2.2 Stages in Nigel's protolanguage: NL1, 0.9–10½
Source: Halliday 1975.

meanings have become systemic. That is to say, each individual act of meaning is the instantiation of some meaning potential; the challenge now is to represent that meaning potential in such a way that the meaning of each instance can be explained and referenced to it. Instances, individual acts of meaning, have to be observed within their contexts of situation; the observer's stance then has to be shifted, to allow observation from a distance, so that the child's meaningful activity can be viewed as a whole and a comprehensive, explanatory picture can be built up.

At least some, and typically perhaps the great majority, of the protolinguistic expressions are – like those of the adult language – vocal. How are these vocal expressions to be represented? Most linguists have used standard phonetic representations (like those in Figure 2.2 above) on the grounds that the child is in fact producing articulatory and prosodic (intonational) patterns using the same bodily resources as the adult. But such notations are not really appropriate. At this stage children's vocalizations are postural rather than phonemic: they begin as patterns of movement among the three basic postures of the theory as 'y- prosody' (lips spread + front of tongue raised), 'w- prosody' (lips rounded, back of tongue raised) and 'a- prosody' (lips open + tongue lowered), and also between higher and lower levels of pitch. What this means is that articulation begins as a kind of prosody rather than the other way round. Prosody in adult languages has typically been represented (if at all) as if it was a funny kind of articulation, with 'suprasegmental phonemes', and pitch shown as points instead of contours. This is problematic even with adult speech; with children it is clear that the prototype is prosodic and that articulatory segments are then specialized out. By the time of the protolanguage, the child's phonological resources have typically expanded to include intermediate vowel postures and some consonantal articulations (associated plosives and nasals); but they are still not sequences of segments entering into separate oppositions, as the phonemes of the adult language do. As far as I know, we have as yet no adequate form of phonetic representation for this phase.

How long does the protolanguage last? Typically, I think, about six to nine months, although this should not be taken as exact, since it has no clear limits in time. It develops gradually from simple signs, and in its turn is gradually abandoned in the transition to the mother tongue. During its time of ascendancy (a typical age range might be 10–18 months), it is constantly changing as new meanings are added to the system and some old ones modified or dropped. This poses a further problem for representation: when to take cross-sections in time. When I did my own first round of work on the protolanguage, I tried various time intervals for resetting the system network and eventually settled on an optimum interval of once every six weeks: less than that and one could be picking up too many isolated instances (i.e. that did not, in fact, become systemic); more than that and one could be losing track of the way the system was developing. I was able to track the protolanguage of one child through six six-week stages (over about eight months, from 0.10½ to 1.6 – by the next time round, at 1.7½, the child had clearly embarked on the transition to the mother tongue) (Halliday 1975; cf. also Painter 1984, Torr 1997).

What do we learn from such a step-by-step representation of individual children's protolanguage? I think there are mainly two kinds of insight that can be gained. On the one hand, we get a clear picture of the functionality of the protolanguage, of how the child is already using language to live by and has a rather clear sense of the domains of life within which language figures prominently and with effect – what in the first paper I ever wrote on child language I referred to as the child's 'relevant models of language'. These are the contexts which have value for small children as the domains of semiotic activity. On the other hand, we can come to see how children expand their meaning potential – and what are the limits imposed on this expansion by the nature of the protolanguage itself; since it has no lexicogrammatical system, it cannot function to construct a model of experience or to develop a dynamic of dialogue. These possibilities are opened up by a higher-order semiotic, one with a grammar in it; there is strong pressure for the child to move into the mother tongue! Putting these two perspectives together, we can gain a coherent picture of the child's early semiotic development: how children are steadily increasing the number of 'semogenic vectors' and the various parameters that open up the total potential for meaning. First, they tease apart the content from the expression, then they separate the system from the instance, then they open up further strata, further levels of organization within the content and within the expression; then they prise apart the distinct functional components inside each stratum. With each step they are opening up a new domain in which to move, so construing a multidimensional semiotic space analogous to the increasing dimensionality of the bodily space in which their material existence is located.

Throughout this developmental history, the body is involved twice over. In the first place, it is involved as itself, so to speak, as the 'doer', or mover, in the child's material existence. In the second place, it is involved as the 'meaner', the signifying agent in the child's semiotic existence. By the time of the protolanguage, these two functions have specialized out and became separated: observe any parent and you will find they are very seldom in doubt about which domain any instance of the child's bodily activity belongs to, the material or the semiotic (they know it unconsciously, of course, they are not aware of making any such distinction, and it is certainly no use trying to find out by asking them!). Both kinds of activity, of course, are controlled by the infant's brain, but it would be wrong to think of this as a ready-made brain guiding the body through its various phases of development. On the contrary, the brain itself is developing, being shaped, moulded, wired up – whatever the metaphor we like to deploy – precisely by the ongoing, cumulative instances of material and semiotic behaviour.

What we are trying to do, it seems to me, is to represent the child's semiotic behaviour as a meaning potential, something that is functional because it is constantly changing as the child's interaction with the environment expands and develops. Once it becomes systemic, such that each performance of an act of meaning is an instance of an underlying system that is instated in the infant's brain – in other words, once it becomes a language, even if still 'proto-', child tongue not yet mother tongue – we can represent it in the form of a network; and, while each network taken by itself is a representation of just one 'movement' in the developmental progression, the sequence of several such networks presents a moving picture of the expanding consciousness of the child. A good way of showing this is to use the retrospective technique that was devised by Joy Phillips (1985): she drew up the network for a particular phase of development, then used it to foreshadow the development that led towards it, filling it in step by step as the child progressed. This also reveals where features are brought into the system and then drop out again, which is an interesting aspect of the earlier phases in learning the mother tongue. Figures 2.3a and 2.3b exemplify Phillips' approach.

Let me go back now to the transition from protolanguage to mother tongue – the move into 'language' in its typical sense of post-infancy human speech. This is, in fact, the transition from primary to higher-order consciousness using Edelman's model of the evolution of the brain (Edelman 1992). It involves what is in evolutionary terms a considerable leap forward, so that there appears to be a massive discontinuity – in the popular view, the child is beginning to talk. (Protolanguage is not recognized in the culture as a form of talk, even though parents carry on long conversations with their infants at the

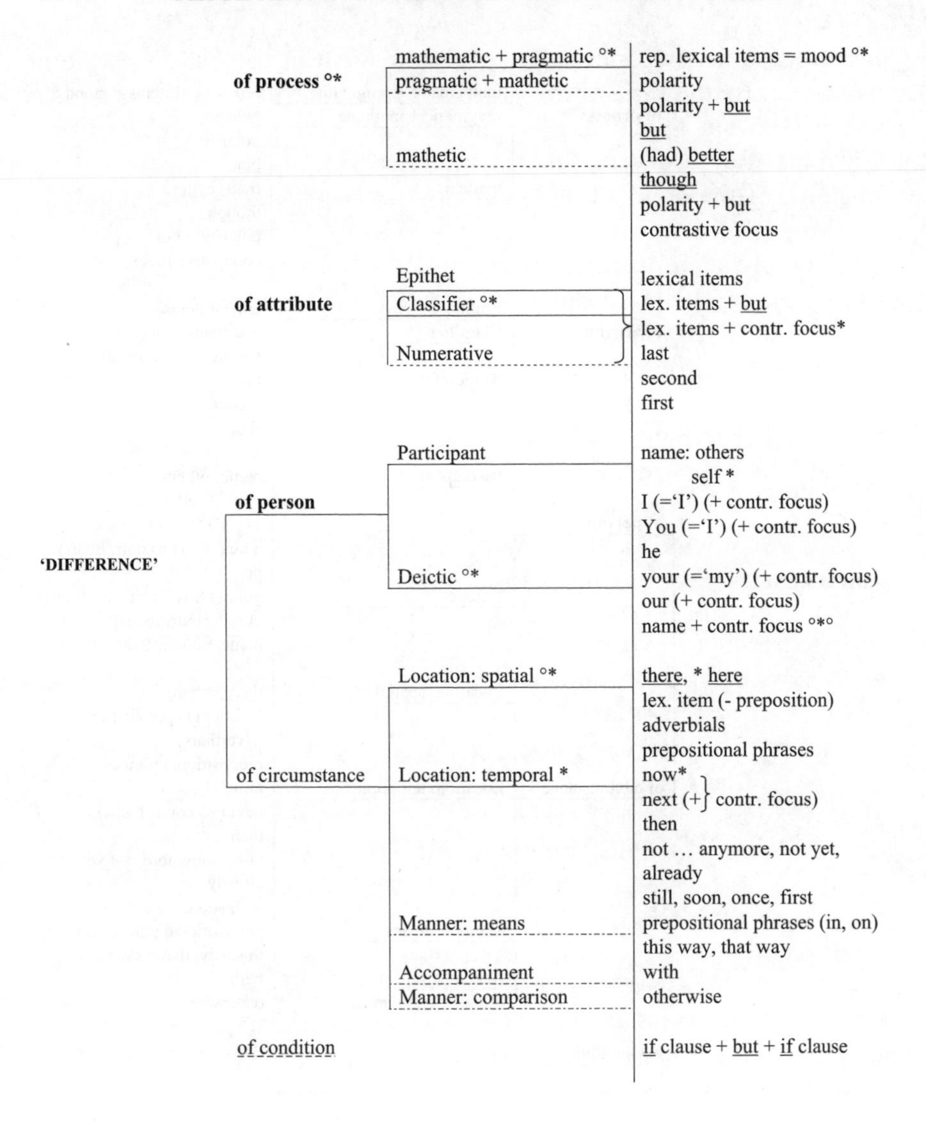

Figure 2.3a Nigel's construal of 'difference' at 1.7½–1.9
Source: Phillips 1985.

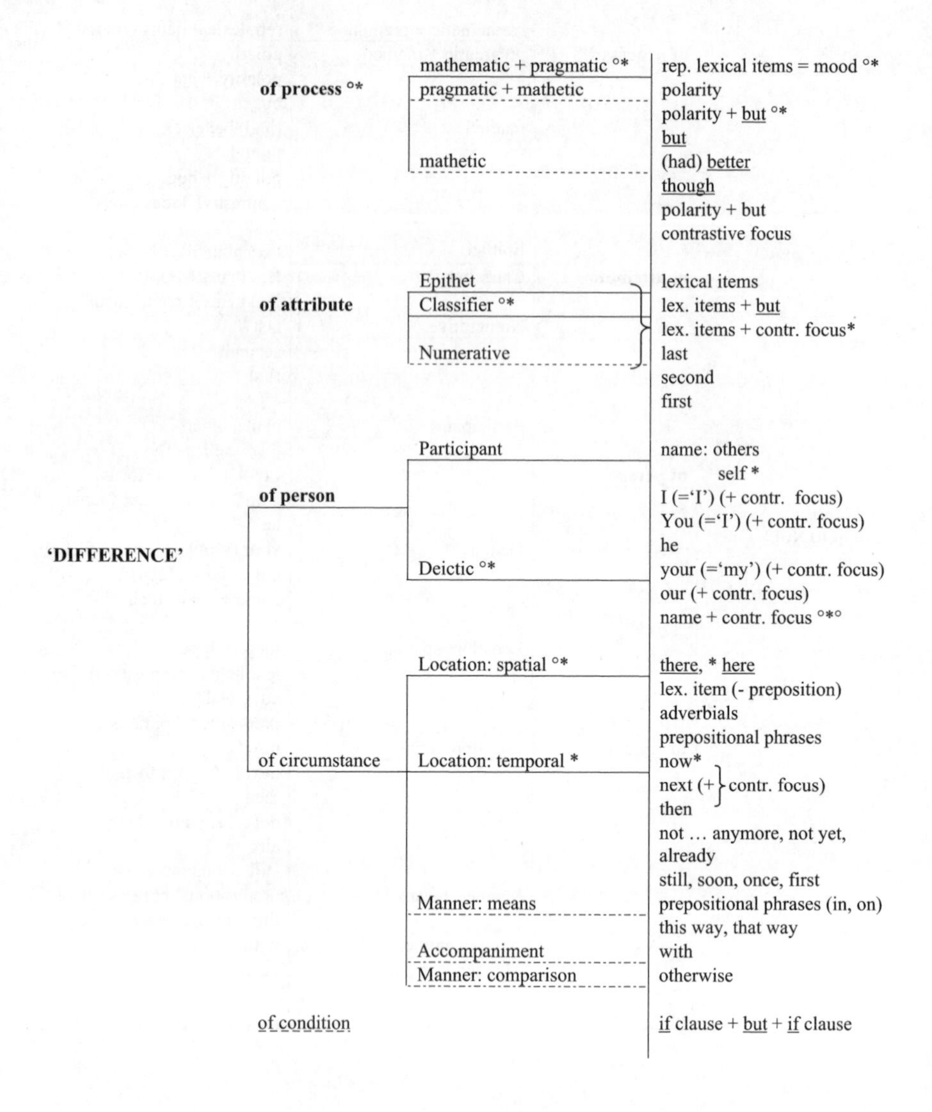

Figure 2.3b Nigel's construal of 'difference' at 1.9–1.10½
Source: Phillips 1985.

protolinguistic stage.) The discontinuity is real enough; but it also tends to mask what is an equally real continuity in the child's development of meaning, including the functions that meaning takes on in everyday life. To return to the analogy I was drawing between meaning, potential and moving potential: whereas protolanguage is associated with crawling, language is associated with walking; and the transition to an upright posture is so sudden, and so striking, that it tends to obscure the essential continuity in the framing of the human body, and in the significance of freedom of movement for human existence.

To represent the transition from child tongue to mother tongue we need to take account of two interdependent factors: the stratal and the functional. In stratal terms, what happens is that the child deconstructs, or rather deconstrues (using 'construe', as throughout, for constructing in the semiotic mode), the protolinguistic sign and insinuates a grammar 'in between' the meaning and the expression. By this move the primary semiotic system (that is, the semiotic system as construed by the infant's primary consciousness – a level of consciousness shared with many other species) is transformed into a higher-order semiotic system, a semiotic system construed by higher-order consciousness which evolved as the 'sapiens' in homo sapiens. Note that there has been no trace of grammar before this moment in the infant's life. The brain is no more capable of construing a grammar at birth, than the human body is of walking – or the brain of directing it to do so. By some time in the second year of life, however, as a result of the early experiences of primary semiotics, the brain has developed to the point where it can construe purely formal, or abstract, systems into which to map the systems of content and of expression, thus creating a new dimension of free play between them. (This free play is what is referred to in linguistics as the arbitrariness, or conventionality, of the linguistic sign. To give an analogy from the material world, it is rather like introducing a gearing mechanism whereby input energy of one kind can be transformed into output energy of any other kind.)

Let us now see what point we have reached – or what point our higher-order consciousness has reached that enables us to embark on our mother tongue. We now have, on the content side, a formal level of content (the lexicogrammar) distinct from, but non-arbitrarily related to, a level of signification (the semantics); and on the expression side, a formal level of expression (the phonology) distinct from, but non-arbitrarily related to, the phonetics – which is the level of bodily signification. The two levels of signification, the semantics and the phonetics, can now be seen as **interfaces** between the formal systems and the material world, in the two aspects in which it constitutes the **environment** for semiotic systems and events: on the one hand, the material world as content (the objects and the persons, including the child's own self, which are construed and acted on by the grammar); and on the other hand, the material world as expression (the signifying body, analogously 'construed' by the phonology).

This has been presented in somewhat abstruse theoretical terms; but before I illustrate it let me refer to one other factor that I mentioned in connection with the transition into the mother tongue, namely the functional one. We have seen how, in the protolanguage, children first systemize their acts of meaning by reference to a small number of functional contexts: obtaining goods-and-services ('instrumental'), manipulating others ('regulatory'), exchanging attention ('interactional'), manifesting their own affective states ('personal'), playing and imagining ('imaginative'). These contexts arise in the course of daily life and the meanings the child produces arise out of them; that is how the caregivers are able to interpret them, just as pet-owners identify the meanings produced by their household pets, which are evolutionarily parallel to the human protolanguage – they also are the manifestations of forms of primary consciousness. The functional orientations of the mother tongue are very different from those of the protolanguage; in fact the entire concept of linguistic 'function' has to be reconstrued. In language (here as opposed to protolanguage), while it is still possible to talk informally about the 'functions' of individual utterances in their contexts of situation, functionality has became intrinsic to the system: every instance is in fact multifunctional, because this feature is built in to the grammar – you cannot switch it off. It is impossible to activate just one 'function' at a time. In our higher-order semiotic, every act of meaning is at once a construing of experience and an enacting of interpersonal relationships (grammatically speaking, every clause selects both in transitivity and in mood). This is the extraordinary semiotic leap that children take in the second year of their lives, from the point where their range of meaning is an inventory of simple signs to the point where they have constructed for themselves an effectively 'infinite resource' for making sense of the world and interacting with the people in it. Our next step in representing the child has to be that of representing how they make this catastrophic transition.

I remarked at the beginning that the infant brain is simultaneously directing the body both to move and to mean – to act materially and to act semiotically. The semiotic act, or 'act of meaning', involves the two planes of expression and content; and each of these two planes interfaces with the material world. The interface on the expression plane is what I have called, following Thibault, the signifying body – at first the whole body, then gradually specializing out to certain parts of it (face, hands, vocal organs) and then, when the child attains the higher-order semiotic, that of language, the vocal organs take over as the dominant player (this interface is what we call 'phonetics'), except in sign which uses mainly hands, arms and face. On the content plane, the interface is what we call 'semantics'; here children are making sense of their experience of the world they find round about them (and also that they find inside themselves, the world of their own consciousness); and in the same breath, so to speak, interacting with those around them, and so enacting their own social being. As they move into this transitional phase of semiosis, leading from the primary semiotic of the protolanguage to the higher-order semiotic of the mother tongue, there is a remarkable collaboration set up in the brain between these two interfaces, something that is made possible by the brain's development to the level of higher-order consciousness. The critical factors in this development, as far as the semantic interface is concerned, are two: memory and consciousness of self.

With memory, the child is able to construe classes of phenomena out of repeated instances, using a re-entrant mapping to impose categories on its experience of the world. Linguistically, this means that the child is now able to construe 'common' terms – generalized common nouns as opposed to individuated proper nouns; and this is the beginning of reference, referential meaning. (The early individuated signs of the protolanguage are not yet referential; a protolinguistic means something like 'I want (you) mummy'). With self-consciousness, the child is able to make a systemic distinction between two modes of meaning, the declarative ('this is how things are') and the imperative ('this is how I want things to be'). This distinction is something that was noticed a long time ago by observers of children's first incursions into language (e.g. Lewis 1936), and more recent evidence confirms that it is a typical strategy for the transition into the mother tongue (Halliday 1975, 1983; Painter 1984, 1989; Torr 1997). In grammatical terms, these two steps constitute, respectively, proto-transitivity and proto-mood; taken together, they make it possible for the child to transform experience into meaning – to reflect on and to act on the world and the people in it in one semiotic swoop.

But for them to be able to do this the other interface must also be involved: the body as domain of expression – now becoming specialized, as we have seen, to expression in the form of vocally originated sound. We noted that in the content there were these two motifs: construing experience, by setting up categories and their interrelations to model the child's experience of the world; and enacting social processes, by getting along with others and in so doing shaping the child's own self. Let us call these two motifs the 'ideational' and the 'interpersonal', as used in systemic functional grammars. Now, somehow these two motifs have to be carried along simultaneously yet independently, so that all possible meanings of the one kind can be combined with all possible meanings of the other kind. How can this freedom of movement – or rather, freedom of meaning – be achieved?

Adult languages do it in highly elaborated ways. They have an array of resources in their grammars: choice of words, the words' phonetic shape, the ordering of elements, repetitions, morphological variation, particles, patterns of intonation and the like; and all this allows for a great deal of play – every language has its own characteristic way of deploying these different resources. But underlying this variation is a basic principle which runs something along these lines: that interpersonal meanings tend to have a slightly longer, or even significantly longer, time frame than ideational ones. Thus, if one thinks of an instance of a clause, ideationally it will consist of various elements (an event, participants in that event, circumstantial elements of various kinds – like *I saw the great man on television the other night*, which is made up of five distinct constituent parts), but interpersonally it is likely to take on colouring as a whole. If it is a statement, or if it is a question, then the whole thing is a statement, or the whole thing is a question; if it is said with disapproval, or sarcastically, then the whole thing is disapproving, or sarcastic, and so on. So in some respect or other, interpersonal meanings tend to be enacted prosodically, by repeating things, choosing a particular voice quality or pitch contour, beginning or signing off with a distinctive type of particle, and so on: some form of expression whose domain is more extended than that of elements of referential meaning.

How do children work their way in to the immense complexity that this interplay of meanings involves? This is where the body again plays a critical part – the part of the body that has become specialized for signifying through language, namely the voice. The organs of articulation – primarily tongue and lips, also soft palate and larynx – move around very quickly; their posture can change many times a second, producing rapidly varying acoustic impacts. By contrast, features of timbre and voice quality, patterns of melody and rhythm, take longer both to unfold and to produce contrasting sound effects. These latter are what are referred to collectively as **prosodic** features (using the term in a less abstract and more strictly phonetic sense than I was doing earlier). The one year old has already developed some mastery of both prosodic and articulatory features in the protolanguage, but has not yet learnt to separate them: a protolinguistic sign is a fixed combination of the two, such as spoken glottalically and on a falling tone. As a critical step – the critical step, as far as the expression plane is concerned – the child now separates out these two types of phonation, and learns to combine one pattern of articulation with two distinct prosodies – different tones, or different voice qualities. This might have happened randomly before, but now it becomes systemic: the articulation pattern carries one consistent meaning and the prosody carries another. To give an actual example from my own data: at 13 months Nigel created an articulatory/prosodic system as follows: three articulatory patterns, meaning respectively 'Mummy', 'Daddy' and Anna', combined with two prosodic patterns, rising tone/falling tone, meaning respectively 'where are you?', 'there you are!' (Figures 2.4a and 2.4b).

This system yielded a set of six terms, each combining proto-reference with proto-speech-function: the articulations have taken the first step on the way to becoming names; the prosodies have taken the first step on the way to becoming moods.

A favourite transition strategy, by which the child breaks through into the transitivity and mood systems of the adult grammar, is to develop this pattern into a general principle. Table 2.2 gives some examples showing the way that Nigel did it. The two tones, rising and falling, were functionally quite distinct. With the rising tone, the meaning was 'somebody do something!', 'I want (some particular good or service)'; some answer, in deeds or (increasingly, over time) in words, was being demanded and had to be forthcoming for the speech act to have been, in Nigel's view, successful (i.e. he would go on saying it until it was responded to). I referred to this type as 'pragmatic'. With the falling tone, the meaning was 'that's the way things are'; no response was expected, although the listener often provided one – 'yes, that's a green bus', 'no, that's blue/that's a van' and so on. I called this type 'mathetic' because they had a learning function; where the pragmatic foregrounded the instance (do that now!), the mathetic assigned the instance to a system ('that's a case of . . .'), locating it within a semantic space made up of categories and relationships. Over a period of six months or so (1½–2), the mathetic developed into the adult declarative mood; the pragmatic developed into interrogative and imperative, both of which for a time kept their rising tones before Nigel eventually shifted the imperatives and the WH-interrogatives over into the falling tone to conform to adult English.

So the prosodic contrasts turned into a system of mood. They became the foundation for the interpersonal component in the

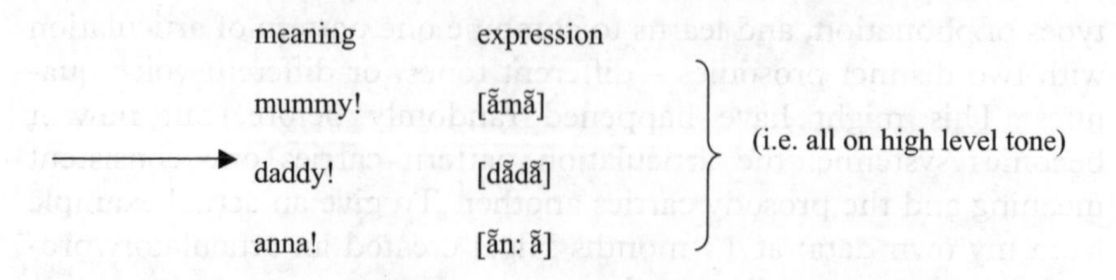

Figure 2.4a Nigel's first stratification of the content plane: 13 months

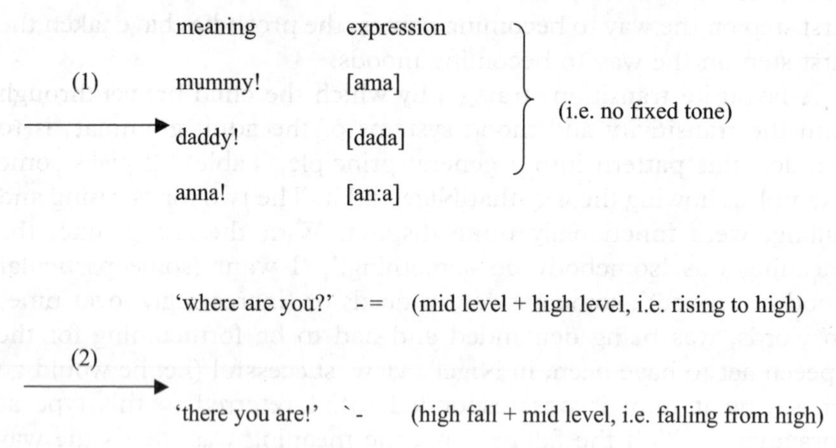

Figure 2.4b Nigel's first stratification of the content plane: 14 months

Note: Here for the first time a system of experiential meaning (three personal names) becomes separated from, and freely combinable with, a system of interpersonal meaning (two moods). This is the child's first step towards a lexicogrammatical stratum.

grammar, with its speech functions, modalities, systems of appraisal and so on. The articulatory contrasts became the foundation for the ideational component; they developed into the process, participants and circumstantial elements that make up the transitivity system, construing the categories and relations with which we model our experience of the world. At first, the experiential domains of the pragmatic ('what I want') and the mathetic ('what's going on') remain distinct; but it is not long before they start to overlap, and

Table 2.2 Examples of pragmatic and mathetic: Nigel 1.6–1.9

chuffa stúck	N. calling for help in freeing toy train
find fór you	'I've lost something; find it for me!'
throw úp	'throw the rabbit up in the air again'
low wáll	N. about to jump off suitcase, asking to be caught; first used when jumping off walls, low and high, in park
squéeze	'squeeze the orange for me'
gláss	'I want my milk in a glass'
orange lémon	'sing "Oranges and lemons"'; accompanied by music gesture, which is alternative realization of pragmatic; hence falling tone
turn róund	N. repeating instruction given when fitting shapes into puzzles: 'is that what I have to do?'
play chuffa	'let's play with the train'
open fór you	(usual form of request for box, etc., to be opened)
back tóothpaste	'put the toothpaste back in the cupboard'
more grávy	also: more omelet, lettuce, tomato, bread, bun, etc.
bounce táble	'I want to bounce my orange on the table'
cárry	'carry me!'
háve it	(usual form of 'I want that thing')
tóast	'I want some toast'; also breakfast, tomato etc.
hit flóor	'I'm going to hit the floor with the hammer'
that sóng	'sing that song you've just sung'
háve that	(same as have it above)
hedgehog bóok	'I want the book with the hedgehog picture in it'
play ráo	'I want to play at lions'
train under tunnel . . . get it fór you	both halves rising tone
dówn . . . table . . . sugar . . . spóon	'put the sugar down on the table for me to put my spoon it; rising tone on down and spoon

molasses nóse	'I've got molasses on my nose' (with accompanying expression of delight)
big ball	frequent when playing with ball; also little ball
mummy bóok	frequent on picking up book and finding no pictures inside (it's Mummy's book')
red swéater	on seeing it; also red jumper (same object)
black brush	also green, red, blue, yellow with stick, light, peg, car, train, etc.
big one	applied to goods train, bubble; tonic on big as in adult form
baby duck	in picture; also mummy duck
too big	frequent: sometimes appropriate as when trying to push object through wire mesh; sometimes inappropriate, as when trying to reach ball with stick (= 'too far')
that bróke	'that's broken'
loud music	frequent comment as loud passage starts
chuffa stóp	in game (Father bouncing N., N. being 'fast train'; Father stops)
two green pég	
green stick find	'the green stick's been found'
old green tráin . . . green old tráin	both halves falling tone, the second, though less probable, would have been the appropriate one in the context
dada black brush to	'Daddy's black brush'
no more wáter	
toothpaste . . . ón . . . tóothbrush	falling tone on on and again on toothbrush; not fully formed as a single structure
tree fall dówn	later: big tree fall down
dada got báll . . . nila got báll	
ball go under cár	cf. water gone plughole

pairs appear such as '*mummy bòok*' (falling tone), '*that's Mummy's bóok*', and '*mummy book*' (rising tone), '*I want Mummy's book*', and by the time the child is ready to ask questions (i.e. when the meaning 'I want' extends to information as well as goods-and-services), the experiential domains of the two become in principle identical: whatever you can tell, you can also ask, and whatever you can ask, you can also tell. And this again is made possible by the signifying body; our vocal resources have evolved in such a way that any articulation can be combined with any prosody. This in turn is what has enabled human language to evolve the way it has done, such that every act of meaning, in our higher-order consciousness, is a complex activity involving both construing (referring to some features of experience) and enacting (setting up some form of interpersonal relationship). Resources for the former evolved out of vowel and consonant articulations like *wiyuwiyu, nananana, abu* and so on; resources for the latter evolved out of rising and falling pitch, breathy and creaky voice quality and the like. Thus the twofold nature of the body's interfacing with the **content**, as repository of experience and as participant in the social process, is matched by the twofold nature of its interfacing with the **expression**, producing (and also, of course, responding to) articulatory and prosodic patterns. All this activity is stage-managed by the child's rapidly developing brain.

For a long time children's language development, or 'language acquisition' as it came to be rather misleadingly called, was thought of as a kind of progressive approximation to a goal, a goal that was extrinsically fixed and defined, so that each new step was seen as an imperfect attempt to attain it. Although the child's efforts are no longer dismissed as irrelevant 'mistakes', but rather are seen as strategies and tactics for learning, there is still the view that the mother tongue is what the child is striving to 'acquire' right from the start. In my view this conception is wide of the mark. What small children are doing is learning how to mean; and the guiding principle is neither approximative (imitating what is around) nor preformative (guided by an innate grammar) but epigenetic. The child is building up a potential, and in doing so is essentially tracking the processes whereby language first evolved. Up until the beginning of the transit into the mother tongue, typically well into the second year of life, the child's language development owes nothing to the language spoken around, except in the indirect sense that the meanings of the child's protolanguage are negotiated with adults who speak that language. You cannot tell from observing a child's protolanguage what its mother tongue is going to be. It is only when the transition begins, and the child starts to leap over thousands of generations of human evolution, that we start to see the influence of the mother tongue, and even then the child persists along its own developmental trajectory – even to the point where the patterns being generated conflict with those that the mother tongue displays (cf. Nigel's use of rising tones on his early imperatives and WH-interrogatives – but many such examples could be cited).

So what are the outstanding problems in representing the child as one who is learning how to mean? Critically, I think, we have to find ways of representing this process as the building up of a semiotic potential, analogous to the building up of the physical potential that is taking place in the child's own body. Ultimately, both are aspects of the development of brain power, and no doubt every part of the brain is talking to all the other parts as these immense resources are being built up. The language development of a small number of individual children has been studied intensively in recent years, but it will be a task for the next millennium to expand this effort and integrate it with studies of individual brain development on the one hand and large-scale corpus studies of natural data from very small children on the other. And we hope that linguistic theory may mature to the point where it can be involved in, and might even contribute to, what E.O. Wilson calls 'consilience', the coming together of scientific understanding not just in physics and biology but also in the social (and I would add the semiotic) sciences. One gain we can surely expect from this will be a deeper understanding of human infancy and childhood.

References

Bateson, M.C. (1975) Mother-infant exchanges. In D. Aaronson and R.W. Rieber (eds), *The Epigenesis of Conversational Interaction. Developmental Psycholinguistics and Communication Disorders*. New York: New York Academy of Sciences.

Edelman, Gerald (1992) *Bright Air, Brilliant Fire: On the Matter of the Mind*. New York: Harper Collins (Basic Books).

Halliday, M.A.K. (1975) *Learning How to Mean*. London: Edward Arnold. Reprinted Nottingham Trent University: Department of English and Media Studies, 1999.

Halliday, M.A.K. (1983) On the transition from child tongue to mother tongue. *Australian Journal of Linguistics*, 3(2): 201–16.

Lewis, Michael M. (1936) *Infant Speech: A Study of the Beginnings of Language*. London: Routledge and Kegan Paul, 2nd edn, enlarged, 1951.

Painter, Clare (1984) *Into the Mother Tongue: A Case Study in Early Language Development*. London and Dover, NH: Pinter.

Painter, Clare (1989) Learning Language: A Functional View of Language Development. In Ruqaiya Hasan and J.R. Martin (eds), *Language Development: Learning Language, Learning Culture.* Norwood, NJ: Ablex, 18–65.

Phillips, Joy Ann (1985) The Development of Comparisons and Contrasts in Young Children's Language. University of Sydney, MA Hons. thesis.

Thibault, Paul (2004) *Brain, Mind and the Signifying Body: Towards an Ecosocial Semiotic Theory of Meaning, Embodiment and Consciousness.* London: Continuum.

Torr, Jane (1997) *From Child Tongue to Mother Tongue: A Case Study of Language Development in the First Two and a Half Years.* University of Nottingham: Dept of English Studies [Monographs in Systemic Linguistics 9].

Williams, George C. (1992) *Natural Selection: Domains, Levels, and Challenges.* New York: Oxford University Press.

3

Reading Picture Reading: A Study in Ideology and Inference

Ruqaiya Hasan

Nigel's mother and I were planning a visit to the aquarium. Nigel (age 23 months) did not know what an aquarium was but he heard us discussing it.

'We're not going to say a rào ['lion'],' he said to himself. 'Vòpa ['fishes']. There will be wàter.'

3.1 Introduction

Going beyond the information given is something we human beings do quite spontaneously and unconsciously. We engage in this activity with an ease that might persuade us to believe that making inferences on the basis of the information in hand inheres in the genetic make-up of the human species. It may well be that the belief is justified to some extent. We may by nature be predisposed to reasoning of the type '*given that A is the case, then B must follow from it*'. Certainly, little Nigel, untutored in the art/science of reasoning is able to deduce that 'given there will be fish, then there will have to be water'. The value of such a genetic trait is obviously enormous for the survival of the species. But the actual act of inferential reasoning as a whole – which is what, after all, impinges on our life – involves much more than this formula suggests. Inferential reasoning is complex and, like most complex processes, it cannot be accounted for purely on the basis of our species' specific endowments. This becomes clear on closer examination. Seen as a whole, the process has at least two stages. First, the need to recognize the information for what it is – to understand what the significant elements of the scenario are that the given information is construing. The phrase 'given information' is used here for any object that requires interpretation, be it language, image, gesture or even a material situation. The only way we can go beyond a given instance of any of these phenomena is to first interpret it, to understand its significance. Second, there is also the need to figure out what practice(s) the construed scenario implies – what steps are 'logically' necessary for the completion of the recognized scenario. Strictly speaking the word *inference* refers precisely to this latter activity, but it is obvious that the recognition of what is and the prediction of what follows from the recognized 'fact' are the two logically related stages in the game. And it appears quite obvious that the requirements of neither of these stages can be met automatically in a manner that has been, as it were, ordained by our biological make-up; an equally crucial contribution is made by our social location – how we are positioned in society – as this is what would predicate how we perceive and interpret the situation. Our social positioning impinges on both stages of inferential reasoning. So far as 'taking in' given information is concerned, we know that it is seldom a neutral act. Information is typically processed from some specific point of view, and to say that point of view is crucial to the recognition and understanding of the given state of affairs is to grant that the process is ultimately ideologically informed. Then, again, the experience of living is crucial also in guiding the prediction of what would follow from the information in hand. It is true that both the memory and the ability to perceive similarities are important elements in inference, but memory needs something to remember and perception of similarity presupposes a (partial) acquaintance. It follows that the act of inference turns crucially upon the inferring subject's point of view, the ideology which they bring to bear on the recognition of what is. So, ultimately, it is on the social subject's ideology that the actual act of inferential reasoning depends.

One might be tempted to reject the crucial role I have assigned here to point of view and ideology in inferential reasoning on the ground that there exist universal truths, which are understood in the same way by all human beings, and which in all cases must lead to the same inference. Certainly the examples provided by logicians and philosophers appear to encourage this view. To take one of the very famous and recurrent examples: suppose the given information is that (1) *precious metals do not rust* and that (2) *gold is a precious metal*, then anyone who perceives the logical relation between these two elements of the given information would naturally complete the thought by inferring the implied conclusion, that (3) *gold does not rust*. At a cursory glance it seems reasonable to suggest that variation in ideology and point of view is not likely to affect our interpretation of the information given in the major and minor premises in (1) and (2) respectively; and that the conclusion in (3) follows naturally and unavoidably from the acceptance of (1) and (2). In the literature on reasoning (see, for example, Evans *et al.* 1993), this kind of inference would be referred to as 'deductive', and it is assumed that, all things being equal, such deductions are arrived at quite naturally.

The question we need to raise at this point is whether all human beings would reason in this way. If they do not, then clearly there must be some significant elements in such reasoning that are not given by nature. We might argue, of course, that failure to reason in this way simply indicates 'feeble intelligence' (Evans *et al.* 1993: 1) and that all human beings, except those suffering from feeble intelligence, would arrive at a uniquely given 'correct' inference. But, on the one hand, granting this exception raises questions about what we mean by feeble intelligence – how and why some might come to suffer from it; and, on the other hand, it puts under threat the claim that the process of logical inference comes naturally to all members of the species *homo sapiens*. If what is called feeble intelligence is traced to the experience of living, then we might have to consider the possibility that given the 'same' point of departure, all human beings may not necessarily arrive at the same destination, for it may be that the point of departure itself does not bear an identical significance for all and so is, in truth, not the 'same' point of departure!

3.2 Thinking in society

It so happens that in 1930–31, the famous Russian scholar Luria conducted research which is highly relevant to our debate. His subjects came from Uzbekistan and represented social groups with different experiences of daily life. Some were mature peasants with little or no formal education; others were younger and/or had received some formal instruction. Luria's research clearly demonstrated (Luria 1976: 100ff) that the first group of subjects 'refused to resort to logical inference from the given premises' (ibid.: 108), especially if the premises were far removed from their personal experience. Remarkably, Luria did not attribute this refusal to 'feeble intelligence'; on the contrary he pointed out that 'These subjects can make excellent judgments about facts of direct concern to them and can draw conclusions, displaying no deviation from the 'rules' and revealing much worldly intelligence' (ibid.: 114). In his opinion, three factors 'substantially limited their [i.e. the subjects'] capabilities for theoretical, verbal-logical thinking' and these Luria listed as:

1. a mistrust of an initial premise that does not reproduce personal experience...
2. the unacceptability of the premise as universal...
3. ...[as] a consequence of the second, ... [a] ready disintegration of the syllogism into three independent and isolated particular propositions with no unified logic and thus no access for thought to be channelled within this system. (ibid.: 114–15)

Reflecting on these three factors, it seems to me that the last two follow from the first, and the first is rooted within the experience of life that Luria's subjects had encountered prior to engaging in this research: it is this factor that was relevant in Luria's subjects' interpretation and recognition of the nature of the given information. To us, who are in the business of dealing with the processing of this kind of 'disembedded information' (Donaldson 1978: 1992), it is crystal clear that the major and minor premises of a syllogism constitute 'given information' and that if they represent generalizations, then in our culture they would be ascribed the status of universal truth. But the point of view that Luria's subjects brought to those premises negated their very status as information: to them the general assertions were neither relevant nor credible. It was this point of view, this way of engaging with the given information, that made a qualitative difference to the direction of their thinking. Were we to explain their response as arising from feeble intelligence, then in view of their social positioning, we would have to see feeble intelligence not as natural mental deficit but rather as a state of mind induced by the experience of their specific social positioning, which was instrumental in fashioning their ideas about what is worthy of attention, what is sayable what and is thinkable. And, indeed, Luria did go on to claim that this group of his subjects were those 'whose cognitive activity was formed by *experience and not by systematic instruction or more complex forms of communication*' [author's emphasis].

I will return at a later point to the opposition Luria sets up between 'experience' on the one hand – by which he meant learning through everyday life – and 'systematic instruction or more complex forms of communication', on the other. This latter term in Luria's opposition corresponds approximately to what Bernstein (e.g. 1990, 1996) used to call instructional discourse in official pedagogy. Inspired by Vygotsky's sociogenetic theory of cognitive development (see Vygotsky 1978; Wertsch 1985; Mertz and Parmentier 1985; Hickman

1987), Luria claimed that the 'shaping of the foundations of theoretical thinking . . . can be regarded as one of the most important processes in the historical shaping of consciousness' (Luria 1976: 115). He thus clearly dissociated himself from the view according to which the capacity for making a logical inference is taken as a gift of nature: what you need for logical inference is, according to Luria, schooled minds. This is how he put it:

> Only through school instruction and the concomitant creation of special 'theoretical' activity could the situation change markedly and the process of problem solving become an independent discursive activity, assuming forms similar to the familiar forms of verbal and logical and discursive thought that we see in school children. (ibid.: 118)

The socio-historical genesis of theoretical thinking – and this in Luria's terminology includes generalization, abstraction, problem-solving and logical inference, etc. – is thus to be attributed, according to Luria, to 'systematic instruction and more complex forms of communication'. Far from being a natural mental activity, it is in fact learned in the experience of instructional discourse, which is characteristically associated with schooling, i.e. with official pedagogy. But how right was Luria in attributing this achievement to schools? In what follows I will examine some classroom discourse to see if there is any indication that the shaping of the foundation of theoretical thinking begins at school. But first a few words about the data to be used for this examination.

3.3 Classroom discourse: the data

The extracts from classroom discourse to be discussed here form part of a large body of data collected for the second phase of a multi-phase research project that I directed at Macquarie University.[1] In the first phase of this research, a substantial sample of naturally occurring everyday talk between 24 mother – child dyads was analysed semantically.[2] This analysis established a statistically robust pattern of semantic variation which was responsive to the subjects' social class position. In the second phase of the research, eight of the subject children were followed into the classroom in the first year of their schooling. In Australia, this stage is known as kindergarten; the word is often abbreviated in the usual Australian manner to 'kindy'. A recording of some kindy classroom sessions was made in the first and the last month of the year; the data presented here are from the first month of schooling. Twenty-four schools participated in the project; 11 of these were located in working-class areas and 13 in middle-class ones. The recording was done by the teachers themselves, all of whom were female. The reason for the recording was given as part of an attempt to find out what the children were able to say and do when they first entered school. The end-of-year recording was to be used as a measure for the distance the children had travelled in one year's schooling.

During the first batch of recording, the subject children were five to five-and-a-half years old, which is normal for the start of official education in Australia. For the eight phase one subjects followed up to the kindy class, we also had reliable information regarding their everyday life-experience at home (see Hasan 1989, 1992a, 1992b; Cloran 1994, 1999, 2000). The data of classroom discourse from the first month of schooling would, therefore, appear to be particularly suitable for examining if and how the 'shaping of the foundations of theoretical thinking' might take place through participation in 'systematic instruction or more complex forms of communication'. At this early stage the school would not have made any notable mark on the children's consciousness, but it is conceivable that it might be taking the initial steps in that direction. The teachers were advised to do the recording during whatever activity they thought would generate more participation in talk by the children. It turns out that the majority of the data comes from 'number talk' and 'picture reading' sessions. Obviously at this early stage, no hard-and-fast lines are drawn between 'subject areas' or 'fields of discipline'; in fact one might go so far as to say there are no recognizable subjects/disciplines, with possibly the sole exception of mathematics. In any event, one would look in vain for any discourse concerned with the transmission of a systematic body of what we tend to call 'knowledge'. However, to pass over the classroom discourse of these young kindy pupils and their teachers as trifling or irrelevant to the serious business of education would be a gross underestimate of its true significance. For, indeed, under the cover of quite mundane-seeming discourse, some highly important things are going on, which do indicate the role of schooling in the historical shaping of consciousness.

3.4 Classroom discourse: the object of teaching

In the last few decades there has been a good deal of interest in classroom discourse, and this had added to our understanding from different points of view (see, for example, Sinclair and Coulthard

1975; Mehan 1979; Edwards and Westgate 1987; Lemke 1990; Christie 1996). To appreciate the schools' possible contribution to the shaping of the foundations of logical thinking, we need to focus on a more abstract issue which is fundamental to education as such. We need to consider the nature of that which is taught, so the question I want to raise here is: what exactly is the object of teaching? Clearly, this is a large question. Schooling is far from homogeneous; there are different styles, different traditions, and, of course, as you move up and down the various significant stages of education, the same tradition might have very different manifestations in pedagogic practices. I will ignore here that variety of educational practice associated with what became known as 'progressive education' (see, however, some relevant comments on this pedagogic tradition below at the close of the next section). A fairly typical manifestation of the underlying assumptions of progressive education was found in 'process writing' in the specific discipline of language education, which I will also ignore for lack of space, limiting my comments to a range of traditional educational practices.

One popular view, endorsed explicitly by most traditional teaching institutions, is that the object of teaching is simply the transmission of some existing body of knowledge. In terms of the analysis of pedagogic discourse offered by Bernstein (1990, 1996 and elsewhere), the traditional view reduces the process simply to 'instructional discourse', ignoring the equal, if not more important, component that Bernstein called 'regulative discourse'. Oversimplifying somewhat, 'instructional discourse is concerned with the transmission/acquisition of specific competences, and regulative discourse is concerned with the transmission of order, relation, and identity' (Bernstein 1990: 211). Where the object of teaching is simply the transmission of specific competences, this knowledge is viewed as consisting of a reservoir of interrelated concepts that concern various aspects of our material and social environment, which for some reason or other are foregrounded in the culture. Each such aspect comes to represent a 'field' or 'subject'. The knowledge in each field is recontextualized for use in schools and universities, having been packaged into the various curriculum genres such as those of physics, chemistry, biology, history, geography, politics and so on. The object of teaching is the mastery of these genres, whether this is recognized in as many words or not. In recent years, critical literacy scholars have been scathing about the value of focus on educational genres as the object of teaching (see, for example, Luke 1996), so it needs to be pointed out that the reproduction of existing knowledge is a significant aspect of the maintenance of any culture. Cultures vary to the extent that they attach value to this aspect, but no living culture can afford to ignore it entirely. A culture that does not attend to its own maintenance – and such cultures are more the figments of our imagination than real historical facts – has no sense of history; where there is no sense of history there can be no sense of change. Cultural change and cultural maintenance are mutually defining phenomena: the one is unknowable without the other. So the reproduction of knowledge as the object of teaching has a definite value in the life of a community. Nonetheless, if it were to remain the sole object of teaching, this could give rise to some serious problems.

If the object of teaching were to be conceptualized *only* as reproduction of existing knowledge, this would lead to a kind of learning that Gregory Bateson (1972) described as 'zero level learning': you simply learn the categories and items and perchance their relations, but you do not learn the principles which underlie the production of these objects. Bateson suggests that a much more important form of learning is learning to learn, which he described as 'deutero learning'. Clearly, deutero learning would be enabling, as it would enhance the capacity to learn. And this is crucial in view of the nature of knowledge. We may certainly view already produced knowledge as an abstract semiotic product; but it is important to realize that the nature of knowledge is not static as the metaphor of knowledge as product might suggest. For human progress to continue, knowledge must always be on the move. Espousing this view in his discussion of the concept of World 3, Popper (1992) makes an observation that appears crucial at this point in our debate. Popper thought of knowledge as an existing reservoir of concepts: once produced it will go on to exist, as he put it, 'without a knowing subject'. But he also observed that as systems of interrelated concepts, knowledge contains within itself the principle of its own development: the concepts and their relations within a field point to the direction of the field's future growth. There is no doubt that Popper is right: the developmental potential that inheres in knowledge is undeniable, but for this potential to become actual, some source of activation is needed. Clearly, this cannot come from within the systems of knowledge. It is, therefore, equally undeniable that the activation of the developmental potential of knowledge systems calls for a knowing subject: to realize its potential, a knowledge system needs someone who can ask how and why questions at appropriate points in exploring existing concepts and relations. It follows that for the continued evolution of knowledge, we need people who are capable of performing this function. And it is also not difficult to see that pupils who have only encountered teaching as the reproduction of knowledge will lack this capacity to interrogate the existing knowledge systems: they would have engaged only in zero level learning.

So how does the production of knowledge continue in society? For continue it must, even in the most traditional societies. One possible answer is that at least so far as pedagogic institutions are concerned, knowledge production is always a late development: it occurs only at the advanced stages, when the student is working for a research degree. The attitude of enquiry coincides with the maturity of years and with the development of the intellect, which has had to prove its excellence over the entire educational career. All this is perfectly true, but unless we maintain that producers of knowledge are born and not culturally produced, the question still remains: when does the transformation of a person into a scholar actually begin? At what stage of schooling do our pedagogic institutions begin to lay the foundation of theoretical thinking? The data collected for our research has some surprising indications. It suggests that the business of shaping the intellect begins very early.

3.5 Classroom discourse: the production of the pedagogic subject

Consider extracts 1a and 1b. Both form part of the same classroom interaction but they are separated from each other by intervening talk that is omitted here in order to save space. As the first message of 1a shows, this is not where the interaction begins; the messages in both extracts have been renumbered here for ease of presentation.

Transcription conventions are as shown below:

(1)	successive numbering of messages for the current presentation
[?abc]	unintelligible; interpreted by reference to context/cotext
[?]	unintelligible; could not be interpreted
<(3) abc>	message (3) is surrounded by message (2)
(ABC)	contextual commentary based on cotextual evidence
abc –	message is left incomplete
...	a pause longer than would be normal at this point
**abc	matched pairs of double asterisks indicate the start of overlapping talk
abc?**	speaker allowed no time for response to this question

Extract 1a:

Teacher: (1) well now, here is another picture (2) now, what do you think this is a picture about? (3) have a look at it
Pupils: (4) a bus
Teacher: (5) yes, its a picture of a bus (6) all right, well, who do you think is going to catch the bus? (7) who's catching that bus?
Pupils: (8) Kindies
Teacher: (9) you think it might be Kindies (10) what about you Tony?
Tony: (11) um ... school[?bus]
Teacher: (12) you think it could be a school bus (13) I think it could be too ... (14) have a good look at it ... (15) what do you think Kim?
Kim: (16) I think it's pre-school
Teacher: (17) you think it could be pre-school (18) might be pre-school (19) what about you Verity?
Verity: (20) first class
Teacher: (21) first class (22) and what do you think about it, Jennie?
Jennie: (23) [?I think it's pre-school]
Teacher: (24) you think it's pre-school

Extract 1b:

Teacher: (1) do you think they are going to school? (2) or are they coming home from the school?
Pupils: (3) home
Teacher: (4) why do you think that? (5) why do you think that Verity?
Verity: (6) because...
Teacher: (7) why do you think they're going home? ... (8) Kim?
Kim: (9) um ...'cause it's this afternoon
Teacher: (10) yes it could be afternoon (11) the shadows are long (12) the shadows are long (13) it could be afternoon ... (14) Steve?
Steve: (15) [?because there's a high fence (16) and you don't usually have that kind of fence around houses]
Teacher: (17) oh, isn't that a good answer! (18) (ADDRESSING WHOLE CLASS) did you hear that?
Pupils: (19) **no
Pupils: (20) **yes
Teacher: (21) did you hear? (22) Steve said because *there's a high*

> *fence* (23) *and you don't usually have that kind of fence around houses*. [emphasis added]

In extract 1a, to use Sinclair and Coulthard's terminology (1975), there are five exchanges. Four of these have some version of the same question, namely, *who's catching the bus?*, functioning as re/initiate. However, contrary to Sinclair and Coulthard's prediction, the teacher's persistence with the question is not indicative of her dissatisfaction with the previous responses. The teacher, in fact, appears to have a relaxed attitude, simply exploring what possible readings of this aspect of the picture can be entertained. This is not accidental behaviour, specific to this occasion or even to this teacher: our data indicate that it is by no means uncommon for teachers to, as it were, implicitly indicate the possibility of variant readings of the same picture. That variant readings are being entertained is shown by the fact that the teacher's feedback to the various pupils in extract 1a simply acknowledges each reading: *you think it's an X, you think it's a Y*. There is no indication of a higher or lower valuation at any stage of these exchanges.

In 1b, by contrast, the issue centres round what substantiates a claim: what justification can the pupil offer in favour of their claim? And here it is quite clear that the teacher is not going to accept just any response. Variant readings will be offered and they might even be considered seriously but the pattern of differential evaluation will establish which response is the best. So when Kim justifies her claim that *they're going home* by saying *'cause it's this afternoon*, this is not seen as solving the problem. Rather, it is implicitly treated as giving rise to a new problem: how do we know it is afternoon? By her follow up messages (11)–(13) the teacher implicitly indicates that Kim's explanation raises a new problem. She models the possible move Kim might make to justify her assertion that it's afternoon: *yes, it could be afternoon, the shadows are long, the shadows are long, it could be afternoon*. The suggestion hangs in the air tentatively until Steve offers his response: *(they're going home) because there's a high fence and you don't usually have that kind of fence around houses*. The teacher is delighted with Steve's response, which she holds up for the class to examine by repeating his words: *did you hear? Steve said 'because there's a high fence and you don't usually have that kind of fence around houses'*.

Why does the teacher prefer Steve's response to Kim's? We can paraphrase Kim's response as follows: *because I believe that it's afternoon, therefore I claim that the children are going home, not coming to school*. But what justification Kim might have for believing that it's afternoon is known only to her: she has not said anything to validate that claim. By contrast, Steve exploits objective evidence; he uses as justification for his claim something that is there in the picture for everyone to see; and seeing is believing. The proceedings in the classroom leave no doubt that the teacher's real concern is with the viability of the evidence for the claim. The lesson continues with further discussion of what 'proof' there might be for claiming that the kids are heading back home, not coming to school. The teacher adds her own observation to Steve's: *the children are coming **out** of the gate; if they were coming **to** school, they would be coming **in** in* [sic!] *the gate . . . so we see they're catching the bus going home **from** school* [emphasis in recorded data]. This complements Steve's response: the high fences he spoke about are **behind** the bus not in front. Together these comments clinch the argument.

I am inclined to describe this early lesson, which occurred within the second or third week of the children's schooling, as an initial step in teaching the principles of argumentation. During this lesson, which seems to completely absorb both the teacher and her pupils, at no point has the teacher explicitly enunciated her principles, which, if they had been worded, might have run as follows: claims you make must be substantiated; and evidence you cite must be objective, which is to say, it should be accessible to others. It is no part of my claim that the teacher is conscious of the significance of what she is doing. She may be or she may not; what does seem beyond doubt here is that the importance of the principles of argumentation – such a central pillar of scholarly discourse – is being pressed upon these young children, who have, in the words of Gordon Wells (1986), just begun their apprenticeship to meanings – meanings that are specific to the educational trade. Here is another example:

Extract 2:

Teacher:	(1) do you think he's having fun?
Pupil 1:	(2) yes
Pupil 2:	(3) mummy's got some shells
Teacher:	(4) (IGNORING PUPIL 2) what tells you? (5) what tells you he's having fun? (6) he's enjoying himself?
Pupil 1:	(7) my brain
Teacher:	(8) your brain tells you! (9) well, how can we tell <(10) by looking at the picture> that he's enjoying himself (11) having fun?
Pupils:	(12) smile
Teacher:	(13) good (14) he's got a smile on his face (15) do you think he'd be enjoying himself (16) if he didn't smile?

Pupils: (17) no
Teacher: (18) I don't think so either.

Pupil 1's response to message (6) that his brain tells him the boy in the picture is having fun receives short shrift from the teacher, who dismisses this category of evidence. A response of this kind is of no interest, the teacher implies: what is really at issue is *how can we tell* ***by looking at the picture*** *that he's having fun* [emphasis added]. What we need is not subjective things like beliefs or feelings, but objective phenomena which others can also view. Note too in passing the fate of Pupil 2's message. It remains 'unheard' as it goes against an important rule of classroom discourse: speak when you are spoken to and speak only of the matter in hand, which is to say, on the topic introduced by the teacher. One more example to round off the discussion of the principles of judicious reasoning:

Extract 3:

Teacher: (1) why do you think this man is dressed up like this? (2) what do you think? (3) anyone like to help Paul? . . . (4) Ellen?
Ellen: (5) a scarecrow
Teacher: (6) can't hear you darling
Ellen: (7) a scarecrow
Teacher: (8) he's a scarecrow? (9) oh, he's not moving (10) he's just standing there, is he?
Ellen: (11) mm
Teacher: (12) do you all agree with that?
Pupils: (13) **mm yes
Pupils: (14) **no (MOST)
Teacher: (15) if you don't agree (16) you have to say why.

In many such episodes – sometimes fleeting, sometimes more elaborated – the rules of argumentation prevalent in our pedagogic ideology are being laid out for the children to imbibe: claims must be justified; justifications must be objectively validated; if an argument is rejected, the rejection must be justified. These are indeed the rules which govern scholarly discourse, and they are essential to the production of knowledge as we understand the term. Despite the fact that the teachers are dealing with perfectly mundane phenomena, such as children travelling in a bus, boys having fun, and the conventions for dressing scarecrows, I would suggest that here we are witnessing the initial steps towards laying down the foundations for theoretical thinking. The teachers are not (re-)producing knowledge per se; they are not dealing with specific subject areas of serious concern such as physics; at least on the surface their discourse does not represent 'complex forms of communication'. Strictly speaking in terms of Bernstein (1996) we are here witnessing not so much the functioning of instructional discourse as that of regulative discourse. And regulative discourse acts on the learning subject: it, first and foremost, regulates the mind. The teachers are engaged in the important business of beginning to shape the consciousness of the young child, transforming him into a pedagogic subject, a subject who might one day interrogate the existing body of knowledge, who might one day actively participate in the production of knowledge. It would seem then that Luria was right in putting his faith in the system of education: systematic instruction seems to be oriented towards laying the foundations for logical thinking. Whatever the consciously confirmed views about the object of teaching in traditional schools, the extracts I have examined here show that from a very early stage a form of deutero learning is on the cards; children are expected to imbibe the rules of valid argumentation.

But can we say without reservation that Luria was right? Would all those who enter an official pedagogic site necessarily learn these rules for thinking logically? In the last paragraph I deliberately used the word *imbibe* rather than *learn*. By doing this, I wanted to draw attention to the fact that this teaching of the fundamental conventions of scholarly discourse is not explicit; where the teaching is implicit, any learning that could possibly occur is of that which struck the listener as relevant, which the learner could absorb due to their own interest. It is true that human beings are learning machines and the most effective dynamo for powering that learning is discourse, but from this widely acknowledged maxim (Bateson 1972; Halliday 1975; Vygotsky 1978) it does not follow that all learners learn the same thing from a discourse. A necessary but not sufficient condition for targetted learning is that the thing to be learned is clearly foregrounded in the teacher's discourse, so that the prospective learner has a better chance of recognizing what they are supposed to learn. Such foregrounding is a necessary step for counteracting, at least to some extent, the principle I stated in the introduction, namely that given information will be interpreted from the addressee's point of view. It is a principle that applies everywhere, and classroom discourse is no exception to it. So the fact that the teacher's discourse is materially available to all pupils alike, does not really mean that they all necessarily engage with the discourse in the same way. If the teaching is implicit, the hearing will be selective, and if the hearing is selective, the learning will be selective too: what the message will say to whom, what will or will not appear relevant will depend on the social identity of the hearer.[3] To return to Luria's optimistic prediction, there is no doubt that systematic instruction and complex forms of communication involving concepts and their relations have the potential to shape a scholarly consciousness, but there is good reason to doubt that they actually perform this function for **every child** in the school. The single most important reason for this failure is the educational system's reluctance to hear the different voices in the classroom, to recognize multiple points of view that exist in every classroom in our pluralistic societies (Hasan 1996b). These comments hark back to the introductory discussions: receiving information is not a neutral process. In the following section I present a segment of classroom discourse which brings this point home quite starkly.

3.6 Classroom discourse: symbol, interpretation and experience

As the segment of classroom discourse I now want to examine is fairly lengthy, it will be broken up into appropriate extracts for discussion below. Note the consecutive numbering of the messages from extract 4a through to 4d; this shows the continuity. However, the messages of extract 4e are renumbered because some messages intervening between 4d and 4e have been excluded in order to save space. As it happens, extract 4a is not where the reading of this picture begins, as can be seen from the first message presented below. The picture that the teacher and her class are reading constitutes a narrative tableau: a saucepan is on the stove with steam rising from it. A little girl who is so tiny that she can scarcely reach the stove is on the point of approaching the saucepan; she might be about to lift it. In the doorway of this kitchen stands another girl, older, watching the scene. The teacher has just established in discussion with the class that the girl is about to lift the saucepan off the stove. This is where extract 4a begins:

Extract 4a:

Teacher: (1) you look at how tall the little girl is [sic!] . . . (2) she can only just reach that saucepan (3) what might happen to her?

Alan: (4) burn herself (5) burn herself

Teacher: (6) why do you think she might burn herself (7) how . . . how would she burn herself?

Alan: (8) [?if she be big] . . .
Teacher: (9) (ENCOURAGINGLY) you're right (10) just tell me again (11) I couldn't hear
Alan: (12) if she be big
Teacher: (13) (CORRECTING) if she was big . . .? (14) well, she's just a little bit tiny, isn't she? (15) she . . . what if . . . you know how sometimes you're just trying to reach something (16) and you can't quite reach it (17) and your hand slips (18) what do you think will happen (19) if her hand slips? (20) what will that saucepan do (20) if her hand slips? (21) Suzie?
Suzie: (22) burn herself
Teacher: (23) how will she burn herself? (24) what will the saucepan do?
Suzie: (25) tip down (26) and burn herself
Teacher: (27) right the saucepan will fall (28) and tip things all over her (29) and if the things in that saucepan are all hot (30) then she will – ? . . . (31) Alan?
Alan: (32) tip it over her
Teacher: (33) tip it over her (34) and what will happen to her?
Alan: (35) [?it'll] burn her
Teacher: (36) and she'll get burnt (37) and she will burn herself.

In this extract, the teacher seems to have two major concerns: one, the children must attend to the wording of their meanings; and two, the steps in inferring what might happen must be spelt out. The appeal to the children's own experience of a situation similar to that in the picture with the sequel half spelt out is particularly noteworthy: here the basis for the recognition of the situation and for the prediction of likely action is being sought in the experience of living. By the end of this interaction, the teacher seems to have established in negotiation with her pupils that the little girl is in a situation where she could hurt herself. The teacher now shifts the pupils' attention to the big girl. What is going to be her role in this drama?

Extract 4b:

Teacher: (38) what do you think this girl . . .? (39) who do you think this girl is? (40) who might she be? (41) Mandy?
Mandy: (42) um a girl that's gonna walk over (43) and smack her
Teacher: (44) do you think she might smack her? . . . (45) could be

As the teacher attempts to make her next move, which is to identify the big girl in the picture, there comes the first surprise of the lesson.

Mandy, as it were, hijacks the intended meaning of the teacher's question: *who might this girl be?* Mandy identifies the big girl by reference to a specific future action of hers. This is a rather unexpected response. Semantically speaking the question, *who is this girl?*, would typically receive a response that would identify the person in question by reference to some status, for example, *she's a neighbour/friend/sister/visitor* and so on. Lexicogrammatically, what we would have is an attributive clause with *she/the girl* as a Carrier and the status term as Attribute: the latter would identify the entity in question by assigning it membership in a class. It is of course possible to identify persons by their activity, but if so, the activity is an occupational one, and English has specific ways of managing this kind of classification: *she is a dancer/receptionist/cook/teacher* etc. It would be rare indeed to come across a response that classifies the entity by reference to a specific one-time activity. The teacher concedes the possibility that the big girl could be someone who might smack the little girl, but she does not welcome the response. She asks the question once again, throwing broad hints (see message 47 and 52–4) where to look for the answer.

Extract 4c:

Teacher:	(46) who do you think she is? (47) do you think she lives in this house with that little girl? (48) or do you think she's a friend? (49) who might she be? (50) Shirley?
Shirley:	(51) ooh ... live there
Teacher:	(52) she might live there (53) so who would she be to this little girl? (54) she would be her what?
Shirley:	(55) friend ... sister
Teacher:	(56) maybe her sister

As we shall see below, agreement on the classification of the big girl as a sister is critical to the direction in which the teacher wants the class to move. She expects this to clear the ground for her next move, but it will become obvious very soon that there is no plain sailing. Here is the ensuing discourse.

Extract 4d:

Teacher:	(57) what do you think that big sister's thinking? (58) as she is looking at her little sister (59) and seeing her touching that hot saucepan? (60) Alan do you know? ... (61) you don't know (62) does anybody know what she might be thinking? (63) Suzie?
Suzie:	(64) getting mad (65) getting mad

Teacher: (66) getting mad? (67) who's getting mad?
Suzie: (68) the big sister
Teacher: (69) why do you think she's getting mad?

Since George Orwell's great work, the descriptor 'big brother' has acquired a somewhat pejorative connotation in English. 'Big sister' is, however, different: in my understanding it has no connotation of overbearing authority and still retains its meaning as in *loco matris*, thus expected to have the same tender, loving, nurturing attitude as a mother. The teacher uses the expression 'big sister' in framing her question about the future intentions of the big girl. The children, however, do not appear to have any association of tenderness with the phrase 'big sister'. Alan is unable to provide any response, and Suzie offers one that must be considerably different from the teacher's expectations. Suzie believes that the big sister is *getting mad*. Note the idiomatic expression which in the child's experience is very likely to have occurred in an everyday situation. What, the teacher wants to know now, is the justification for this prediction about the big sister's reaction to the situation? It takes a good deal of to-ing and fro-ing before she can get Rosa to come up with a reason for why the big sister is getting mad: it's *because she*'s [the little girl] *touching the thing* [hot saucepan on the stove]. Patiently and very carefully, through a series of questions and answers, the teacher re-establishes all the significant elements in her reading of the picture, finishing with the conclusion: *the big sister knows if she* [the little girl] *touches it* [the saucepan], *it might . . . slip . . . and pour everything over and burn her*. It is clear from this discourse that for the teacher the picture construes a context in which the little girl's well-being is threatened; the big girl, because she is big, has the power to avert this threat, and of course we have now established that she is a big sister – so what will she do? This reading has been arrived at in negotiation with the children, and the process has taken time – some two to three minutes – and a considerable amount of talk. This intervening talk, which I have summarized above, is excluded for lack of space (note that the messages are now renumbered). In extract 4e the teacher once again puts her question. For her the answer to the question is quite clear: being a big sister, the big girl will protect the little girl, but for the children this is not a transparently obvious solution:

Extract 4e:
Teacher: (1) what could this big sister do (2) to help her little sister? (3) what could she do? (4) Derek?
Derek: (5) smack her . . .

Teacher: (6) maybe she could smack her (7) what else could she do (8) so she didn't burn herself? Shirley?
Shirley: (10) she could pick the saucepan up
Teacher: (11) and what could she do with it then?
Shirley: (12) put it (13) where she can't get it
Teacher: (14) good girl! (15) that's very good thinking (16) she – the big sister – <(17) because she's nice and tall (18) and she can reach that saucepan can't she> she could pick that saucepan up <(19) and put it somewhere where the little girl can't reach it> couldn't she?

As we can see from message (2) the teacher is now making her question more precise: *what could the big sister do* ***to help her little sister***? [emphasis added]. Even so Derek's response is: *smack her*. Conceding this possibility, the teacher once again asks the question, spelling out the situated meaning of *to help her*: she asks: *what* ***else*** *could she do* **so she** [the little girl] ***didn't burn herself***? [emphasis added]. This does produce the response she has been trying to elicit from her pupils. With some help from the teacher, Shirley is able to provide this desirable response: *she* [big sister] *could pick the saucepan up and put it where she* [little girl] *can't get it*. For the first time since the beginning of this picture reading episode the teacher offers an unreservedly positive evaluation: *good girl! That's very good thinking*. And like the teacher of another lesson which was discussed above (see extract 1b), she goes on to repeat this response, which in a very real sense is a response 'natural' to her, not to the children.

It is interesting to note the form of this repetition: an interpretation of its lexicogrammar reveals that by her choice of tag questions the teacher is attempting/expecting to get the children to subscribe to her view. She uses mood tags with reversed polarity (on grammatical terminology, used here, see Halliday 1994): *she can . . . can't she?* (message 18) and *she could . . . couldn't she?* The choice of reversed polarity mood tags makes disagreement a less likely and, therefore, a marked response on the addressee's part. It is thus used in contexts where you do not entertain the possibility of dissent. Thus a question such as *you love your mum don't you* is unremarkable because there is a very high probability the answer would be *yes I do*, whereas *you tell lies, don't you* is definitely odd since very few people, if any, would be expected to ascribe this immoral action to themselves. In using the reversed polarity mood tags, the teacher is, as it were, pre-empting disagreement from her class. The form of the question that elicits the desirable response from Shirley is also noteworthy: *what* ***else*** *could she do* **so she** [the little girl] ***didn't***

burn herself? [emphasis added]. The question concedes that the children's initial response: *smack her* is a possibility; at the same time it suggests that there are **other** possibilities; and, further, it unpacks the teacher's meaning of *help her little sister* (see message 2 in extract 4e): ***what else could she*** [the big sister] ***do so she*** [the little girl] ***didn't burn herself***. This is reminiscent of an experiment conducted by Holland (1981) (see further discussion in Bernstein 1990: 18–19) where children were asked to group coloured pictures of familiar food items whichever way they wished. Working-class children first grouped the items by reference to the items' direct relation to the specific local context of their own lives, for example, *this is what my mum makes, this is what we have for breakfast*, and so on. Middle-class children grouped the same items by reference to criteria that were relatively independent of local contexts, for example, *these come from the ground, all of these have butter in them*, and so on. However, when the same children were asked to think of *some other way of grouping* the same items, the point of reference shifted notably: significantly more working-class children grouped the items by reference to criteria that were independent of local contexts, while those in the middle-class moved more towards the use of local contexts for their grouping of the items. By the end of the experiment 'almost one third of the working-class children had changed their principle' for the recognition and classification of the given food items (Bernstein 1990: 19).

It would seem that in our picture reading lesson, the teacher has achieved success of a similar kind: she has managed to bring the class round to a view of the situation which does not come naturally to them, but which they are willing to see as a possibility. The teacher achieved this result by making her question as precise and explicit as possible. But this success is short lived, which is not really surprising. Although orientation to meanings can be changed, for this change to take root so that the alternative orientation becomes automatic, one would need many reiterations of alternative experience: a single lesson is not sufficient to shift the pupils from the position that seems natural to **them**. So in the case of the above discourse, despite Shirley's response and the teacher's careful re-play of it, the children do not now automatically believe that the big sister's role is to help the little girl. Thus during the struggle to establish what the big girl would do – and by now one begins to suspect that most probably it is not a question of what she **would** do, but one of what she **should** do – one of the children asserts: *the big girl could tell mummy . . . her sister was a naughty girl*. The teacher argues against this prediction, explaining that the little girl was not really naughty, she was just too small to realize the seriousness of her action, therefore she does not deserve to be punished. At the end of this exchange she turns to Rob, presumably to check on what he has learned about appropriate behaviour in a similar situation: *Rob, what would you say to Jenny* [Jenny is Rob's little sister] *if she touched a hot saucepan?* Rob's response is both laconic and, by now, quite predictable: *smack her*. The basis of his prediction is not in what the teacher has been saying in this class, here, but what life has been teaching him day in and day out. It is clear then that the children's prediction of what the big girl would do is at odds with the teacher's prediction; this is because the points of view that the teacher and the children bring to the reading of this narrative picture are considerably different. The central problem is the incompatibility of their recognition of the situation in Bernstein's terms; their sense of what social practice is likely to flow from this understanding naturally depends on what they recognize the situation to be. The principle *if A then B* holds but the meaning of *A and B* does not. I summarize the position in table 3.1, which shows that semantically the two parties are far apart and there is a considerable semantic distance between them:

Table 3.1 Semantic distance: different points of view, different significance

Teacher's point of view	Pupil's point of view
context for protective action: the big sister will help avert danger from her little sister	context for control: the big sister will punish the little girl's naughty action
because	**because**
the little girl is too young to realize the consequence of her action and she is likely to burn herself	the little girl is being naughty in trying to lift a hot saucepan and she is likely to burn herself
therefore	**therefore**
since the big sister realizes the little girl's danger, being older and wiser, she will remove the source of danger by moving the hot saucepan out of the little girl's reach	since the big girl can see that the little girl is being naughty, being bigger and stronger she will smack her to stop her from touching the saucepan
and	**and**
she will explain to the little girl why she is doing this so that the little girl will be careful in the future.	she will tell mummy that the little girl is being naughty so that mummy can punish her to make her act properly in the future.

In the data of picture reading interactions, we note a recurrent feature: teachers are very careful about establishing what it is that the children are physically 'seeing'. The picture-reading lesson discussed above is no exception: here too the material attributes of the picture are identically present to both parties. The teacher and her pupils do not differ on what it is they see with their eyes. The real question is how they interpret what they see: what context does the material situation represent? What is the meaning of that particular physical arrangement of relevant objects and persons that they find in the pictorial tableau? The introduction of this paper claimed that the recognition of what the given information is construing depends on the receiver's social positioning, which is inalienably related to their experience of living. Let me add now that the picture reading lesson in extracts 4a–e comes from a school in a working-class area. Here, from phase one, are a few examples of working-class discourse in the context of control when the mean age of the children was three years eight months. In extract 5 Pete is running around near his mother while holding a glass full of juice; the mother fears the juice will spill; she wants Pete to stop.

Extract 5:

Mother:	(1) don't do that ... (MOTHER WAITS FOR PETE TO RESPOND. HE PAYS NO HEED) (2) now look you'll get it all over me
Pete:	(PETE LAUGHS AND CONTINUES RUNNING)
Mother:	(3) it's not funny (4) what's funny about that?** (5)[?] you do it again (6) and I'll whack you

In extract 6 Davie is hungry; he would like macaroni for lunch. His mother wants him to have a sandwich. Davie rejects this suggestion somewhat rudely.

Extract 6:

Mother:	(1) go to your room
Davie:	(2) no!
Mother:	(3) I beg your pardon! (4) you do what I say (5) or I'll smack you (6) now do you want maca – do you want sandwich or not?
Davie:	(7) yes (STAMPING ANGRILY) (8) Peanut butter ... (9) peanut butter ... please mummy! (CHASTENED VOICE ??DID MOTHER PHYSICALLY THREATEN)

In extract 7 mother is trying to get Karen into her bed. In fact she has been trying for some time. She has reasoned, scolded, humoured, and now she is really 'getting mad'.

Extract 7:

Mother:	(1) Karen, do as you're – (SLAPS KAREN) (2) (IN ANGRY VOICE) put your legs down (3) or I'm going outside right this minute without a kiss (4) now put your legs down (ANGRY VOICE)
Karen:	(5) mmhm (KAREN REFUSES TO OBEY)
Mother:	(6) (ARRANGING KAREN'S LEGS UNDER THE BLANKET) now, give a kiss goodnight
Karen:	(7) I'm not
Mother:	(8) you're not gonna kiss me?** (9) why?
Karen:	(10) 'cause
Mother:	(11) 'cause why?
Karen:	(12) 'cause I don't like you

It is not necessary to multiply these examples. Overwhelmingly situations of control are situations of conflict in the working-class subjects' lives. It is the environment where the power of authority, and the irrationality of power are brought home to the child. The meanings of the sayings make authority of power palpable: commands are direct, often unadorned by modification; reasons are terse, often upholding the power of hierarchy and/or conventions. With respect to these semantic features,[4] the difference between middle-class and working-class mothers' discourse in the context of control is statistically highly significant (Hasan 1992a, 1992b). The children's prediction about the big girl's behaviour is rooted in their personal experience. Like Luria's subjects, the children responding to the picture in extracts 4a–e are simply being 'natural', but their way of being natural is significantly different from the teacher's way of being 'natural'. The teacher's reaction is closer in its approach to the middle-class modes of control, where the power of authority is made invisible, commands are transformed into consultations about needs, desires, willingness, and reasons typically celebrate the 'logic' of physical relations between things and events (Hasan 1992a). It seems reasonable to conclude that in the picture-reading lesson neither party is inherently more intelligent, more im/moral than the other: they are simply responding in the way that comes naturally to them, that is to say, in keeping with their social positioning – their cognition is fashioned by their experience of living in society. This is not a fact simply about the working-class children; it is also a fact about the teacher and about middle-class pupils.

3.7 Experience and systematic instruction: social life, learning and discourse

The two sets of classroom discourse I have discussed appear to be quite dissimilar, but their juxtaposition here is deliberate. If the only discourses we knew about were of the type exemplified by extracts 1–3, we would not hesitate to agree with Luria that anyone who has had the benefit of 'school instruction and concomitant creation of special 'theoretical' activity' would achieve a particular kind of mental development. This would imply the belief that school instruction is equally efficacious for all children, which in its turn would imply that classroom discourses are heard in the same way by all pupils. It is this latter position that is thrown into doubt by lessons of the kind exemplified by 4a–e. A consideration of this classroom discourse tells us that what might be taken to be the 'same' in terms of its appearance is not necessarily the 'same' for everyone in terms of its meaning: what gets in the way of arriving at the same meaning is the difference in the experiences of persons who are socially differentially positioned, because meaning is refracted through the experience of one's social location. It follows that a given instance of systematic instruction may in fact not be the same for children coming from different social locations. In light of this finding, Luria's opposition of experience to systematic instruction (see 'Thinking in society' above) which suggested a clear boundary between the two appears rather questionable. Certainly, for purposes of analysis, this distinction has to be recognized, but it does not seem justifiable to believe that in the life of social subjects the two forms of consciousness created by the two ways of 'learning' remain forever compartmentalized, each having a separate existence from the other. Luria's own research and the data of phase two from my research demonstrate quite clearly that experience of everyday living will colour the meanings in systematic instruction. It is also possible, at least in theory, that systematic instruction might change our way of experiencing everyday life, though this latter position is less likely. To understand why this should be so, we need to understand the working of social positioning – what produces it and what it, in its turn, produces.

In the last decade or so, positioning theory has gained a good deal of popularity, but in many of these discussions the term 'positioning' boils down to performative positioning of the interactive other or of the speaking self (see for example Harré and Langenhove 1999); it is as if its genesis were independent of what else goes on in the social organization of communal life. This approach to positioning is significantly different from Bernstein's use of the term, which locates it within the politico-economic structure of the society. For Bernstein, the production and distribution of capital is the fundamental social fact from which flow the distribution of power and the principles of control. The concept of social positioning is thus ultimately grounded in class relations: positioning can in fact be paraphrased as inter-subject class relations (Bernstein 1990: 17). To quote Bernstein, 'class relations generate, distribute, reproduce, and legitimate distinctive forms of communication, which transmit dominant and dominated codes ... subjects are differentially positioned by these codes in the process of acquiring them ... from this point of view, codes are culturally determined positioning devices ... Ideology is constituted through and in such positioning' (1990: 13). In this view, ideology is not content: it is not that some ideas or attitudes are ideological, others are not; it is simply that through experience we develop a particular way of relating to whatever we encounter in life. The question is not whether someone has ideology or not; it is simply a question of what the ideology actually is, how we see what we claim to see.

For reasons that need not detain us here, Bernstein's concept of code has not been well understood. Let me explain about Bernstein very briefly here: codes are a device for positioning; to say this is to say also that codes are related realizationally[5] to positioning. It is through the coding orientation that our social positioning can be construed and it is our social positioning that activates for us the habitual choice of one code rather than another. But code itself is an abstract concept: it refers to orders of relevance, to what appears thinkable and sayable. What makes a person's coding orientation palpable is their actual ways of meaning, the way they manage their discourse with an other, the texts they are able to manage as producers and as receivers. The successful management of discourse with an other demands a certain degree of reflexivity. Linguists recognize this when they draw attention to the fact that the comprehension of an other's discourse presupposes a 'sharing of the same world' by the interactants: each must 'know' the other's world. This process of the internalization of the world in which we live, act and speak begins very early in life, and it is synonymous with learning the coding orientation of one's immediate group: the newly born infant is, as it were, automatically socially located at birth. This automatic assigning and assuming of social positioning is a condition for human survival. And a condition for the assuming of the social position is participation in the communication game. If we perceive a circularity in the relations of discourse, positioning and coding orientation, this is because underlying their relations is the fact of co-genesis (Hasan 1989). A person's ways of saying and meaning are not independent of their social positioning, and social positioning is itself construed by semiotic acts which enact the interpersonal relationships, without which the idea of social positioning is vacuous. Infants have to be drawn into this complex web from a very early stage (Halliday 1975, 1980; Hasan 2001), some might even suggest before birth (Greenfield 2000). As Firth put it perspicaciously, 'the young human has to be progressively incorporated into a social organization, and the main condition of that incorporation is sharing the local magic – that is, the language' (1957: 185).

Firth went on to make a distinction between speech fellowship and language community, 'A speech fellowship sees itself and hears itself as different from those who do not belong. . . . Within . . . [a] speech fellowship a speaker is **phonetically and verbally content** because when he speaks to one of his fellows he is also speaking to himself' (ibid. 186; emphasis mine). One could go further; one could claim that within the immediate group, the child is content not only phonetically and verbally, but also **semantically and ideologically**. It is in this experience of interaction that the child's social structure becomes a reality for him, as Bernstein pointed out some decades ago (Bernstein 1971), and through his own and the other's acts of speech the child comes to 'internalise the world [he] experiences in the living of social life' (Hasan 2002). When young children first begin to learn how to talk, they are not simply learning language; they are also learning through language (Halliday 1980) about the way their world is organized: the shape of reality is defined for them in and through these interactions. This internalization provides criteria for both the recognition of the nature and identity of a context and the relevant rules for active participation in it. As Bernstein maintained, in providing the orders of relevance, the coding orientation logically sets aside as unnatural that which departs from the internalized orders of relevance which happen to be shared by one's immediate community; alternative views of the world are thus suppressed (Bernstein 1971, 1975, 1990, 1996). Much of the innocence of childhood resides in the fact that for the child there is no other reality except that which they know through daily experience.

The above is a simplified picture of what the positioning-positioned form of communication does in the very early years of a social subject's life. What this suggests is that the point of view, the ideology that I spoke of as being active in the processing of any information, becomes active fairly early. The analysis of phase one data in our research revealed significant semantic variation in the discourse of children from the two social classes (Hasan 1989), suggesting that in some sense ideology begins to take hold early (recall that the mean age of the 24 children was three years eight months). It is not that these internalizations are engraved images destined to remain with the social subjects for ever; but it is that relatively more effort is needed to bring about this change. Two considerations appear relevant here. First, recent work in neurolinguistics shows (Deacon 1997; Greenfield 2000) that the early connections are also the longer-lasting ones; second, and related to the first point, is the fact that 'as we develop, the contribution of the mind will be to enhance each conscious moment by imbuing each snapshot of the outside world with meaning' (Greenfield 2000: 164). This meaning is regulated by the developing coding orientation. If this is so, then it is very likely that simply because the world is already being refracted through an already established point of view, systematic instruction will need to make special effort to bring about the kind of change Luria spoke about if it so happens that the learners' experience has not already paved the way to such acceptance, as it tends to do for the middle-class child coming to school.

In this connection it is important to remember that, as Bernstein pointed out, official education is 'essentially a moral activity which articulates the dominant ideology/ies of dominant groups' (1990: 66). This is one reason for suggesting that the discourse in official educational sites may encounter a resistance from dominated groups, or, at the least, it may not be heard in the way that the teacher takes it for granted it would be. This would not be surprising because, in a curious way, classroom discourse presents the converse of the habitual orientations of meaning so far as the dominated group is concerned. For the dominating classes, the discourse of control makes principles of power and authority invisible, while information is made explicit, its attributes made as visible, detailed and precise as possible. In this description, we can certainly recognize the classroom data that have been presented here: the semantic analysis and comparison of mothers and teachers in my research shows that teachers' talk presents itself as a somewhat exaggerated version of the semantic style characteristic of mothers from the dominating classes. So, as far as the dominated classes are concerned, our results reveal that the discourse of control makes the principles of power and authority highly visible, while information is left implicit, its attributes invisible, lacking precision and detail (Hasan 1989, 1992a, 1992b; Cloran

1994, 2000; Williams 1995, 1999, 2001). It is not surprising that there existed an appreciable semantic distance between the children and the teacher in 4a–e.

If we are really serious about bringing social change through school instruction, then it is important that a form of communication be devised which bridges this distance, which breaks through the barrier without alienating the already dominated child. Currently there seems very little effort from this point of view. Official educational systems insist on retaining a 'univocal' discourse in the classroom, because either it is assumed that the dominating voice is the only voice that actually exists in the classroom or perhaps that it **should** be the only voice: that the alternative voices deserve to be suppressed. In any event, to my knowledge at least, no dialogue between the voices has ever been entertained. But, as I have suggested elsewhere (see Hasan 1996b), this is the single most severe problem in official pedagogic systems. On the face of it, these systems appear to invest a good deal of vocal energy in attempts to devise strategies for overcoming the problem of failure in schools, but all these strategies are predicated on the assumption of univocality: it is as if we do not really wish to confront the real problem, or perhaps because the real problem is so difficult we shortsightedly try to solve other problems. When attention is drawn to this aspect, as for example it was in the work of Bernstein and his colleagues some forty years ago, instead of attempting to understand the problem, it appeared easier for many colleagues to simply attribute his comments to a deep class prejudice (for details of such critique and Bernstein's refutation of them, see Bernstein 1990, 1996). There are certainly those who refuse to believe that in our pluralistic societies different ways of saying and meaning exist, and that in the hierarchized organization of our societies, the differences between ways of saying and ways of meaning are exploited by the dominating segments for their own benefit. Ironically, these same persons who pose as the saviours of the disadvantaged, tend to see the meanings that characterize dominated coding orientations as if they were meanings that could not possibly be meant by anyone. The twisted argument goes that the dominated classes are rational, and therefore, they must mean the same rational meanings that we the dominating classes do. This is the only interpretation that can be put on their claim that meanings regulated by dominated codes have been dreamt up maliciously by biased researchers who are bent upon showing that the disadvantaged do not know how to speak!

There is an urgent need to problematize the question: What is the best way to encourage a dialogue between speakers whose discourse is regulated by different coding orientations? Linguists have written volumes on shared discourse axioms, conversational implicatures, and shared worlds. It is time to ask: how can we talk across unshared worlds, across discursive axioms that are not in agreement, and conversational implicatures that have distinctly different points of departure? How can a teacher capitalize on the presence of multiple voices in the classroom without creating in any of her speakers either a sense of superiority or a sense of being devalued? While I admire the patience of the teacher whose discourse I have examined in 4a–e, it is doubtful that by the end of the lesson the pupils had any idea what exactly was the issue, and what difference it makes to punish or to protect. The central issue of the teacher–pupil talk during this session was the choice between punishment and avoidance as strategies for the prevention of something undesirable. The teacher at no point explicitly engaged with this central issue; she simply indicated, in an implicit manner, by her pattern of evaluations that she did not favour the children's spontaneous response. What might have possibly helped at this point was the practice of reflection literacy (Hasan 1996b). The teacher could have raised the why question: Why is punishment better than removing the source of the problem? Who would it benefit to punish the little girl? How soon do little children come to discriminate between good acts and bad ones that need to be punished? But to set up this kind of dialogue, the teacher herself needs to understand the history of the children's response. This understanding can only come if the conspiracy of silencing research of this kind under false pretences is abandoned. Those who examine classroom discourse have a responsibility to understand that discourse cannot be separated from social life. Speaking may appear effortless, always responding to the 'present' of the discourse to its 'now' and to its 'here', but every utterance has behind it the history of the speaking person, which is to say, the history of the speaker's speech fellowship – in the words of Bernstein, between the system of language and the coding orientations there lies the social structure of the speaker's society. Discourse analysis of classroom talk has, over the past quarter of a century, simply swept these deeper sociolinguistic issues under the carpet, focusing on the form of the discourse and/or its instructional content. We need an examination of classroom discourse which is able to highlight the unilateral design of this interaction and we need to ask why this design is preferred? Whom does it benefit? Whom does it disadvantage?

References

Bateson, Gregory (1972) *Steps to an Ecology of Mind: A Revolutionary Approach to Man's Understanding of Himself*. New York: Ballantine Books.

Bernstein, Basil (1971) *Class, Codes and Control: Volume 1 Theoretical Studies Towards a Sociology of Language*. London: Routledge and Kegan Paul.

Bernstein, Basil (1975) *Class, Codes and Control: Volume 3 Towards a Theory of Educational Transmission*. 2nd ed. London: Routledge and Kegan Paul.

Bernstein, Basil (1990) *The Structuring of Pedagogic Discourse: Volume IV Class, Codes and Control*. London: Routledge.

Bernstein, Basil (1996) *Pedagogy, Symbolic Control and Identity: Theory, Research, Critique*. Revised edn. Oxford: Rowman and Littlefield.

Butt, David G. (1989) The object of language. In Ruqaiya Hasan and J. R. Martin, (eds), *Language Development: Learning Language, Learning Culture*. Norwood, NJ: Ablex, 66–110.

Christie, Frances (1996) *The Pedagogic Discourse of Secondary School Social Sciences: Geography*. Melbourn: University of Melbourne Press.

Cloran, Carmel (1994) *Rhetorical Units and Decontextualisation: An Enquiry into some Relations of Context, Meaning and Grammar*. Monographs in Systemic Linguistics no 6. Nottingham: Department of English, Nottingham University.

Cloran, Carmel (1999) Contexts for learning. In Frances Christie (ed.), *Pedagogy and the Shaping of Consciousness: Linguistic and Social Processes*. London: Cassell, 31–65.

Cloran, Carmel (2000) Socio-semantic variation: different wordings, different meanings. In Len Unsworth (ed.), *Researching Language in Schools and Communities: Functional Linguistic Perspectives*. London: Cassell, 152–83.

Deacon, T. (1997) *The Symbolic Species: The Co-evolution of Language and the Human Brain*. New York: W. W. Norton & Co.

Donaldson, Margaret (1978) *Children's Minds*. Glasgow: Collins.

Donaldson, Margaret (1992) *Human Minds: An Exploration*. London: Penguin Books.

Edwards, A.D. and Westgate, D.P.G. (1987) *Investigating Classroom Talk*. London: Falmer Press.

Evans, J. St B.T., Newstead, Stephen E. and Byrne, Ruth M.J. (1993) *Human Reasoning: The Psychology of Deduction*. Hillsdale NJ: Lawrence Erlebaum.

Firth, J.R. (1957) *Papers in Linguistics 1934–1951*. London: Oxford University Press.

Greenfield, Susan (2000) *The Private Life of the Brain*. London: Penguin Books.

Halliday, M.A.K. (1975) *Learning How to Mean: Explorations in the Development of Language*. London: Arnold.

Halliday, M.A.K. (1980) Three aspects of children's language development:

learning language, learning through language, learning about language. In Yetta Goodman, Myna M. Haussler and Dorothy M. Strickland (eds), *Oral and Written Language: Impact on Schools*. International Reading Association & National Council of Teachers of English. (A fuller version to appear in *Collected Works of M.A.K. Halliday, Volume 4: The Language of Early Childhood*. Ed. Jonathan Webster. London: Continuum 2002.

Halliday, M.A.K. (1992) How do you mean? In Martin Davies and Louise Ravelli (eds), *Advances in Systemic Linguistics: Recent Theory and Practice*. London: Painter, 20–35.

Halliday, M.A.K. (1993) The act of meaning. In James E. Alatis (ed.), *Language, Communication and Social Meaning: Georgetown University Round Table on Language and Linguistics 1992*. Washington, DC: Georgetown University Press, 7–21.

Halliday, M.A.K. (1994) *An Introduction to Functional Grammar*. 2nd edn. London: Arnold.

Halliday, M.A.K. and Matthiessen, Christian (1999) *Construing Experience with Meaning: A Language-Based Approach to Cognition*. London: Cassell.

Harré, Rom and van Langenhoven, Luk (eds) (1999) *Positioning Theory*. Oxford: Blackwell.

Hasan, Ruqaiya (1983) *A Semantic Network for the Analysis of Messages in Everyday Talk between Mothers and Their Children*. Mimeo, Macquarie University N.S.W.

Hasan, Ruqaiya (1989) Semantic variation and sociolinguistics. *Australian Journal of Linguistics*, 9(2): 221–76.

Hasan, Ruqaiya (1992a) Rationality in everyday talk: from process to system. In Jan Svartvik (ed.), *Directions in Corpus Linguistics: Proceedings of Nobel Symposium 82*. Berlin: Mouton de Gruyter, 257–307.

Hasan, Ruqaiya (1992b) Meaning in sociolinguistic theory. In Kingsley Bolton and Helen Kwok (eds), *Sociolinguistics Today: International Perspective*. London: Routledge, 80–119.

Hasan, Ruqaiya (1995) The conception of context in text. In Peter H. Fries and Michael Gregory (eds), *Discourse in Society*. Norwood, NJ: Ablex, 183–283.

Hasan, Ruqaiya (1996a) Semantic networks: A tool for the analysis of meaning. In Carmel Cloran, David Butt and Geoff Williams (eds), *Ways of Saying, Ways of Meaning: Selected Papers of Ruqaiya Hasan*. London: Cassell.

Hasan, Ruqaiya (1996b) Literacy, everyday talk and society. In Ruqaiya Hasan and Geoff Williams (eds), *Literacy in Society*. 377–424. Harlow, Longman.

Hasan, Ruqaiya (2000) The uses of talk. In Srikant Sarangi and Malcolm Coulthard (eds), *Discourse in Social Life*. London: Pearson Education, 28–47.

Hasan, Ruqaiya (2001) Wherefore context? The place of context in the system and process of language. In Ren Shaozeng, William Guthrie,

I. W. Ronald Fong (eds), *Grammar and Discourse: Proceedings of the International Conference on Discourse Analysis*. Macau: Universidad de Macau, 1–21.

Hasan, Ruqaiya (2002) Semiotic mediation and mental development in pluralistic societies: some implications for tomorrow's schooling. In Gordon Wells and Guy Claxton (eds), *Learning for Life in the 21st Century: Socio-cultural Perspectives on the Future of Education*. Oxford: Blackwell.

Hickman, Maya (ed.) (1987) *Social and Functional Approaches to Language and Thought*. Hillsdale, NY: New York Academic Press.

Holland, J. (1981) Social class and orientations to meanings. *Sociology*, 15(1): 1–8.

Lemke, Jay L. (1990) *Talking Science: Language, Learning and Values*. Norwood, NJ: Ablex.

Luke, Allan (1996) Genres of power? Literacy education and the production of capital. In Ruqaiya Hasan and Geoff Williams (eds), *Literacy in Society*. London: Longman.

Luria, A.R. (1976) *Cognitive Development: Its Cultural and Social Foundations*. Ed. Michael Cole. Cambridge, MA: Harvard University Press.

Mehan, Hugh (1979) *Learning Lessons: Social Organization in the Classroom*. Cambridge, MA: Harvard University Press.

Mertz, Elizabeth and Parmentier, Richard J. (eds) (1985) *Semiotic Mediation: Sociocultural and Psychological Perspectives*. Hillsdale, NY: New York Academic Press.

Popper, K. (1992) *Unended Quest: An Intellectual Autobiography*. London: Routledge.

Sinclair, McH. J. and Coulthard, Malcolm (1975) *Towards an Analysis of Discourse: The English Used by Teachers and Pupils*. London: Oxford University Press.

Vygotsky, L. S. (1978) *Mind in Society: The Development of Higher Psychological Functions*. Eds Michael Cole, Vera John-Steiner, Sylvia Scribner and Ellen Souberman. Cambridge, MA: Harvard University Press.

Wells, Gordon (1986) *The Meaning Makers: Children Learning Language and Using Language To Learn*. London: Hodder and Stoughton.

Wertsch, James V. (1985) *Vygotsky and the Social Foundation of Mind*. Cambridge, MA: Harvard University Press.

Williams, Geoff (1995) *Joint Book-Reading and Literacy Pedagogy: A Socio-Semantic Interpretation*. Unpublished PhD dissertation. School of English, Linguistics and Media, Macquarie University. (Available as CORE 19:3 and 20:1.)

Williams, Geoff (1999) The pedagogic device and the production of pedagogic discourse: a case example in early literacy education. In Frances Christie (ed.), *Pedagogy and the Shaping of Consciousness: Linguistic and Social Processes*. London: Cassell, 123–55.

Williams, Geoff (2001) Literacy pedagogy prior to schooling: Relations between social positioning and semantic variation. In Ana Morais, Isabel

Neves, Brian Davies, and Harry Daniels (eds), *Towards a Sociology of Pedagogy: The Contribution of Basil Bernstein to Research*. New York: Peter Lang.

Notes

1 The project, titled 'The Role of Everyday Talk between Mothers and Children in Establishing Ways of Learning' was conducted during 1984–88. Funding was received from the Australian Research Council and Macquarie University Research grant scheme, which is hereby gratefully acknowledged. For further details of this project see Butt (1989), Hasan (1989, 1992a, 1992b, 2000), and Cloran (1994, 1999). My thanks are due to Carmel Cloran for her valuable contribution to every phase of this project.

2 The 24 dyads were evenly distributed by social class and sex of the children. The children's mean age was three years eight months. The recording of the conversation was made by the mothers themselves during the course of going about their everyday household activities. The categories for semantic analysis were devised by me (Hasan 1983); a partial amount of these categories will be found in Hasan (1989, 1992b, 1996a), Cloran (1994, 2000), and Williams (1995, 2001).

3 This is precisely the criticism one might level at progressive pedagogy in schools, where the role of the teacher is said to be that of a facilitator. This is supposed to remove control from the child's learning, so that they can grow as their inner self dictates. There remains, however, the problem that when education becomes facilitation, the facilitator has no way of knowing what learning it is that is being facilitated – such knowledge comes to the teacher only in the moment of evaluation, and typically at the cost of the pupil.

4 For details of semantic analysis see Hasan (1989, 1992b, 1996a), Cloran (1994, 1999), Williams (1995, 1999).

5 On realization see Halliday (1992, 1993), Hasan (1995), Halliday and Matthiessen (1999).

4

Learning Language: Learning Culture in Singapore

Linda Thompson

4.1 Introduction

The nursery rhyme genre, including lullabies, game-rhymes and rhyming alphabets, is essentially an adult-inspired traditional rhyme passed from parent to child as nursery entertainment (Cambridge Encyclopaedia 1997: 775). Opie and Opie (1951: 3) suggest that these rhymes are sung or said by adults to soothe and amuse the child. The traditional form of the text comprises rhymes and alliteration that are easily memorized. Huber (1955: 81) suggests that they appeal to the child as pleasure rather than significance. However, in contrast, Hasan (1985: 21) states they are not concerned with 'experiential content' and 'shine only as a text'. Nursery rhymes are texts that are learnt informally, usually before the child enters the world of formal education and literacy. For Hasan (1985: 28) the nursery rhyme 'is simply learnt in such a diffuse way that ... it is one of the most invisible acts of learning'. It is this invisibility that makes the nursery rhyme of particular significance. The aim of this chapter is to explore the invisible act of learning.

4.2 The text

The rhyme selected for analysis is not strictly a nursery rhyme. It is taken from a compilation of Singaporean rhymes written by Khoo Kim Choo and illustrated by Patrick Yee. Khoo is an educator in early childhood education (Khoo 1996). She runs the Regional Training and Resource Centre in Early Childhood Care and Education for Asia and provides consultation on early childhood. She is also the Executive Director of the National Trade Union Council (NTUC) Childcare Co-operative and its subsidiaries. The NTUC Childcare Co-operative Ltd is the largest single provider of affordable childcare in Singapore. Currently, it has 25 centres with an intake of approximately three thousand children whose age range from 18 months to six years old (NTUC Childcare). The centres not only provide childcare services but also offer a bilingual pre-school education programme. The rhymes selected are specially written as part of the curriculum for the NTUC Childcare Centres.

There are two important reasons for this choice of text. The first is that a rhyme written by a Singaporean author can provide a rich insight into Singaporean cultural values. The second is that since the rhyme was specifically written by a pre-school educator for educational purposes, it is anticipated that it will be widely learned in Singapore. According to Bruner (1996: 15) 'An official enterprise presumably cultivates beliefs, skills and feelings in order to transmit and explicate its sponsoring culture's ways of interpreting the natural and social world.'

In this chapter I use a systemic functional framework analysis to demonstrate the ways in which Singaporean societal values are realized systematically through language. The aim is to make more explicit the invisible acts of learning that are taking place and to demonstrate the ways in which learning language plays a central role in this socialization process.

4.3 The Singapore context

Since context is central to a Systemic Functional Linguistics (SFL) approach to understanding language use, it is important to begin with some contextual understanding of Singapore. Gaining independence in 1965, one of the stated political and social priorities of government has been to establish a strong Singaporean identity based on a cohesive, pluralist nation. Singaporeans are actively encouraged to create new ways of nurturing this collective identity, of fostering this national ethos and of being united in their diversity.

A prevailing feature of the Singapore philosophy is the theme of nation-building. As part of this nation-building process since independence, Singapore has pursued a 'unity-in-diversity' approach to national integration (Kuo 1980: 58). The policies of the People's Association Party (PAP) government aim to create a common consciousness among Singaporeans. Campaigns are frequently supported through national icons and symbols. Initiatives have included the multiracial policy, the bilingual policy and the public housing programme (Quah 1990).

Within the terms of the multiracial policy, the Singapore population is represented officially by the four race model CMIO – Chinese, Malay, Indian and Others (Siddique 1989 cited in Chua 1995: 8). A person's culture is not self-ascribed but determined by affiliation to race. The official four race model was introduced to reduce differences in languages and dialects within each racial group by consolidating heterogeneous communities internally through the recognition of one language, rather than a number of dialects. This has become established as the *one language one culture* policy (Ho 1998: 210).

Singapore's bilingual education policy has been adopted to reinforce multiracialism and multiculturalism. Under this policy, English is the medium of education and Mandarin, Malay or Tamil is learned as a second language. English, which is not the dominant language of any one ethnic group, has become the lingua franca and was chosen to facilitate inter-ethnic communication and strengthen social cohesiveness. Moreover, English, the international language for trade, science and technology, is viewed as necessary for the nation's economic success. However, English is also viewed, in some quarters, as transmitting undesirable values, while the second languages (known as the mother tongues in Singapore) are considered to be transmitters of the better values, such as diligence and filial piety. This is a view encapsulated by former President Wee Kim Wee (1989) in the following statement, 'Traditional Asian ideas of morality, duty and society which have sustained and guided us in the past are giving way to a more Westernized, individualistic, and self-centred outlook on life' (cited in Shared Values 1991).

The perceived move away from dominant Asian values such as group solidarity to dominant Western values such as individualism is a major concern for the government and is perceived as undermining the nation's economic competitiveness and social cohesion. Thus, a set of national values has been identified so as to provide the 'moral anchors [to] buttress Singapore's Asian value system against over-Westernization and de-culturalization' (Prime Minister Goh Chok Tong 1991, cited in Bokhorst-Heng 1998: 309). The four core values include placing the nation before community, and society before self; upholding the family as a basic building block of society; resolving major issues through consensus instead of contention; and racial and religious tolerance and harmony (Shared Values: 1991). These core values, picked from the various ethnic groups in Singapore, form the basis of Singapore's official culture as well as provide a definition of the Singaporean identity. In other words, at the national level, nation-building involves the inculcation of non-culture-specific values such as loyalty, discipline and effort as well as a commitment to the cultural heritage of the various ethnic groups in Singapore (Gopinathan 1980: 192). Clammer (1985: 28) suggests that although at the macro-level, the Singaporean culture is defined as one that contains traditional values from the different ethnic groups and at the same time embracing progress, at the micro-level, Singaporeans are 'cultural brokers', where their cultural identities are fluid, encompassing more than one system of cultural values. These cultural values need not necessarily be identifiable with those selected by the government to develop the Singaporean identity.

There are two main tenets to the PAP government national unity policy: language planning and the public housing programme. Before the Housing Development Board (HDB) was established in 1960, the population was concentrated in ethnic enclaves. This ethnic segregation policy was a direct result of the British colonial government. Since 1960, high-rise flats have been built by HDB to house the population and to unite the different races. Ethnic quotas in the HDB neighbourhoods and blocks ensure that each housing estate is ethnically integrated. These integrated high-rise flats have become a distinguishing feature of the Singapore landscape. Further, to cultivate a sense of social responsibility towards the nation, national campaigns are carried out regularly. One of the many national campaigns is the 'Clean and Green Week . . . Green for Life' campaign. This campaign aims to promote and inculcate environmental consciousness by addressing issues such as maintaining a litter-free environment.

Nation-building policies implemented at the national level are further reinforced at the institutional level through the formal educational system. Education is heavily emphasized in Singapore. The widespread establishment of pre-school centres such as NTUC Childcare Centres and PAP kindergartens reflects the literate culture of Singapore. It is common for children as young as three or four years old in Singapore to be enrolled in pre-schools where they acquire basic literacy skills (Gupta 1994: 152).

However, the educational system in Singapore is not just concerned with academic achievement. It also strives to provide a well-rounded education for Singaporeans where social values such as co-operation, friendship, respect, moral values and a love for Singapore are taught in school. *The Desired Outcomes of Education* (Singapore Ministry of

Education 1998: 2) states that, 'formal education must cultivate instincts in our young so that they identify Singapore as their home; a home to live in, to strive to improve and, if called upon, to defend. An educated person is also one responsible to the community and country'.

The text chosen for discussion here is *Going Downtown* (Khoo 1996). This Singaporean rhyme for children, 'Mr Frog', shares some of the textual features of conventional nursery rhymes including acoustic characteristics, as well as repetition, alliteration and assonance. Hasan (1985: 24) suggests that these features have 'a special . . . appeal to the very young and its appeal is mostly through the abstract medium of playing upon the lexico-grammar and the sound system of language'. Halliday (1985: 97) suggests that different modes of transmission create different versions of realities. Written language presents a *synoptic* view of the world, while spoken language presents a *dynamic* view. The world is captured as a phenomenon in the written form and as a process in its spoken form. In highly literate cultures, the written text is highly valued and functions as an important tool for learning about the environment where the encoded meaning is interpreted as stored knowledge, while relatively less recognition is given to the role of spoken language in the acquisition of knowledge. The aim here is to demonstrate linguistically how a newly created Singaporean rhyme plays a social role in transmitting cultural values central to the socialization process. Culture was defined by E.B. Taylor (1871 cited in Slonim 1991: 4) as 'that complex whole which includes knowledge, beliefs, art, morals, law, customs and any capabilities and habits acquired by . . . a member of society'.

The text 'Mr Frog' comprises ten clauses:

1 /Mr Frog Mr Frog all dressed in green/
2 /off to Orchard/
3 /to buy blue jeans/
4 /the salesman said/
5 /sorry sir/
6 /I don't have your size/
7 /but I have something/
8 /you'll find very nice/*
9 /how about orchid shirt and shorts [to match]/
10 /makes flies easier [for you to catch]/

* 'nice' rhymes with 'size' given the Singapore pronunciation.

	Mr	Frog	Mr	Frog	all	dressed	in	green
TH1	Topic Theme				Rheme			
M1	Subj Mood				Adj Mood	Pred Mood-Residue	Comp Residue	
T1	Carr –				Proc Reln Attr Circ		Att –	
LEX	Lex1 Int						Lex2 Exp	

Figure 4.1 SFL analysis of Clause 1

The frog is an ubiquitous character in Singapore, partly because it was adopted as the emblem for the Clean and Green Campaign. The frog appears in government campaigns reminding us to keep Singapore clean, litter-free and a better place for all to enjoy and live together. In clause 1 we have a personification of this emblem in Mr Frog. This reinforces the character as the theme and focus. As the analysis progresses it will be seen that Mr Frog is re-positioned in the text. Singapore is renowned for its cleanliness, public orderliness and now it wants to link these established characteristics with environmental awareness. This position assumes greater significance in a region where forest burning has been criticized internationally because of the destruction to the local rainforest environment and the regional pollution that is euphemistically named 'the haze' has caused severe environmental pollution in Singapore, Malaysia and the region.

Mr Frog is all dressed in green. Green skin colour is a key marker of ethnic identity. Skin colour, eye colour, hair colour and texture feature in Singapore's descriptions of ethnicity. Pale skin colour is considered desirable and accorded high status. Advertisements for skin-whitening-cream beauty treatments for skin-lightening abound. Personal columns where prospective marriage partners can be contacted, advertise themselves as pale, white-skinned or with a fair complexion. Mr Frog is environmentally green. The intensifiers *all* emphasize his colour as central and as a defining aspect of who he is. This theme of ethnic identity, 'Who am I and who do I want to be?' is a theme that recurs throughout this short rhyme.

To those who have visited Singapore, Orchard Road needs no explanation. Indeed it is so embedded in the Singaporean consciousness that it is referred to elliptically as Orchard. Road is considered redundant. Orchard (Road) is the hub of Singapore

	off	to	Orchard
TH1	Rheme		
M1	Pred Residue	Comp Residue	
T1	Proc Mat	Locn Time	
LEX	Lex1 Exp	Lex2 Exp	

Figure 4.2 Clause 2

consummations – everything and anything can be purchased there. A weekly visit to Orchard, usually on Saturday afternoon when Singaporeans end their 6.5 day working week, is a ritual. Even those who do not shop parade along Orchard carrying carrier bags, emblems of previous purchases. The state of the national economy impinges on Singaporeans in an immediate way. When times are hard and the economy is in relative recession, Singaporeans and civil servants experience lower salaries, reduced (or even no) annual bonus and employee privileges, such as the Central Provident Fund (CPF) that provides individuals with pensions and long-term savings, are reduced. Singaporeans are openly encouraged to contribute to the economy by shopping. In the recent past, Singaporeans and permanent residents who invited overseas guests to stay in their homes were rewarded with tax incentives. This was based on the assumption that visitors shop, thus supporting the local economy by providing employment for Singaporeans. Shopping in Singapore is big business. It is *everyone's* business.

	To	buy	blue	jeans
TH1	Rheme			
M1	Pred Residue		Comp Residue	
T1	Proc Mat		Range	
LEX			Lex1 Exp	

Figure 4.3 Clause 3

Mr Frog's intention is to buy blue jeans. Blue jeans epitomize the Western image. Singaporeans are currently experiencing some kind of cultural schizophrenia. On the one hand they are exhorted to be proud of themselves as Singaporeans, but on the other hand they are being encouraged to embrace globalization and the technology that will link them to the international stage. At school, children learn English in pre-schools and primary school to be able to communicate with the world. Mandarin is encouraged as the economic possibilities emerge in the Chinese-speaking world. In Singapore, it is not unknown for Chinese youth to describe themselves as bananas – white on the inside, Westerners at heart. Blue jeans are seen to encapsulate the Western image of youthful aspiration. The theme of colour (blue-green) continues. Blue contrasts with Mr Frog's own ethnic green.

	the	salesman	said
TH1	Topic Theme		Rheme
M1	Subj Mood		Fin Pred Mood-Residue
T1	Sayer		Proc Verbl
LEX			

Figure 4.4 Clause 4

Here we have a verbal process that leads straight into projection. The lexical string buy – salesman – leads us to the heart of Orchard (Road) activity – *consumerism*. The alliteration of 'salesman said' will be repeated in Clause 5. This clause positions the salesman in the rhyme as central. This becomes increasingly apparent from the number of clauses dedicated to the creation of the salesman in the rhyme.

	sorry	sir
TH1	Rheme	
M1	Comp Residue	Voc Adj
T1		
LEX	Lex1 Int	Lex2 Int

Figure 4.5 Clause 5

The salesman is very polite, as one would expect. He is almost deferential. The colloquial Singapore English (CSE) 'Sorry' with 'I'm' ellipsed – again draws the reader into the text as a fellow Singaporean. It has the affect of the poet and reader sharing the same variety of 'Singlish'. 'Sir', a respect marker, is vocative. The salesman is highly respectful while simultaneously positioning the customer/consumer. The acoustic resonance is reinforced again with the repetition of the alliteration in 'sorry sir'. An alliteration pattern also found in clause 4, 'the salesman said'.

	I	don't	have	your	size
TH1	Topic Theme	Rheme			
M1	Subj Mood	Fin Mood	Pred Residue	Comp Residue	
T1	Carr Possr	Proc Reln Attr Poss		Attr Possd	
LEX				Lex1 Exp	

Figure 4.6 Clause 6

Size – the right size is a social issue in Singapore as any Westerner who has tried to buy clothing will know. The recent Singapore government health campaigners focus on healthy eating and Singaporeans are urged to ask for four things when they eat out at hawker stalls (as most do, daily). These are:

- more vegetables
- less fat and oil for less calories
- less sugar for natural sweetness
- less 'salt' for natural taste.

Even Singaporean schoolchildren are urged to keep slim, fit and healthy, although sport is not part of the official school curriculum. Children can be sent home from school if their Body-Mass-Index is too high and parents are urged to keep children slim. Size is an issue in Singapore – appearance is important and slim is highly desirable. It is an image driven by the motive of health.

The ever-helpful salesman makes a suggestion, 'But I have something'. The choice of the topic is again significant and serves to centralize the salesman. It positions him and reinforces his status in the customer/consumer relationship. The salesman is being helpful but also doing his job and selling. He is telling his customer, Mr Frog, what he wants and what Mr Frog will probably buy. The role relationship and relative status of these interlocutors is encapsulated in this clause.

	but	I	have	something
TH1	Conj Str Theme	Topic Theme	Rheme	
M1		Subj Mood	Fin Pred Mood-Residue	Comp Residue
T1		Carr Possr	Proc Reln Attr Poss	Att Possd
LEX				

Figure 4.7 Clause 7

	you	'll	find	very	nice
TH1	Topic Theme	Rheme			
M1	Subj Mood	Fin Modl Mood	Pred Residue	Comp Residue	
T1	Sens	Proc Ment Aff		Phen Range	
LEX				Lex1 Int	

Figure 4.8 Clause 8

'You will/very nice' is the amplification through which intensification acts on the reader and reinforces the lexical string that is preoccupied with physical, visual appearance, etc. In their descriptions of narrative this is what Martin and Rothery (1981) refer to as the *Resolution* stage. It functions to resolve Mr Frog's problem. This stage is realized by the causative process that establishes the meaning of Singaporean identity as currently defined officially. The Singaporean identity is a 'supra-ethnic national identity' (Kuo 1980: 59) where loyalty to the nation supersedes local and individual loyalties. Identification with one's ethnic group is subsumed under a national identity. The preservation of the ethnic identity within a national identity is manifested in the causative process where a direct relationship between 'orchid shirts and shorts' and 'flies' is established. Identification with the ethnic group is expressed symbolically through 'flies', since flies are what frogs naturally eat. On the other hand, identification with the nation, Singapore, is expressed symbolically through 'orchid shirts and shorts'.

	how	about	orchid	shirt	and	shorts	[to	match]
TH1	Rheme							
M1	Comp WH Residue		Comp Residue					
T1								
LEX			Lex1 Exp					

Figure 4.9 Clause 9

The orchid has been adopted as the national emblem of Singapore. It is depicted frequently on clothing. The salesman's suggestion that Mr Frog forgets about blue jeans and instead buys an orchid shirt and shorts to match also suggests that Mr Frog replaces his own 'all green self', his ethnic self, with the national emblem of Singapore. There is strong appeal to Singaporeans to put

Nation before family
Family before self

as stated in the national campaign slogan. Mr Frog is being encouraged, persuaded, exhorted (forced) to forego green (himself) and blue jeans (his aspirational self) in favour of the national emblem of orchid shirt and shorts to match. At the National Day Parade (9 August 1999) the theme song 'Together We Make the Difference, One Hope, One Family', reinforces the national aspiration of the collective (family, nation) before the individual (self).

	makes	flies	easier	[for	you	to	catch]
TH1	Rheme						
M1	Fin Pred Mood-Residue	Comp Residue	Comp Residue				
T1	Proc Reln Attr Int	Carr	Att				
E1	Proc	Medm	Range				
LEX		Lex1 Exp	Lex2 Exp				

Figure 4.10 Clause 10

Here again the ellipsed [it], i.e. the suit, is colloquial Singapore English usage. The benefit to Mr Frog is that if he buys the orchid shirt and shorts to match and rejects the blue jeans, his life as a frog, his ethnic self, will be made easier. Why? Because he will be able to catch flies, his natural food. Hence there are personal benefits and gains to being a Singaporean and acting in the collective interest. However, there are attributes to ethnicity. Not all ethnic groups are considered as socially equal. The sting for Mr Frog is that the salesman has positioned him within the social stratification of Singaporean society. Catching flies is not high status. But you are still who you are. You can change your appearance to fit in, buy Western clothes or orchid shirt and shorts, you will fit in but you can remain true to your ethnic self. Mr Frog has now found himself – a green frog.

As the clause 'make flies easier for you to catch' is an elliptical declarative clause, the token 'orchid shirts and shorts' is understood from the preceding clause. In the wider cultural context, the causative relationship establishes the meaning of the Singaporean identity. Eggins (1994: 260) suggests that Value gives meaning, referent, function, status or role to Token. Hence either participant can be used to identify the other. The 'supra-ethnic national' identity is realized symbolically by Token and Value where Token is realized by a symbol of the national identity and Value is realized by a feature that is associated with frogs. Token and Value are symbolic representations of the Singaporean identity as both participants represent the multicultural and multiracial manifestations of the Singaporean identity.

The different ways in which the main character is constructed in this text suggests that there is more than one way in which Singaporeans can make a statement of identity. Mr Frog is quite happy to comply with the shop assistant's suggestion to opt for Singaporean-style dress, shorts and shirt. In this sense, the text reinforces the official construction of a national identity so prevalent in national document statements.

This text demonstrates differing portrayals of Singaporean identity at the macro and the micro levels. It can be seen as a socializing agent that contributes to the readers' construction and understanding of the society in which they live.

4.4 Language as a medium of cultural transmission

One of the important functions of language is its role in the construction of reality. Language is not simply a tool for communication, it is also a guide to what Sapir terms *social reality*. Language has a semantic system, or a meaning potential which enables the transmission of cultural values (Halliday 1978: 109). Therefore, while the child is learning language, other significant learning is taking place through the medium of language. The child is simultaneously learning the meanings associated with the culture, realized linguistically by the lexico-grammatical system of the language (Halliday 1978: 23).

There is further support for this role of language as the means of cultural transmission. Vygotsky (1981) claims that the child's cultural development occurs first on the social plane and then on the psychological plane. Learning takes place by internalizing processes witnessed in the social world as activity. Speech is one of the main tools used in mental regulation and refinement of behaviour. Through the process of memorization and repetition of the rhyme, the rhyme is easily rooted in the child's linguistic repertoire. Cultural values inherent in the language are subsequently transmitted to the child in the form of the rhyme.

The mode through which culture is transmitted also contributes towards the cultural development of the child. From the Vygotskian perspective, there are three ways in which communication activities are regulated: object-regulation, other-regulation and self-regulation. The rhyme analysed here can be regarded as an example of object-regulation, since the written text helps the child to develop a conscious reflection where they can think about the form or meaning that is carried by the language (Wertsch 1991: 79). Cultural values inherent in the daily experiences of the child thus become objectified as a stable system of meanings to be learned by the child (Halliday 1991: 19). Halliday (1991) further suggests that these rhymes have a role in inculcating culture. It is likely that these rhymes, which are used as texts in formal learning, have additional significance since they serve to fulfil certain educational goals.

Obernstein (1994) supports this view that books are written for children with an educational purpose. She argues that there is a conscious effort by the author to educate the child, as the relationship between the author of children's books and the reader is hierarchical, i.e. based on an adult-child relationship. Amusement and enjoyment are seen to be subordinate elements of a moral and emotional education. Stephens (1992: 3) also suggests that writers try to inculcate societal values, such as contemporary morality, ethics and aspirations about the future. Hunt (1992: 18) supports this view: 'one of the most useful insights of modern criticism has been that ... even the most apparently simple book, cannot be innocent of some ideological freight'.

This view of language as being influenced by social structure is further supported by Bernstein (1971: 174) who argues that social relations are embedded in the meanings of the message the system carries. Different speech systems are created by different forms of social relations. He notes,

> which speech codes are realized is a function of the culture acting through social relationships in specific contexts. Different speech forms or codes symbolize the form of the social relationship, regulate the nature of the speech encounters, and create for the speakers different orders of relevance and relation. The experience of the speaker is then transformed by what is made significant or relevant by the speech form.

This view further reinforces the socializing function of rhymes. Hence, through their form and content, the rhymes can socialize the child into modes of thinking and behaviour that are compatible with the prevailing culture and societal values.

In addition to support for this view of literature as an agent of socialization, Hollindale (1992) and Stephens (1992) also focus on ideology in children's fiction. Hollindale (1992: 28–30), identifies three levels in which ideology can be imbued in the text:

i) ideology can be explicit, disclosing the writer's social, political and moral beliefs.
ii) ideology can be passive whereby beliefs and values are taken for granted in society.
iii) existing ideology is reinforced through language in the text.

The term *ideology* is closely associated with the Marxist view of culture, defined as 'false consciousness' or an illusion of reality created by the ruling class (Gee 1990: 6). This views culture as a set of hidden beliefs imposed on the oppressed by the dominant group. Thus it can be seen that there is a view shared between linguists (Halliday, Hasan), children's literature specialists and the sociologist Bernstein that children's rhymes are a vehicle of cultural transmission and that there is a dynamic relationship between culture and language.

4.5 Understanding (nursery rhymes): a socio-semiotic perspective

Semiotics is the study of meanings (Halliday and Hasan 1985: 4). Language is a carrier of meanings that interrelates with other systems of meaning. The socio-semiotic approach explains how meanings are created and exchanged between members of a society by establishing a systematic relationship between the social environment and the functional organization of language (see Figure 4.11). Within the systemic-functional framework, language is seen as playing a functional role in the socio-cultural environment. Language described as text is a semantic unit, both a product and a process. As a product, it is organized in a systematic manner that reflects the social meaning of context. As a process, it is a system of choices that allows for making meaning through selection. Meanings are subsequently realized in the lexico-grammatical and phonological systems. Rothery (1996: 92) states that text is 'a culturally specific object which mediates the expression of experience and the response to it'. Hence, the semiotic environment is structured in terms of context of situation and context of culture.

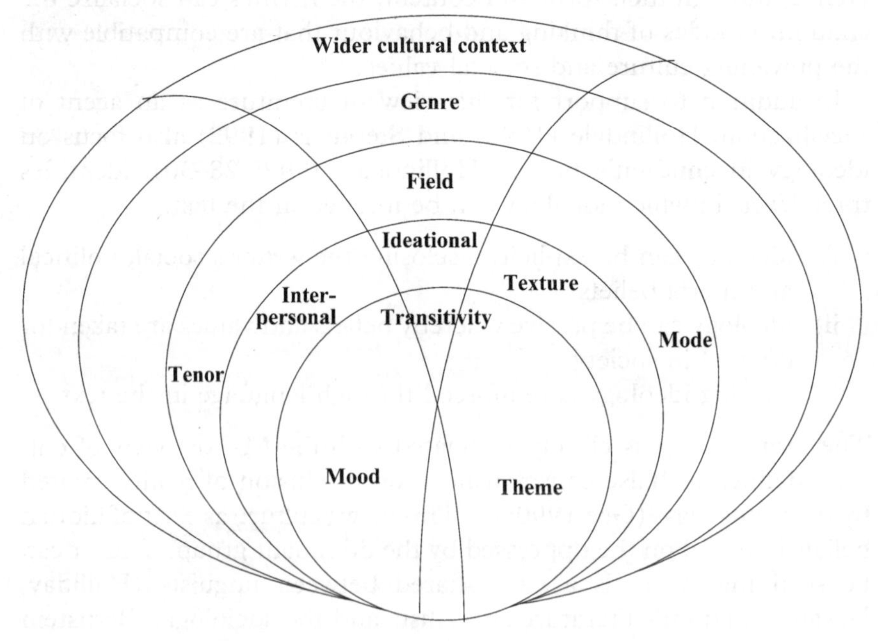

Figure 4.11 A summary of the socio-semiotic perspective
Source: Adapted from Martin (1997).

4.5.1 Context of situation

Context of situation is the semiotic environment in which the text is embedded (Halliday 1978: 123). It is organized in terms of field, tenor and mode or register (Martin 1992: 502). Each situational variable is systematically related to the ideational, interpersonal and textual components of the semantic system (Halliday 1978: 123). The ideational component is the component that encodes the cultural experience and individual experience as well as phenomena about the world, facts and assumptions (ibid.: 112). The interpersonal component allows the speaker to express attitudes and influence the behaviour of others, while the textual component gives the text its form (ibid.: 112). These three components are subsequently realized in the lexico-grammar as transitivity, mood and theme respectively. An elaboration on register is outlined in the next section to provide the context of situation in which a particular Singaporean rhyme for children was created and in which it will be read for and with young children who may eventually come to learn it by heart.

4.5.1.1 An elaboration of register: field

Field refers to sets of activity sequences that are oriented to achieve some global institutional purpose (Martin 1992: 536). The field of discourse can be ranked along a continuum that ranges from common-sense knowledge to technical knowledge (ibid.: 544). The field of discourse for this rhyme is common-sense knowledge. It is assumed that childhood is a crucial period for basic education where the child learns about social role, responsibilities and the modes of thinking that are expected within a given cultural context (Stephens 1992: 8). The philosophy of the NTUC Childcare Centre is to 'to develop a keen mind, a co-operative and friendly spirit and a cheerful disposition' (NTUC Childcare). As the director of the NTUC Childcare Centres, presumably, this is a direct statement of their philosophy from the author in the 'Mr Frog' rhyme.

4.5.1.2. Tenor

Tenor refers to the negotiation of social relationships (Martin 1992: 523). Martin (ibid.) cites Poynton (1984, 1985, 1990a) to state that tenor can be seen in three dimensions: status, contact and affect. Status is defined as the relative position of the participants in the culture's social hierarchy (ibid.: 525). Contact is the degree of institutional involvement between people, while affect is the degree of emotion present in the relationship between participants (ibid.: 525). Affect is more likely to be manifest in an involved relationship than in an uninvolved relationship, and between participants of equal status, than with participants of unequal status.

4.5.1.3 Mode

Mode refers to the role that language plays in realizing social action (ibid.: 508). Mode mediates the extent to which text constructs or accompanies its field. Martin (ibid.) identifies two types of distance between language and situation: interpersonal and experiential distances. Interpersonal distance measures the possibilities of feedback from the audience, while experiential distance measures the distance between language and social processes occurring.

For this rhyme, it is suggested that both the interpersonal and the experiential distances are high because of the written mode. However, the aural qualities of the text together with the visual reinforcement of the text through the illustration, reinforce contact between the author and the reader(s). This allows for the possibility of feedback from the reader and interaction with the text, albeit perhaps mediated. Also the language is organized synoptically for reflection rather than for social action.

4.5.2 Context of culture: genre

Context of culture refers to the cultural history behind the participants and the practices in which they engage (Halliday and Hasan 1985: 6). This concept has been extended by Martin (1992a: 505) to refer to genre, defined as a staged, goal-oriented social process that is realized through register. Halliday (1978: 134) identifies genre as language that is beyond the linguistic system and projected on a higher-level semiotic structure. Genre consists of stages that enable meanings to be transmitted in a systematic and organized manner. It provides a way of accomplishing social goals through the step-by-step organization of the text. Different genre structures reflect different ways of using language. For example, the different generic structures in which the rhymes are written create different reading positions for the reader. Kress (1985) argues that the construction of a reading position has two effects. First, readers are placed directly in the text and instructed on the roles to assume in reading. Second, readers are constructed as certain types of social beings within larger social institutions.

4.6 Socialization through the selection of choices in the transitivity system

The transitivity system contains a range of process types and participant roles which enable a world of actions, social relations and events to be encoded in the language (Eggins 1994: 220). This selection of choices in the transitivity system creates a particular version of reality that is related to the field of discourse or common-sense knowledge. The transitivity system helps to identify the social and cultural aspects of Singapore in the rhymes. It shows how nation-building policies are transformed into everyday knowledge for the pre-school child through the selection of meaning choices in the creation of the text.

4.7 Conclusion

This chapter has attempted to demonstrate how one Singaporean rhyme can play an important role in the transmission of culture. Although the rhyme selected resembles a nursery rhyme in some textual aspects, for example, structural features, it is argued that unlike nursery rhymes, which are typically recited for entertainment purposes, the 'Mr Frog' rhyme has additional social significance because it was written as an educational text to be included in the NTUC childcare curriculum, one of the largest and most significant in Singapore. The rhyme genre socializes the reader into modes of thinking dominant in a literate society, especially within the educational context. Hence it is suggested that the rhyme plays a role in shaping the attitudes, behaviour and thinking of its readers.

The fact that this nursery rhyme among many others was specially commissioned and used widely throughout nurseries and kindergartens in Singapore gives it greater significance. Such nursery rhymes are not merely meant to soothe and entertain. They are doing more than educating. They are transmitting, through language, Singaporean values of:

- being a Singaporean
- being a consumer
- being one's ethnic self
- accepting Asian values of collectivism
- rejecting (some) Western values and emblems (blue jeans)
- being Singaporean *first* (Singaporeans cannot hold dual nationality)
- nation-building through diversity of ethnic groupings.

Singapore 21 emphasises the collective good with the slogan and theme of 'Together we make the difference'. It has five themes of national policy:

1 Every Singaporean matters.
2 Strong families.

3 Opportunities for all.
4 Singapore heartbeat.
5 Active citizenship.

While this chapter presents an adult reading and view of the text, key questions remain:

- What do children understand when they read the 'Mr Frog' rhyme?
- How do the adults and parents who read 'Mr Frog' with and for children understand the text?
- What grammar of social practice are young Singaporeans internalizing when they read the 'Mr Frog' text?

That is the next task – to explore these questions.

Acknowledgements

I owe thanks to my colleague and friend Kay O'Halloran for the analysis of the text that was generated using 'The Systemics' 1.0 Software System (O'Halloran and Judd 2001).

References

Bernstein, Basil (1971) *Class, Codes and Control: Vol. 1. Theoretical Studies Towards a Sociology of Language*. London, Henley and Boston: Routledge and Kegan Paul.

Bokhorst-Heng, Wendy (1998) Language planning and management in Singapore. In J.A. Foley, T. Kandiah. Bao Zhiming, A.F. Gupta, L. Alsagoff, Ho Chee Lick, L. Wee, I.S. Talib and W. Bokhorst-Heng (eds), *English in New Cultural Contexts. Reflections From Singapore*. Singapore: Oxford University Press, 201–17.

Bruner, Jerome (1996) *The Culture of Education*. Cambridge, MA and London: Harvard University Press.

Chua, Beng Huat (1995) *Culture, Multiracialism and National Identity in Singapore*. Working Papers No.125. Department of Sociology, National University of Singapore.

Clammer, J. (1985) *Singapore: Ideology, Society and Culture*. Singapore: Chapmen Publishers.

Crystal, D. (ed.) (1997) *The Cambridge Encyclopaedia* 3rd edn. Cambridge: Cambridge University Press.

Eggins, Suzanne (1994) *An Introduction to Systemic Functional Linguistics*. London: Pinter.

Gee, James Paul (1990) *Social Linguistics and Literacies: Ideology in Discourses*. London: Routledge Falmer.

Gopinathan, S. (1980) *Language Policy in Education. Language and Society in*

Singapore. Singapore: Singapore University Press, 175–201.

Gupta Fraser, Anthea (1994) *The Step-tongue: Children's English in Singapore*. Clevedon: Multilingual Matters.

Halliday, M.A.K. (1978) *Language As Social Semiotic: The Social Interpretation of Language and Meaning*. London: Edward Arnold.

Halliday, M.A.K. (1985) *Spoken and Written Language*. Geelong, Victoria: Deakin University Press.

Halliday, M.A.K. (1991) *Linguistic Perspectives On Literacy: A Systemic-Functional Approach. Literacy in Social Processes*. Papers from the inaugural Australian Systemic Functional Linguistics Conference held at Deakin University, January 1990. Darwin Centre for Studies of Language in Education, Northern Territory University.

Halliday, M.A.K. and Hasan, Ruqaiya (1985) *Language, Context and Text: Aspects of Language in a Social-semiotic Perspective*. Oxford: Oxford University Press.

Hasan, Ruqaiya (1985) *Linguistics, Language and Verbal Art*. Victoria: Deakin University Press.

Ho Wah Kam (1998) The English Language Curriculum in Perspective: Exogenous Influences and Indigenization. In S. Gopinathan, A. Pakir, Ho Wah Kam and S. Saravanan (eds), *Language, Society and Education in Singapore* 2nd edn. Singapore: Times Academic Press.

Hollindale, Peter (1992) *Ideology and the Children's Book*. London and New York: Routledge, 19–40.

Huber, Miriam Blanton (1955) *Story and Verse for Children*. Revised edn. Basingstoke: The Macmillan Company.

Hunt, Peter (1992) *Literature for Children. Contemporary Criticism*. London and New York: Routledge.

Khoo Kim Choo (1996) *Going Downtown. Going Downtown and Other Rhymes*. Singapore: NTUC Childcare Co-operative Ltd.

Kress, Gunther (1985) *Linguistic Processes in Sociocultural Practice*. Geelong, Victoria: Deakin University Press.

Kuo, E.C.Y. (1980) The Sociolinguistic Situation in Singapore: Unity in Diversity. In E.A. Afendras and E.C. Y. Kuo (eds), *Language and Society in Singapore*. Singapore: Singapore University Press.

Martin, J.R. (1992) *English Text. System and Structure*. Amsterdam: Benjamins.

Martin J.R. (1997) Analysing genre: functional parameters. In F. Christie and J.R. Martin (eds), *Genre and Institutions: Social Processes in the Workplace and School*. London: Cassell.

Martin, J.R. and Rothery, J. (1981) *Writing Project Report, No. 2*. Department of Linguistics, University of Sydney, Sydney.

NTUC Childcare Home page. http://www.ntuc.childcare.com.sg/cccent.ntm

Obernstein, Karin Lesnik (1994) *Children's Literature. Criticism and the Fictional Child*. Oxford: Clarendon Press.

O'Halloran, K.L. and Judd, K. (2002) *Systemics 1.0*. Singapore: Singapore University Press.

Opie, Peter and Opie, Iona (1951) *The Oxford Dictionary of Nursery Rhymes*. Oxford: Clarendon Press.

Quah, Jon S.T. (1990) *In Search of Singapore's National Values*. Singapore: Times Academic Press.

Rothery, Joan (1996) Making changes: developing an educational linguistics. In Ruqaiya Hasan and Geoff Williams (eds). *Literacy in Society*. London and New York: Longman, 86–171.

Shared Values (1991) *Singapore Ministry of Education, White Paper, Cmd.1 of 1991*.

Singapore Ministry of Education (1995) *Hallmarks of Excellence. Educating Our Next Generation*. Singapore: Public Affairs Division, Ministry of Education.

Singapore Ministry of Education (1998) *The Desired Outcomes of Education*. Singapore: Public Affairs Division, Ministry of Education.

Slonim, Maureen B. (1991) *Children, Culture and Ethnicity: Evaluating and Understanding the Impact*. New York and London: Gardland Publishing, Inc.

Stephens, John (1992) *Language and Ideology in Children's Fiction*. London and New York: Longman.

Vygotsky, L.S. (1981) *The Genesis of Higher Mental Functions. The Concept of Activity in Soviet Psychology*. Armonk, NY: M.E. Sharpe

Wertsch, James V. (1991) Sociocultural Setting and the Zone of Proximal Development: The Problem of Text-Based Realities. In Landsmann, Liliana Tolchinsky (eds), *Culture, Schooling and Psychological Development, Vol. 4: Human Development*. Norwood, NJ: Ablex Publishing Corporation, 71–86.

5

A Framework for Tracing the Development of Children's Writing in Primary Schools

Joseph A. Foley and Cheryl Lee

5.1 Introduction

The purpose of the research described in this chapter was to develop a framework which could be used to give some indication of how a child's control of written language developed from their initial entry into primary school until the end of primary schooling. As indicated in the following statement by McCarthy and Carter:

> A focus on text and discourse can help us to notice and analyse aspects of usage which have previously gone unnoticed and untaught – the better a text analyst the teacher can be, the better equipped – all other things being equal – his or her students are likely to be in using the language appropriately. (1994: xii)

The setting for this study was Singapore where English is the dominant language of education. So much so that one could argue that many of the younger generation of Singaporeans have English as their primary language of communication in what is essentially a multilingual community (Foley 2001).

Although studies of the development of writing in the context of Singapore have been fairly extensive over the last 20 years (Saffiah bte Mohammed Amin 1984; Laxmi 1985; Narandran 1986; Varghese 1994; Wong 1994), the focus has mainly been on the grammatical or lexical development in terms of the formal aspects of language. Other studies (Samraj 1989; Yee 1991; Wee 1991; Goh 1992; Foley 1991, 1994) have looked at the development of generic structures in primary schools. The ability to use these conventionalized forms of language is important, as they are associated with specific social and institutional settings.

What early studies on genres or text-types used in the primary schools has shown is that much of the teaching has centred almost exclusively around the two generic structures of *Recount* and *Narrative.*

It is now well established (Martin and Rothery 1981, 1982, 1986; Christie 1989, 1999; Derewianka 1990) that children's ability to write a variety of genres is essential in developing maturity in writing. Such maturity is also essential if children on reaching adulthood want to participate fully in society. Programmes such as the Sydney Metropolitan East Disadvantaged Schools Program or the LINC programme, which was proposed for the National Curriculum in England and Wales, had as a central focus a text-based approach to the teaching of English. More recently, the 2001 English Language Syllabus issued by the Ministry of Education in Singapore has also stressed such an approach. As an example of the text-types typically used in society, the following guidelines were given by the Ministry of Education in Singapore:

Table 5.1 Text types

TYPE	Recount		Narrative	Explanation	Report	Exposition	Procedure
Feature	Personal	Factual					
Participants	speaker/ address	specific 3rd party or generalized	specific 1st or 3rd person	generalized	generalized	specific 3rd party or generalized	hearer/ reader
Time	past	past	usually past	timeless	timeless	timeless, obligation, future	mainly imperative
Connectives	mainly temporal	mainly temporal	mainly temporal	mainly causal	various	mainly causal	mainly temporal and causal
Purpose	retell	retell/record	entertain	reveal	describe	persuade	instruct

However, this present study has as its main focus not just text-types or generic structures directly but also how a child's growing control over the written form of the language can be observed by looking at a number of choices that a young writer makes within the language network system.

The Singapore Ministry of Education 2001 English Syllabus has laid considerable stress on the functional use of language.

5.2 Language use

Pupils need to know how to communicate fluently, appropriately and effectively in internationally acceptable English. They need to understand how the language system works and how language conventions can vary according to purpose, audience, context and culture, and apply this knowledge in speech and writing in both formal and informal situations. Language teaching and learning is organized around three major areas of language use (see Figure 5.1).

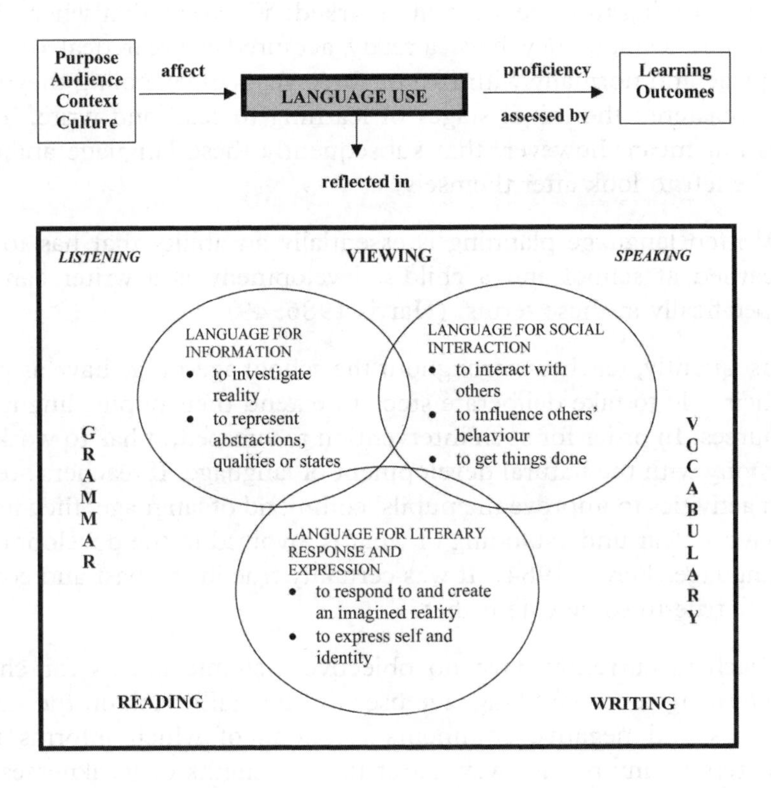

Figure 5.1 The organization of language teaching and learning.
Source: Curriculum Planning and Development Division, Ministry of Education 2001: 4–6).

Apart from the formal guidelines as indicated above, societal demands on literacy are on the increase. In the school system itself, pupils' progress is constantly monitored and evaluated through their ability to write, be it a project, an essay or a written examination. Later on in the tertiary level of education, the demands on writing increase with essays, reports and research papers. In the working world, especially in large organizations, sometimes the only form of communication one has with superiors is in the written mode and all too often an individual's performance is based on how well they communicate.

> Now more than ever, possession of literacy capacities is an essential qualification for full and rewarding participation in one's community. (Christie 1989: 3)

Considering how painlessly children learn to talk, the difficulties they face in learning to write are quite marked. We know that when children start school, they have already acquired a great deal of oral language and normally with two or three years of schooling they will have mastered the initial stages of learning to read and write. This does not mean, however, that subsequently these language abilities can be left to look after themselves.

> Written language planning is essentially an ability that has to be learned at school and a child's development as a writer can be specifically in these terms. (Harris 1986: 49)

Consequently, teachers throughout the school age-range have as part of their role to take deliberate steps to extend their pupils' linguistic resources. In order for such intervention to succeed, it has to work in harmony with the natural development of language. If teachers are to plan activities to improve the pupils' command of language, they need to have a clear understanding of what is involved in the development of language (Perera 1984). It was certainly true in the past and could still be true to some extent that:

> Teachers currently have no objective systemic means for characterizing successful language use ... [they fall] back on the same values and negative comments ... none of which informs the writers in any precise way about their strengths or weaknesses or offers strategies for improvement... [the] nature of their language becomes increasingly invisible. (Bernstein 1979, 1986 quoted in Rothery, 1988: 206)

The purpose, therefore, of this study was to identify key features in the language network which might help in the analysing of children's writing such that one could identify which textual and grammatical features have been acquired, which are in the process of being acquired and which apparently have not been acquired or are not in active use. By identifying these features it was hoped that the information gained could contribute to an assessment of the pupils' growing linguistic maturity in the development of their writing.

5.3 Collection of data

As this study was meant to be an initial study of the proposed framework for the development of writing in primary schools in Singapore, the language background of the children was controlled by only selecting Chinese-speaking children who were in a Special Assistance Plan (SAP) school. That is to say, that Chinese as well as English is taught in this school as a first language until Primary four. All these children were considered to be bilingual and literate in both languages. A study of the development of discourse patterns in Chinese at what we have called the 'macro level' indicated that *Recount* and *Narrative* dominated as the text-types. However, as the immediate focus of this study was on the students' need to understand how a language system works in constructing discourse, their writing in one language was considered to be extensive enough to establish a workable framework for teachers to trace the development.

For the actual project, the children were given a set of four pictures (see Figure 5.2) taken from a textbook quite widely used in Singapore. The children were asked to write a story based on the pictures. The task was that of 'story-telling' as this generic structure, as we have previously indicated, was the one most familiar to the children in primary schools. Also, there was a need to achieve homogeneity in the data so as to reduce an unequal knowledge base as far as subject matter was concerned between the older and younger children.

In total six classes (one from each level of the primary school) were given the task. A total of 240 samples were collected and of these 30 texts were selected (five from each class) for analysis at the macro level of textual structure and micro level of lexico-grammatical structure. It was surmised that such an analysis would give some indication of the progression of the children's' language development from Primary one to six.

5.4 Analysis of data

5.4.1 Macro-level analysis

The schematic structure of each text was analysed using the approach, as we have earlier indicated, suggested by Martin and Rothery (1981). According to Martin (1997) the move from

Figure 5.2 Four pictures used for a story writing task

non-metaphorical to metaphorical text is often symbolized by the separation of primary and secondary schooling. This reflects the move from organized multidisciplinary working primary school to work which is more strongly classified in secondary schooling. Research into the pre-school child (Painter 1999) seems to indicate that the move into primary schooling is characterized by the child's ability to begin to deal with abstractions. But once in school, the development of the child's language in using abstractions will be crucial. That is to say, a child would have to be able to distinguish between things which are concrete and everyday ('event focus') as might be described in *Recount* and *Narrative* and the more technical 'thing focus': *Description, Report* and *Exposition.* In primary school both these strands often develop from the *Observation/Comment* genre. In the 'event focus' strand, *Recount* usually precedes *Narrative,* while in the 'thing focus' strand, *Report* can often precede *Exposition.* In other words, within the genres themselves there are some which seem to be linguistically more demanding than others for the young writer (see Martin 1997: 31–4).

5.4.2 Micro-level analysis

The micro-level analysis took that part of the network system which seemed particularly relevant to the early stages of the development of writing. Since the *interpersonal, ideational* and *textual* metafunctions contribute simultaneously, though in different ways, to the overall meaning and structure of a text, all three were felt to be necessary in trying to establish a framework by which to analyse the pupil's written language.

5.4.3 Macro analysis

5.4.3.1 Schematic structure in the texts

(References: P1=Primary One, T20=Text 20)

Observation/Comment as a beginning genre was expected at Primary one level but more often the texts produced were just a series of clauses without temporal sequence such as the following:

> The family is eating dinner.
> The girl is standing on the chair.
> The girl fell of the chair.
> A boy is chasing a rat and a girl was crying.
> (P1; T20)

5.4.3.2 Recount

This generic pattern is found in Primary one and many Primary two texts.

> (**Orientation**)
> One night, my mother, sister and brother had dinner together.
>
> (**Events**)
> Suddenly, a rat appear.
> My sister jump up on the chair
> and the leg of the chair broke.
> My sister fell down from the chair
> and my brother took a broom and went after the rat.
> My mother ask my sister not to cry
>
> (**Re-orientation**)
> but in the end the rat was chased out of the house.
> (P2; T20)

5.4.3.3 Narrative

What was found in the early stages of primary school was evidence of young writers picking up narrative skills, although we might call these 'incomplete narratives'.

(**Orientation**)
One night, the Lim family is having dinner together

(**Complication**)
Suddenly, sister stood up on her chair.
She saw a mouse nearby the chair and was terrified,
so she upset the chair and the dishes on the table.

(**Resolution?**)
She stood in a corner crying as her brother tries to catch the mouse.
(P1; T26)

In Primary two 'incomplete narratives' were common, very often they lacked a 'resolution' despite sometimes having a coda.

(**Orientation**)
Monday night, the moon was shining brightly in the sky,
at that time I was eating my dinner.

(**Complication**)
Suddenly a mice ran to the table,
I stand on the chair screaming for help
Then the mice ran to my chair.
I was scared and my chair gave way.
I pulled the cloth of the table

(**Resolution?**)
then my brother used the brome and ran after it all over the house,
it was here, there and everywhere.

(**Coda**)
It was really a sad day.
(P2; T3)

Background reading and the 'story-telling' genre often produced phrases such as:

Once upon a time, there was a girl stand on a chair (P1; T25)
They lived happily ever after (P1; T8)

Complete narratives do appear in Primary two.

(**Orientation**)
Last night, my mother, brother and me were at home.
We are at home eating a wonderful dinner.

(**Complication**)
Suddenly, I saw a mouse crawling beside the table.
I quickly shouted and stand on the chair.
The mouse crawl nearer to me.
I was scared and I fall holding the cloth on the table when all the food drop.

(**Resolution**)
I cried and I cried while my mother console me.
My brother was so angry that he took a broom and scar it away.
(P2; T23)

From Primary three onwards, the majority of texts are complete narratives with a development from simple to more complex. That is to say, a simple narrative as defined here would consist of *orientation*, a *complication* and a *resolution*. A complex narrative would comprise multiple complications and resolutions. A complete complex narrative would have all the resolutions to multiple complications. For example:

(**Orientation**)
1 'It's dinner time', my mother called out.
2 My sister and I ran to the table and started eating.
3 The food was simply fabulous.

(**Complication 1**)
4 Suddenly my sister shrieked, 'Ahh . . . a rat!'
5 She climbed up to the seat of the chair and stood there.

(**Complication 2**)
6 Unfortunately, the leg of the old chair broke!
7(i) My sister came falling down
7(ii) pulling the tablecloth and all the dishes with her.
8(i) And my sister started crying

(**Complication 3**)
8(ii) The floor was in a mess

(**Resolution to Complication 2**)
9 As my mother was comforting my sister,

(**Resolution to Complication 1**)
10 I picked up the broom and started chasing the rat.
11 I chased the rat to the doorstep and, with a mighty hit, I pushed the rat out of the house.

(**Resolution to Complication 3**)
12 My mother cleared the mess and suggested that we eat out.
13 So we went to the nearest coffeehouse to eat.

(**Coda**)
14 That day when my father came back, he praised me for being so brave.
15 I was very happy.
(P6; T22)

This final example illustrates a complex narrative where the events are unfolded as possibly having several complications.

(**Orientation**)
1 One night, the Lee family were having dinner except for their father Mr Lee, who was busy studying in his room.

(**Complication 1**)
2 Adrian, their son and Mrs Lee had just finished their dinner when their daughter, Pauline climbed onto the chair when she saw a rat scuttling across the floor.
3 She screamed at the top of her voice.

(**Complication 2**)
4 Suddenly the chair gave way and Pauline grabbed the table for support.
5 But she only managed to grab the tablecloth and all the food utensils rolled down the table.
6 She bumped onto the floor and started crying.

(**Resolution to Complication 2**)
7(i) Mrs Lee started to console her

(**Resolution to Complication 1**)
7(ii) while Adrian went after the rat.
8 A natural rat catcher, he only caught the rat in a few minutes.

(**Final Resolution**)
9 Finally, Pauline cooled down and Adrian kept the rat as a pet.
(P6; T17)

The overall impression of the development of writing within the generic structure of 'story-telling' is that by the time children have reached Primary six, they are proficient in writing 'stories'. No doubt this can be explained by the emphasis which is given to this genre in classroom teaching. The introduction of the new 2001 English Syllabus and the focus on 'Language in Use' with a much wider array of text-types being taught should better equip the young learner for later life.

5.4.4 Micro-analysis

5.4.4.1 Lexico-grammatical analysis

The framework for the lexico-grammatical analysis was constructed around selected components of the language network system. The *interpersonal* component was analysed on the grounds that this is the earliest function developed by the child through the processes of interaction in the home (Halliday 1994). The *experiential* component reflected the growing ideas of the child together with attempts at explaining these ideas in a logical fashion. The final component, that of the *textual*, was felt to be crucial for the development of writing in a cohesive and coherent manner.

The parts of the network system chosen as being particularly important at this stage in the child's language development are summarized in Figure 5.3.

5.4.4.2 The interpersonal component

5.4.4.2.1 MOOD analysis

Table 5.2 summarizes the results of the analysis of MOOD, showing the total figures for ranking (non-embedded) clauses. MOOD is listed if at least one example occurs in the text.

Table 5.2 MOOD in the Primary 1–6 texts

MOOD Class	Pri. 1	Pri. 2	Pri. 3	Pri. 4	Pri. 5	Pri.6
Full declarative	39	57	99	113	111	128
Elliptical declarative	0	0	0	0	0	1
Full wh-interrogative	0	1	1	4	0	1
Imperative	0	0	0	0	0	1
Exclamative	0	0	0	1	0	1
Total ranking clauses	39	58	100	118	111	132

Clearly evident is the dominance of the *full declarative MOOD* type in all the texts from the six Primary levels. The indications from this

- **Interpersonal component**
  - MOOD (analysis of ranking clauses)
  - Adjuncts
  - MOOD adjuncts

- **Experiential component**
  - Transitivity analysis: verbal processes
  - Circumstantial adjuncts

- **Logico-semantic relations in clause complexes**

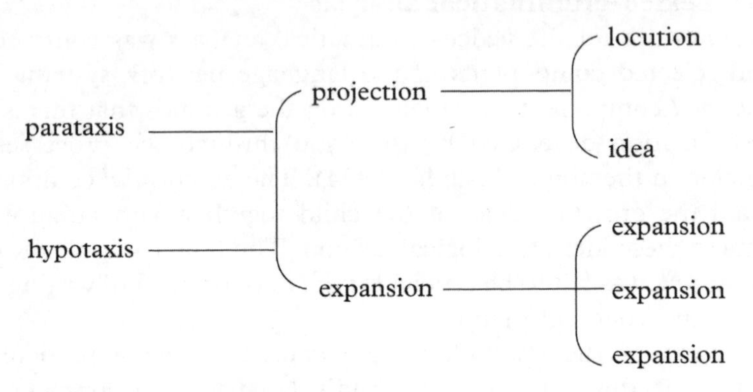

- **Textual component**
  - Theme analysis
  - Conjunctions
  - Tense

Figure 5.3 Components of the language network system

small sample are that there is little development in the use of MOOD in the later years of primary schooling. The *wh-interrogative* is the most common alternative and tends to come in characters' locutions or ideas-type clauses, e.g.:

> Tom asked her, 'Why did you stand on the chair?' (P4; T5)
> . . . I didn't know why my sister jumped on the chair. (P3; T24)

The results show that the majority of adjuncts are mainly circumstantial and conjunctive, with an increase in frequency of use as the child's written language develops. Both these types of adjuncts will be discussed later when we consider the process of Transitivity and the Textual component.

Other adjuncts such as the vocative are often the result of the young writers attempt to create dialogue, e.g.:

Table 5.3 Types of adjuncts in the Primary 1–6 texts

Type of adjuncts	Pri. 1	Pri. 2	Pri. 3	Pri. 4	Pri. 5	Pri. 6
Circumstantial	21	43	73	75	76	91
MOOD	2	3	6	6	10	12
Comment	0	0	0	2	0	3
Conjunctive	17	26	43	48	53	54
Continuity	0	0	0	0	0	2
Vocative	0	0	0	1	0	3
Total adjuncts	40	72	122	132	139	165
Ranking clauses	39	58	100	118	115	132

> '*Mum*, your chicken taste very good today!' I complimented (P4; T19)
> '*Well*, I hope you have learnt your lesson, Jane ...' (P6; T13)

Or comment adjuncts such as:

> *Unfortunately*, the chair which she was standing on could not take her weight and gave way. (P6; T4)

Such adjuncts add expression of attitude and evaluation to indicate some expression of the writer's own opinion.

The only other adjunct found in all six levels of texts is the MOOD adjunct. Like the comment adjunct, it also allows for a writer's personal injection. Its usage in the texts is an indication of the children's control of the grammar to temper what would have been a more impersonal narrative without it.

In order to gain a clearer picture of modality in the texts, Table 5.4 tabulates the total realizations of verbal modality and modulation of the MOOD adjuncts which are divided into categories of *usuality, probability, intensification* and *inclination.*

Table 5.4 gives some indication that as the children get older the amount of modality increases, showing a greater input of their own opinions in the texts. However, it is the MOOD adjunct of intensification that predominates as this is probably the easiest of the MOOD adjuncts to use e.g.:

> ...were a *little* frightened (P5; T29)
> ...became *very* frightened (P6; T6)

Verbal realization where found is mainly in terms of obligation:

> We *should* always stay calm when we feel frightened. (P5; T29)
> you ... *will* not be so foolish (P6; T29)

Table 5.4 Categories of the total number of MOOD adjuncts

	Pri.1	Pri.2	Pri.3	Pri.4	Pri.5	Pri.6
Modalization (verbal)	0	0	0	0	0	0
MOOD adjunct: usuality	0	0	1	0	1	1
MOOD adjunct: probability	0	0	0	0	0	0
MOOD adjunct: intensification	2	2	5	5	5	10
Modulation (verbal)	0	1	0	0	1	1
MOOD adjunct: inclination	1	1	0	1	3	0
Total expressions of Modality	3	4	6	6	10	12
Total ranking clauses	39	58	100	118	115	132

5.4.4.3 The ideational component

5.4.4.3.1 Transitivity analysis

Table 5.5 presents the total number of clauses of each process type for each level.

Table 5.5 Transitivity in the Primary 1–6 texts

Process type	Pri. 1	Pri. 2	Pri. 3	Pri. 4	Pri. 5	Pri. 6
Material	28	41	75	91	72	93
Mental	6	7	8	17	9	11
Verbal	0	3	3	9	8	9
Behavioural	4	7	9	7	6	11
Existential	1	0	2	0	2	2
Relational (attributive)	2	6	8	8	24	21
Relational (possessive)	0	0	3	1	1	1
Total no. of processes	41	64	108	133	122	148

As the table shows, *material* processes are dominant in all the texts. This is what would be expected as narratives are centrally concerned with actions and events, and the participants who carry them out. However, the proportion of the material processes to the other process types is higher in Primary one to Primary four than in Primary five and six. This indicates a growing maturity in the use of the verbal processes available to the writer. Anomalies do occur as one would expect in such a small sample, such as in a Primary four text, which produced a particularly large input from a single text of *mental* processes.

Significantly the relational (attributive) is one of the processes whose usage increased. This is an indication that the texts become more descriptive at the higher levels. This can be illustrated in the following examples:

As the chair ... *was* very old, one of the stands ... *was* unstable ... the chair's stands broke and Mary fell ... (P6; T3)

Compared to a text from Primary two:

Suddenly, the chair broke. (P2; T27).

Another common function of the relational (attributive) process is to describe the emotional make of the characters. This was in addition to the behavioural processes commonly used by writers at all levels e.g.:

She was crying (P1; T7)
Jame ... scream ... (P2; T11)

The texts at upper levels include attributive processes such as:

She was so frightened and scared (P5; T36)
Hassam and his Mother were shocked (P5; T3)

Lastly, the use of verbal processes can be attributed to the young writers' attempts to incorporate dialogue in their narratives:

Tom asked her, 'Why did you stand on the chair?' (P4; T5)
'I told him I saw a mouse ...' (P4; T23)

5.4.4.3.2 Circumstantial adjuncts

Table 5.6 Circumstances in the Primary 1–6 texts

Type	Pri. 1	Pri. 2	Pri. 3	Pri. 4	Pri. 5	Pri. 6
Location	17	32	58	50	48	65
Extent	0	0	1	1	0	1
Manner	3	6	14	20	16	15
Role	0	0	0	5	0	1
Accompaniment	1	0	2	0	2	3
Cause	0	2	1	5	3	1
Total	21	40	76	81	69	86
No. of ranking clauses	39	58	100	118	115	132

As Table 5.6 indicates, the number of circumstances used generally increases as the level progresses. Circumstances function to increase the experiential content of the text as they add specificity to the information.

In all the texts, the dominant circumstance is that of location. This means that the texts concentrate on situating events in time and space, a common feature in narratives.

The other circumstance that is used fairly often is that of *manner*. The Table shows the uses of *manner* from Primary three to six are more than double. This is an indication that as the children get older, on top of providing information on the 'where' and 'when' of something happening, they also start providing information on the 'how'. For instance, in the texts of the lower Primary levels, it is common for the writers to inform the readers of the events only, e.g.:

She was crying. (P1; T7)
I was eating my dinner. (P2; T3)
My brother ... hit the mouse (P1; T4)

Whereas in the upper Primary levels the writers provide information on the manner in which the events are performed.

Mary was crying *bitterly* (P4; T5)
... she cried even *louder* (P6; T31)
They were eating *happily* (P5; T29)
her brother ... hit the mouse *with a broom* (P5; T5)

Despite the increased use of circumstantial adjuncts as the young writers mature, the actual proportion of circumstantial adjuncts to ranking clauses diminishes. The indication seems to be that children at the upper end of primary education begin to use a more informal style of writing, possibly in an attempt to bridge the gap between writer and reader, or in other words move towards being more 'reader friendly'.

5.4.4.4 Logical relations analysis

The logical relations of explicitly marked and non-finite clauses in each text were analysed and the total results are tabulated in Table 5.7.

Table 5.7 shows a high use of explicit conjunctions in all the levels, suggesting some possible forward planning by the pupils, with or without the teacher's help. The greater proportion of the explicit conjunctions in relation to the number of sentences from the Primary four level onwards suggests that the pupils are becoming more aware of the cohesion needed in texts and one way of doing this is by linking the clause sequence.

The dominant logico-semantic sequence in clause complexing is *enhancement*; this could indicate that the narratives of the children are more concerned with qualifying the events with some circumstantial feature of *time*, *place*, *cause* or *condition* rather than restating it in another way or simply giving more information. There is also quite

Table 5.7 An analysis of logical relations in the Primary 1–6 texts

Type	Pri.1	Pri.2	Pri.3	Pri.4	Pri.5	Pri.6
Elaboration						
Paratactic	1	1	0	1	2	0
Hypotactic	1	0	0	1	0	0
Extension						
Paratactic	0	10	9	18	19	22
Hypotactic	0	0	0	2	1	0
Enhancement						
Paratactic	8	16	24	10	14	17
Hypotactic	3	7	17	22	23	26
Locution						
Paratactic	0	0	3	5	3	9
Hypotactic	0	1	0	2	2	1
Idea						
Hypotactic	0	0	4	3	3	3
Embedding						
Elaboration	0	0	0	2	2	2
Enhancement	2	1	2	5	3	5
Explicit (Conjunctions)	22	32	50	66	67	83
Number of sentences	25	30	53	58	54	68

markedly a greater use of hypotactic and embedded clauses at the upper levels of primary schooling which is what would be expected if there is growth in the language development in writing skills.

The use of *elaboration* is very limited and often involves internal (rhetorical) conjunctive relations, which can reflect a writer's thinking process. This limited usage is revealing as this would seem to indicate that the writers were not composing the texts as some internalized structure in their own minds but rather depended on an outside agency with some pre-set ideas, in this case either the restrictions of the task itself or too much reliance on the 'guided composition'.

However, there are quite positive signs of growth as we see in the development of the early use *enhancement* which grows in complexity as the child's language develops.

> I jumped up and I fell on the ground and hit my head. (P1; T4)
> Mary's brother was very angry and wanted to kill the mouse with the broom. (P2; T16)
> They lived in a HDB flat, so it was usually very quiet. (P3; T40)
> While we were eating our dinner, our dinner was interrupted by a loud shriek by my sister. (P4; T19)

When Jill saw the mouse she was so frightened and scared that she jumped up and stood on the chair. (P5; T36)
As Mary fell she also pulled the table cloth and the food fell to the floor. (P6; T3)

One additional consideration has to be in the choice of the narrative technique. In the lower Primary levels, events of the narrative were mostly reported, setting the time frame in the past.

I told him I saw a mouse. (P4; T23)

However, in the Primary six level, with the choice of paratactic locutions like:

''Yum! The food taste great, Mummy,' said John' (P6; T13)

The young writer shows an awareness of a linguistic technique to transport the reader to the time when the event occurred thereby enriching the reader's experience of the event. This livens up the text, ultimately making the narrative more interesting.

5.4.4.5 The textual component

5.4.4.5.1 Theme analysis

Table 5.8 THEME in the Primary 1–6 texts

Category	Pri.1	Pri.2	Pri.3	Pri.4	Pri.5	Pri.6
Marked	4	10	16	11	20	19
Interpersonal element as Theme	0	0	3	20	0	4
Dependent clause as Theme	1	1	0	9	9	11
Ranking clause	39	58	100	118	115	132

The Table 5.8 indicates that marked themes are used at all levels with a greater proportion in the later years of primary schooling. This usage of the marked Theme suggests a more planned rhetorical development of the text with the foregrounding of circumstantial information. But these marked Themes at Primary one and two are used mainly in the orientation of the narrative and many seem to be simply formulaic.

One night, the Ting family was eating dinner (P1; T7)
Last night, my mother brother and me was at home (P2; T23)

By Primary three the marked Theme is more elaborate.

At the background, Meifeng was crying (P3; T5)
After the long chase, the rat was finally killed. (P5; T3)

By Primary five the marked Theme can often be of *manner:*

Like a bolt from the blue, Mary jumped out. (P5; T29)
With a loud scream, Jane toppled off. (P6; T13)

Thus the young writers seem to be acquiring the skill to use marked themes in a variety of ways, which helps to increase the maturity of their written prose.

Another indication is that as the writers get older, their narratives become more informal and conversational with a significant increase in the use of dependent clauses as Themes. That the upper level of primary school texts appears to be more informal in their style is supported by the increased occurrence of interpersonal themes such as:

Fortunately, she stopped crying. (P4; T5)

5.4.4.5.2 Conjunction analysis

The use of the appropriate conjunctions in a text has great implications for the text's overall coherence and cohesion. Halliday in his grammar lists conjunctive adjuncts under four main headings: additive, adversative, causal and temporal. In this sample of texts, the children throughout their writing use the *and* as an additive as the predominant conjunction although it may sometimes occur as causal.

. . . the chair broke and the girl fell. (P1; T16)

Occasionally one finds temporal connectors such as *then* and *when* in Primary one and two.

I stand on the chair . . . then the mice ran to my chair. (P2; T3)
When we were eating . . . I saw a rat. (P2; T27)

In Primary three and four, the only non-temporal and non-additive conjunctions used other than *and*, were the adversative *but* and the causal connectors *because* and *so*.

He tried to kill the mouse. *But* . . . he failed to do it. (P4; T5)
Their father was not in *because* he was working. (P3; T27)
They lived in a HDB flat, *so* it was usually very quiet. (P3; T40)

Greater variety of adversatives was found at Primary five and six.

Although Hassam and his mother were very hungry *but* they were

glad that the rat was killed. (P5; T3)
Their mother and John were ... calm ... *even though* they were a little frightened. (P5; T9)

5.4.4.5.3 Tense analysis

Narratives are typically written in the past tense (whether real or imagined past). In the data collected from this sample, Primary one and two wrote in the present tense and only in Primary three did the majority of texts use the past tense with occasional slips back into the present. However, the young writers' inability to maintain agreement between tenses in successive verb phrases had a considerable effect on the overall coherence of the text.

... the mouse *die* because it *did not have* air to breath. (P3; T6)
Hassam *took* a broom and *chase* after the rat. (P5; T3)

There is also evidence of the use of the past progressive in place of the simpler past, which could be an indication of a growing maturity in the use of the English tense system.

Jackson and I *were eating* ... dinner when a mouse suddenly *ran out* from no where. (P4; T23)
They *were eating* ... and having a conversation ... Like a bolt from the blue Mary *jumped out* and *stood* on her chair. (P5; T29)

5.5 Conclusion

The general findings of this initial study using limited text-types in the macro-analysis and a simplified lexico-grammatical network for the micro-analysis of the linguistic features seem to indicate that the children are gaining greater control over their writing. However, any further macro-analysis would need to look at how the young writers were developing when exposed to a greater variety of genres.

On the other hand, in the micro-analysis what was observed was an increasing use of the full declarative MOOD type as well as an increased use of hypotactic and embedded clauses. There is also an increasing and more diverse use of conjunctions and marked themes, which signals a more rhetorical organization of their texts. This in turns improves the coherence and cohesion and, consequently, is more likely to create texts which are richer in content and far less monotonous.

There are still, of course, a number of problem areas such as those indicated earlier: agreement of tenses which affect the overall coherence of the texts; the lack of internal conjunctions and the rather formulaic use of some adjuncts. The indication is that for this sample, a controlled writing environment is still maintained even at Primary five and six. In fact one very notable feature which stands out in this data is how little development there is from Primary four onwards. In general, having completed Primary four, the indications are that in Primary five and six all the features we have analysed show little or no development in the children's writing when compared to Primary four. In the context of Singapore this is probably explained by the fact that teachers in Primary five and six concentrate on preparing the children for the end-of-Primary-school examinations. The focus then becomes the types of questions set in the examinations. In the past much of the extended writing has been assessed by questions that lead to recount or narrative generic structures.

As far as this particular project is concerned, there seems to be some potential in developing a framework by which to analyse the development of children's writing over the six years of primary education. In any further study, the important linguistic element of nominalization would have to be included in the framework, as this is particularly relevant in the factually oriented text-types.

The division into macro-level and micro-level analysis does seem useful as it allows an investigation into the 'textual' aspects of the pupils' writing in terms of the generic structure and, at the same time, the micro-analysis allows a close examination of the grammatical features associated with that text-type. Such a close examination allows the researcher/teacher to see not only the weaknesses of the young writer but also the strengths. The creation of a writing portfolio for each child would allow the teacher to follow the development of the child's discourse through the years of primary education far more accurately than any examination. Also such a detailed record could be 'passed on' to the secondary school as a more tangible account of the child's progress.

References

Christie, F. (1989) *Genres in Writing. Writing in Schools*. Victoria: Deakin University Press.

Christie, F. (ed.) (1999) *Pedagogy and the Shaping of Consciousness*. London: Cassell.

Curriculum Planning and Development Division (2001) *English Language, Primary and Secondary*. Singapore.

Derewianka, B. (1990) *Exploring How Texts Work*. Sydney: Primary English

Teaching Association.

Foley, J.A. (1991) Developmental features of children's writing in Singapore. In A. Kwan-Terry (ed.), *Language Development in Singapore and Malaysia*. Singapore: Singapore University Press.

Foley, J.A. (1994) Moving from 'Common-sense Knowledge' to 'Educational Knowledge'. In S. Gopinathan, A. Pakir, Ho Wah Kam and V. Saravanan (eds), *Language Society and Education in Singapore*. Singapore: Times Academic Press.

Foley, J.A. (2001) Is English a First or Second Language in Singapore? In V.B.Y. Ooi (ed.), *Evolving Identities*. Singapore: Times Academic Press.

Goh, Li Wah (1992) *The Re-contextualising of Academic Knowledge in History and Geography in Secondary One and Two*. Singapore: Academic Exercise, Department of English Language and Literature, National University of Singapore.

Halliday, M.A.K. (1994) *An Introduction to Functional Grammar* (2nd edn.) London: Edward Arnold.

Harris, J. (1986) Organisation in Children's Writing. In J. Harris and J. Wilkinson (eds), *Reading Children's Writing*. London: Allen and Unwin.

Laxmi, J. (1985) *Analysing the Use of Cohesive Devices in the Language of Primary School Children*. Singapore: Academic Exercise, Department of English Language and Literature, National University of Singapore.

Martin, J.R. (1997) Analysing genre: functional parameters. In F. Christie and J.R. Martin (eds), *Genre and Institutions*. London: Cassell.

Martin, J.R. and Rothery, J. (1981, 1982, 1986) *Writing Project Reports, Working Papers in Linguistics, Nos 1, 2 and 4*. Sydney: Department of Linguistics, University of Sydney.

McCarthy, M. and Carter, R. (1994) *Language as Discourse: Perspectives for Language Teaching*. Harlow: Longman.

Narandran, N. (1986) *A Study of Grammar and Register of Primary School Children's Essays*. Singapore: Academic Exercise, Department of English Language and Literature, National University of Singapore.

Painter, C. (1999) *Learning Through Language in Early Childhood*. London: Cassell.

Perera, K. (1984) *Children's Writing and Reading*. Oxford: Basil Blackwell.

Rothery, J. (1988) Learning about Language. In R. Hasan and J.R. Martin (eds), *Language Development: Learning Language, Learning Culture*. New Jersey: Ablex.

Saffiah bte Mohammed Amin (1984) *The Teaching of Writing in Primary Six and the First Year of Secondary School*. Singapore: Academic Exercise, Department of English Language and Literature, National University of Singapore.

Samraj, B. (1989) *Picture Talk as Curriculum Genre*. Singapore: Academic Exercise, Department of English Language and Literature, National University of Singapore.

Varghese, S.A. (1994) Reading and Writing Instruction in Singapore

Secondary Schools. In S. Gopinathan, A. Pakir, Ho Wah Kam and V. Saravanan (eds), *Language Society and Education in Singapore*. Singapore: Times Academic Press.

Wee Bee Geok (1991) A preliminary study of generic structures used with and by secondary two students in Singapore. MA thesis. National University of Singapore.

Wong, R. (1994) Meaning-constructing Strategies in English and Chinese Writing: Effective versus Ineffective Writing. In S. Gopinathan, A. Pakir, Ho Wah Kam and V. Saravanan (eds), *Language Society and Education in Singapore*. Singapore: Times Academic Press.

Yee Mei Pao (1991) *A Study of Genre in the Writing of Primary Five and Six Children*. Singapore: Academic Exercise, Department of English Language and Literature, National University of Singapore.

6

An Analysis of a Children's History Text

Bridget Goom

6.1 Introduction

In his account of monolingual children's language development, Halliday (1996) suggests that elaboration and extension of each child's language are ongoing. But he proposes that there are three phases of enhancement, all necessary for full access to participation in modern society. The three phases he identifies are:

1. from prototypical language to commonsense knowledge that is embedded in the mother tongue (at age 1–2)
2. from the commonsense knowledge of the home to educational knowledge of the primary school and its symbolic worlds of literacy and numeracy (at age 4–6)
3. technical knowledge: from congruent construals to metaphorical ones (at age 9–13).

While other linguists and educationalists may have their own theory, their own account with its practical technicalities, there is very general agreement about the existence of the first two phases, and about what should be done in those instances where children are not yet achieving within the normal linguistic range. In Britain, for example, the child who is perceived (at nursery school or beginning primary school) to be deficient in operating the mother tongue will be prescribed speech therapy. A child who is perceived (in primary school) to be deficient in basic literacy and numeracy will also be prescribed remediation (currently termed 'special needs provision'). The existence of these two phases is thoroughly naturalized. But the existence and the nature of the movement into technical knowledge (as described by Halliday) does not, it would seem, have anything like the same consensus among concerned professionals.

That many children fail to master the range of disciplines on offer in the secondary school is evident enough. But there is no general perception that this is a matter of linguistic difficulty – not at least of the order of linguistic difficulty that Halliday is discussing. Educational failure is variously ascribed to: lack of pupil intelligence; lack of pupil motivation; lack of parental motivation; poor teaching; poorly managed schools; and under-funding. While these ascriptions cover most of the interested parties, they do not pay attention to what children have to contend with as they begin secondary school, in attempting to construe, and in turn to produce, technical texts. An attempt to focus on the linguistic demands of the secondary curriculum was made in Britain in the 1970s. However, this 'Language Across the Curriculum' movement quickly foundered on the internal organization of strongly classified institutions. Many secondary teachers, especially in poor urban areas, have worked extremely hard to contend with the difficulties they have perceived in their pedagogic situation: they have routinely recontextualized knowledge from textbooks they find too demanding for a large section of their pupils to worksheets that may be within their grasp. However, it is only relatively recently that it has been supported by the theoretical work of linguists such as Halliday (1993), Derewianka (1995), Christie (1999) and Martin (1999) to mention but a few. Such researchers have been prominent in following up on Bernstein's sociological perspectives first outlined in the 1970s.

Among the fields that cause most difficulty to young learners is history. History is full of judgements and valuations (Veel and Coffin 1996; Martin 1997). These judgements and valuations are sometimes explicit, but often implicit. Moreover, the criteria for the judgements and valuations are frequently implicit. They are derived, consciously or otherwise, from the grand narratives of the history writer's and history learner's culture or they may be derived from the grand narratives of other cultures. While, in this case, unconscious osmosis may seem at first sight much less likely, if the other culture has political and/or economic dominance, then rejection of its implicit assumptions embedded in history texts may only be possible through conscious and sustained resistance (something extremely difficult for young learners).

Incoherences (Lemke's 1995 dislocations) in implicit assumptions are not infrequent. As Davies (a leading academic historian) remarks, in a discussion of the effects of national bias on historical texts:

> The problem of national bias is probably best observed in the realm of school textbooks and popular histories. The more that historians have to condense and simplify their material, the harder it is to mask their prejudices. (1996: 33)

Many teachers in the upper primary school are not, of course, history specialists. Even in lower secondary school, it is very common for teachers of geography and English to take a few history classes. While some history specialists may be very good at making explicit to children what the written texts do, not many children in this age range will have come across a history specialist at all.

Halliday and Derewianka among others have proposed that the linguistic challenge facing nine to thirteen year olds is crucial for the young learner entering the field of 'technical knowledge'. History, as we have already pointed out, is a field particularly dense in culturally loaded implicit assumptions. Thus the rationale for this study, which undertakes an analysis of a history text designed for this crucial age group of nine to thirteen year olds, is that it may shed some additional light both on the task facing children and on the difficulty of writing coherently for such an age group.

6.2 The verbal text and the context of situation

The text selected was from a series of children's illustrated (pictures, diagrams, maps, explanatory boxes) history textbooks designed for upper primary schools in the UK: *Christopher Columbus: The Discovery of the New World* (Twist 1993).

6.2.1 The Field

School history texts are recontextualizations from the academic field of history. In Western culture, the academic field of history traditionally sees itself as autonomous, strongly disapproving of academic history elsewhere that is overtly tied to the support of the political status quo. However, national bias within the Western academic field is acknowledged, even though this is generally in the form of the other writer's transgression. As Davies (1996: 44) puts it, 'National states are themselves 'imagined communities' they are built on powerful myths, and on the political rewriting of history.'

Bernstein formulated this as follows, albeit in another context:

> The school is a crucial device for writing and re-writing national consciousness, and national consciousness is constructed out of

> myths of origin, achievements and destiny. Essentially national consciousness transforms a common biology into a cultural specific in such a way that the specific cultural consciousness comes to have the force of a unique biology. (1996: 10)

For the last half-century or so Western academic history has come under attack on the grounds of hagiography and ethnocentrism. This attack has been under two influences. The first is the rise in importance of social historians, accompanied (within the field) by the continuing shift from narrative to analysis and (externally) by the general rise of the social sciences. The second is the articulation of viewpoints not included in the traditional all-white hegemony of Western Europe and North America. (see James's (1938) treatment of Christopher Columbus as an example of this.)

Such overt debate of historical interpretation has made considerable headway. Davies says of hagiography:

> The really vicious quality shared by almost all accounts of 'Western civilization' lies in the fact that they present idealized, and hence essentially false pictures of past reality. They extract everything that might be judged genial or impressive; and they filter out anything that might appear mundane or repulsive ... judging from some of the textbooks, one gets the distinct impression that everyone in the 'West' was a genius, a philosopher, a pioneer, a democrat, or a saint, that it was a world inhabited exclusively by Platos and Marie Curies. Such hagiography is no longer credible. (1996: 28)

With such general acceptance of anti-hagiographic and anti-ethnocentric arguments in the academic field, it might be expected that by the 1990s a recontextualization in a children's book would reflect this acceptance. Such an expectation might be strengthened by the back cover of this book on Christopher Columbus, emblazoned with the statement:

> The year 1492, when Columbus first landed in the New World, as America was known, marks one of the great turning points in history: Europe, America and the rest of the world would never be the same again!

The publishers appear to be implying a reconstructed trifocal approach of 'Europe, America and the rest of the World'.

6.2.2 Tenor

The traditional general assumption behind history texts for readers in this age group is of an extreme difference in power between readers (beginners in the field) and writer (an expert).

The authoritarian-sounding expert is much less fashionable in schools than he was. Teachers are more likely than they were half a century ago to aim not just at transmitting nuggets of information but at elucidating approaches to knowledge. Some textbook-writers share these concerns for demystification; others do not. A writer's attitude with respect to his own role will have implications for the organization of the text. Texts will give more, or less, space to reporting debate; they will be more, or less, open in quoting source (both within the period under discussion, and since); they will be more, or less, open in inviting readers' opinions on any aspect of the topic or related question.

History texts will also vary in what play they make with solidarity: what use is made of 'we' and 'our' and how clearly the referents are defined. Then there is the degree of sympathy between 'us' and the various historical participants, what Martin (1997) and White (2000) would possibly list under 'affect', and certainly also judgement and appreciation.

6.2.3 Mode

The mode of published written text carries with it the expectations of a carefully planned, carefully drafted, carefully polished text: the expected level of coherence is high.

Within general history for young learners, biographical narrative as iconic exemplification is constituting the social process by reconstructing unshared vicarious experience; whereas the surrounding historical generalization is constituting the social process by construction. In other words, the writer has more choice with respect to historical generalization than with respect to biographical narrative; but this greater choice is still, of course, constrained by the context of culture.

Where a book is entitled by the name of an iconic individual, as in this case, the writer can choose to give more, or less, space to historical generalization and to make the relationship between generalization and the choice of icon more, or less, explicit.

However, the total lack of contact between writer and readers other than through the printed page puts the onus on the writer to be sensitive to his target audience in two respects. The first is what they might know and what they might not know (which therefore requires explanation). The second is who they are: what their experience might be in terms of social positioning. The argument here is not that every reader is necessarily restricted by general experience to interest in one point of view only, but that a writer who provides for only one point of view is necessarily failing many of his readers.

6.3 What young readers might not know

We can consider 'what young readers might not know' under three headings: General (non-historical) knowledge; historical knowledge; and linguistic and textual knowledge.

6.3.1 General knowledge

The writer of *Christopher Columbus* makes several suppositions about the background knowledge of his young readers. We will illustrate this by citing a number of examples from the text.

In the passage on page 8 introducing the Renaissance, Humanism, the Reformation and the Counter Reformation, 'philosophy' is introduced without gloss, that is, it is treated as a non-problematic term. If the term is to be used, it needs considerable unpacking. That the attempted explanation of Humanism is based on it, makes the lack of explanation of 'philosophy' doubly unfortunate.

In the report on the three ships that comprised Columbus's first fleet on pages 12–13, various technical terms are used: bow, stern, draught, main mast, lateen sail, etc. A useful line drawing is provided – but none of the parts referred to are labelled.

As for the state of navigation in the 1490s, on page 15 there is a paragraph on the problem of measuring longitude.

> The best method was to work out the distances sailed by multiplying the ship's speed by the length of time it had been sailing.

This explanation is so compact that it is probably inaccessible to many children in the target age range. Distance, speed and time problems are notoriously difficult for ten and eleven year olds. Those children who are strong and experienced mathematicians, may successfully construe the explanation. The rest would benefit from less incongruent wording: 'how far', 'how fast', 'how long'.

In his division of indigenous American cultures into groups according to the standard anthropological taxonomy on page 32, the author does not explain what the basis for the grouping is. Technology does surface except with reference to 'primitive hunter-gatherers, existing on wild food and using only stone tools'. Nor does he attempt to explain the technical term 'culture': 'Many had their cultures wiped out.' To assume that children in this age range have a general idea of what a culture is, is to assume too much: some will, many will not. 'Culture' continues to crop up, unexplained, in later parts of the text:

> Although the Olmecs and the Zapotecs both had highly developed cultures, they were overshadowed by the rise of the Maya Empire to the east.

In the box on the transatlantic spread of diseases on page 42, the central medico-biological concept of immunity is not explained. It is used unproblematically: 'many Europeans had acquired some immunity' and 'native Americans had no such immunity'. The writer is surely right to give this subject space; but the space could have been more effectively used.

These are only a few examples of the expectations that the writer has of the background knowledge he supposes the young reader to have. Too often more explanation is required, at least when writing at this level.

6.3.2 Historical knowledge

The opening section of the opening chapter of the book on page 4 ends with this sentence:

> The result of this introduction was the creation of what Europeans called the 'New World' – a land of dreams and opportunity, and also a land of nightmares and destruction.

For those who are initiated into the history of the Americas over the last 500 hundred years, this sentence is a clear predictive signal for the whole text: there will be happy events recounted and unhappy events. Alternatively, for those with no historical background but a good knowledge of how texts operate, the predictive signal will also work. But for those without the historical background and without the textual knowledge, the signal will fail. The 'New World' is glossed, but in a dense cluster of nominalizations. Because actions, both planned and realized, are represented as nouns, all the participants (both the happy, and the unhappy, the doers and the done-to) can be elided from the text. This formulation will fail to convey to many young readers that white American society was built on the ruins of native America, and that an additional cost was the forced disruption of the life of many Africans.

This page is further complicated by ambivalent uses of 'America' and 'Europe': referring either to physical landmass, or to the society constructed there, or to both. This kind of ambivalence is common in history texts, but not all children will know this.

Also the ambivalence in history of geopolitical terms could be a source of difficulty for young readers again on page 7. In the opening sentence of the section entitled 'The position of Spain', both geographical and political ends of the spectrum are used:

> Spain was larger and more powerful than Portugal.

As the paragraph develops, young readers have to supply for themselves the knowledge that in history texts 'interest' is either diplomatic interest, economic interest, or both:

> But as yet Spain had no real interest in the Atlantic. During most of the 1400s, Spain's attention was concentrated elsewhere.

This applies also to page 10:

> The Portuguese were more interested in Africa than in some fabled lands which might lie to the west.

Readers are also expected to know that the Turkish Ottoman Empire was Muslim:

> Although the old Islamic Empire of the Arabs was in decline, it had been replaced by the Turkish Ottoman Empire based in Istanbul (formerly the Christian city of Constantinople. (8)

The correct construal of 'replaced' here is 'replaced as leading member of the new Islam Empire in the continuing confrontation between Islam and Christianity'. Islam is in the glossary – but the entry does not mention Turkey. The Ottoman Empire is in the glossary – but the entry does not mention Islam.

It is also pointed out in the Introduction that 'Columbus . . . lived in times very different from our own' (5). Children must often bring the relevant differences to the text for themselves or be left unenlightened.

Lack of background on the norms of fifteenth- and sixteenth-century Europe directly affects how a reader is to construe Columbus's actions. It is stated on page 11 that:

> He [Columbus] would be loyal to whoever employed him: earlier in his career, Columbus happily fought a sea battle on the side of the Portuguese against his home city of Genoa.

But the normality of mercenaries (as opposed to the modern arrangement whereby fighters' loyalty normally matches citizenship) is not explained.

'Spain' vies with 'Europe' for the distinction of being the most 'slippery' concept. On page 9, Spain is implicitly characterized as being intolerant and regressive:

> the Catholic reaction [to Humanism and Protestantism] was strongest in Spain ... In 1481 Spain reintroduced the Inquisition.

By page 11, the implicit characterization is quite different:

> The year 1492 would have been exceptional for Spain, even without Columbus's achievement. At the beginning of the year, Spanish armies finally reconquered the territory of Granada held by the Moors. Spain was at last united and free of Islamic occupation.

There are two routes to correct construal; neither is easy for beginners. The first is via Columbus's achievement:

- Columbus's achievement was a good thing (see title; 4, 8).
- It was an important event for Spain in 1492.
- The other important event for Spain in 1492 was the conquest of Granada.
- Therefore the conquest of Granada was a good thing.
- Therefore Spain was a good thing.

The second is the anti-Islamic route:

- Spain was now free of Islamic occupation.
- Islamic occupation had been a problem (see 7)
- Therefore the conquest of Granada was a good thing.
- Therefore Spain was a good thing.

Whatever route is taken, Spain emerges as Christian and progressive.

6.3.3 Linguistic and textual knowledge

Every item in the previous two sections is, of course, an item in this section too. However, we will not replicate the discussion above. We will briefly indicate the lexical density of a few samples from the text, on the argument that young readers are likely to have difficulty with high-density texts. We will consider some of the clusters of technical terms, lexical metaphors and grammatical metaphors found in this text.

First, lexical density. It is not difficult to find sentences with a high lexical density – that is, the number of lexical items divided by the number of ranking clauses (Halliday 1994: 351).

Here are some examples:

1 The result of this introduction was the creation of what Europeans called the New World – land of dreams and opportunity, and also a land of nightmare and destruction. (4)
lexical density: 12

2 New ideas about art, science and religion, and new inventions such as printing, had combined to produce an atmosphere of change. (4)
lexical density: 12

3 The only way for Christian Kingdoms to increase their power and wealth was to turn their attention to the gray waters of the Atlantic Ocean. (8)
lexical density: 13

In the light of Halliday's (1996) finding that typical lexical density in technical texts for adults is 6–10, these figures are extraordinarily high.

Second, metaphorical density. Lexical metaphor abounds. In (1) above, there is the lexical metaphor of creation: 'land' is both physical, differentiated from sea, and social. The lexical metaphor in (2) is chemical: elements combine to produce a new compound ('atmosphere of change'). In (3) the lexical metaphor is a continuation from the previous sentence: 'The blue waters of the Mediterranean Sea were besieged by the rival powers.' Waters besieged is a curious image; it might even be questionable as to cultural availability. Presumably the meaning is something along the lines of 'The trade capacities of the Mediterranean Sea were contended by these rivals powers.' Such a construal has to be built anaphorically, from 'The only way ... to increase their power and wealth.' It is clear here that the process of struggling to construe a not very illuminating lexical metaphor is not very far different from the process of struggling to construe a passage overloaded with technical terms or grammatical metaphor.

Turning to grammatical metaphor, in example (1) above 'introduction' is a technical term which is not explained, and because it does not look technical many young readers will not recognize it as such. Moreover, the 'introduction' involves two place names; and place names in history are complex technical terms. With a text so densely packed with complex technical terms and grammatical metaphors, the combined effect is very far from congruent and, in any case, the task of construal is highly demanding.

Consider (1) again and its preceding sentence:

> What Columbus did was to introduce America to Europe, and Europe to America. The result of this introduction was the creation of what Europeans called the 'New World' – a land of dreams and opportunity, and also a land of nightmares and destruction.

To provide a congruent agnate, participants and circumstances missing from this version must be supplied. 'America' and 'Europe' could have a range of meanings, for example:

- the landmass itself
- the people of the landmass
- the political unit or units
- the people and the culture of the landmass and so on.

The densest passages are, not altogether surprisingly, in the first two chapters: the 'Introduction' and 'The historical background', which is in fact a brief survey of the Renaissance and the Reformation.

'A time of transformation' (2) introduces these themes. The first technical term used here (other than Europe, already discussed) is 'the Middle Ages':

> In 1477, the year that Columbus settled in Lisbon, Europe stood poised at the very end of the Middle Ages. Life had changed little during the previous 300 years. There was one church, the Roman Catholic Church, headed by the Pope. Printing had only just been invented and books were rare.

A later paragraph describes the Renaissance: the collapse of the Roman Empire; the crudity of medieval art; the northern Italian return to the Ancients as inspiration; Leonardo as exemplification of the 'more realistic'; and the summing up:

> This development is known as the Renaissance (rebirth) of European art.

Only a reader already familiar with the framework of European art history could possibly make sense of this account. To learners it is totally inaccessible. If such a complex term as 'the Renaissance' is vital to the argument of the text, it must be given much better treatment than this.

The Reformation is introduced, mainly it would seem, to help explain that Columbus was 'A man of his time' (10), that:

> The same society that shaped the Renaissance and the Reformation also shaped Christopher Columbus.

This claim is partially and more congruently re-expressed by reference to the already established iconic exemplifications; the link is made in terms of personal characteristics:

> Like Leonardo, Columbus was adventurous and ambitious; and, like Luther, he was convinced that he was right.

Renaissance-and-Reformation Man, as opposed both to Medieval Man and to Counter-Reformation Man, is characterized as adventurous, ambitious and firm in his convictions. This neat formulation is, in fact, hard to substantiate: there is no evidence to suggest that Columbus was at all critical of Catholicism; and, if he had been, he is not likely to have obtained Queen Isabella's support for his expeditions!

6.4 The readers' experience in terms of social positioning

> In fourteen hundred and ninety two
> Columbus sailed the ocean blue.

The text beneath begins:

> These traditional lines of school day verse remind us that the year 1492 is one of the great signposts in the history of the human race.

This implies schooldays long behind us: 'we' are adults – a curious opening in a children's history book.

The establishment of insider/outsider relations has two main forms: the explicit use of the pronouns 'we' and 'us' and the use of implication in the immediately surrounding text.

Explicit use of 'us' and 'we' occurs mainly in the introductory chapter. The first occurrence is in the opening sentence of the book on page 4 that is stated above. The most obvious meaning of 'us' is the circle of writer and readers but how much this can be applied to the 'human race' as a whole is more doubtful.

There is an expansion of the 'we' in on page 4:

> It is important to understand exactly why 1492 is so significant. We

are not really remembering the exploits of a single Italian sea captain, no matter how skilful and daring he may have been. Columbus did not 'discover' America. There were already about 100 million native inhabitants living in the continent, and they had explored most of it.

Here the 'we' is more inclusive, accepting the multicultural perspective on the relative importance of the event.

Nevertheless, by the succeeding paragraph the distance between 'us' and the old-fashioned idea of 'discovery' has collapsed:

> Columbus was not the first European to 'discover' America.

There is a recurrence of 'our' and 'we' in the last paragraph of the Introduction (5):

> Columbus, and the Spanish conquerors who followed him to America, lived in times very different from our own. By today's standards, they were appallingly ignorant. If we think that they behaved badly, it is only because we have since learned better.

The distance between the historical participants and those currently reflecting on the events is stressed. This is the one place in the text where it is acknowledged implicitly that readers may have an opinion on the topic. At the same time, any non-favourable opinion is discounted:

> If we think that they behaved badly, it is only because we have learned better.

After this first chapter, an explicit 'we' occurs once more in the sixth chapter, 'Native Americans' on page 33:

> Mayan civilization developed at different times in different places, but we know that the Mayan people first began building temples and cities around 300 BC.

Here 'we' are those with access to information – information where long and difficult debates are represented as definitive facts.

6.4.1 The writer as the 'insider'

The writer as the 'insider' is clearly conveyed through the first paragraph (4) which raises the matter of emotional responses to the Columbus story (only negative emotions are explicitly mentioned):

> Sometimes when people read about events in history they feel angry and ashamed.

The main comment on this is worded as incontrovertible fact, rather than one interpretation:

> The discovery of America by Christopher Columbus is a story of European achievement.

The main statement is then qualified:

> Yet there are parts of his story, and parts of the history of America after 1492, that must make most Europeans feel at least slightly ashamed.

The next paragraph (5) starts congruently ('Christopher Columbus was a tough, greedy man') and ends highly incongruently ('The effects of this slave trade are still being felt today'). But movement between these two extremes is not simply one way. In the middle of the paragraph there is 'caused the death of about eight out of ten native Americans'. From here the text falls back to what appears to be a much less incongruent level:

> When there were no longer enough natives to work in the mines and the fields, the Europeans began importing black slaves from Africa.

Neither the cause of death nor the effects of the trade are made explicit. But the part of the paragraph that hides most is 'When there were no longer enough natives'. That forced labour on a vast scale was one of the 'new inventions' of the 'restless European society' represented by Columbus – and a cause of death – is not mentioned; the lack of native labour is presented as something quite external to, quite independent of, the European entrepreneurs who instituted colonial slave labour.

The third paragraph (5) does not expand on 'effects of this slave trade ... still being felt today'. Instead, it picks up the implicit identification buried in the middle of the previous paragraph:

> However, the judgement of history must not be too harsh.

Note the high-level modal and the fact that the writer chooses to put the summing-up here, rather than at the end of the book. The implication of insider/outsider status comes in the final sentence of the chapter:

> Christopher Columbus and his crew were, after all, just a small group of human explorers in tiny ships, floating on the vastness of the Atlantic Ocean.

6.5 The visual context: page design as immediate context

This section will consider some of those aspects of the visual design of the pages of the book that surround and include the main linguistic text, and the relationship between these surroundings and the main text.

Bathes (quoted in Kress and van Leeuwen 1996: 16–17) discusses two kinds of elaboration in the relationship between the verbal and the pictorial: primary verbal text with secondary pictorial illustration (dominant before the Renaissance); and primary images of nature with secondary accompanying text (dominant since the Renaissance and the rise of science). Kress and van Leeuwen find this framework useful, with qualification:

> But Barthes' account misses an important point: the visual component of a text is an independently organized and structured message – connected with the verbal text, but is no way dependent on it: similarly the other way round. (ibid.: 17)

While there clearly are many texts where the two act independently so that the writing may carry one set of meanings and the images another, there are other texts where the two are closely integrated. It is the argument of this study that more, or less, integration between the two is an aspect of more, or less, overall coherence; and that overall coherence is still culturally desirable, even if the production team is divided between writers, photographers, writing editors, graphics, editors and overall editors.

As Kress and van Leeuwen point out (ibid.: 218–23) linear texts, which do not provide choice of reading path, are becoming less common as non-linear, 'inter-active', computer-influenced texts become more common: both in general and in educational books.

A few examples will be given here to illustrate what we mean. The cover gives the central, dominant position to a line drawing of the *Nina* – the vertical mainmast and convergent rigging pointing to the sky. Around it, in clockwise order from bottom right, are: a triptych of pineapples; the logo of the series (the head of Columbus/Renaissance Man, wreathed in the series title, 'Beyond the Horizons'); a compass; a Native American mask; a Native American statue; a gold coin (reign of Ferdinand and Isabella); and a bejewelled gold statue of a toucan.

The ship and the coin are repeated inside the book. Pineapples, compass, mask, statue and bird were selected for the cover alone. The recurrence of spherical or near-spherical shapes (only the bird is strongly elliptical) neatly suggests the planets circling the sun and the dominance of the Earth as a globe in this story. The circle of the ship and its satellites are (almost) contained by a rectangular frame. There are three interruptions: at the bottom, by the neck of Columbus/ Renaissance Man; at the top, by the gold coin of Ferdinand and Isabella; and on the right, by the extreme edge of the aft lateen. These interruptions give additional salience to the three images concerned. The cover designer has correctly identified the three main images of the book: out of a total of 61 images (excluding modern maps), Columbus/Renaissance Man has 12; gold and silver have nine; sailing and sailing technology have 12. Native American Man is not present on the cover in any realistic sense: both the mask and the statue show formalizations of the human face, but the mask is terrifying, and the statue's eye sockets are empty. The king and queen represent imperialism with the comfortable familiarity of playing cards or nursery rhymes ('the Queen of Hearts', 'the King was in his counting-house'). Renaissance Man is sharply focused, looking intently and clear-sightedly into the distance (and towards the New). The image, with its central right eye (right is correct, left is sinister – even for Europeans who know no Latin) is repeated at the top of each page.

Other examples of the juxtapositioning of the visual and the textual can be found in the Introduction: the first double-page spread (4–5) gives the basic format – illustrations in a generous margin, which is also used from time to time for suggested extensions of the topic; the main text divided into sections in a user-friendly layout, section headings giving salience; a capsule ('The Vikings and Vinland') as an illustrated footnote. However, even in the visuals there are a number of apparent contradictions. One is the visual salience of the replica Viking ship, another is the clash between two elements – the section heading 'A bad beginning' and the image of the loaded slaver with its caption ('Slaves in a nineteenth-century ship. Slaves being transported to America were crammed tightly below decks.')

Yet another is the leading sentence of the chapter's final paragraph:

> However, the judgement of history must not be too harsh.

The next double-page spread (6–7) is rather less traditional: images start to impinge on verbal space. The smaller Alhambra picture acts as a vector giving salience to the larger, which is captioned: 'Inside, the Alhambra is beautifully decorated.' This positive appreciation

(Martin 1997) of Islamic culture is implicitly contradicted in the main text just above:

> One main problem was that part of the country was still under Islamic control.

In another double-page spread (8–9), Luther appears to be kept in the margin while Leonardo impinges on text space (section headings are 'A time of transformation' and 'The Renaissance and the Reformation'). The Renaissance in the main text is defined in terms of art, and art is defined in terms of painting and sculpture.

Although there are many other visuals combined with text on every page in this book, as a final example we will turn to the final double-page spread. The image chosen to represent contemporary America is the five hundredth anniversary of 1492: 'sailing ships from all over the world gathered in New York Harbour to celebrate Columbus's discovery of America'.

America in the 1990s is white America, proud of its technology, sentimental about its European origins and making only minimum concession to those for whom 1492 may not have been wholly a cause of celebration. The final image of native Americans is as the noble savage, firmly in the grip of the sober Puritan (with the right hand holding a gun). The noble savage's pipe of peace looks more like a toy than the real thing.

One final point about the visual context and page design of this book is the inadequate map coverage. The extent of the Moor's empire is not clear. There is no attempt to show the extent of the Ottoman empire. A map of the Portuguese expeditions along the African coast (which are mentioned from time to time) would have also made it clear that Columbus as a young man had already made several voyages, including working out of Portugal, along the African coast.

6.6 Appraisal in the text

There are a number of places where this text constructs (or recontextualizes) distinctions/dichotomies/classifications; expands one part; and fails to develop the rest. Judgements and evaluations are being made in the text and, as we have earlier indicated, these can often be implicit. The argument is not that any and every writer is obliged to write encyclopaedically, but that points of view raised by the writer (unless clearly signalled as paths that the text will not take) raise expectations in the reader. One such dropped distinction is on the topic of reader reactions to history.

> Sometimes when people read about events in history they feel angry or ashamed. (4)

The author goes on to expand briefly one sub-part of shame, slight shame:

> there are parts . . . that must make most Europeans feel at least slightly ashamed.

Negative reader reactions to history get no further mention in the book. Columbus is negatively characterized (5) as 'greedy' and 'a careless administrator'.

The theme of greed is developed (though not every instance is negatively appraised) on a number of pages. On page 10, in the context of Columbus the Renaissance Man and Columbus the visionary, appraisal is clearly positive:

> Meanwhile he dreamed of sailing to the unknown west in search of riches.

On page 11, in the real politik of the court where Isabella was considering his job qualifications as a potential glorifier of Castile, it is positive too:

> He was also ambitious and greedy.

On page 19, appraisal has swung back to strongly negative:

> Even at the hour of his greatest triumph, Columbus remained a very greedy man. He insisted on claiming the 10,000 gold coins as reward for himself.

The financial motivation on page 21 reads much less negatively, perhaps even positively:

> He was also eager to revisit Navidad in the hope that the men he had left behind would have collected a huge amount of gold.

But 'the men he had left behind' are then described as 'too greedy', definitely negative:

> The sailors left behind at Navidad had become too greedy. They had demanded that the natives deliver more gold than they could obtain.

Columbus's greed, then, is ambiguous and ambivalent – but the theme is not totally lost. His carelessness in administration on the other hand is hard to trace at all by page 23.

> The king and queen had decided that, while Columbus was a great explorer, he was a bad governor.

There are only two details of negative appraisal that could be construed as contributing to the 'bad governor'. Both are in the section headed 'Another failure' (22). The first is forthright:

> he had made a bad choice of sight.

The second is markedly euphemistic:

> Columbus did not help the situation when he sent 500 native slaves back to Spain as a present to the king and queen . . . the natives started a violent rebellion which was only quelled with difficulty.

Returning to the evaluation of 'A bad beginning' (4–5) as anger and greed, greed and carelessness, there is also 'ignorance and greed':

> Through ignorance and greed they destroyed the Aztec and Inca civilizations and caused the death of eight out of every ten native Americans.

In the immediately following text, greed is forgotten: the charge is reduced to the lesser count of ignorance – and then dismissed:

> By today's standards, they were appallingly ignorant. If we think that they behaved badly, it is only because we have learned better.

However, in the text as a whole it is ignorance that is dropped: necessarily, as it clashes with the intellectual pretensions of Renaissance Man. After page 5, the role of ignorance is over. Greed, on the other hand, conveniently dropped in 'A bad beginning', does make further appearances later in the text. The first settlers were 'too greedy' (21). On page 26 there is half a paragraph on the conquistadors' greed:

> At this point, the history of the exploration of America is largely replaced by a story of conquest and forced conversion. All too often, the Spanish Church ordered that natives who would not be converted to Christianity should be killed. With the blessing of the Church and the king and driven on by dreams of gold and glory, a new type of European arrived – the 'conquistador', the 'conqueror'.

Yet on the opposite page (in the final sentence of 'The conquest of Peru') the discussion about greed is transmuted implicitly into something different: that is, the quest for 'gold and glory' which was successful.

> This was wealth beyond even the wildest European dreams.

The dual significance of 1492 'for Spain' is another dropped distinction which reflects the writer's evaluation. It is set up on page 11:

> The year 1492 would have been exceptional for Spain, even without Columbus's achievement. At the beginning of the year, Spanish armies finally reconquered the territory of Granada held by the Moors.

Columbus's part, in line with the rest of the text, is positively appraised: it is 'achievement'. So is the capture of Granada:

> Spain was at last united and free of Islamic occupation.

In alignment with this positive role, the forced conversion of Muslims and the expulsion in 1493 of all Jews are not mentioned. Where 'forced conversion' is mentioned, on page 26, it merits negative appraisal:

> All too often, the Spanish Church ordered that natives who would not be converted to Christianity should be killed.

Similarly, while the black slave trade gets a paragraph (30), the black experience of America in slavery gets not a word. The slave trade is not presented as an all-Spanish affair. But neither is the British part in it explicitly mentioned:

> Ships from many nations took part in the trade.

In the final chapter, native Americans are mentioned four times: once in the main text; once in a marginal capsule (the kind with least salience); once in an apparently sympathetic capsule, 'Invisible killers'; and once in a marginal illustration, with caption. The main text says simply (43):

> The claims of the native Americans were ignored, and European civilization flourished.

The marginal note is a listing of 'cross-connections with the story': 'Geronimo, Apache chief'. The 'Invisible killers' capsule is illustrated with 'An Indian suffering from smallpox'.

The capsule text has three paragraphs. The first is a highly elliptical discussion (the only one in the book) of the causes of the success of the European conquest of America. The word 'conquest' does not appear.

> Throughout America, small numbers of Europeans achieved overwhelming success against much larger numbers of natives. Superior European technology played a part in these victories. However, the Europeans had another weapon, so secret that not even they were aware of it.

The second paragraph gives an account of the mortal spread of European diseases. The last three sentences are (42):

> Within quite a short time, imported diseases were to kill the vast majority of native Americans. When Cortes marched into Mexico, the country had a population of around 30 million people. A little over a century later, the native population had fallen to about one and a half million, a decrease of around 95 per cent.

The implicit argument appears to be:

- The diseases were the killers.
- European weapons (swords and guns) were superior (and the main reason for the success of the conquest) but rarely used except for show.

A final mention is made of the fact these new diseases continued to plague and to bring 'nightmare and destruction':

> America later suffered a second wave of new diseases when black slaves brought malaria and yellow fever with them from Africa.

But the final judgement is still the fact that:

> The year 1492 is one of the great turning points in history because the discovery of America was to change the course of European history.

In other words, in the implied judgement of the writer the 'history of the human race' has dwindled to 'European history'.

6.7 Conclusion

It is quite common for the teacher or even the parent to presume, at least in the first instance, that the inability of the young reader to 'understand' the text comes from mainly from the child rather than the writer. But as Halliday and Hasan have remarked:

> There are many instances where it is the textbook that doesn't hang together. (1985: 48)

Clearly, from our examination of this text and what has been cited above, writing history for young learners is a demanding task. Painter (1991) quoted in Derewianka (1995: 247) says of the limitations of implicit learning:

> If this model of implicit learning is adopted within the school, then there is every likelihood that the successful language learner will be unresistantly co-opted into the cultural values and assumptions which lie implicit in the texts which constitute the sources of school knowledge. Without explicit ways of reflecting on educational texts and other public forms of speech and writing, the school will be apprenticing children into particular ways of looking at the world and of dealing with experience, without simultaneously giving them tools for being conscious that this is so, and for making choices about whether and how they will make use of this learning.

Even though children's books are often visually more attractive than those read by adults, this does not guarantee their quality in any other respect. Indeed, more than a small minority of space going on images and captions can in itself severely lessen the chances of complex issues getting enough space for elucidation.

Again citing Painter quoted in Derewianka (1995: 190)

> Many sentences are stored ready made; they are more or less formulaic . . . and any given instance of their occurrence harks back to previous instances of the same working rather than being engendered afresh but choosing within the system . . . Intertextual potential is strongest where the act of meaning exploits the full resources of the system; it tends precisely to be weakened where the act of meaning is locked into a formula, since this inhibits the search for other semiotic input.

As children in primary school spend less time on history and more time on information technology, the standard of those few history texts that are used becomes even more crucial.

As already mentioned in the introduction to this chapter, work in this area by a number of linguists, particularly in Australia (Eggins *et al.* 1993) have foregrounded the myopia, prejudice and misunderstanding that have been institutionalized. This present text seems to be no exception.

The fact that it is a text written for relatively young children makes the need for explanation, discussion and careful appraisal all the more important.

References

Bernstein, B. (1996) *Pedagogy, Symbolic Control and Identity*. London: Taylor and Francis.

Christie, F. (ed.) (1999) *Pedagogy and the Shaping of Consciousness*. London: Cassell.

Davies, N. (1996) *Europe: A History*. Oxford: Oxford University Press.

Derewianka, B. (1995) Language development; the transition from childhood to adolescence: the role of grammatical metaphor. Unpublished PhD thesis, Department of English and Linguistics, Macquarie University.

Eggins, S., Wignall, P. and Martin, J.R. (1993) The Discourse of History. In M. Ghadessy (ed.), *Register Analysis. Theory and Practice*. London: Pinter.

Halliday, M.A.K. (1993) Towards a language-based theory of learning. *Linguistics and Education*, 5: 93–116.

Halliday, M.A.K. (1994) *An Introduction to Functional Grammar* 2nd edn. London: Arnold.

Halliday, M.A.K. (1996) Language and Knowledge: the 'unpacking of text'. Paper given at the Language and Knowledge conference, National University of Singapore.

Halliday, M.A.K. and Hasan, R. (1985) *Language, Content and Text: Aspects of Language in a Social-semiotic Perspective*. Victoria: Deakin University Press.

James, C.L.R. (1938) *The Black Jacobins: Toussaint l'Ouverture and the San Domingo Revolution*. 2nd edn. New York: Vintage, 1963.

Kress, G. and van Leeuwen, T. (1996) *Reading Images: The Grammar of Visual Design*. London: Routledge.

Lemke, J. (1995) *Textual Politics*. London: Taylor and Francis.

Martin, J.R. (1997) Beyond exchange: Appraisal systems in English. In S. Hunston and J. Thompson (eds), *Evaluation in Text*. Oxford: Oxford University Press.

Martin, J.R. (1999) Monitoring semogenesis: 'genre-based' literacy pedagogy. In F. Christie (ed.), *Pedagogy and the Shaping of Consciousness*. London: Cassell.

Twist, C. (1993) *Christopher Columbus: The Discovery of the New World*. London: Evans Bros.

Veel, R. and Coffin, C. (1996) Learning to think like an historian: the language of secondary school history. In R. Hasan and G. Williams (eds), *Literacy in Society*. London: Longman.

White, P. (2000) Media objectivity and the rhetoric of news story structure. In E. Ventola (ed.), *Discourse and Community: Doing Functional Linguistics*. Language in Performance 21. Tubingen: Gunter Narr Verlag.

PART TWO

DISCOURSE IN SECONDARY AND TERTIARY LEVELS OF EDUCATION

7

Revisiting Some Old Themes: The Role of Grammar in the Teaching of English[1]

Frances Christie

7.1 Introduction

One of the most enduring of the problems that beset the teacher of English in schools is what to do in the name of teaching Knowledge about Language, where the term refers to any area of overt teaching about language, including grammar. Recognizing the apparently contentious nature of the issues of teaching Knowledge about Language, Carter (1990) even coined a term for it: 'KAL'. Over the period 1998–2000, together with my colleague Anne Soosai, I was involved in a study in Melbourne to address the problem working with junior secondary teachers of English. The study was conceived out of an interest in addressing the relevance of overt teaching of functional grammar as a means of enhancing the general literacy proficiency of junior secondary students. The focus was on teaching functional grammar and literacy for the junior secondary English classroom only. The intention was, first, in consultation with the English teachers involved, to identify the kinds of text types they expected their students to write and to read, as aspects of the junior English programme. Then, second, the intention was to engage directly with the grammatical features of these text types with the teachers, so that they might teach these overtly as a dimension of their total teaching programmes.

When I planned the study back in early 1997, I was responding to a number of issues that had emerged in my experience as a teacher educator. They were as follows:

- *How best might one challenge the claims for an 'integrated' or 'holistic' approach to the junior secondary English curriculum?*
  I knew from earlier work I had done in Melbourne, as well as information gathered in other Australian states, that the accepted wisdom was that the English curriculum should not involve separate lessons devoted to different aspects of the total English programme. Instead, the programme should focus for a week or more (sometimes several weeks, or even a school term) on a particular text, such as a novel or a play, which was to give 'integration' to the total programme. Opportunities should be made available in the course of the total teaching–learning programme, to take up such aspects of KAL as might be relevant to pursuing that text. I was aware that the claims for a 'holistic' approach were attractive to many teachers, in that it sought primarily to establish students' interest in a text and/or activity, and then introduced such teaching about language as seemed necessary. Yet I could also see that such an approach had considerable problems, in that in practice it never seemed very centrally to address questions of language – or KAL – at all. In that the teaching of KAL was intended to arise as an aspect of engagement with something else – normally a text and its themes – it seemed to me that teaching about language was therefore largely conceived as an addendum to another enterprise, which was by implication held to be far more important.
- *How should one teach functional grammar to students in the junior secondary school?*
  While those of us working in Australia with so-called 'genre-based approaches' had done a great deal of work in identifying genres of relevance for schools, and in identifying the grammatical choices in which they were realized, I was not persuaded that we had fully addressed questions of teaching about grammar. Overall, we had had considerably greater success in identifying genres than we had had in developing either in teachers or in students a knowledge of grammar, or an interest in its teaching and learning. Moreover, the successes we had had were mainly among primary teachers, and, at the secondary level, among teachers of subjects other than English.
- *How should one design the curriculum in order to develop a principled approach to the teaching of KAL, including grammar, over a year, and/or over several years of schooling?*
  Doughty once wrote of the need for the English programme to be 'ordered without being structured' (1974: 10–11). In his terms a 'structured' approach was 'the predetermined programme,

designed and put together by someone who is not himself the teacher', while the 'ordered' approach provided 'the options and then (left) the teacher in a position to make a clear and considered choice from what is available, according to the needs of the learning situation as he reads them.' Doughty was quite clear that, without order, English teaching could become 'totally directionless'.

Before I outline the nature of the study we developed, I want to turn to the wider question of why it is that teaching of KAL is problematic.

7.2 Historical antecedents of the problem

I have argued elsewhere (Christie 1993) what I believe were the major developments in the growth of practices for teaching KAL in schools over the late eighteenth, nineteenth and early twentieth centuries. Partly because of the declining significance of rhetoric, and partly because of the requirements to teach large numbers of students in the expanding systems of mass education, grammar became a matter of learning to recognize parts of speech, to parse and analyse sentences, and to correct 'faulty sentences'. It was increasingly dissociated from any interest in meaning or in text.

The pattern of grammar and of composition teaching did not change much well into the twentieth century, if we are to base that judgement on the English syllabus statements and the various textbooks used for teaching in both the UK and Australia. Yet in the period after the Second World War there were changes and traditional school grammar was placed under significant challenge. Especially from the 1960s onwards, there were new trends and preoccupations in the teaching of English generally, and of grammar in particular. What transpired, however, was that while in some senses it represented an advance, it also led to a number of educational problems, the nature of which we are still addressing today.

In the 1960s and 1970s, language and its role in living and learning came to the fore in a great deal of educational theorizing and discussion, at least in English-speaking communities. It is ironic, then, that it was also the period in which teaching *about* language generally seems to have fallen from favour.

Among several new educational initiatives in the UK of the 1960s, Halliday directed the Nuffield/Schools Council Programme in Linguistics and Language Teaching (1964–7, 1967–71). That project was committed to using linguistics to develop new and imaginative approaches to the teaching of English. Halliday and colleagues had earlier discussed the limitations of available models of the English language for teaching and learning. They had argued that 'the principal contribution of the linguistic sciences' to language teaching was that they enabled 'a good description to be made of the language being taught' (Halliday *et al.* 1964: 170). The principal programmes that emerged from the project were *Breakthrough to Literacy* (for the very early years of schooling) and *Language in Use* (for the upper years of secondary schooling). Another programme for the middle years, *Language and Communication*, appeared in 1980.

While Halliday and his colleagues at the University of London were working on their project, there was already an alternative set of proposals to do with the teaching of language developing in the UK, which would be influential in Australia and also parts of North America. It found its first expression, it seems, at the Anglo-American Seminar on English Teaching held at Dartmouth, New Hampshire in 1965. Dixon's book *Growth Through English* (1967) was the principal publication to emerge from that seminar, and while some have argued that its views were not necessarily representative of those who attended the seminar, the fact remains that it became a very influential publication. Its general views about the role of language in learning and about the responsibility of the teacher in fostering students' growth in living and learning in their language was one that was variously taken up and developed by such writers as Barnes *et al.* (1987), Barnes (1978) and Martin *et al.* (1976). As a general principle, the latter group was suspicious of the value of any teaching about language. They were also suspicious of the claims of linguistics for relevance to educational practices. Barnes (1977: 91–2), in the course of a visit to Australia, suggested that linguistics had 'its own issues', not in themselves directly relevant to education.

Debates about the role of linguistics and also about how educationally useful was the teaching of KAL, often became very lively and occasionally even rather acrimonious. Doughty, referring to the British experience, wrote of the 'paradox' that while there seemed to be a consensus in the English teaching community about placing 'increasing emphasis upon language', there was nonetheless 'a curious diffidence about the place of language' (1974: 24). He wrote:

> ... discussion focuses on language as something other than language: as the way in which pupils write about experience; or as the means by which they can develop social relationships; or as the means by which they can acquire a powerful critique of

> contemporary society. What has been conspicuously lacking ... is any broad agreement that there needs to be a specifically linguistic perspective on the way in which language is used for both living and learning, by both teachers and pupils; and that this perspective is relevant to the development of a necessary explicitness in the discussion of practice ... (ibid.: 24)

The similarity between the trends that Doughty reported in the UK and those that emerged in Australia in the 1970s was striking. In the national Language Development Project (LDP) in which I was involved, we adopted Halliday's model of language development as involving: 'learning language, learning through language, and learning about language'. The work we did in the LDP over some four or five years was considerably more successful in addressing issues of 'learning language' and 'learning through language' than it was in addressing 'learning about language'. For the most part, English teachers and teacher educators resisted any involvement with discussion of teaching about language. There were times in both the UK and Australia when talk of teaching about language was said in some way to compromise the capacity of students to use 'their own language' in personally rewarding ways (Medway, cited in Torbe 1987).

The members of the Schools Council Project led by Halliday sought to teach school students about language, though that did not involve any overt teaching of grammar. In fact, Halliday (personal communication) has advised that when the project was conceived, he was opposed to the teaching of grammar in schools, though about that he later changed his mind. In the 1960s and 1970s there were loosely two groups of people researching and writing about language and language-learning in schools. I shall call them the 'linguists' and the 'non-linguists'. What they had in common was a belief in the importance of children's language in life and in learning, and the importance of the teacher in promoting students' growth in language. Both groups also recognized and respected dialects and dialect differences, and both argued the importance of a respect for regional dialects and their values as measures of membership of different social groups. Both groups were alike disenchanted with what I have elsewhere referred to as 'the received tradition of English teaching' (Christie 1993), with its joyless pursuit of parts of speech and correction of 'faulty sentences'. Both groups even agreed about the need for teachers to have a thorough grasp of the nature of language, the better to foster their students' learning.

However, the two groups differed sharply about what should

constitute knowledge of language for teachers and about how such knowledge should be used. The linguists asserted a strong commitment to a linguistic body of knowledge for teachers and active use of this to devise teaching programmes. The non-linguists eschewed linguistic knowledge, on the grounds of its alleged preoccupation with 'structure' and indifference to meaning. What they termed a useful body of language knowledge for teachers was in many ways the more indeterminate of the two groups, resting primarily upon a preoccupation with studying how children talked in classrooms or, alternatively, wrote in personally valued writing.

At bottom, it seems to me that the two groups functioned with very different ideologies of the person, as well as models of language. The non-linguists were committed to a view of the child, embarked on a journey of personal discovery, in which language was the instrument with which experience was expressed and refined in some individualistic way. The role of the teacher was to be the adult who was 'trusted' in Dixon's words (1967: 13), facilitating the child's growth in language. For the linguists, the ideal child was a social being, growing in participation in complex sets of social processes, where language was an essential resource for articulating experience and knowledge, and where language itself was an interesting phenomenon to speculate about and to learn. The role of the teacher was to challenge and provoke students as they learned.

No one, as far as I can tell, among the linguists actually used the word 'intervention'. Certainly, the non-linguists did not use it, as they would have actively rejected it. But I can find no use of the word among the linguists of the 1960s and 1970s either. It was a comment on the times that by 1975, when the British released the report of their enquiry into the teaching of English – known as the Bullock Report – the report writers stated that they rejected 'the notion that the forms of language can be left to look after themselves' and they went on to say that the teacher 'should intervene in teaching students language' (Bullock Report 1974: 8).

Intervention was to become one of the themes in much language education discussion in the 1980s, although it has remained contentious among teachers of English. I shall turn briefly now to that decade.

7.3 Developments in the 1980s and up to the present

Some of the developments of the last 20 years have been already documented (e.g., Christie 1991; Martin 1992). From the point of view of those interested in Systemic Functional (SF) theory in Australia, Martin and Rothery embarked on their study of children's writing development in the late 1970s. Partly because of their work and partly because of that which I was able to do when I moved to Deakin University,[2] SF theory, which had of course engaged with educational issues from the late 1960s, entered a new phase of such engagement. 'Genre-based approaches' to the teaching of literacy were launched, and not without controversy. Kress (1982), who had written the first book on genres in children's writing, was to continue to work on genres, though he was to part company with aspects of what he termed the 'Martin/Rothery' model (Kress 1993), as was Threadgold (1993). Debates about genres and their values appeared quite regularly in the pages of *English in Australia* as well as in other publications (e.g., Reid 1987). The wider community of English teaching specialists in the UK and in North America (Freedman 1993; Freedman and Medway 1994) were to be drawn into debates about genres and what had become known as the 'Australian school'. Hasan (1995) mounted a critique on the models of genre and register associated with Martin and his colleagues, including myself.

The debates and the controversy were, on the whole, good for us: they meant at least that people were noticing us. Moreover, the effort to respond to often thoughtful critiques was always worth it.

The wider socio-political contexts in which we all work changed with the entry to the 1990s. In both the UK and Australia there was a move towards national English curriculum development, marked in the UK by the Kingman Report (1988) and the subsequent developments of the working party chaired by Cox (1989), as well as other developments since (see Christie 1999 for a discussion). In Australia, there was a call for a new national English curriculum. In 1990–1, I led a research team which reported to the government on the preservice preparation of teachers to teach English literacy (Christie *et al.* 1991). The report generated considerable debate in Australia for a time, and it won acceptance in many quarters. Nonetheless, its recommendations were not accepted and, at least among those most active in the profession of English teacher educators, its use of a functional grammar was viewed with suspicion.

Calls for a revival of interest in the teaching of grammar appeared in Australia, as in the UK, with associated if sometimes confused calls for 'intervention' in promoting students' language growth. Curriculum statements which espouse an interest in the teaching of grammar have reappeared in both the UK and Australia. What is meant by the term 'grammar' is generally not functional, though it also needs to be said that the term is used so vaguely (at least in the Australian context) that teachers can be forgiven for not finding it helpful or informative in any sense. Moreover, within the English-teaching community there is considerable confusion about what it means to teach KAL. Equally, and for related reasons, there is general confusion about what it is to 'intervene' in the development of students' language learning.

While there are no doubt many teachers doing good work in a number of places, I believe that the teaching of English is often confused and indeed 'directionless', to use the term Doughty employed over 20 years ago. Two related trends have developed in English teaching, having their origins in the changes that occurred in the 1960s and 1970s. First, there has been a preoccupation primarily with promoting development *through* language, and an associated disinclination to engage in overt teaching and learning *about* language. Second, and because of such a preoccupation, the English curriculum is not 'ordered', in the sense that Doughty intended.

7.4 Developing a study on teaching KAL in the junior secondary English curriculum

To return to the matters I touched upon at the start of this chapter, I had several reasons for focusing on the English programme of the first two years of junior secondary education, school years 7 and 8, when students are aged about 12–14 years. They are as follows:

- *These years mark the transition into secondary school.* That transition is for many students a hard one, involving a move to a new, often larger school, a considerably altered timetable, a range of school subjects and different teachers for each, all of them setting somewhat different expectations for their students. All these aspects of transition put pressures on students' oral language and literacy, though the matter is often not understood in these terms. It is in general discussed in terms of changes in cognition. Moreover, the move to secondary school is a time developmentally when students pass from childhood to adolescence, with all the attendant changes, psychological and emotional, this can bring.
- *Literacy performance becomes an issue of increasing importance, as more and more of the curriculum is taught and learned in literate modes, while literacy is of growing significance for assessment purposes.*
- *The changing kinds of literacy that students must deal with will be marked by the need to adjust to, and ideally manipulate, grammatical*

metaphor (Halliday 1994: 342–67), which is central to handling the abstractions of much secondary school discourse.[3] I do not think this is well understood by teachers because it has not on the whole been adequately explained to them in most teacher education programmes. Most good secondary teachers recognize that the discourses of their subjects have specialist language demands, but they are generally hard pressed to be very articulate about these.

- *Finally, I would argue that students need a metalanguage in order to deal in particular with their literacy needs.* While such a metalanguage will probably have value in other areas of the curriculum, the particular school subject best suited for its teaching and learning is English.

The study as we developed it had three phases. These were to some extent planned, though it is also fair to say that their nature and their implementation emerged in the light of several unforeseen developments. School-based research – rewarding though it is – is actually very hard, because much of what happens can be unpredictable. In what follows, I shall outline the three phases, seeking to clarify both why we took the courses of action we did, and what the results proved to be.

7.5 Phase 1 of the study: implementation

In the early months of 1998, Anne Soosai and I started work with junior English teachers in two secondary schools: one state, the other Catholic. Both were in the western suburbs of Melbourne, drawing on communities with reasonably high unemployment levels, and large numbers of students of non-English-speaking backgrounds (NESB), though the students in the classrooms in which our teachers were working were not recent arrivals. Many had in fact been born in Australia of migrant parents.

Our early workshops with teachers introduced notions of traditional and functional grammar; invited the teachers to identify the sorts of texts their students read and wrote; sought to clarify grammatical features in particular of the target texts the students were to write; and sought to identify linguistic features of texts being read in class, around which teaching of KAL might take place.

With hindsight it was clear that I made two assumptions which experience proved to be unjustified. First, I assumed that the teachers knew considerably more about traditional grammar, at least in terms of word classes or parts of speech, than they did. Even though I was aware that most teachers would have probably had less formal teaching about grammar themselves at school than did school students of my generation, I had not reckoned on how little they did know. In that, I was naïve. Second, I had assumed that I could employ a pedagogy with the teachers participating in the workshops that was at least related to, if not the same as, that which they were ostensibly employing with their students. Namely, I wanted to work from the target texts their students were to read and write, and develop teaching and discussion of grammar around these. These assumptions got us into difficulties. The English teachers involved were reluctant to admit how little they did know, and some became disturbed by any talk of a metalanguage. Given their considerable ignorance, the efforts to develop useful discussion in workshops around the target texts they used in classrooms were hampered. I remember one session when a young woman interrupted me to say, rather sharply, that I had used the word 'clause' and she did not understand this. She went on to say, 'I was born in 1965, and no one born since then knows what a clause is, let alone a lot of the other things you have referred to.'

In both schools, the pattern applied was that a selected text formed the basis of a 10-week term's work. The text was normally a novel, but it might be a play, and in one school term it was a film. These were read (or viewed) in class and discussed. Writing activities were based on a reading and discussion of such texts. Thus, book reviews or character descriptions were sought for the class novels, though recounts intended to reconstruct events from the novels were also sought in at least one school. In the case of the film, whose theme was cruelty to animals, discussion texts about the treatment of animals in zoos or circuses were sought, as well as film reviews. The state school also involved the students in writing imaginative narratives of their own.

The teachers, for whom the notion of a text as having a structure of its own was new, were interested in learning about schematic structures, as these had been extensively developed in genre theory (see for example, Rothery and Stevenson 1994; Christie and Martin 1997; Feez and Joyce 1998; Feez 1998). As the year progressed, the feedback from the teachers was encouraging. Comments such as 'I'd never thought about the kind of introduction a text should have before' were not uncommon from the teachers. As Anne Soosai was regularly recording teaching sequences with at least some of the teachers, we were able to collect data about the extent to which, and the ways in which, they were implementing the ideas about grammar and its relevance to text types.

It became clear reasonably soon into the year that the teachers were extremely reticent about trying to teach grammar. Their tendency was to teach the schematic structure, sometimes modelling it, but often introducing it just once. The latter, as anyone who has pursued the pedagogy involved in using genres knows, is very ineffective. It completely trivializes the nature of the genre and the functional significance of the elements of structure. Moreover, for students learning the issues for the first time, a 'one-off' teaching episode does not allow adequate time to learn it.[4] The teachers were, for the most part, reluctant to try more. It seemed to Anne Soosai and me that there were two problems that emerged in the teachers we were working with. First, as noted, they knew even less about traditional grammar than we had reckoned. Second, despite our efforts to work with functional grammar with the teachers in workshops, demonstrating how such features as theme choices, process types or conjunction choices worked with respect to different text types, the teachers were, it seemed, unable to use such knowledge, either to anticipate the kinds of decisions their students might want to make in writing, or to respond to the writing after the event. As for the novels their students were reading, the teachers generally saw no particular opportunities to work with these from the point of view of using KAL to explore how they were written.

It might be argued that our experience demonstrated the relative lack of value in a focus on language as we had planned it. Certainly, I was aware that among the critics of genre-based approaches and/or any approaches that adopted principles of explicit teaching, it had been argued there was little evidence to support the claims for teaching KAL – grammar in particular – in the writing programme. Freedman (1993), for example, has so argued, as have Sawyer and Watson (1987) in Australia. Yet I had two reasons for not accepting this. First, a significant number of the teachers themselves evinced interest in finding out more about KAL, as they were aware of their lack of information in the area and keen to learn more. Second, when one examines the arguments of Freedman and others, it is clear that they are not writing about functional descriptions of English grammar when they critique explicit teaching about language. We therefore planned to move into a second and different phase of the study.

7.6 Phase 2 of the study

In the opening months of 1999, with approval from the school principal at one of the schools involved, we instituted a series of much more intensive training sessions than we had attempted in 1998. The group of teachers at the school was enlarged, drawing in other staff members as well as some teachers from three other schools. We arranged to run ten sessions of 2½ hours at roughly fortnightly intervals over the first half of the year: a total of 25 hours. In planning the sessions the second time around, I sought to deal with matters both more intensively and more leisurely than we had in the first year. I wanted the opportunity to spend more time on matters the teachers expressed concern about.

The sessions for 1999 were planned in a sequence such that the first sessions were to address grammar and the latter sessions were to pursue teaching implications. Thus we planned to begin with a focus on the differences between traditional and functional grammars, exploring such terms as 'parts of speech', 'syntax' and the term 'grammar' itself, and the functional notion of rank.[5] We then planned to introduce notions of text and context, the metafunctions and grammatical differences between speech and writing. Beyond that, the plan was to go on to transitivity, nominal groups and their function in realizing participant roles, adverbial groups and prepositional phrases in realizing circumstances, mood and the different speech functions, as well as modality, theme and conjunction.

In the period in which we were developing plans for the training sessions, I was approached by a publishing representative who asked me to develop some new textbooks for the junior secondary school, teaching grammar and other aspects of KAL. The invitation was unexpected, but as it happened, it was also timely. That was because it had become clear by the early months of 1999 that there was a dearth of appropriate textbooks available for the junior secondary English programme. In addition, the advice available to us from the teachers with whom we had been working, as well as others encountered in the profession, was that teachers sorely needed books they could use, which would also serve the purpose of teaching them what to teach. Hence, as Anne Soosai and I planned and started to run our teacher training sessions, we also commenced work to develop what would become two new textbooks for the junior secondary classroom. The development of these books while we were intensively engaged in the training sessions with the teachers was very fortunate, both because the teachers' responses in the sessions helped us to shape our thinking about the contents of the books and because we could ask the teachers to pilot some of the materials we were developing. I shall say more about the textbooks that emerged in a later section of this chapter. First I shall go on to say more of the training sessions.

In practice, the plan for the training sessions was considerably modified as we went along for several reasons. It took much longer to cover several topics than we had reckoned, and indeed I had been far too ambitious in the range of matters I planned to address. Furthermore, we had not always anticipated those areas of English grammatical knowledge the teachers would themselves find problematic. For example, we were quite unprepared for the considerable difficulties the teachers had in recognizing all the elements of a verbal group. Relatedly, they were very unsure about the English tense system and, as they gained in confidence in talking with Anne Soosai and me, admitted to a great concern about how to teach tense. Most teachers of English as a second language are aware that the tense system is difficult, and since numbers of the students in the mainstream classrooms of our teachers were NESB, this was one source of the problem. But it also happens that English tense is quite critical to the writing of book reviews and character studies, which seem to feature quite considerably in the junior secondary English programme. Tense is problematic for native speakers of English, when it comes to teaching the conventions of English literary critique and discussion.

Some teachers found hard even the traditional rules of syntax, such as that which says a verb should agree with its subject in person and number. I had not expected to spend time on both the person and the number systems, as well as other aspects of sentence grammar (such as the rule that says one should not use a double negative), but in fact we did need to do so. We were also asked to devote time to the English punctuation system and ways to teach paragraph structure.

We adopted the practice of giving the teachers 'homework' to complete between sessions, and while they did not always do this, most did. Feedback on the homework took a long time to provide each week, but it often proved very productive to spend time on it. It was in working through the homework that such problems as how to recognize the verbal group emerged, as well as the confusions over tense. Expressions such as *He might have been going to see me* caused considerable confusion in terms of identifying all the elements of the verbal group. Even recognition of the nominal group proved problematic. It was not that the teachers were unable to identify a noun or an adjective: most could recognize these. But the structure of a relatively elaborate nominal group often confused the teachers. They could recognize the noun and any adjectives realizing the modifier position, as for example, in the expression: *the happy children*. However, identifying the post-modifier, expressed in either an embedded clause (*the children* [*who lost their bags*] *were punished*) or an embedded phrase (*the children* [*in the cricket club*] *were all good players*) often eluded them.

Theme proved difficult to teach also, though I had anticipated that from my regular teaching of the functional grammar to post-graduate students in the Faculty of Education at the University of Melbourne. Without a sense of the constituent structure in which a theme choice is realized, I found the teachers were often guessing in their efforts to recognize themes. The values of understanding active and passive voice, and the ways in which the use of the passive voice changes what we make a topical theme in the English clause (e.g., *The house was destroyed in the storm*, as opposed to *The storm destroyed the house*), did prove of interest to some. However, from the standpoint of those who were growing alarmed about the amount of metalanguage they were being asked to learn, the need to add to their repertoire the terms 'active voice' and 'passive voice' was troubling. Anxiety about use of a technical language for dealing with language is an issue to which I shall return later.

Modality proved problematic to the teachers also, not so much because they had difficulty understanding the idea of this, but because they did not always recognize items having modal significance. It has to be said that English has a very complex range of ways to express modality. Discussion of modality led to some reasonably spirited talk of whether a metalanguage was necessary at all, at least some teachers expressing the view that modal expressions emerged 'naturally', and it was doubtful whether any terms were needed to deal with it at all. The discussion over this was of interest, and one of the group – a young woman who taught both English and science – observed that she could not teach science at all without a technical language for dealing with its concepts. Why then, she asked, should English teachers resist the claims of a metalanguage for teaching about language? This was an issue that remained on the table and was returned to from time to time throughout the workshops. As for the mood system, the whole notion of speech functions and of the different roles taken up depending on one's mood choice was quite foreign to the teachers, though of interest when pointed out to them. English mood and its realizations is, of course, of critical importance for NESB learners.

Most of the teachers started to use at least some of what they were learning in their classrooms: some making greater and better use of the notions of schematic structure than they had in the previous years, others making more overt use of grammar, though in most cases those who sought to use the grammar confined their efforts to use of the traditional terms associated with sentence grammar and word classes. Some of the later training sessions in the series were specifically devoted to ways of examining sample text-types from the point of view of the grammatical choices in which they were realized. Here, for instance, moving across the metafunctions, we looked at the patterns of process choices, including their participant roles and circumstances, the tense choices and the significance of shifts in tense in different text types, uses of modality and patterns of theme choices. Where we could use passages from novels being read in the class, or written texts produced by students in the classes, we did so – and this certainly added a great deal of interest to the sessions. One class novel being used by some classes was *Chasing Redbird* by Sharon Creech. This is a novel of adolescence, documenting the coming to maturity of a girl whose aunt and cousin have both died. The novel makes very complex use of chronology, constantly shifting back and forth between the present experiences of the narrator and past events. An understanding of the novel and its themes depends quite crucially upon an awareness of the ways the English tense system works, and teachers complained of difficulties in helping their students to comprehend it. Anne Soosai developed and taught a very successful session, in which she modelled and explained English tense, making constant use of the novel to demonstrate. This was a classic example of how overt awareness of an aspect of the English grammatical system can actively assist reading comprehension.

By the end of the second phase, we had accumulated data in several ways. We had kept careful records of all the training sessions we ran, including the substantial handouts of materials we had prepared for the sessions. Anne Soosai had collected many hours of classroom activity, video recorded for intensive analysis of the classroom talk, and we collected large numbers of written texts and notes from the classrooms concerned, where these written materials had emerged from the classroom talk. The written texts we analysed closely, using the systemic functional grammar. At the end of the training sessions, we discussed with the teachers what they believed they had learned and found most valuable, and in addition we distributed a questionnaire to them all, seeking advice about the values of what they had covered and learned. Using all the data we had collected, we wrote a report for the benefit of the schools involved, documenting what we had covered in the study and making extensive use of texts written and/or read by the students in the classrooms of the teachers involved, as well as extracts at least of the classroom talk. I shall comment here first on the teachers' own reactions to the training sessions and briefly outline some of the matters we documented in detail in our report.

Teachers generally considered the training sessions had been rewarding, if 'hard', 'challenging' or even 'frustrating'. The traditional parts of speech were judged useful and important, and while two or three teachers (the older ones) said they had been taught these at school, they said they appreciated the 'revision', as they had not used them for a long time. Matters of subject–verb agreement, punctuation, and double negatives were all judged important and teachers said they had benefited from learning about ways to teach these. English tense was held to be very problematic, and many teachers admitted to still feeling confused about verbal group structures after the training sessions were over. Notions of the clause and of the conjunctive relations between clauses were also judged hard to understand and hard to teach. Terms such as 'nominal group' (or 'noun phrase'), transitivity, mood, modality and theme were all judged hard, though a few teachers started to use these terms in their classrooms with some success. All participating teachers expressed appreciation of what the functional orientation on texts offered them and of practical ways to link the teaching of grammar to the teaching of text-types or genres.

Turning more directly to the classroom experiences, teachers reported a number of matters, supported by our own video observations and analysis. Systematic attention to the schematic structures of different text-types, assisted by the adoption of slower, more measured teaching about their elements than had been true in the first phase of the study, led to better writing than had been observed in the classrooms in the past. The texts generally: had a clearer overall sense of direction and structure than in the past; showed greatly enhanced paragraph organization and structure; had an appropriate sense of completion; and showed a good developing sense of thematic organization relevant to different types of genres (this was true even where the term 'theme' had not been overtly used, and teachers had instead used terms like 'sentence opening' or 'paragraph opening'). Tense choices in such relatively difficult genres as book reviews or character discussions (where tense choices typically shift between present and past) showed improvement, some teachers taking the trouble to teach sequences of lessons about tense preparatory to the writing of such genres.

Matters of the metalanguage and of how much technical terminology is appropriate, as I noted above, were often alluded to in the workshops, and they were also referred to in the written evaluations. Even at the end of the training sessions, most teachers were more comfortable with using a metalanguage in one of only two senses: (i) in the sense of teaching about the elements of the structure of a target genre (e.g., terms such as 'Preview of Issue', 'Arguments For', 'Arguments Against' and 'Recommendation' in a discussion genre), and (ii) in the sense of teaching the traditional parts of speech. The more confident were willing to use functional terms such as 'process', or 'theme', or even 'modality'. However, on the evidence of the video records of teaching sequences, even where teachers might have indicated a willingness to use these terms, they did not use them much, if at all. As it happens – and Anne Soosai and I were to demonstrate this in the two textbooks we were developing – you can go quite a long way using the traditional terms while developing essentially functional orientations in young learners. In any case, you must use them, as they are essential to grasping the constituent structures within which the functional elements are realized.

The latter observation noted, it still remained an issue as to why teachers were for the most part reluctant to make use of the terms of the functional grammar, and in many cases admitted to a continuing concern about using the traditional terms as well. In the case of the functional terms, the answer to the question lies partly in the fact that we did not cover all matters in the detail originally planned. As I noted before, I had been rather ambitious in what we planned to do. Transitivity, for example, was not handled other than very briefly, while our treatments of mood and modality, while more substantial than that for transitivity, were very selective in their focus.

Over and beyond these considerations, however, I believe there were two other reasons why teachers were reluctant to deal with much technicality in language. The first reason I have already partly suggested; it is not possible to go any great distance in using a functional grammar unless the notion of the constituent structures which realize the functional categories are well understood. The teachers were, for the most part, actively coming to terms with the traditional terms for the greater part of the training sessions. The other, related reason, very disturbing in its implications for pedagogy, is that we have a current generation of English teachers who have been so poorly educated themselves that they are frightened of technical language for teaching language. Hence they resist much use of a technical language on the grounds that it is 'too hard for children', or perhaps that language develops 'naturally', without the need for overt teaching, when they really mean they are fearful themselves.

To take the first of these reasons, I have frequent supporting evidence in my Master's students at the University of Melbourne. The L1 students whose own background in traditional terminology these days is decidedly weak, often have greater difficulty in coming to terms with such notions as participant roles, or circumstances, because they do not always recognize the nominal group structures in which the former are realized, or the prepositional phrases and/or adverbial groups in which the latter are realized. The overseas students from China, Vietnam, Malaysia and Indonesia who join my classes in increasing numbers, come with very strong training in traditional terminology, and they are typically attracted to the possibilities opened up by a functional orientation. Ironically, from my own point of view, the community of overseas students is often easier to teach the functional grammar than the community of native speakers.

As for the second of my reasons for believing we now have a generation of English teachers who fear the use of technicality for teaching about language, I have constant and growing evidence for this, not only from the study reported here, but also from the frequent and growing numbers of requests I get from school principals and literacy co-ordinators for assistance in rethinking what should be done in the name of teaching KAL. Very often, such requests have all the character of cries for help, as schools face problems of what to do in the name of teaching KAL, and, associatedly, what to do in lifting the general levels of literacy in the secondary schools. Among those who call for help, the numbers of English teachers are growing, though regrettably, I believe many are reluctant to speak out.

7.7 Phase 3 of the study

The third and final phase of the study commenced in the latter part of 1999 and lasted until the end of 2000. In this phase, three broad developments were planned, all of them intended to allow opportunity to test the results of the work done with teachers. First, teachers were free to develop their teaching programmes using any of the ideas taught them in the series of training sessions, and their progress would again be documented using video records and subsequent analysis; it was intended that the teaching programmes for the new intake of Year 7 at the start of 2000 would be, in particular, subject of analysis, though it was known that the teachers would also be using many of the ideas we had introduced in Years 8 and 9. Second, the first of the two textbooks, having been completed by the end of 1999, was made available for training in the first half of 2000. The volume *Language and Meaning 1* (Christie and Soosai 2000) was written for Year 7, and its contents were intended to enrich and complement the teaching programmes, which, as noted, were to be based on our training sessions. The third development was that Anne Soosai and I finished the second volume, this time for Year 8, under the title *Language and Meaning 2* (2001). Like the first book, the contents of this emerged directly from all those areas of work in the junior secondary English classroom which our considerable experience had shown us were problematic. Both books were thus direct outcomes of the study. It will now be appropriate to say something about these two books, their contents, and in particular the principles upon which they were written.

Language and Meaning 1 was launched in mid-2000. The principles which guided its development were:

- The book should offer a lively introduction to the study of KAL for the audience of Year 7 students coming to terms with their first year of secondary schooling. Among other matters, it should seek to bring to consciousness a great deal about verbal and non-verbal means of communication, functions of language, language-learning and language systems.
- It should seek to establish an interest in KAL, eliciting curiosity about language, thereby creating an incentive to learn about English language, its grammar, writing systems, spelling and punctuation systems, dictionaries, thesauruses and their uses.
- It should interweave chapters, some of them devoted to KAL, of a non-grammatical kind, while others should focus on the teaching aspects of grammar. It thus should be not only a grammar book, but also one which addressed a selection of areas of KAL, of which grammatical knowledge was one.
- It should avoid teaching grammar in chapters devoted to teaching other aspects of KAL. The exception to this general principle occurs once some grammatical knowledge has been introduced in a given chapter; it may well then be revised in a later chapter, where the focus is otherwise, but it should not be introduced as new information. The reasons for this decision are not necessarily self-evident, and they merit some explanation. Despite our own early reservations about so-called 'integrated' approaches to the teaching of English, our initial advice from the publisher was that we should

attempt to adopt such an approach. We tried, for example, to introduce themes to do with different forms of communication such as gesture or dress, and to use study of these themes as a means to introduce teaching of grammar. As we also planned some work on dictionaries and the growth of writing systems, we also considered introducing teaching of aspects of grammar into these chapters. In fact, it would not have mattered what we had selected, for the effort to combine grammatical knowledge with knowledge of other things did not work. The attempt was probably worth it, if only because we learned the folly of trying to do two different things in the one context: one risks not doing justice to either.

- The knowledge of grammar taught should be confined to the major grammatical systems of mood, tense, number and person on the one hand, and the ranks of words, word groups and phrases on the other hand. The factors responsible for these selections are worthy of comment, and they are explained below as separate points.
  1. For reasons I have reiterated already, students – like teachers – need a knowledge of the basic 'parts of speech', for these provide the basic elements in which constituent structures are realized. The object was to teach for a recognition of nouns, adjectives, adverbs, verbs, prepositions and so on, but to teach them in such a way that their roles in the larger unities of groups and phrases were also taught and recognized. Hence, for example, it was important to be able to recognize a noun (*the boy*), but it was also important to be able to recognize ways such a noun could be expanded by using either a modifier realized in adjectives and adverbs (*the very untidy boys*) or a post-modifier realized in a prepositional *phrase* (*the very untidy boys in the football team*). We dealt with all parts of speech (except conjunctions) and word groups and phrases, but we did not venture into teaching about clauses or conjunctive relations. The latter were left to be dealt with in the second book, where we intended to open up notions of sentence organization and paragraph structure as well.[6]
  2. To turn to the grammatical systems of mood, tense, number and person, there were at least two reasons for teaching these. First, they are quite major systems in terms of using English language successfully, and they can be sources of error in controlling written English, among both L1 and L2 speakers. Second, the four represent a very good and amenable means to teach and demonstrate the idea of language as choice: as resource for exploiting to make different meanings. Thus, even for those

students for whom person and number in particular are not in themselves problematic (in that they make no errors in exploiting them), the learning of them in choice and system terms is in itself enlightening. Of the various systems, mood was developed and taught first, arising from a chapter in which language-learning in early life, and the importance of interaction in learning language, were explored. This provided a basis for exploring the various mood choices in English, and the range of speech functions open to speakers/writers of English. The tense system was examined once notions of verb groups had been established; tense merited a separate chapter devoted to it, called 'Verbs and Telling Time', though it was in this chapter too, that the systems of both number and person were examined. After considerable effort and thought, we confined the treatment of tense to a consideration of only the basic three: simple present, simple past and simple future. It proved impossible to address more than this without producing a very long chapter, and as with the example of conjunctions, we decided to leave the other tense choices for consideration in the second book.

Language and Meaning 2 (Christie and Soosai 2001) was intended to offer a sequel to the first book, though it had also to be written in the knowledge that not all schools would necessarily use *Language and Meaning 1.* The principles that guided its construction were as follows:

- It should seek to establish interest in, and curiosity about, language and literacy, bringing to consciousness some understandings about KAL, and teaching other areas of KAL.
- Like the first book, it should also interweave chapters, some devoted to KAL of a non-grammatical kind, while others addressed grammar.
- The latter principle should apply with respect to the KAL to do with imagery in language. Ways of playing with words by means of metaphors, similes and puns were taught in one chapter, and the knowledge was subsequently exemplified and taught in another chapter devoted to reading a narrative.
- For the most part, as in the first book, it should avoid teaching grammar in chapters devoted to teaching other aspects of KAL. The exceptions to this general principle occur either where the grammatical knowledge has been introduced hitherto, or, in the case of modality at least (see below), it was introduced in chapters devoted to argumentative texts.
- The non-grammar aspects of KAL involved should be quite different from those in Book 1, addressing matters as various as

aspects of the history of English, its significance as a world language, the origins of some at least of its words, the values of imagery in language (similes and metaphors in particular) as well as puns.

- It should address some of the traditional composition concerns with sentence structure, paragraph structure, topic sentences, and the relevance of all these for considering a sample of text types or genres. It was not in fact conceived as a genre book as such. This was partly because a number of genre books already existed on the market, and partly because, while not withdrawing from a belief in the values of teaching genres, we wanted to teach critical areas of KAL which we believed supported genre and which we had reason to believe were often neglected or forgotten. In any case, we planned a separate book about genres (Christie and Soosai, in prep.)
- The knowledge of grammar taught should include the traditional parts of speech (though not in the same detail as in the first book) and their role in various words groups: noun groups, verb groups and prepositional phrases. Four grammatical systems were introduced, albeit reasonably simply: those of conjunction, voice, theme and modality. Conjunction was introduced through teaching the idea of a clause and the kinds of conjunctive relations one can choose to create between clauses. Theme was taught through teaching paragraphs, topic sentences and sentence structure generally. Voice was taught by examining topical themes and the ways choices in active and passive voice create different possibilities for starting clauses and sentences. The teaching of all these systems was done in such a way that they were introduced and later their significance was exemplified as far as possible by reference to several texts written by secondary students. Modality was similarly taught; it was introduced and explained, and later its role in argumentative and persuasive pieces was demonstrated. In these ways, as in the first book, no attempt was made to teach grammatical knowledge simultaneously with the teaching of other areas of KAL. The tense system merited a chapter of its own and, as in all other chapters, an attempt was made to teach it around the systemic functional notion of choice and all that this implies about the possibilities for meaning-making that the system opens up.

An important aspect Anne Soosai and I needed to address early on in developing the two books was the issue of what technical language to use. From what has been said thus far, it will be clear that all the traditional terms to do with word classes were used, as were the terms associated with the mood and modality systems, voice, conjunction, person and number. We also used the traditional terms for dealing with English tense, having considered, but then rejected, the account of tense offered by Halliday (1994) in his SF description. Neither the traditional nor the SF terminology for tense is easy for the novice, once one moves beyond the basic choices of present, past and future tenses. We opted in the end for the traditional terms, on the grounds that they remain the better known in an English-speaking culture, and are to that extent more accessible to teachers, as much as to students.

The SF term of theme was introduced, though in a simplified manner. However, the SF notions of the processes realized in verbal groups, of the participant roles realized in nominal groups, and of the circumstances realized in prepositional phrases and/or adverbial groups, were not used. We have seen the SF terms used very badly in some junior textbooks recently produced for young readers, indicating that the writers themselves have a confused notion of what they mean. In the circumstances, given the requirement to write only two books, and the strong need we felt to offer textbooks that were in their terms accurate and helpful to young learners, we made the decision to use the traditional terms only for the most part. Three other observations I would make beyond this. First, the orientation adopted in teaching aspects of KAL, including that about grammar, is certainly functional, and in that sense the books are in our view very different from other contemporary books for young readers we have reviewed. Second, as I have noted more than once in this chapter, the traditional terms are in any case essential, if one is to make sense of the constituent structures in which functional elements are realized; what we have done, does, I believe, teach these clearly. Finally, the two books provide a foundation upon which the functional descriptions might be taught as well.

While the two textbooks were not the only outcomes of the study, they were in fact significant, for they provided Anne Soosai and me with an opportunity to employ in a very practical way the principles we had been articulating about teaching KAL. Our experience in observing and recording our co-operating teachers using the books and the work we had developed in our training sessions in the second phase of the study demonstrated the considerable success of a great deal that we had done. It was gratifying to observe students, for example, developing and using a metalanguage for talking about their language learning, where such a metalanguage referred to such things as the several parts of speech, some aspects of tense, uses of dictionaries and thesauruses, or to the elements of structure of the target text-types they were discussing and preparing to write. These are often not features of the classroom discourse of students in Year 7. The general standard of the writing of the students also improved as they developed a stronger and better focused sense of the various texts they were asked to write and a better informed sense of the functions of the elements of such texts.

7.8 Findings of the study

A number of important findings have emerged from the study, and they are summarized here:

- *The teaching of KAL, especially grammar*
  If the object is to teach grammar, then one must teach that, and not wait until the opportunity to teach it arises as a consequence of engaging with the text and/or some activity of concern. It does not follow that opportunities to teach grammar or other kinds of KAL will not arise incidentally in some other task. However, it will never be sufficient to expect to achieve the purpose this way. In any case, English must be the only school subject for which the claim has been made that some essential knowledge can be taught as a consequence of teaching something else. Teaching is surely a deliberate act, and the teaching programme should function in such a way that it foregrounds and makes explicit the need to learn things, where these things will then lead on to something else. Hence, the 'holistic' or 'integrated' curriculum to which I alluded much earlier creates considerable problems. But once this is recognized, the issue arises that English teachers will need assistance to rethink their teaching programmes, moving away from the present preoccupation with teaching cycles devoted primarily to class novels, films or perhaps class plays. Another organizing principle, motivated by a stronger sense of the nature of language and of the decisions to be made in its teaching, will need to be developed. Teachers will also need to be persuaded to abandon the idea, quite misguided in my view, that students in the junior secondary programme cannot be taught KAL, including aspects of grammar. In fact, I would argue that it is precisely because students are entering secondary schooling, with all the attendant changes in the nature of literacy that they will need to deal with, that the development of a metalanguage will assist them in coming to terms with such literacy.

- *The teaching of sentence grammar and constituent structure*
  Teachers will need to teach how to identify and recognize word classes while also teaching notions of function (and I know that you can teach functionally while using traditional terms). I earlier noted that the traditions of grammar teaching that were rejected in the 1960s and 1970s had focused on 'parts of speech' and correction of 'faulty sentences', at the expense of meaning and interest. I am therefore aware that in some quarters my present insistence on the need to teach word classes carefully as a necessary part of teaching the functional grammar may be criticized. I hope it is clear that I am not wanting to invoke some old discredited practices. Using the functional grammar, Williams (1998) has demonstrated how successfully one can teach features of transitivity even in the junior primary school, revealing how rapidly even young children can become interested in the different process types and their role in making meaning. He did such teaching without recourse to any teaching of the word classes involved in building process types and their participants. But it does not follow that the students involved will not eventually need to learn these things. In the past, those of us involved in genre-based approaches in Australia have not always addressed this issue particularly well as an aspect of the pedagogy we have offered teachers. For the purposes of school pedagogy, at least, in our concern to teach the functional grammar, we have, with some success, sought to teach some functional grammatical terms (e.g., Christie *et al.* 1992). However, we have given a rather shadowy significance to the role of the constituent structures of clauses, groups or words. We have tended either to hope that teachers somehow knew something about these and could get by with what they knew, or to believe that we could elicit sufficient interest in teachers in functional grammar that they could be persuaded to do the additional work of coming to terms with constituency. While the latter belief was sometimes justified, it often was not.

One can start one's teaching by first dealing with the functional elements, then going on to dealing with the constituent structure, as Williams demonstrated one can do in the very early years of schooling. Equally, one can start with notions of rank and the various elements of structure, and move from these to the functional descriptions. One can defend both approaches, and I suspect in time we will be able to say what is best for the different age groups in schools. My hunch is that to start with the functional categories of process types as Williams did with young learners is the best approach for such an age group. Such functional notions are in many ways very close to young children's intuitions about language and how it works. But the pedagogical decision will differ as students grow older, and as they need to do different things with their language, their literacy in particular. I would argue that the entry to secondary schooling, and the changing nature of the discourses students must read and write, are reasons to view the teaching of literacy very differently at this stage in students' lives. Literacy at this stage requires a different kind of consciousness, and while that consciousness has many dimensions, it will certainly include an understanding of basic word classes, their groupings into major components of the various groups, nominal, verbal, and so on, and the larger unities of the sentence, the paragraph and the overall written text.

Whether one starts with the functional elements, or with notions of rank, students will need to be taught how to identify adjectives, nouns, prepositions, articles, grammatical and lexical verbs, and so on. To many linguists this may seem obvious. However, in the profession of English teachers it is not so obvious, partly because many of its members have not been taught these things themselves and partly because they have been sold a misguided ideology that teaching 'about language' is undesirable.

7.9 Conclusion

I want to conclude by saying that what one does educationally is itself always in part a condition of the period of history in which one is working. If I seem to be arguing for a movement towards explicit teaching of constituent structure as an essential step for working with junior secondary students at least, this is because currently both teachers and students in that age group seem to be so bereft of knowledge in this area that it is a necessary step to take. But I hold no particular brief for the course of action I am proposing, in that I am not persuaded it is the only way to go. There is, I think, a necessary tension both in understanding the grammar and in teaching it, which is to do with reconciling the claims of an understanding of both constituent structure and function. While I think that in time we should be able to say something of what is the best point of departure in teaching different age groups, I also think that the pedagogical decisions to be made will always be significantly influenced by the historical context in which one works and the educational ideologies that prevail. It may be, of course, that in the new millennium we will have reached a state in which one no longer has to argue quite so hard for the claims of teaching grammar, functional or otherwise. In that event, I can only speculate about what might be the problems of pedagogy in the future.

References

Barnes, D. (1978) The study of classroom communication in teacher education. In M. Gill and W.J. Crockers (eds), *English in Teacher Education*. Armidale, NSW: The University of New England, 85–94.

Barnes, D., Britton, J. and Rosen, H. (1987) *Language, The Learner and The School*. 3rd edn. London: Penguin Books.

'Bullock Report, The', (1975) *A Language for Life*. Report of the Committee of Inquiry appointed by the Secretary of State for Education and Science under the Chairmanship of Sir Alan Bullock. London: Her Majesty's Stationery Office.

Carter, R. (ed.) (1990) *Knowledge about Language and the Curriculum. The LINC Reader*. London: Hodder and Stoughton.

Christie, F. (1991) Literacy in Australia. *Annual Review of Applied Linguistics*, 12: 142–55.

Christie, F. (1993) The 'received tradition' of English teaching: the decline of rhetoric and the corruption of grammar. In B. Green (ed.), *The Insistence of the Letter. Literacy Studies and Curriculum Theorizing*. London: Falmer Press, 75–106.

Christie, F. (1999) The pedagogic device and the teaching of English. In F. Christie (ed.), *Pedagogy and the Shaping of Consciousness: Linguistic and Social Processes*. London: Cassell Academic, 156–84.

Christie, F., Gray, P., Gray, B., Macken, M., Martin, J.R. and Rothery, J. (1990, 1992) *Language a Resource for Meaning: Procedures. Reports. Explanations*. Sydney: Harcourt Brace Jovanovich.

Christie, F., Devlin, B., Freebody, P., Luke, A., Martin, J.R., Threadgold, T. and Walton, C. (1991) *Teaching English Literacy: the Preservice Preparation of Teachers to Teach English*. Canberra: Centre for Studies of Language in Education, Northern Territory University Darwin, and Department of Employment Education and Training.

Christie, F. and Martin, J.R. (eds) (1997) *Genre and Institutions. Social Processes in the Workplace and School*. London: Cassell Academic.

'Cox Report, The' (1989) *Report of the English Working Party 5–16*. London: HMSO.

Dixon, J. (1967) *Growth Through English*. London: National Association for the Teaching of English.

Doughty, P. (1974) *Language, 'English' and the Curriculum*. Schools Council Programme in Linguistics and English Teaching. London: Arnold.

Feez, S. (1998) *Text-based Syllabus Design*. Sydney: National Centre for English Language Teaching and Research, Macquarie University.

Feez, S. and Joyce, H. (1998) *Writing Skills. Narrative and Non-Fiction Text Types*. Sydney: Phoenix Education.

Freedman, A. (1993) Show and tell? The role of explicit teaching in the learning of new genres. In *Research in the Teaching of English*, 27(3): 222–51.

Freedman, A. and Medway P. (eds.) (1994) *Genre and the New Rhetoric*. London: Taylor & Francis.

Gibbons, P. (1991) *Learning to Learn in a Second Language*. Sydney: PETA.

Halliday, M.A.K., Mcintosh, A. and Strevens, P. (1994) *The Linguistic Sciences and Language Teaching*. Longmans' Linguistics Library. London: Longmans.

Hasan, R. (1995) The conception of context in text. In P. Fries and M. Gregory (eds), *Discourse in Society: Systemic Functional Perspectives*. Norwood, NJ: Ablex, 183–283.

'Kingman Report, The' (1988) *Report of the Committee of Inquiry into the Teaching of English Language*. London: HMSO.

Kress, G. (1982) *Learning to Write*. London: Routledge and Kegan Paul.

Kress, G. (1993) Genre as social process. In B. Cope and M. Kalantzis (eds) *The Powers of Literacy: A Genre Approach to Teaching Writing*. London: Falmer Press, 1–21.

Martin, J.R. (1992) Genre and literacy – modelling context in educational linguistics. *Annual Review of Applied Linguistics*, 13: 141–74.

Martin, N. *et al.* (1976) *Understanding Children Talking*. London: Penguin.

Reid, I. (1987) *The Place of Genre in Learning: Current Debates*. Typereader Publications No. 1. Geelong, Victoria: Centre for Studies in Literary Education, Deakin University.

Rothery, J. and Stevenson, M. (1994) *Write it Right. Resources for Literacy and Learning*. Sydney: Disadvantaged Schools Program, Metropolitan East Region, NSW Department of Education.

Sawyer, W. and Watson, K. (1987) Questions of genre. In Reid (ed.), *The Place of Genre in Learning: Current Debates*. Typereader Publications No. 1. Geelong, Victoria: Centre for Studies in Literary Education, Deakin University, 46–57.

Threadgold, T. (1993) Performing genre: violence, the making of protected subjects, and the discourse of critical literacy and radical pedagogy. *Changing English*, London: University of London, Institute of Education. 1(2): 2–31.

Torbe, M. (1987) Language across the curriculum: policies and practices. In D. Barnes, J. Britton and H. Rosen, *Language, the Learner and the School*. 3rd edn. London: Penguin Books, 131–66.

Williams, G. (1998) Children entering literate worlds. In F. Christie and R. Misson (eds), *Literacy and Schooling*. London: Routledge, 18–46.

Notes

1 The research reported in this paper was funded by the Australian Research Council. I am grateful to my colleague, Anne Soosai, for advice on the writing of this paper.
2 During the period 1984–90 at Deakin University, I developed teaching programmes for students of education at the Bachelor's and Master's levels using systemic functional linguistics. Since Deakin University is a distance education provider, this led to the production of several course books which were extensively marketed. Probably the best known of the volumes were the various monographs for the Master's programme, in the Language Education series, which were also taken up for British distribution by Oxford University Press in 1989.
3 The term 'grammatical metaphor' is one invented by Halliday. It refers to the ways the 'congruent' expressions of speech become the 'non-congruent' ones of writing. A simple example would be: 'The soldiers exercised and then they were released from duty' (speech), and 'The soldiers exercise was followed by/led to their release from duty'. The tendency of the grammar is such that the actions of speech (realized mainly in verbs and nouns) become the things or the phenomena of writing (realized in nouns). Grammatical metaphor is important in building the abstractions of much writing.
4 The pedagogy associated with genre theory has been discussed and presented in detail in several places, including Christie *et al.* (1990, 1992), Gibbons (1991) and Feez (1998).
5 The functional notion of rank is explained in Halliday (1994: 19–36).
6 We were aware, incidentally, that we might be criticized for the decision to remove considerations of conjunctions and clauses, and in principle, given a strong enough background, there is no reason why Year 7 students could not learn about these matters. However, we based our decision to use the selection we did on our sense of the need (i) to cover some useful knowledge about grammar in a meaningful and useful way, and (ii) to allow opportunity in the book to teach other aspects of KAL apart from grammar. This was not intended to be only a grammar book.

8

What Should We Teach about the Paradoxes of English Nominalization?

Carolyn G. Hartnett

8.1 Introduction

The nominalizations discussed here are nouns that appear to be made by changing a verb, either internally or by adding an ending, such as one spelled *-ation*. This type of grammatical metaphor I call verb-change nominalizations; other linguists call them *non-zero derived deverbal nouns* or *stativation*. Suffixes add length, which by Zipf's Law should make these nominalizations rare, but they abound. In a specialized science report that I examined closely, 6 per cent of the words are nominalizations of this type. In the Longman–Lancaster academic corpus, 4.4 per cent of the words are nominalizations; its fiction rate is 1.1 per cent, the same as speech in the London–Lund corpus (Biber *et al.* 1998: 60). The difference in frequency has significant implications for teaching and for the future of the language.

Nominalizations shorten explanations and efficiently organize known information, building on it to develop new knowledge. They make a cohesive conclusion relevant to a previous explanation. Nominalizations help to reorganize much expository writing rhetorically, instead of in the real-world's time and location sequence. Because they generalize economically in evaluations, introductions, summaries and conclusions, they appear in a large range of situations in law and administrative bureaucracies, besides academic fields. Nominalizations construct abstractions and generalizations in humanities, interpret changes in social sciences and name processes, classifications and measurements in physical sciences. For example, they allow discussing *motion*, instead of saying *things move*, and naming *the speed of light*, which is not an object. Nominalization interprets or reconstructs 'the world as a place where things relate to other things' (Halliday and Martin 1993: 220).

After a review of the morphology of nominalizations, I will summarize the history of nominalizations in times of change in Western science and in Thai culture, seeking similarities. The frequency of nominalizations is examined in a wide variety of publications; examples of accommodating different audiences come from an intensive comparison of two science reports written for different audiences. I will discuss the effects of nominalization, some predictions about its future, and teaching nominalization to beginning learners, advanced students, future bureaucrats, scientists, and linguists. My conclusion suggests an alternative point of view in some non-European languages.

I focus on the type of nominalizations that proved to be most significant in my research. I have reported elsewhere statistics on other types that I omit here. The most numerous nominalizations are simply words spelled the same as either nouns or verbs, what some linguists call *zero-derived deverbal nouns*, such as *watch, plan, wave.* This type continues the normal historical pattern, common since Anglo-Saxon (Halliday 1998: 199). Although purists object to new uses, such as *a good feed* and *to lunch*, popular usage says, 'All nouns can be verbed, and vice versa.' So do the authorities I consulted: Baugh (1957), Bloomfield (1933, 1939), Bolinger (1968), Jesperson (1969), Longacre (1983), Matthews (1979), Mencken (1982) and Skeat, who says, 'false etymologies have long lives, and die hard' (1912: 29). All English verbs can add *-ing* to a verb root to create a noun, a gerund, so I omit them from current consideration, along with nominalizations that add suffixes to adjectives, such as *-ness (fairness)* and *-ity (purity)*, compounds such as *birthday*, and nominalizations that change the meanings of words that are already nouns, such as *friendship* and *patriotism*. The nominalizations I discuss either change the stem, as in *sell/sale*, *live/life* and *sing/song*, or add a suffix, such as *-al (portrayal)*, *-ance (attendance)*, *-ee (payee)*, *-ment (achievement)*, *-tion (recommendation)*, *-ure (creature)*, *-y (mastery)*, and *-yst (analyst)*.

Nominalizations should not be confused with abstractions, although some are abstract. They often serve as nouns or noun adjuncts to indicate operating principle, working substance, means of operation, characteristic working part, person who formulated the process, material used, purpose, location or professional role.

8.2 Language in times of change in Western science

Science has stimulated changes in language. A brief history of European nominalizations might begin with the ancient Greek scientists (Halliday 1998: 197–229). They transcategorized verbs for processes into nouns for actors and for products (that which is n). The category of nouns expanded to include terms such as measurements, which are not visible things, only theoretical entities. Science and mathematics needed ordered sets of abstract technical terms. Eventually processes were construed as things, as stable, measurable phenomena. Adjectives for qualities and degrees were treated as nouns that could be modified and could participate in further processes. Latin calqued these nominalizations, and they were absorbed into the Saxon languages of the Middle Ages, known also as the Dark Ages.

After the Renaissance, the Enlightenment brought a new age in science and many nominalizations that compact pieces of an argument into a persuasive flow of logical reasoning. In 1704, Newton used nominalizations to explain his observations in a line of logical reasoning, progressing from factual occurrence expressed with a verb, *refract*, to a process with a new theory *refraction*. He explained a condition wherein 'Light will not be refracted enough, and for want of a sufficient Refraction will not converge to the bottom of the Eye' (Halliday 1998: 201). Processes and qualities were transcategorized into nouns, and relators became verbs. The compacted results could be distilled 'to create technical taxonomies of abstract, virtual entities', the goal of language-planning in England and France in the 1600s (Halliday 1998: 228).

Lavoisier established experimental chemistry through language, explaining that we think only through the medium of words. 'Languages are true analytical methods the art of reasoning is nothing more than a language well arranged' (1989: xiii). Two years later, shortly before his execution in the French revolution, Lavoisier explained in the preface to his masterpiece, *Elements of Chemistry*:

> Thus, while I thought myself employed only in forming a Nomenclature, and while I proposed to myself nothing more than to improve the chemical language, my work transformed itself by degrees, without my being able to prevent it, into a treatise upon the elements of Chemistry. The impossibility of separating the nomenclature of a science from the science itself, is owing to this, that every branch of physical science must consist of three things; the series of facts which are the objects of the science, the ideas which represent these facts, and the words by which these ideas are

> expressed. Like three impressions of the same seal, the word ought to produce the idea, and the idea to be a picture of the fact. And, as ideas are preserved and communicated by means of words, it necessarily follows that we cannot improve the language of any science without at the same time improving the science itself; neither can we, on the other hand, improve a science, without improving the language or nomenclature which belongs to it. However certain the facts of any science may be, and, however just the ideas we may have formed of these facts, we can only communicate false impressions to others, while we want words by which these may be properly expressed. (ibid.: xiv–xv)

Lavoisier also quoted an objection by the Abbe de Condillac (1715–80):

> The method, too, by which we conduct our reasonings is as absurd; we abuse words which we do not understand, and call this the art of reasoning. But, after all, the sciences have made progress . . . and have communicated to their language that precision and accuracy which they have employed in their observations: in correcting their language they reason better. (ibid.: xxxvi–xxxvii)

In the nineteenth century, as the life sciences developed, nominalization helped create taxonomies in biology. Chemistry and biology teachers today continue to emphasize vocabulary in their taxonomies because they agree with Lavoisier and continue to believe, 'Whoever controls the language controls the science.' Then the social sciences used nominalizations to develop generalizations (Halliday and Martin 1993: 16–21). Thus systematic knowledge has developed from physical matter to biological life, through social sciences, and now to the semiotic sciences of meaning in what some call 'our age of information' or the 'fourth order of complexity'.

Science needs language that does more than describe experience: it must interpret it to create new theories, which consist of language that has evolved to interpret reality as persisting, as unrealistically still and unchanging, while it is being observed. However, after Einstein changed the prevailing views of time, space and gravitation, Nobel Prize-winning physicist Steven Weinberg wrote, 'quantum mechanics has transformed the very language we use to describe nature: in place of particles with definite positions and velocities, we have learned to speak of wave functions and probabilities . . . matter has lost its central role' (1992: 3). How can physicists use nouns when 'matter has lost its central role'? They need new names for short-lived artificial subnuclear particles that they consider to be vibrating strings of positive and negative waves of energy in fields, not in specific, precise locations. They must discuss particles that exist temporarily as other particles. Their solutions show their sense of humour when they name particles *gluons* or *anti-bottom quarks*, with characteristics of *beauty*, *charm* and *strangeness*. They use colours as labels and then name the field *quantum chromo dynamics*, although it has nothing to do with visual colours. Scientists do not hesitate to use language metaphorically; geneticists, for example, write about *molecular communication* and *transcription*, even describing gene therapy as *correcting spelling mistakes* (Harnett 1999). Communication continues, but the use of nominalizations, in at least some sciences, is in doubt (Martin 1990).

8.3 The Thai language in times of change

'Any major restructuring of knowledge is likely to demand some remodelling of grammar' according to Halliday (1998: 229). Restructuring may be in a scientific field or in an entire culture. Such a change occurred in Thai under circumstances much different from those of the European Enlightenment. Thai has always had nominalizations, but uses more prefixes than suffixes.

Like English suffixes, Thai affixes have inconsistent and overlapping meanings, according to Amara Prasithrathsint (1994, 1997). The most common nominalizing affix (60 per cent, *khwaam*) has been used since 1283, that is, 500 years before Western contact. It expresses abstract intangible concepts such as feelings, states of being, or qualities. The next most common (24 per cent, *kaan*) has been used since the seventeenth century. It names actions and is similar to our *-ing* gerund. The third (*thii*) condenses a clause as a *factive nominal* or *sentential complement*, creating a clause, as in her examples.

> That *he passed the exam is a surprise*
> *(thii khaw soop phaan pen riang pralaat)*.

Nominalization increased tremendously in the nineteenth century during the deliberate Westernization of Thai society; it abolished slavery and reformed administration and education. Then nominalization decreased, and later a smaller increase occurred during the political revolution in the 1930s (Prasithrathsint 1997). Thai has borrowed and calqued words from English, but its officials encouraged coining nominalizations, often without success; some Thais criticize nominalization as unnecessarily elaborate and foreign-sounding.

Prasithrathsint searched a dictionary of coinages and also systematically collected 60,000 words of Standard Thai. She counted only verbs with affixes but excluded affixes meaning 'actor' and the many verbs identical with nouns. Her quantitative data show that the frequency of Thai nominalizations and the preferred patterns vary by discipline to a statistically significant degree: psychology uses most, 23 per cent of them, then sociology with 18 per cent, philosophy and science at 10 per cent each, statistics 8 per cent, mathematics 7 per cent and medical science 5 per cent.

She concluded that increased nominalization has coincided with significant changes in Thai society. The changes increased discussion of abstract political ideologies and philosophies, and this discussion needed appropriate forms. She felt confident in predicting that certain nominalizers would become more productive in Thai, while others would decline. Can we make similar predictions about the future of nominalizations in English?

8.4 How English nominalization works

Nominalization is most frequent in writing, less common in standard speech, and least often in non-standard varieties. Conversational topics differ from written topics. Conversation occurs in real time, usually face-to-face, and without much time for reflection or for collecting separate ideas into generalities or systems of classification, which use nominalizations. Writing, in contrast, is slowly and deliberately created, often with a different logical structure.

Nominalization freezes actions for interpretation, as in hierarchies and theories. It allows knowledge to accumulate by building on previous information, compressed, organized and packaged as a base (Halliday and Martin 1993: 199). When specifics of time and actor are irrelevant in a regular process, that process can be reduced to a noun in a clause that expresses a great deal more. A clause can classify, define and exemplify as it constructs new taxonomies and knowledge. Nominalization foregrounds results and products and expresses its broad presuppositional base and abstractions with precision (Leckie-Tarrie 1995: 118).

This concentration of the ideational component creates sentences with more information in simpler and fewer clauses. A common sentence structure has a heavily modified nominalization followed by a verb that relates it to another heavily modified nominalization. A typical example is a sentence from a technical research report written for other specialists in the field: *Examination of split-brain patients both before and after their surgery is another tool for the unmasking of such processes*. If this specialized sentence were stripped of the fifteen words in its four prepositional phrases, it would read, simply and insignificantly, 'Examination . . . is another tool'. In its entirety, this sentence illustrates how nominalizations attract modifiers of all types, especially noun adjuncts and prepositional phrases. As heavily modified nominalizations like this simplify syntactic complexity, they also pack more lexical content into the clause. In spoken English, the lexical density, the ratio of content words to grammatical terms, is only about two lexical words per clause (Halliday 1998: 207). In contrast, the science articles that I examined have very high lexical densities of 10.8 content words per average sentence of 20.7 words. They are 52 per cent nouns, verbs, adjectives, or adverbs, and 48 per cent prepositions, conjunctions, articles, or modal auxiliaries of verbs.

Although it is hard to avoid nominalizations, the authors of student handbooks for grammar and composition often advise shunning them. However, these authors averaged two nominalizations for every three verbs when they began their own articles in professional journals (see Table 8.1). Textbooks on technical writing urge caution with nominalizations but are much more realistic. A report on teaching English as a second language to European researchers, where the policy is 'Publish in English or perish', recommends that students should practise nominalization instead of narrative skills (Ventola 1994: 298).

8.5 Research materials analysed and results

I examined the first paragraphs of 194 articles in 22 publications and 15 essays by first-year tertiary students. In the 847 sentences there, the frequency of nominalizations correlated roughly with the price of the publication and the number of references cited, which may relate to the readers' interests and prior knowledge. Of the 2384 nominalizations of all five types, one-third (784) were the verb-change type, averaging one in 93 per cent of the sentences. Verb-change nominalizations equalled 53 per cent of the complete finite verbs, but they varied from equalling 17 per cent of the finite verbs in the free magazines available in the malls and grocery stores of Cardiff, Wales, to equalling 130 per cent of the verbs in the *Houston Chronicle* newspaper. Academic journals were consistently greatly above average (70 per cent), while popular computer magazines were slightly below average (42 per cent), and student compositions even lower (29 per cent), as shown in Table 8.1.

Table 8.1 Nominalizations in first paragraphs

Type of Publication	Number of issues examined	Average price per issue	Total articles included	Number of sentences	Number of finite verbs	Number of nominaliz ations	Nominaliz-ations per verb
Science:	1	$7.00					
for specialists			18	117	193	178	.92
for educated readers			17	64	125	55	.44
New York Times	3	$1.00	23	28	65	49	.75
Other newspapers	6	$0.51	28	41	64	43	.67
Linguistics journals	2	$9.55	10	53	90	71	.78
Composition journals	3	$9.00	11	61	144	98	.68
Family magazines	5	$2.81	63	254	467	192	.41
Free magazines	2	$0.00	24	55	98	17	.17
College student compositions	15		15	100	187	55	.29

I also analysed closely the nominalizations in two reports of a research project in the same issue of *Science*, written for two different kinds of scientists: one for specialists in the field and one for scientists educated in other fields (Strauss 1998; Baynes 1998). Different audiences need and receive somewhat different style and content. The editors consider the previous knowledge of the readers and try to meet the differing needs of both intended audiences.

To obtain comparable selections of similar content and size (681 words in the article for educated readers and 687 words in the article by and for specialists), I omitted much of the lengthy narrative of procedures and test results from the middle of the specialists' article. For example, although the specialists' article could identify the authors in the by-line and begin a sentence with the subject *we*, the educated article needed a sentence of 50 words to identify the researcher. Neither article had many nominalizations that are technical terms (such as *lateralization*, 10 total), for most of the technical terms were adjectives, verbs or ordinary nouns. Most of the nominalizations were clear in context, and only one related to previous use as a verb.

Table 8.2 '*Science* articles about the same research' reflects the more nominal style of the article for specialists. The articles differ significantly in the number of verb-change nominalizations (25 in educated and 41 in specialized), nominalizations per sentence (0.8 and 1.2), percent of nouns that are nominalizations (14 per cent and 22 per cent), number of nouns that are objects of prepositions (70

Table 8.2 Analyses of two *Science* articles about the same research

	For educated readers	For specialized readers
Total words analysed	681	687
Sentences	31	35
Verb-change nominalizations	25	41
Verb-change Nominalization in Prepositional Phrases	17	54
Nominalization per sentence	0.8	1.2
All nouns	174	184
per cent of nouns that are nominalizations	14 per cent	22 per cent
Objects of prepositions	70	104
Nominalization that are objects of prepositions	29	61
Complete finite verbs	80	67
Nominalizations per verb	0.31	.62

Sample sentences for educated readers

1 By studying an epileptic patient whose brain was surgically divided to control her seizures, K.
B., a cognitive neuroscientist at U Cal Davis, and her colleagues found that the centres for speech and writing, long thought to be on the same side of the brain, can reside in both hemispheres.

2 It's hard to generalize from this single case.

3 But the findings suggest that spoken and written language can develop separately, and may lead to a new understanding of learning disorders.

Parallel sample sentences for specialists

1 Examination of split-brain patients both before and after their surgery is another tool for the unmasking of such processes.

2 Here we use this method to reveal a dissociation between the neural representations involved in spoken and written language.

3 These results are consistent with the view that the brain processes enabling written language do not call upon brain representation responsible for phonological capacity.

and 104), and nominalizations per verb (0.31 and 0.62). There are significant differences in frequency of nominalizations in grammatical roles of subject, of object or complement of verbs and of object of prepositions (p = .01). In the article for specialists, 54 per cent of the verb-change nominalizations are in prepositional phrases, while the educated article has only 17 per cent there (p = .008).

Syntactic roles are important because nominalizations are easier to comprehend when they occur not as subject or theme but later in the sentence in the new information position of the N-Rheme. The two articles showed a statistically significant difference in the themes. The fourth sentence in the educated article names the researcher as grammatical subject after 14 words describing the method: '*By* studying an epileptic patient whose brain was surgically divided to control her seizures, K. B. . . . found that the centers for speech and writing, long thought to be in the same side of the brain, can reside in different hemispheres.' In the specialized article a shorter fourth sentence introduces the findings with a nominalization as subject, 'Examination of split-brain patients both before and after their surgery is another tool for the unmasking of such *processes*.' (The processes were described two sentences earlier.)

The educated article's verb-change nominalizations in the first example sentence above are the everyday words, *seizures* and *speech*; both are used as objects, not subjects. Compared to the article for educated readers, the specialists' article has slightly fewer ordinary nouns total and slightly more ordinary nouns in prepositional phrases, but twice as many nominalizations of all types in prepositional phrases, three times as many nominalizations of all types in second or third prepositional phrases in sequence, and, impressively, more than five times as many verb-change nominalizations in prepositional phrases. This difference is greater than the difference in proportions of nouns to complete verbs (46 per cent for educated readers, 37 per cent for specialists), although prepositions could be expected to increase in nominal styles.

8.6 Effects of nominalizations

As single vocabulary items, nominalizations are stored as single items in long-term memory, where they get less attention and analysis. When nominalization condenses prior knowledge, it is treated as given and cannot be challenged, even in positions other than theme or subject, where given information usually occurs. For example, when readers see, 'The indistinguishability of electrons allows molecule binding', they cannot question the existence of indistinguishability; they can question only the existence of molecule binding and its relationships. And when a chief executive officer predicts nothing but states, 'A reduction in force increases profitability', stockholders are elated and employees worried.

Nominalizations can mislead by de-emphasizing or hiding relevant information, obscuring what is harmful to the position of the writer. Because they allow writers to avoid commitment to actor, tense and probability modulation, they advantage writers but disadvantage the audience. Moreover, although nominalizations turn processes into objects, nothing requires treating them objectively. Nominalizations are generalities, and, as has been said, all generalities are false, including this one.

The ideational uses of nominalization have interpersonal effects. Any overall recommendation to avoid the standard terminology in a field, to dismiss it as mere insider jargon meant to impress, misses the point that insiders need their own efficient jargon and standard technical terminology, and informed audiences dislike being talked down to. Technical jargon creates a field. Because using and understanding nominalization presupposes a knowledge of the field, nominalization distinguishes the expert from the uninitiated. It reveals status, authority, maturity and other aspects of the writer's identity. Heavy nominalization makes a text sound authoritative, formal, impersonal and prestigious. It adds a learned touch that is often desirable, and it can be interpreted as indicating the writer's assumption that readers understand the content and its background, thus implying group identity as well as perhaps boosting the egos of the readers.

However, after the prestige of science and the advantages of vagueness in nominalizations led industrial and governmental bureaucracies to adopt this style, a backlash arose from overuse, misuse and new needs in our 'information society'. Bureaucrats often overuse nominalizations from habit, to make an impression, or to manipulate readers. When they have reason to limit the amount of information they are revealing, they take the easy way out with a nominal style that does not require them to specify actors and times. Some lawmakers may believe that they are safer relying on traditional wordings they are familiar with. However, the style often called 'gobbledygook' became the target of the 'plain English' movement and has become somewhat less common. Many government publications, insurance policies and health guidelines have become easier for consumers to understand, showing that improvement is possible.

Nominalizations once gave science the advantage of discussing processes and relationships as things that are to be treated as stable objects and as the basis for further knowledge and theory. Scientists once had a reputation for precision and exactness; now, nominalization presents scientists with a problem when they accept probabilities, flux and fuzzy logic. They accept the Heisenberg flaw of not being able to observe all the aspects of a particle (such as its speed and its location) without changing it in some way, and so they accept the conclusion that their knowledge is always incomplete. They need a way of discussing indeterminacies and chaos theory. Imprecision is a problem elsewhere, too. The US government debated using statistical sampling for the census because sampling is more accurate than an actual count that misses many people for various reasons. Meanwhile, teenagers go, 'Like uhm, y'know, well, er, ah, anyway, like, whatever, y'know.'

A criticism of nominalizations is that they tend to associate with what are popularly called 'weak verbs', passives and verbs for existential and relational processes. An example of this tendency is the sentence quoted earlier, 'Examination ... is another tool'. This association does seem to exist, especially in science for specialists. Only the article for specialists had verb-change nominalizations (five of them) that are complements of verbs of existence. Traditional grammar handbooks advocate a strong verbal style, and properly so, but while they castigate a nominal style with nominalization, they themselves cannot avoid it: *usage*, *modifiers*, *variety*, *references*, etc. (Hacker 1995: 62).

Before audiences pay attention to minute descriptions of something, they want verbs that tell what happens to make it worth describing, but nominalizations do not tell interesting stories. Verbs are necessary for narratives, stories of action and news reports of events. Only later, after thoughtful consideration, do conclusions need efficient nominalizations. In some situations, separate clauses without nominalization are essential to provide poignancy, but in others, nominalizations are required because full clauses would impede the flow of information in the discourse (Longacre 1983: 327).

English nominalizations are efficient because they allow new information to be re-used as given, without specifying the actor, time, situation or probability. Meanings can change unpredictably. Even a native reader cannot deduce meaning simply from the form. For example, an actor/agent can be shown by the suffix *-er* (*player*, *speaker*), but *laughter* and *prayer* are usually products, not actors. The words *corrosion* and *classification* can mean either processes or their products, but *information* means only the product, not the process. Does *animal protection* mean using guard dogs or saving endangered species? The context and modifiers may be insufficient to clarify what the nominalizations refer to: the actor, action, recipient, resulting product, or, more abstractly, the outcome or quality.

Speakers have intended their meanings before they make nominalizations, and so their meanings are 'never simply additive', but are more specific and applicable to a narrower field (Bolinger 1968: 55). Furthermore, assuming previous knowledge, as nominalizations do, can make comprehension more difficult. They can, incidentally, confuse uninformed student readers and mislead them.

Nominalizations leave implicit the experiential meanings that beginning learners most depend on (Halliday and Martin 1993: 41, 250–7). Nominalizations presuppose so much prior knowledge that they are difficult for students to comprehend; this may be why many educators dislike them. But unpacking nominalization makes texts longer, although still not clear, because it gives all details equal importance and may still hide relationships. Brevity is both advantageous and problematic.

8.7 Teaching for the future

We have seen languages change in times of change in both Europe and Thailand, and we can anticipate further changes as sciences advance. Halliday has expressed some expectations (Halliday and Martin 1993: 20–1).

1 He expects the semiotic sciences to gain importance; he expects continuation of the trend toward interpreting many phenomena as semiotic events. We have seen this trend in genetics.
2 Because technology, from radio scripts to e-mail, continues the trend of making speech and writing more alike, he expects from science greater use of ordinary language that is more in harmony with what emerging sciences mean and want to say. Scientists may return to the language of their childhood and the non-scientific general public. Such a change would make science less alienating and more democratic.
3 He anticipates a less nominal style with more clauses and verbs, but fewer nouns. The language of science 'is likely to back off from its present extremes of nominalization and grammatical metaphor and go back to being more preoccupied with processes and more tolerant of indeterminacy and flux recasting the nominal mode into a clausal one while developing the verbal group as a technical resource'.

Teachers must be alert to these trends in some sciences, but they also must prepare students for current usage and other fields. Mastering nominalization is 'partly a question of maturity: students well into secondary school may still find it difficult to comprehend' (Halliday and Martin 1993: 81–2). Native speakers of English do not understand or use nominalizations of the verb-change type before about age 10 to 14, although very young ones do hear and use verbs as nouns easily (MacNamara 1982: 116–40). Nominalization develops in children as it does in texts and as it did historically. As Halliday explains, ontogeny recapitulates phylogeny and logo genesis (1998: 222). Children can learn and do not need to be talked down to. In some way they need to be taught the meaning and use of nominalizations.

Students can learn from definitions that list accumulated properties explicitly; they also benefit from use of the verb shortly before its nominalization, creating the prior knowledge to build on. For example, a post-secondary student wrote, 'When you *know* how cocaine *acts*, . . . that *knowledge* can help avoid its *actions*.' School science textbooks and pedagogy must provide appropriate models (Halliday and Martin 1993: 189). Then, students must respond with more than short answers to learn to express relationships and to practise the style of the adult world. Both native and non-native advanced users of English may continue to experience special difficulties with writing nominalizations, such as not knowing whether a verb needs a suffix to form a noun.

Students must understand the unethical manipulative uses of nominalization and, even more, they need to learn to avoid being manipulated by what they read and hear or by relevant omissions. The many students on the road to becoming bureaucrats themselves need to become aware of the advantages and traps of the English bureaucratic style that may surround them. They need to consider whether their primary audience is other bureaucrats or the general public. Meeting the needs of specific audiences has always been good advice for everyone. All communicators need to develop appropriate interpersonal relationships with their audiences.

If advanced academic students want to be treated as well informed, they must use the language of their professors to discuss the field. Nominalizations reveal their comprehension and identity. When students are establishing new identities for themselves, they must respect the appropriate use of the style of the status they aspire to (Ivani 1998: 135–46). They must learn to consider their purpose for writing and the needs and previous knowledge of their audience; they need to include enough information, but not too much, and so they need nominalization.

Scientists and technicians also have a range of purposes and audiences, so they need all that advanced academic students need, and more. They need flexibility to write for both specialists in their own field and outsiders. Molecular geneticists who want acceptance and funding need to know how to make their needs known to the public and to those who fund grants. When computer programmers write handbooks for their products, they should write clearly enough that consumers do not need the thousands of lay instruction books that abound.

Beyond understanding what advanced students and bureaucrats need, linguists need to keep an open mind and become aware of the problems that some sciences have with nominalizations. Sciences differ, and the present language may satisfy some. Mathematics, for example, discusses imaginary and irrational numbers without difficulty and long ago found advantages in using Arabic numerals instead of iconic Roman numerals. However, scientists in some fields are dissatisfied with current usage that implies or clearly expresses more precision and stability than exists, the real paradox of nominalization (Bohm 1980: 123). We may now be on the verge of revolutionary developments in some sciences (such as physics and genetics) and their language. Future linguists must understand *metastability*, for it applies to features that are stable only because of their ability to handle constant change. Unless linguists can help, they must get out of the way. The people who will change the language of science are the scientists themselves, the discoverers of quarks, not linguists or the authors of grammar handbooks.

Halliday cites Whorf's observations about Hopi's 'preference for verbs, as contrasted with our own liking for nouns, [which] perpetually turns our propositions about things into propositions about events'. Elsewhere Whorf wrote, 'The person most nearly free in such respects [free from being limited to certain modes of interpretation] would be a linguist familiar with very many widely different linguistic systems' (1956: 214). If Western physicists believe that matter has lost its central role, they may not want to distinguish nouns and verbs in their traditional manner, but instead consider the differences between orientation to objects and orientation to relationships and processes. They may want to understand a more consonant approach, such as how non-Western, non-European languages manage things and processes. Now in these times of change when physicists need to discuss flux and instability and differing part-whole relationships, our teaching should anticipate some change in language. We should be alert to the paradoxes and the opportunities for the semiotic sciences as we teach for the future. Nominalizations may lose ground. Until then, when they serve valid purposes, they must be recognized, and we must teach their advantages and disadvantages.

References

Baugh, Albert C. (1957) *A History of the English Language.* New York: Appleton-Century-Crofts.

Baynes, Kathleen (1998) Modular organization of cognitive systems masked by interhemispheric integration. *Science*, 280: 902–5.

Biber, Douglas, Conrad, Susan and Rippen, Randi (1998) *Corpus Linguistics: Investigating Language Structure and Use.* Cambridge: Cambridge University Press.

Bloomfield, Leonard (1933) *Language.* New York: Holt.

Bloomfield, Leonard (1939) Linguistic Aspects of Science. In *International Encyclopaedia of Science: VI (4)*. Chicago: University of Chicago Press, 3.

Bohm, David (1980) *Wholeness and the Implicate Order.* New York: Routledge.

Bolinger, Dwight (1968) *Aspects of Language.* New York: Harcourt, Brace and World.

Hacker, Diana (1995) *A Writer's Reference.* Boston: Bedford, St Martin's.

Halliday, M.A.K. (1998) Things and relations. In J. R. Martin and Robert Veel (eds), *Reading Science.* London: Routledge, 185–235.

Halliday, M.A.K. and Martin, J.R. (1993) *Writing Science: Literacy and Discursive Power.* London and Washington: Palmer.

Harnett, Carolyn G. (1999) Nominalization: hiding the actor while making the writer and the reader visible. Presentation for the conference on College Composition and Communication, Atlanta, 24–7 March.

Ivani, Roz (1998) *Writing and Identity: The Discoursal Construction of Identity in Academic Writing.* Philadelphia: John Benjamins.

Jesperson, Otto (1969) *Analytic Syntax.* New York: Holt, Rinehart, and Winston.

Lavoisier, Antoine-Laurent (1790) *Elements of Chemistry in a New Systematic Order, Containing All the Modern Discoveries.* Trans. Robert Kerr. Edinburgh: Creech. Reprinted 1989. New York: Dover Publications.

Leckie-Tarrie, Helen (1995) *Language and Context: A Functional Linguistic Theory of Register.* London: Pinter.

Longacre, Robert (1983) *The Grammar of Discourse.* New York: Plenum.

MacNamara, John (1982) *Names for Things: A Study of Human Learning.* Cambridge: MIT Press.

Martin, J.R. (1990) Literacy in science: learning to handle text as technology. In Frances Christie (ed.), *Literacy for a Changing World.* Victoria: Australian Council for Educational Research.

Matthews, C.M. (1979) *Words, Words, Words.* New York: Scribner's.

Mencken, H.L. (1982) *The American Language* (abridged). New York: Alfred A. Knopf.

Prasithrathsint, Amara (1994) Borrowing and Nominalization of Technical Terms in Standard Thai. In *Language Reform: History and Future.* Hamburg: Helmut Buske Verlag, 9–24.

Prasithrathsint, Amara (1997) The emergence and development of abstract nominalization in standard Thai. In Arthur S. Abramson (ed.), *Southeast Asian Linguistic Studies in Honor of Vichin Panupong*. Bangkok: Chulalonghorn University Press, 179–90.

Skeat, Walter W. (1912) *The Science of Etymology*. Oxford: Clarendon Press.

Strauss, Evelyn (1998) Writing, speech separated in split brain. *Science*, 289: 827.

Ventola, Eija (1994) From syntax to text: problems in producing scientific abstracts in L2. In Svetla Cmerjrkova and František Štícha (eds), *Syntax of Sentence and Text: A Festschrift for František Danes*. Philadelphia: John Benjamins, 281–303.

Weinberg, Steven (1992) *Dreams of a Final Theory*. New York: Pantheon and Random House Vintage.

Whorf, Benjamin Lee (1956) *Language, Thought, and Reality: Selected Writings of Benjamin Lee Whorf*. Cambridge: MIT Press.

9

Discourses in Secondary School Mathematics Classrooms According to Social Class and Gender

Kay L. O'Halloran

9.1 Introduction

In this chapter I present findings from a larger research project (O'Halloran 1996) in which systemic functional theory is used to analyse the oral discourse and board texts in three mathematics lessons differentiated on the basis of gender, social class and school sector. In this project, following from Michael Halliday's (1978, 1994) social semiotic theory of language, mathematics discourse is viewed as a multi-semiotic construction[1] which involves the use of language, mathematical symbolism and visual display. Although not presented here, preliminary systemic frameworks for mathematical symbolism and visual display (O'Halloran 1996: 154–63) were used to analyse the written board texts. However, this chapter is largely concerned with the nature of the oral pedagogical discourse in order to discuss differences in classroom practices. From this analysis, the level of engagement with mathematics and the subject positions of the students across the different schools is contextualized in relation to Bernstein's (1971, 1973, 1977, 1981, 1990) sociological theory of pedagogical practices and the relationship between educational achievement, language and social structure.

The systemic linguistic analysis of the oral discourse was completed for the systems for interpersonal, experiential, logical and textual metafunctions listed in Table 9.1. Following conventional notation, systems are written in uppercase and functional elements are capitalized. The analysis was undertaken using a prototype version of *Systemics* (O'Halloran and Judd 2002), software for systemic analysis

Table 9.1 SFL systems according to function and rank

	Interpersonal	Experiential	Logical	Textual
Exchange or paragraph	NEGOTIATION (Exchange Structure including SPEECH FUNCTION)	(lexical and nuclear relations)	CONJUCTION (logico-semantic relations) and CONTINUITY	IDENTIFICATION (phoricity and reference)
Clause complex			LOGICO-SEMANTIC RELATIONS; INTER-DEPENDENCY	
Clause	MOOD, ELLIPSIS MODALISATION MODULATION POLARITY MOOD TAGGING, VOCATION CLAUSE TYPE INTERPERSONAL METAPHOR	TRANSITIVITY AGENCY EXPERIENTIAL METAPHOR	LOGICAL METAPHOR	THEME, ELLIPSIS; TEXTUAL METAPHOR
Word Group	ATTITUDE COMMENT LEXIS AMPLIFICATION GRAMMATICAL METAPHOR	TENSE, LEXIS GRAMMATICAL METAPHOR	GRAMMATICAL METAPHOR	DEIXIS; RANKSHIFTED ELEMENTS; GRAMMATICAL METAPHOR

which contains pre-programmed options for each of these major systems documented in Halliday (1994). Given space constraints, a summary of the patterns are discussed here rather than presenting the actual statistics for each dimension of the analysis (see O'Halloran 1996).

The study revealed the linguistic selections in the lessons with working-class students and elite private school female students are more consistently oriented towards interpersonal meaning at the expense of the mathematical content of the lesson. Further to this, the selections for interpersonal meaning in these lessons tended towards a deferential position in power relations.

These patterns are most marked in the government school lesson with working-class students. However, in the lesson with male students in an elite private school, the ideational content of the mathematics is foregrounded against the stable tenor configurations of power dominating relations, low levels of affect and involved but formal contact. In what follows, I contextualize the nature of three lessons before summarizing and interpreting the linguistic evidence that supports these findings.

9.2 Contextualization of the lessons

The three mathematics lessons took place in Perth, Western Australia in classes consisting of 'more able' mathematics students in Year 10 where the typical age of the students is 15 years. In what follows, I contextualize the three mathematics lessons in terms of (i) their location in the mathematics curriculum, (ii) the nature of the lesson genre, and (iii) the internal structure of each lesson as a sequence of microgenres. The display of the microgeneric structure is significant for it serves to capture how interpersonal meaning (the enactment of social relations) impacts upon the unfolding of each lesson.

9.2.1 The Curriculum Macrogenre and Lesson Genres

As proposed by Christie (1994) in her analysis of school science lessons, the school curriculum may be considered to be a Macrogenre, a series of stages realized though different Lesson Genres. The stages of the mathematics curriculum Macrogenre as a sequence of Lesson Genres are displayed schematically in Figure 9.1. The range of Microgenres (see section 9.2.2) constituting the Lesson Genres are also displayed in Figure 9.1.

1 Lesson 1(extract): elite private school for male students

Teacher: It's very easy to criticize but come up with something better. Why don't you think that would be a good idea?

Student: It's going to be more than ten metres high. It's . . .

Teacher: Well I think that's a logical answer there.

Lesson 1 took place in an advanced Year 10 class in an elite private school for boys in Perth, Western Australia. The lesson is trigonometry where the teacher presents a 'real-life' problem involving finding the height of a cliff 'h' and width of a river 'r' using an angle-measuring device and a ten metre rope. The problem involves finding a generalized result which may be applied to any number of cases. The verbal problem is first represented diagrammatically and then the symbolic expression is derived from this representation. Lesson 1 represents a Theory Applications Lesson in the Curriculum Application stage.

2 Lesson 2 (extract): elite private school for female students

Teacher: OK what letter would we like best today? 'p' . . . 'p' squared.

Teacher: Put a three there. Umm, plus four 'p'.

Teacher: Why is it safe for me to put minus on the end?

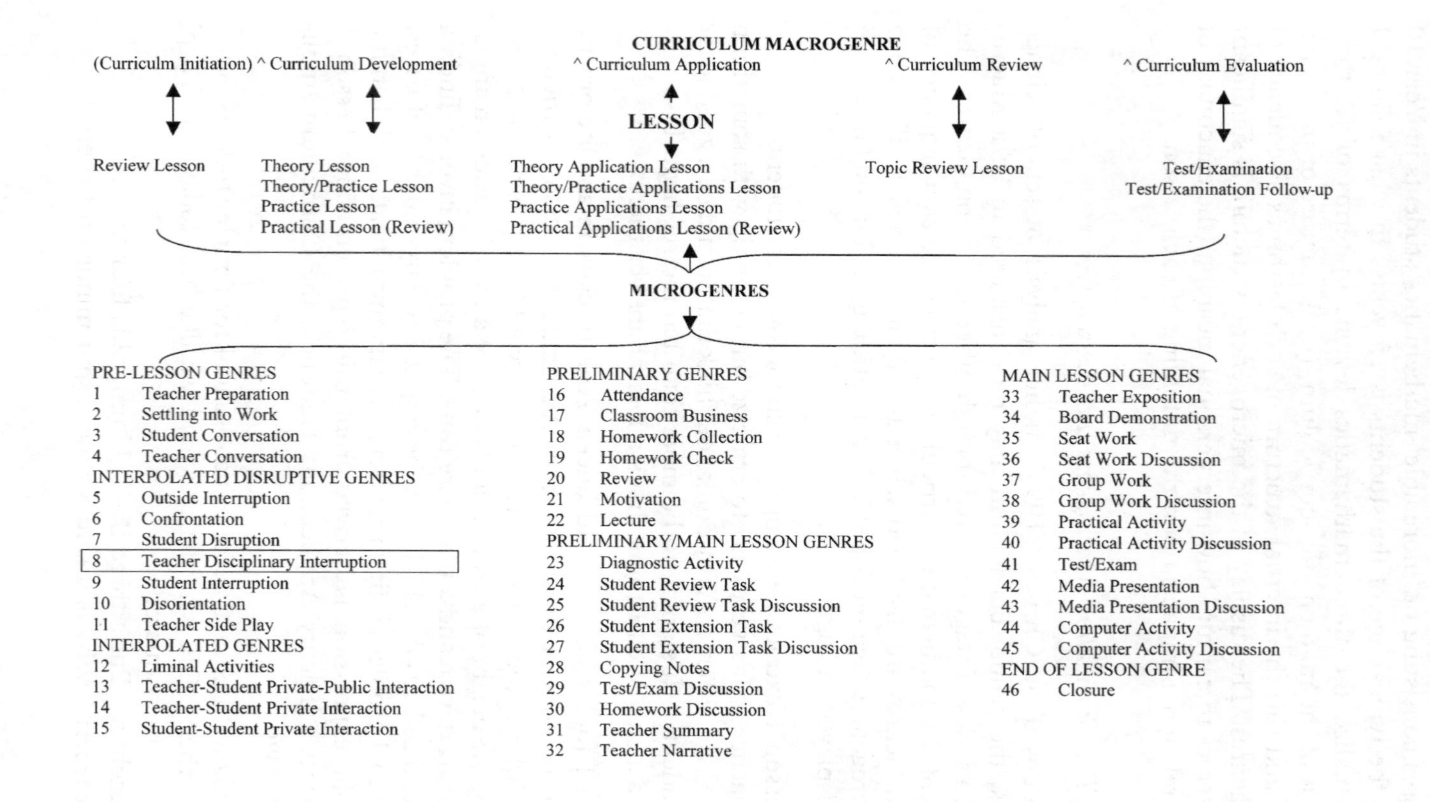

Figure 9.1 The Curriculum Macrogenre, Lesson Genres and Microgenres

Lesson 2 is an algebra lesson with a comparable Year 10 class in an elite private school for girls. The lesson commences with a student complaint that the homework was difficult and so the teacher reviews the solution of quadratic equations using the quadratic formula. The remainder of the lesson is concerned with the solution of word problems involving these equations. The lesson constitutes a hybrid mixture of the Curriculum Development and Curriculum Application stages in the Macrogenre. The Lesson Genre is a hybrid combination of the Review Lesson and Practice Applications Lesson.

3 Lesson 3 (extract): working-class government co-educational school

Student:	But aren't they supposed to change if they're negative?
Teacher:	But there's no negative there.
Student:	Oh. It's in front of it ... the sign. Ahh.
Teacher:	We all do it mate.

Lesson 3 is an algebra lesson in a comparable Year 10 working-class government school. The lesson commences with the teacher directing the students to complete the review questions on the board involving the simplification of algebraic expressions through addition, subtraction and multiplication. After the answers to the homework are given, the teacher demonstrates the new content of the lesson which involves simplification of algebraic expressions by removing brackets. The students then complete practice problems from a worksheet. As such this is a Theory/Practice Lesson from the Curriculum Development stage.

9.2.2 Variation in the lesson structure

It must be acknowledged that here is an inherent variation in the classroom discourse arising from the fact that the lessons under consideration represent various stages in the Curriculum Macrogenre and different Lesson Genres where the material being taught ranges from trigonometry to algebra. For example, in the trigonometry lesson in Lesson 1 these differences include a much greater incidence of prepositional phrases realizing circumstance because the diagram is central to the discussion at various phases of the lesson. However, as I demonstrate below, certain facets of the semantic clusters arising from the linguistic selections in each lesson cannot be reasonably explained from this position alone. That is, the nature of the Lesson Genres and the differing fields of the discourse cannot account for all the dimensions of variation which become apparent in the discourse analysis. To illustrate this point, I display graphically the lesson structure for Lessons 1, 2 and 3.

The Lesson Genre may be considered to be a series of stages as suggested by Lemke's (1990) formulation of Activity Types (see Figure 9.1). I call these stages Microgenres and classify them according to their particular configurations of Field, Tenor and Mode selections (O'Halloran 1996: 559–70). These Microgenres are classified as Pre-Lesson, Interpolated Disruptive, Interpolated, Preliminary, Main and End of Lesson Microgenres. For example, the Microgenre, 'Teacher Disciplinary Interruption' (see highlighted in box in Figure 9.1) is classified as an 'Interpolated Disruptive Genre'. The description of the Field, Tenor and Mode selections for this Microgenre is given below:

Teacher Disciplinary Interruption

The teacher interrupts the genre-in-progress for disciplinary purposes.

Field:	Related to student behaviour.
Tenor:	Participants: teacher and student(s).
Affect:	Low-high/neutral to negative.
Power:	Unequal relations with full exposure of the teacher's positioning as dominating.
Mode:	i. oral (two-way, turn-restricted, turn-controlled, quasi-dialogue). ii. constitutive (construction/reconstruction).

Shifts in the Field, Tenor and/or Mode configuration realized linguistically through selections from the systems for ideational, interpersonal and textual meaning are recorded as movements to a different Microgenre. The lesson transcripts are divided into groups of clauses realizing the different Microgenres according to the list given in Figure 9.1. The shifts between the Microgenres (according to number given in Figure 9.1) are displayed according to the clause number in Figures 9.2, 9.3 and 9.4 for Lessons 1, 2 and 3 respectively. The hollow circles depicted in the graphs represent private talk amongst the teacher/students. The function of the graphs is to map the shifts between the Pre-Lesson, Interpolated Disruptive, Interpolated, Preliminary, Main and End of Lesson Microgenres in order to map the generic structure of each lesson.

The clear and progressive structure of Lesson 1 may be contrasted to Lessons 2 and 3, which consist of a series of disjointed movements between different Microgenres as shown by Figures 9.2 and 9.3. In Lesson 2 this may in part be due to the hybrid nature of the lesson

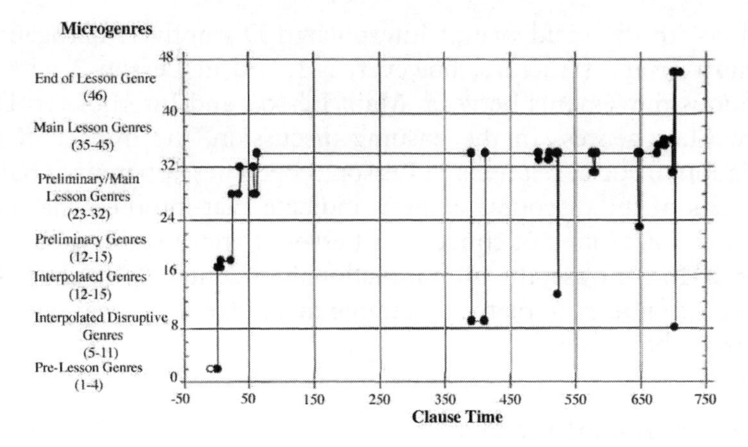

Figure 9.2 Lesson 1 as a sequence of Microgenres

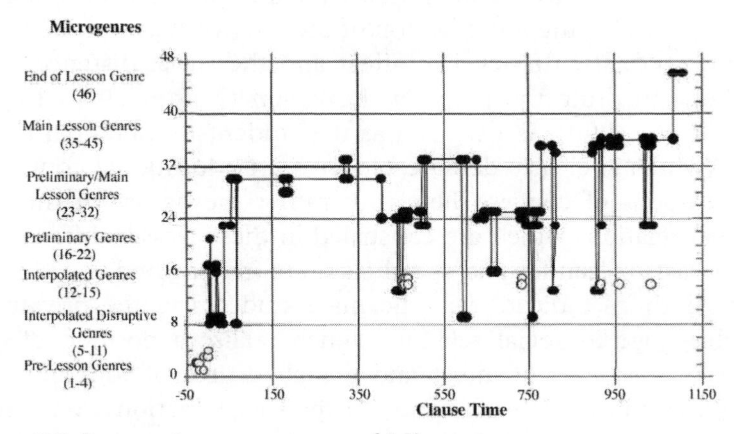

Figure 9.3 Lesson 2 as a sequence of Microgenres

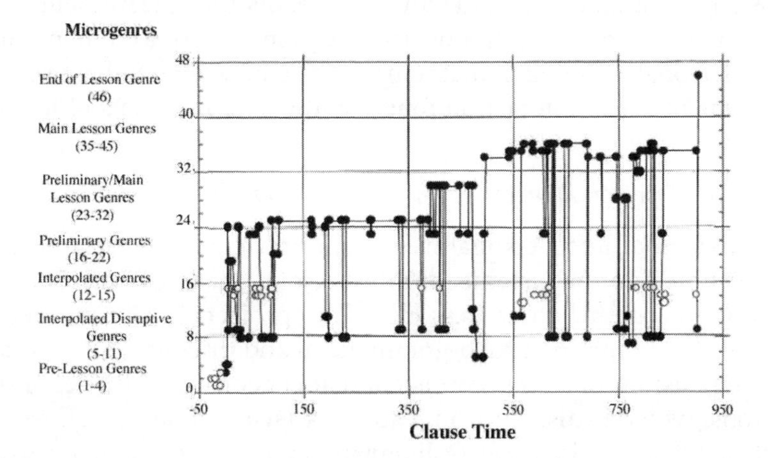

Figure 9.4 Lesson 3 as a sequence of Microgenres

together with the incidence of Interpolated Disruptive Microgenres. The most erratic structure, however, is found in Lesson 3 with its continuous movements between Main Lesson and Interpolated Disruptive Microgenres. In the ensuing discussion, the impact of the negotiation of social relations in Lesson 3 becomes apparent. That is, the results of the discourse analysis indicate that interpersonal relations are a major area of concern in Lesson 3 and, to a lesser extent, Lesson 2. In contrast, the monofunctional tendency (O'Toole 1994) in Lesson 1 appears to be the ideational meaning, or the mathematics content of the lesson.

9.3 Interpersonal meaning

The linguistic choices from systems for interpersonal meaning provide the basis for the investigation of the relative status of the teacher and the students, the level of affect and the social distance, which together constitute the tenor of the lesson (Martin 1992; Poynton 1984, 1985, 1990). Issues such as the students' differential right to speak (which is clearly demarcated in most educational contexts) is not the focus of concern here, but rather the nature of the interpersonal relations which are construed in these classes differentiated on the basis of gender and social class are investigated.

The findings indicate that the male students in the private elite school engage in social relations which realize a position of dominance, a low level of affect and a high degree of formality. This position contrasts with the nature of the social relations construed in the class of female students in the elite private female school and the working-class students in the low socio-economic government school. This raises further questions (see section 9.6.3) as the nature of interpersonal meaning in mathematics discourse match these semantic patterns of social interaction found in the elite male school lesson.

9.3.1 Interpersonal meaning in the classroom discourse

The nature of interpersonal meaning in the three classrooms arising from choices in the systems for interpersonal meaning (see Table 9.1) varies across the three lessons. The projection of interpersonal meaning through the lexico-grammatical and discourse systems along the dimensions of status, contact and affect constitute the tenor of the lessons, which is displayed in Table 9.4 (see section 9.3.2). Martin's (1992: 529) classification of linguistic patterns of status are used to determine the relative status of the interlocutors.

In terms of status, uniformly the teacher occupies a position of power as evident from the initiation, control and sheer number of contributions in the Exchange Structure (see Table 9.2). At a more delicate level, however, we may see that finer distinctions exist between the status of the teacher and negotiation of power with the students across the three lessons.

In Lesson 1, there is a greater tendency for the teacher and the students to interact on a direct basis compared with the other two lessons. This is evidenced by linguistic patterns such as interpersonal congruence as opposed to interpersonal metaphor through the use of unmarked MOOD choices for the different SPEECH FUNCTIONS. That is, questions, statements and commands tend to be realized congruently through interrogative, declarative and imperative MOOD respectively in Lesson 1. For example, instances of interpersonal MOOD metaphor where the teachers select interrogative MOOD for commands occur in 2.4 per cent, 10.9 per cent and 8.2 per cent of cases respectively in Lessons 1, 2 and 3. The relatively low incidence of metaphorical realizations in Lesson 1 indicates that the teacher interacts with the students on a more direct basis where power is openly enacted. There is also a lack of contestation of power in Lesson 1 with students respecting and participating in turn-taking procedures so that the lesson proceeds in the manner prescribed by the teacher as displayed by the smooth unfolding of the Lesson Genre in Figure 9.2. There seems to be a directness and congruence in the relationship between the teacher and the students which is not found in the other two lessons.

Table 9.2 Exchange Structure

	NATURE OF EXCHANGE		
	LESSON 1	LESSON 2	LESSON 3
Number of Exchanges	200	404	257
Average Length of Exchange	3.54 clauses	2.64 clauses	2.91 clauses
Teacher-Initiated Exchanges	198	398	239
Student-Initiated Exchanges	2	6	18
Ratio of teacher clauses: Student	1:0.25	1:0.13	1:0.27

The greater incidence of interpersonal metaphor in Lessons 2 and 3 is sometimes related to covert disciplinary strategies. In Lesson 2, for instance, the teacher covertly disciplines the female students while maintaining an aura of pleasantness, patience, co-operation and tolerance as illustrated by the following commands to the class:

Teacher: Alright girls can I just have your attention please?
Teacher: Can you open up the work please?
Teacher: OK will you just look at the screen please?
Teacher: Can you tell me . . . ?
Teacher: Can we just ask questions?
Teacher: So can you just put your pens down for a second?
Teacher: Can you put your hand up?

These attributes, together with safety and convenience, are also promoted in part through lexical choice in Lesson 2. Although comment is presented, it is often in the form of euphemistic expressions. According to Martin's (1992: 529) classification of linguistic patterns of status, an overall tendency to a deferential position is manifested with the female students in Lesson 2 through the use of covert lexis together with the use of interpersonal metaphor.

In Lesson 3, although students demonstrate some degree of power through the initiation of exchanges as displayed in Table 9.2, these are largely disruptions which are quickly stopped by the teacher. The teacher's response in this class, however, is different to the genteel politeness and patience of the disciplinary actions in Lesson 2. The teacher uses gentle sarcasm and dry humour as a control mechanism, and this often entails the use of dysphemic and euphemistic selections. As explained by Allen and Burridge (1991), covert lexis reveals uses of language as a 'veil, shield and weapon' largely oriented to manipulation of others. This use of covert lexis also contributes to establishing a deferential position in power relations for the students.

Teacher: Sorry I'm going so fast Terry.
Teacher: I just like things to be clear. [Students' laughter]
Teacher: It's for my benefit.

The underlying balance in the status or power relations between the teacher and the male students in Lesson 1 extend beyond the realm of interpersonal congruence. For example, student contributions tend to reflect those of the teacher. The interactions are extended with minimal ellipsis, and the chorus answers and paralinguistic behaviour of Lessons 2 and 3 do not occur. Responsibility is individual rather than group. This may be contrasted to the situation in Lesson 3 where low-social-status students are positioned as members of a group whose few contributions are characterized by brevity, ellipsis, and paralinguistic and chorus responses. In Lesson 3 the interactions are moderately extended while in Lesson 2, due to a lower incidence of dynamic moves and clause complex relations, the exchanges with

the female students are the shortest. In addition, it appears that maximal (that is, an absence of modality) to high values for modalization and modulation are a feature of mathematics classrooms, but in Lesson 2 with the female students, we find the greatest incidence of explicit values of modality which paradoxically promotes a lower level of certainty.
The selection of MOOD Adjuncts (displayed in Table 9.3) in Lesson 1 function to promote a high level of presumption and a lowered level

Table 9.3 MOOD Adjuncts

	LESSON 1		LESSON 2		LESSON 3	
	Total	per cent	Total	per cent	Total	per cent
MOOD ADJUNCT	90	100	126	100	50	100
Intensity	38	42.2	69	54.8	37	74.0
Degree	3	3.3	11	8.47	2	4.0
Time	14	15.6	17	13.5	7	14.0
Presumption	21	23.3	4	3.2	4	2.0
Probability	12	13.3	19	15.1	3	6.0
Usuality	2	2.2	6	4.7		
Mood Adjuncts per ranking clause	$\frac{90}{708}$	12.7 per cent	$\frac{126}{1067}$	11.8 per cent	$\frac{50}{749}$	6.7%

of intensity in the classroom discourse. This high level of presumption is not found in Lessons 2 and 3. Rather, while the humour may act as a disciplinary measure to maintain the interpersonal relations in Lesson 3, the view that mathematics is too difficult for the majority of these students may be implied. The opposite view is promoted with the male students in Lesson 1 with its high levels of presumption and non-acceptance of excuse, while in Lesson 2 difficulties for the girls are commonly related to external factors.

The social contact with the boys in Lesson 1 is involved but non-intimate as suggested by the selections of Vocatives (for example, 'people', and given first names). These function to realize formal and reserved interpersonal relations. In Lesson 2, Vocation selections tend to be familiar and more intimate through choices of hypocorisms for names and colloquial forms of address (for example, 'guys' to refer to the girls as a group, and abbreviations such as 'Libby', 'Steph', 'Fie', 'Fran'). Although the teacher's overt position of dominance is evident in this lesson, these types of linguistic patterns function to reduce the formality. The types of Vocative selected in Lesson 3 occur in roughly the same proportion as Lesson 2. However, in Lesson 3 the teacher's position of dominance is reinforced by the multiple selections of 'sir'. This division between the teacher and the student is offset by the choice of 'mate' as a form of address for the students. As will be seen, this operates in conjunction with colloquial expressions to manifest a spirit of comradeship which functions with the covert operation of power.

In Lesson 1, the level of affect is minimal, as demonstrated by the lack of linguistic selections for attitude, comment, lexis and amplification. The paucity of amplification of lexical items through intensification and repetition means that surges of interpersonal meaning generally do not occur in this lesson with the male students. In addition, the lack of attitudinal lexis, displays of mental affection and absence of exclamatives and paralinguistic behaviour means that the tone is controlled, steady, serious, assured and minimally expressive in terms of emotion. With minor exceptions, affective meaning is quietly controlled with comments being reserved for the mathematical content of the lesson. This position may be compared to Lessons 2 and 3 where exclamatives, amplification of lexical items and colloquialisms realize surges of interpersonal meaning. The high incidence of colloquial expressions and fixed expressions is indeed a feature of the discourse of Lesson 3, and these forms of expression may be interpreted as facets of a restricted code (see section 9.6.3). Further to this, in Lesson 3 the strategies of disciplinary manipulation operate with the use of these colloquialisms and fixed expressions. While the students are being covertly controlled, the colloquial lexical items function to promote familiarity, solidarity and group cohesiveness. That is, the colloquialisms function to align the teacher with the students despite the obvious power differential and control strategies. The impact of the surges of interpersonal meaning is apparent in the erratic generic structure of Lessons 2 and 3 where there is constant need to control the flow of the lesson.

9.3.2 Tenor

In Lesson 1 visible control is exercised by the teacher, unlike the more covert strategies used in Lessons 2 and 3 as summarized in Table 9.4. However, while the teacher has explicitly a higher status as indicated by the nature of the exchange structure across all three lessons, the nature of the implicit power relations is more equal in Lesson 1 where the emphasis is towards interacting congruently with individual students.

The directness of the Tenor relations and the nature of the linguistic selections for interpersonal meaning therefore suggest that the

Table 9.4 Tenor relations

Dimension of Interpersonal Meaning	Middle/Upper-Class Students		Working-Class Students	Mathematical Discourse
	Lesson 1 (Male students)	Lesson 2 (Female Students)	Lesson 3 (Male/ female students)	
REGISTER				
TENOR CONTROL AND STATUS	Visible control and explicit unequal status, with implicit equal status	Invisible control and explicit unequal status, with implicit unequal status	Invisible control and explicit unequal status, with implicit unequal status	Visible control and high status
ORIENTATION	The individual with high student input	The individual and group with minimal student input	The group with moderate student input	The individual

male students in Lesson 1 operate from a position of dominance as opposed to the more deferential position of the students in Lessons 2 and 3. It appears that in combination with learning mathematics, the male students are also learning how to negotiate power. Given the elite nature of the school, presumably the majority of the male students in Lesson 1 are implicitly being groomed for future positions and the teacher is mentor for that ascendancy. As demonstrated by their results in university entrance exams (O'Halloran 1996: 524–7), the social status of the teacher is lower than the one that these students will most likely attain in their future professions.

9.4 Ideational meaning

There is not sufficient space here to give a complete description of all facets of the experiential and logical meaning of Lessons 1, 2 and 3 where the different content of the lessons must necessarily be reflected. Rather, I select particular dimensions of the analysis that shed light on the more general similarities and differences across the lessons, and also those that highlight particular features of the pedagogical discourse and board texts that are specific to mathematics classrooms. For this last objective, I concentrate on Lesson 1 because the nature of the texture of mathematical discourse is most apparent in this lesson.

In order to theorize the nature of mathematical discourse, I introduce the notion of Operative processes in mathematical symbolism (see O'Halloran 1996, 1999, 2000, in press (a)). These processes, which are also realized linguistically in the oral discourse, are mathematical operations such as addition, subtraction, multiplication and division, for instance.

9.4.1 Experiential meaning in the classroom discourse

The prominent trend across all lessons is that the most frequently selected process is Relational (Attributive and Identifying). Relational processes constitute 37.9 per cent, 38.5 per cent and 41.7 per cent of the total processes selected respectively in Lessons 1, 2 and 3 in ranking and rankshifted clauses. Across the spectrum of Relational processes, the Intensive Attributive and Intensive Identifying processes are the most common. More specifically, however, the dominant category of Relational process is Attributive. However, Material processes, or processes of 'doing', occur in nearly equal proportions to the Relational Attributive processes in each lesson. In Lesson 2, if Attributive and Identifying processes are considered as separate categories, then Material processes occur most often. Although the difference is slight, this tends to suggest that Lesson 2 is more orientated towards action than the other two lessons.

In Lesson 1, Mental processes of Cognition and Perception also feature. It appears that in Lesson 1, the experiential meaning is concerned with 'being', 'doing' and 'thinking' with the major participants being mathematical entities, the teacher and the students. In Lessons 2 and 3, as another indication of the emphasis on interpersonal meaning, Mental processes of Affection are more common. Although it would be a valuable exercise to examine in more detail the differences across the lessons in terms of the participants and circumstantial elements attached to each process type, given the constraints of this chapter, I instead focus on more general features of the experiential meaning of the discourse.

One significant pattern that emerges in the separation of rankshifted clauses from ranking clauses is the predominance of embedded Operative processes. For Lessons 1, 2 and 3, from 4.5 per cent, 3.4 per cent and 3.8 per cent of the total number of processes in ranking clauses, Operative processes rise to 24.1 per cent, 42.3 per cent and 37.6 per cent of processes in rankshifted clauses. As Lessons 2 and 3 are concerned with algebra, there is a relatively higher incidence of rankshifted Operative processes in these lessons. For example, in Lesson 3 the teacher gives the answers to the homework which contain multiple rankshifted Operative processes: 'number eleven [eight 'x' squared minus five 'x' minus four]'. These results clearly indicate that participants in mathematical discourse are often rankshifted nuclear configurations of Operative processes and mathematical participants. This trend is found in both the oral and the symbolic discourse. These configurations are in a constant process of reconfiguration as the symbolic solution to the problem is derived. In combination with the depth of rankshift involved, the continual rearrangement of the configurations of Operative processes and participants can generate difficulties in penetrating mathematical discourse. These difficulties arise in both the symbolic text, with its own unique lexicogrammar which is distinct from that of natural language, and the oral discourse, where levels of rankshift are compounded with possible syntactic ambiguity when the symbolic text is verbalized (O'Halloran, 1996, 2000, in press(a)). Also, other possible problems of interpretation arise because the reconfigurations of mathematical participants and processes often occur on the basis of mathematical results, properties and definitions which are implicit. In terms of the similarities and differences across the three lessons, the

Table 9.5 Classification of mathematical register items

	LESSON 1 (Male)		LESSON 2 (Female)		LESSON 3 (Co-ed)	
	Total	per cent	Total	per cent	Total	per cent
CLASSIFICATION	532	100	586	100	315	100
Technical	439	82.5	425	72.5	163	51.6
Jargon	39	7.3	13	2.2	45	14.5
Non-technical	54	10.2	148	25.3	107	33.9

analysis of the mathematical lexical items displayed in Table 9.5 reveals that Lesson 1 has the highest percentage of technical expressions and the lowest percentage of non-technical terms. The relative proportion of technical terms for mathematics register items is 82.5 per cent, 72.5 per cent, and 51.6 per cent for Lessons 1, 2 and 3 respectively. As I discuss below, this is one indicator of the relative positioning of each lesson in relation to the formal discourse of mathematics.

The Field of the mathematics lesson in Lesson 3 is simplification of algebraic expressions. However, as apparent from the range of different Microgenres constituting the Lesson Genre displayed in Figure 4, the Field selections change frequently throughout the lesson. However, when the Field is the mathematical content, we may see from Table 9.5 that technical lexis is not always selected. That is, more than one-third of all mathematical register items in Lesson 3 are non-technical lexical items. This indicates that the discourse of Lesson 3 deviates to the greatest extent from the formal discourse of mathematics. In particular, non-technical selections such as 'letters' and 'numbers' for 'variables' and 'constants' respectively appear not only in the oral discourse, but also are written on the board. This feature of the classroom discourse in Lesson 3 must necessarily impact on the nature of taxonomic relations. First, major classificatory and compositional items of the mathematical taxonomy for simplification of algebraic expressions are absent, or those that do appear are most commonly non-technical terms. For instance, the term 'algebraic expression' is not used to identify the symbolic statements. The components of the terms of the algebraic expressions are not referred to by their technical names of 'constants' and 'variables'. Non-technical items such as 'x squareds' and 'subtracts' are used to identify particular terms of the algebraic expressions. Other selections for mathematical participants are context dependent, for example, 'this bit', 'this [happens as one chunk]', 'around something', 'more than one bit' and 'this one'. In addition, the algebraic properties and definitions used in simplifying the algebraic expressions are not referred to. Instead, the simplification proceeds on the basis of 'rules'.

In Lesson 2, non-technical lexis accounts for 25.3 per cent of mathematical register items. These include selections such as 'adding and taking', 'that bit', 'minus b' and 'this thing'. We may see that these selections are also non-taxonomic and context dependent. This may be compared to Lesson 1 where technical taxonomic relations include those for triangles ('right triangle'), parts of triangle ('adjacent side', 'hypotenuse', 'right angle'), trigonometric relations ('tangent ratio', 'cotangent'), arithmetic processes ('addition', 'subtraction', 'divide') and algebraic relations ('statement', 'expression', 'equation', 'subject').

Lessons 2 and 3 also contain different register items. In Lesson 3, for example, these include items from an education register, such as 'correction time' and 'put your hand up', as well as items from diverse fields such as gambling, medicine and film (for example, 'I'll lay odds', 'bruising', 'candid camera' and 'that would probably take the award').

In Lesson 3, from several of the exchanges (for example, one student asks 'can you just explain that sign thing again'), it becomes apparent that the new content of the lesson is not understood by all students. One contributing factor is the differing functions of particular symbolic components as illustrated by the shifts in functions of the symbols '+' and '–' from Operative processes of addition and subtraction to Classifier in participant functions: for example, 'positive and negative one'. These shifts in status of the '+' and '–' are acknowledged (for example, Borowski and Borwein 1989: 452). However, in the oral and written discourse of Lesson 3, these symbols are assigned different functions indiscriminately. Further to this, with statements like '+ = same' and '– = opp. sign' as displayed in Figure 9.5, it is apparent that the board text of Lesson 3 is non-generic and context dependent. This may be compared to sections of the board text from the other two lessons (see Figures 9.6 and 9.7) which shows that only Lesson 1 contains generic, context-independent board texts. Once again, this indicates the location of each lesson with respect to the formal discourse of mathematics.

Parentheses

$+ (3x - 2)$
$= 3x - 2$

$- (3x - 2)$
$= -3x + 2$

+ = same

– = opp sign

Figure 9.5 Section of board text: lesson 3

$a \quad a + 2$

$a^2 + (a+2)^2 = 340$

$a^2 + a^2 + 4a + 4 = 340$

$2a^2 + 4a - 336 = 0$

$a = {}^2 \quad b = 4 \quad c = -336$

Figure 9.6 Section of board text: lesson 2

Examples of grammatical metaphor in Lesson 1 which realize experiential meaning are listed in Table 9.6. In these examples, the

In the right Δ CBR:

$$\tan \alpha = \frac{h - 10}{r} \quad (1)$$

In the right Δ ABR:

$$\tan \Theta = \frac{h}{r} \quad (2)$$

Algebraically obtain ONE variable as the subject of EACH equation

From (1): $h - 10 = r (\tan \alpha)$

$\therefore h = 10 + r (\tan \alpha)$

(2) $h = r (\tan \Theta)$

Figure 9.7 Section of board text: lesson 1

grammatical metaphor involves a shift from process to entity. That is, the processes of 'differing', 'extending', 'equating' and 'fracturing' become the entities difference, extension, equation and fractions respectively. Further to this, by virtue of the meaning potential of the semiotic codes of visual diagrammatic display and symbolism, new entities such as 'angles of elevation and depression' arise. These selections function to make the oral and written discourse dense through the packing of experiential meaning in nominal group structures. However, the density arising from the unique lexico-grammatical strategy of clausal rankshift in the symbolic text is perhaps more problematic for students, in addition to the nature of the metaphorical expressions which occur as shifts in semiotic codes (that is, linguistic, visual and symbolic) occur (O'Halloran 1996, 2000; in press(a) and (b)).

In summary, although the students in Lesson 3 are engaged in learning the basic grammar of algebraic operations, the lack of mathematical technical expressions and taxonomic relations, and the non-generic board texts indicate that shifts or scaffolds to mathematical discourse are not being made. In addition, it is apparent that the discourse often moves away from the mathematical content of the lesson. This position may be compared with Lesson 1 where features

Table 9.6 Grammatical metaphor and experiential meaning

RANK AND METAFUNCTION	**GRAMMATICAL METAPHOR**
process	**entity**
	1. 'Thing' in nominal group
differ	// such that we have **a ten metre difference** [in height] here
extend	// so you are making **extensions** [to diagrams]
equate	// we've got **two equations**
fracture	// which then leads to **fractions** doesn't it
	2. 'Thing' in Qualifier of nominal group
elevate, depress	// the problems [with calculating angles [**of elevation and depression**]]
express	// so a strategy would be <in other words> would be [algebraically obtain 'r' [as a subject [**of each expression**]]
equate	// you choose one variable [as the subject [**of each equation**]]
	3. 'Thing' in prepositional phrase
possess	// the man has two things [**in his possession**]
inform	// so [with **this information**] [he has a ten metre rope and a device [that measures angles]] we are asking the question
express	// so we will get both of them [in **expression** [of 'r']]

of the discourse include technical expressions, precise taxonomic relations and generic board texts. Lesson 2 appears to lie between these two extremes. In Lesson 1 we also may see facets of mathematical pedagogical discourse such as rankshifted reconfigurations of mathematical processes and participants, and instances of ambiguity and metaphor in the moments between mathematical symbolism and language.[2]

9.4.2 Logical meaning in the classroom discourse

The analysis of the LOGICO-SEMANTIC relations for clause-complex relations (Halliday 1994: Ch. 7; Martin 1992: 179) reveals that the most common form of relation is EXPANSION, whereby a secondary clause expands a primary clause through Elaboration, Extension or Enhancement. However, there are relatively differing degrees of exploitation of this resource with 46.6 per cent, 35.3 per cent and 32.1 per cent of ranking clauses in Lessons 1, 2 and 3 respectively containing such a selection. This tends to suggest that logical meaning plays a more significant role in Lesson 1. These results further indicate that the pedagogical discourse in this lesson with male students is more aligned with mathematical discourse than the other two lessons.

If the clause-complex relations of teacher and student contributions are considered separately as displayed in Table 9.7, we may see that in Lesson 1 students select for logical meaning approximately three times more often than their counterparts in Lessons 2 and 3. For relations of EXPANSION, the proportions of total contributions by students are respectively 18.2 per cent, 6.6 per cent and 6.4 per cent. This tends to indicate that resources for logical meaning are exploited more often by the male students in their extended classroom interactions.

Table 9.7 LOGICO-SEMANTIC relations: teacher and student

	LESSON 1		LESSON 2		LESSON 3	
NATURE OF RELATION	Total	per cent	Total	per cent	Total	per cent
Expansion (n = 30)	330	100	376	100	235	100
Teacher	270	81.8	351	93.4	220	93.6
Students	60	18.2	25	6.6	15	6.4
Projection (n=73)	73	100	91	100	45	100
Teacher	61	83.6	89	97.8	42	93.3
Students	12	16.4	2	2.2	3	6.7

In what follows, I briefly discuss the type of clause-complex relations for EXPANSION and INTERDEPENDENCY found in Lesson 1. These results are contextualized with respect to Lessons 2 and 3. The predominant type of relation in Lesson 1 is paratactic while the most common category of EXPANSION is Enhancement. These logical relations are realized through selections for consequential relations (for example, 'so', 'if', 'because', 'so as'), temporal relations (for example, 'then') and additive relations (for example, 'and'). Given the field-structured nature of the discourse, the occurrence of the latter relations is not surprising. However, the nature of the logical relations is such that the lesson is orientated towards consequence, either as occurring 'naturally' or as a result of some predetermined condition. The high incidence of these relations results in long implication chains of reasoning in the oral discourse of Lesson 1. While the majority of relations are external and as such are orientated to experiential meaning, the incidence of selections realizing internal relations is the highest in Lesson 1, indicating the greatest level of rhetorical organization. This position resonates with the nature of logical relations realized in mathematical texts.

Although not as prevalent, the LOGICO-SEMANTIC relations for EXPANSION in Lesson 2 reveal similar patterns to those found in Lesson 1. So while logical relations are not as prolific, the basis for making these (in press(a) and (b)) connections remains similar in Lesson 2. However, the majority of logical relations are external, indicating an orientation towards experiential meaning which is most marked in Lesson 2. It appears that the oral discourse is not primarily orientated towards constructing rhetorical arguments, which is surprising in view of the Field being algebra. This position does not resonate with the symbolic mathematical text of the lesson where the logical organization is predominantly internal.

While the patterns of LOGICO-SEMANTIC relations in Lesson 3 basically reflect those found in Lessons 1 and 2, the lowest incidence of logical relations are found in this lesson. In addition, nearly 40 per cent of logical relations are implicitly realized with few student contributions in Lesson 3. However, as a common trend across all lessons, logical relations tend to be realized congruently.

Selections from the system of CONTINUITY (Martin 1992: 230–4) realized through thematic Continuatives such as 'OK', 'well', 'right' occur in 19.5 per cent, 6.6 per cent and 8.0 per cent of ranking clauses in Lessons 1, 2 and 3. This is one further indication that logical progression and coherence is more prominent in Lesson 1 compared with the other two lessons.

9.4.3 Field

In addition to the impact of interpersonal meaning, the graphical representation of the generic structure of Lessons 1, 2 and 3 in Figures 9.2. 9.3 and 9.4 also give some indication of the degrees of shift in Field across the lessons. With minor exceptions, Lesson 1 is confined to some dimension of the activity sequence of teaching and learning trigonometry. The fields of the Microgenres are the course content, the homework, tests, student performance on a set task or a narrative associated with the specific problem under consideration. The teacher and students are fully engaged with the activity sequence of learning and teaching to the exclusion of any other activity. Although not discussed here, the strategies that the teacher employs such as narrative, questioning and analogy are aimed at developing the mathematical content.

On the other hand, as indicated by the range and nature of the

Microgenres and the range of register items, the Field of the discourse shifts away from mathematics in Lessons 2 and 3. Here the students are engaged in other activities apart from learning mathematical discourse, and this is most pronounced in Lesson 3. Furthermore, when the field is the mathematical content, technical lexis is not typically selected in the oral discourse in Lesson 3. This means that taxonomic relations are not constructed and, furthermore, these non-generic context-dependent forms extend to the written board texts. Therefore contextual parameters play a greater role in ideational meaning in Lessons 2 and 3. Thus the context-independent generic board texts, the nature of selections for mathematical register items, the taxonomic relations and the emphasis on logical meaning means that the semantics of the ideational meaning of the discourse in Lesson 1 is more aligned with the formal discourse of mathematics compared with Lessons 2 and 3.

9.5 Textual meaning

It is not possible to discuss each dimension of textual organization of the discourses across the lessons, so once again I shall limit the discussion to the major features.

9.5.1 Textual meaning in the classroom discourse

From the system of THEME, the classification and nature of the Theme selections for the oral discourse of Lessons 1, 2 and 3 are displayed in Table 9.8. These results suggest that the textual organization in Lesson 1 is sophisticated, with patterns that include the highest incidence of marked Themes and the lowest incidence of unmarked and ellipsed Themes. These patterns tend to align the oral discourse of Lesson 1 with written discourse since the choice of Theme as the point of departure for the message shows variation and operates as a strategy to foreground selected meanings. The low occurrence of thematic ellipsis is another manifestation of the more formal basis of the spoken discourse. Further to this, Lesson 1 has the highest percentage of multiple Thematic elements since, in addition to the ideational meaning realized through the Topic, interpersonal and textual thematic components also occur.

Lesson 2 is situated between the extremes of the other two lessons with respect to the sophistication of textual organization. However, although the individual components of the multiple Themes are not displayed here, Lesson 2 has the greatest proportion of interpersonal

Table 9.8 Classification and components of Theme selections

	LESSON 1		LESSON 2		LESSON 3	
	Total	per cent	Total	per cent	Total	per cent
	708	100	1067	100	734	100
THEME CLASSIFICATION						
Unmarked	413	58.3	704	66.0	431	58.8
Marked	78	11.0	64	6.0	34	4.6
Dependent	35	4.9	47	4.4	41	5.6
Embedded	5	0.7	16	1.5	11	1.5
Ellipsed	54	7.6	135	12.6	138	18.7
No theme (minor clause or dependent Non-finite clause	123	17.5	97	9.1	77	10.5
Unknown	0	0	4	0.4	2	0.3
NATURE OF THEME						
No Thematic components						
Ellipsed topic	37	5.2	111	10.4	128	17.5
Minor clause and Non-finite dependent clauses	73	10.3	69	6.5	53	7.2
Single Theme (Topic only)	242	34.2	447	41.9	339	46.2
Multiple Theme	356	50.3	436	40.9	211	28.8

thematic elements. This may be compared to Lesson 1 where selections are more frequently related to textual organization. In general, the textual organisation of Lesson 3 is the least complex with the colloquial nature of the discourse extending to thematic patterns. Together with the lowest incidence of marked Themes and multiple thematic elements, Lesson 3 contains the highest incidence of ellipsed Themes and single Themes.

The nature of the field of the Topic selection for Lessons 1, 2 and 3 was categorized as 'interlocutors' (the teacher, the students, the collective group), 'mathematics' (a mathematical lexical item, a wh-item, th-item, a pronoun or related to the mathematical content), 'student work', 'an action' and 'others'. In Lesson 1 the majority of Topics are connected to the mathematical content, and the teacher, the students or both form the second most common point of departure for the message. In Lesson 3, the difference between the relative frequency of mathematical content versus the interlocutors is minimal. However, in Lesson 2, the interlocutors are selected as Theme most often. This tends to suggest that the mathematical content is foregrounded to the greatest extent in Lesson 1 and, furthermore, perhaps this is another indication of the prominence of interpersonal meaning over ideational meaning in Lesson 2. It appears that thematic selections operate to foreground the students and their work as opposed to the mathematical content of the lesson in Lesson 2.

When the teacher and/or students are selected as the Topic, however, the students as a collective group are selected proportionally more often in Lessons 2 and 3. There is a greater tendency in Lesson 1 for the teacher to identify with the students as Topic, which tends to support the findings of the power-dominating tenor relations documented above. It appears that despite the emphasis on interpersonal meaning in Lessons 2 and 3, the line between the teacher and the students is more often drawn in these lessons. Further to this, the ratio of 'other' Themes is greatest in Lesson 3. Nearly one-fifth of the total number of Themes do not concern the teacher, the students, the mathematics or the student work. This once again suggests the varying emphasis directed towards the mathematical content in Lesson 3.

Although not common, Textual Metaphor (Martin 1992: 416–7) occurs most frequently in Lesson 1. 'Meta-message relations' realized as anaphoric nouns and text reference occur (for example, 'this' or 'that') together with 'negotiating texture' which exploits monologic text as dialogic (for example, the frequent use of 'let's'). Also, internal conjunction which orchestrates text organization is most common in Lesson 1. In combination with other lexico-grammatical and discourse patterns, this aligns the oral discourse of Lesson 1 more closely with written discourse compared with the other two lessons.

Although not explored here in detail (see O'Halloran 1996, 2000), at the discourse semantics stratum the tracking of participants realized through the system of IDENTIFICATION (Martin 1992: 93–157) is complex, especially in Lesson 1. This is partly the result of movements between both the constituent modes and the semiotic codes. That is, there is a dynamic interplay between the constitutive and ancillary modes and codes of oral/visual and linguistic/diagrammatic/symbolic respectively. However, the patterns of reference in Lesson 1 are also complex because of the co-joining and splitting of chains. That is, the symbolic solution to the problem involves recombining the participants through mathematical Operative processes into new nuclear configurations. Initially, distinct participants become blended into single participants and composite participants are split into separate participants and then recombined with others. Participants recombine through Operative processes which are not always explicitly marked in the symbolic text but rather depend on an understanding of the lexico-grammar of mathematical symbolism to identify multiple rankshifted nuclear configurations.

In general the reference patterns of Lesson 2 are simpler than those found in Lesson 1, as the mathematical participants are not recombined into new nuclear configurations to the same extent as found in Lesson 1. In addition, the teacher adopts non-generic visual strategies as an aid for tracking in the written text. That is, he draws arrows to link the mathematical participants. Given the transitions between the constituent and ancillary roles of the oral and visual mode, these visual strategies interface with gesture as a strategy for tracking in the oral discourse. Across all lessons, the absence of selections from the system of DEIXIS in the oral discourse is compensated for by gesture which plays an important role in tracking, as does repetition for both the linguistic and the symbolic discourse.

In Lesson 3, one major participant is the student group, as realized by 'you' as the topical element in the Theme. This would usually have the effect of increasing the depth of the level of the rankshifted mathematical participants. However, the reference chains do not often contain linguistic versions of the participants of the symbolic text. Instead, the teacher simplifies the reference patterns through selection of items such as 'it', 'everything', 'thing', 'what' and 'your next line'. In addition to this lexical non-specificity and dependence on contextual factors, the teacher also uses non-technical mathematics register items to refer to participants. These include the 'letters' and 'numbers' for the variables and constants respectively and items such as 'the invisible one'.

The nature of the reference selections in Lesson 3 means that gesture and other contextual factors play an even more important role in realizing textual meaning than in Lessons 1 and 2. Here the students track participants through visual cues rather than extended linguistic reference chains which involve the co-joining and splitting of nuclear configurations of mathematical processes and participants. Significantly, the teacher and the students are not replicating the textual organization which is specific to mathematical oral discourse as found in Lesson 1. Visual cues in the form of gesture organize the oral discourse as metadiscourse for the mathematical symbolic text. The result is discourse which mirrors to a greater extent the textual organization of everyday meaning.

9.5.2 Mode

The constituent mode of each lesson alternates dynamically between the oral and written/visual modes. Particularly in the case where the teacher is demonstrating work on the whiteboard, the two modes are involved in a dynamic interplay in terms of their role as accompanying and constituting the social process. The other feature is that the primary and ancillary codes switch very rapidly between linguistic, visual and symbolic, and this means that classroom discourse is extremely complex and dynamic. The constituent mode through which meanings are made is a function of the stage reached in the solution to the problem and the meaning potential inherent in each of the semiotic codes. For instance, in Lesson 1, the teacher introduces the trigonometric problem linguistically and visually in the form of a diagram. The solution is then derived linguistically and symbolically (O'Halloran 1996).

In summary, from the analysis of textual meaning, we may see that the textual organization of the discourse of Lesson 1 is more closely aligned with formal mathematical discourse. This may be compared to the discourse of Lesson 3 which is more context-dependent like casual spoken discourse. As a general feature of mathematical pedagogical discourse, we may note that the texture is dense due to the inclusion of rankshifted clausal constituents and the multi-semiotic nature of mathematics.

9.6 Implications of analysis

The findings of the discourse analysis of Lessons 1, 2 and 3 are reflected in the performance of the same student cohort from Schools 1, 2 and 3 in the 1995 Tertiary Entrance Examinations (TEE) in mathematics in Western Australia (O'Halloran 1996). Both the number of students who complete TEE mathematics in School 1 and their mean scores are higher than the girls in School 2 though both sets of results are in excess of the average state performance. On the other hand, markedly few students complete TEE mathematics in School 3 and those that do gain lower-than-average results.

In order to interpret the findings of this research project, I turn to Bernstein's (1971, 1973, 1977, 1981, 1990) sociological theory of the relations between social structure, language and education. This concerns Bernstein's (1990) conceptualization of the nature of pedagogical practices and his earlier theorizations of the relations between discursive practices of the school and that of the individual. In the context of this study, I extend Bernstein's discussions of discursive practices to include the discourse of mathematics. Finally I discuss issues of gender which arise from these analyses of mathematics pedagogical practices in single-sex schools.

9.6.1 Bernstein's pedagogical practices

Bernstein (1990) categorizes pedagogic models as oppositions between the conservative/traditional and the progressive/child centred, with the essential logic consisting of hierarchical, sequencing and criterial rules. Those practices with explicit and implicit rules are categorized respectively as visible and invisible pedagogic practices where the former is concerned with the external gradable performance of the learner against model texts and the latter is concerned with internal procedures of students such as cognitive, linguistic, affective and motivational features.

In so far as the ultimate result of the education system in Australia is stratification by rank through the TEE scores which determine subsequent entrance to university, despite political rhetoric to the contrary, the school system may be classified as being based on visible pedagogical practices. Significantly, the nature of the classroom discourse in Lesson 1 reflects this traditional explicit visible pedagogy with the individual as the primary focus. The strong classification (recognition rules of acceptable combinations of Field, Tenor and Mode selections) and framing (regulative control) typical of a visible pedagogy is evident in the tight lesson structure and the nature of Tenor relations of Lesson 1. It appears that Lesson 1 is an example of the traditional model of pedagogy in which the ideology of the educational system as a whole is reflected. Lesson 3, on the other hand, is an example of an invisible pedagogical practice. The weak classification (multiple combinations of Field, Tenor and Mode selections) and framing (plays with regulative control) are evident in the erratic movements between major and interpolated lesson Microgenres and the covert form of control. Though not as accentuated, similarly Lesson 2 contains features of an invisible pedagogical practice. The ramifications of the different types of pedagogical practices are developed below.

9.6.2 Bernstein's discursive practices

Bernstein theorized the social basis for different speech forms and so linked social structure with ranges of meaning potential as the determining factor in educational achievement. Bernstein claimed that patterns of differential educational achievement may be explained by the match or mismatch between the discursive practices of school and those of the student as 'social relations acted selectively on principles and focuses of communication and these in turn created rules of interpretation, relation and identity for the speakers' (Bernstein 1990: 95). Bernstein developed the notion of a restricted and elaborated code, which is discussed in section 9.6.3 in relation to the discourses of Lessons 1, 2 and 3, and mathematics discourse. As part of that discussion, Halliday's (1985) formulations of the differences between spoken and written discourse are also introduced.

The results of the systemic functional analysis of the classroom discourse in Lessons 1, 2 and 3 support Bernstein's findings with respect to the relationship between educational achievement and the discursive practices of the school, the classroom and the individual. That is, different fashions of meaning and pedagogical practices in Lessons 1, 2 and 3 are accompanied by different levels of educational achievement. The insights afforded through a metafunctionally based Systemic Functional Linguistics (SFL) approach to the pedagogical discourse (that is, consideration of interpersonal, ideational and textual meaning) allow for further investigation of the differences in the discursive practices postulated by Bernstein. In addition, as developed in section 9.6.3, Bernstein's consideration of the discursive practices of the school, teacher and students may be extended to include those of the subject being taught, in this case mathematics.

The SFL analysis for interpersonal meaning reveals that the discourse of Lesson 1 is formal compared with Lessons 2 and 3. The lack of variation and amplification of interpersonal meaning in Lesson 1 allows the ideational meaning or the mathematical content to be foregrounded as the focus of the lesson. This is evident in the smooth unfolding of the generic structure of the lesson displayed in Figure 9.2 as compared with Lessons 2 and 3. Interpersonal meaning is not a primary site for contestation in Lesson 1. This same orientation towards ideational meaning does not occur in the other two lessons with the female students and the low social class students. That is, the linguistic choices function to orientate the discourse more towards interpersonal meaning rather than the mathematics content in Lesson 2 and 3.

The most marked difference in classroom discourse occurs in Lesson 3 where the dynamic interplay between the teacher and the students appears to be dominated by interpersonal concerns. That is, at times the prominence of interpersonal meaning functions to override the ideational and textual metafunctions of language with respect to the mathematical content. The teacher's central concern seems to be to maintain the social relations in the classroom. In addition to the use of humour and sarcasm, the teacher balances his techniques of control with the use of colloquial language which functions to create familiarity and solidarity. Linguistic selections of affect and intimate contact mean that the teacher aligns himself with the students while at the same time maintaining control in the classroom. The covert strategies and surges of interpersonal meaning arising from these linguistic selections allow social relations to be maintained. The prominence of interpersonal meaning suggests that the social goal of learning mathematics is not enough to ensure group solidarity in Lesson 3.

The apparently different social purpose of Lesson 3 (one that is based on interpersonal concerns and maintenance of social relations) has significant consequences. First, the teacher and students appear not to be primarily engaged in teaching and learning mathematics. Second, the nature of the linguistic selections means that the students are participating in patterns of deference rather than dominance. In a larger cultural context, the implications of these findings are significant for working-class students. In the more immediate situation of the classroom, these patterns of interpersonal relations are also important because they do not accord with the nature of interpersonal meaning in mathematical discourse as we see in section 9.6.3. In Lesson 3, instead of shifting back and forth between everyday discourse and the bounded semantic realm of mathematical discourse in the classroom discourse (mathematics-in-progress), the students appear to be positioned outside the perimeter of mathematics (mathematics-as-finished-product). On the other hand, the discursive practices in Lesson 1 conflate with those of the school and, significantly, also conflate with those found in mathematics.

9.6.3 The discursive practices of mathematics

Bernstein's theorizations of the social structure and educational achievement resulted in his conceptualization of restricted and elaborated codes which were distinguished respectively according to the differing semantic basis of particularistic/local/context-dependent meanings versus universalistic/less local/more context-independent meaning. These conceptualizations have relevance not only with respect to the discourse of Lessons 1, 2 and 3, but also with the semantic realm of mathematics.

Viewed from a systemic perspective, mathematics may be contextualized as a particular register, or rather a particular configuration of Field, Tenor and Mode selections for ideational, interpersonal and textual meanings. In terms of Field, the nature of the process and participant types (Relational and Operative processes) means that mathematics appears as universal, remote and context-independent. Also, being a written mode of discourse, mathematics is not located in the immediate context of situation, but rather it is context-independent. Halliday explains that 'in its core functions, writing is not anchored in the here-and-now' (Halliday 1985: 32). Mathematical discourse has a sophisticated textual organization with particular thematic patterns and specific patterns of reference. With respect to interpersonal meaning, there is a limited range of options in mathematical discourse if the meaning potential of natural language is invoked. For instance, preliminary investigations reveal that mathematical symbolism evolved as a semiotic system in which dimensions of the interpersonal meaning of language disappeared (O'Halloran 1996). In terms of Tenor, mathematics appears to operate from a position of dominance, a low level of affect, and involved but non-intimate social contact. The semantic realms of mathematics may be considered in relation to Lessons 1, 2 and 3.

The analysis of the dimensions of interpersonal meaning in Lessons 1, 2 and 3 indicate that differing semantic orientations are construed within each lesson. Significantly, the Tenor of Lesson 1 tends to conflate with that found in mathematics, while the dimensions of interpersonal meaning in Lessons 2 and 3 fall outside those boundaries. If the interpersonal meaning is viewed as the gateway to exploration of our experience of the world (Halliday 1975), then perhaps the male students are better prepared to engage with mathematical discourse. Further to this, although the nature of the interpersonal relations in Lesson 3 may initially be perceived to function as scaffolding to the discourse of mathematics, the analysis of experiential, logical and textual meaning of the oral discourse and board texts in the three lessons provide evidence to suggest that this does not occur.

In a larger cultural context the analysis of interpersonal meaning also suggests that the male students possess the linguistic resources to position themselves as powerful while the female students, and to a greater extent the working-class students, are somewhat disenfranchised as a result of their linguistic repertoire and semantic orientation in interpersonal relations. This point is further developed in section 9.6.4 in relation to gender.

The orientation towards particularistic/local/context-dependent meanings in Lesson 3 does not accord with the universal, remote and seemingly context-independent meanings of mathematics. That is, the greatest degree of contextual dependency is displayed in the lesson with working-class students. For example, in this lesson the non-specificity of the patterns of reference means that the coherence of the discourse depends to a much greater extent on accompanying visual features such as gesture and physical features of the context of the situation. Similarly these patterns are also reflected in the board texts. The hybrid, non-generic and ellipsed forms of representation in the lesson with working-class students mean that the written texts are only coherent in the context of the lesson. The semantic orientation of the 'here-and-now' of working-class students appears to be fundamentally different to 'there-and-forever' orientation of the discourse of mathematics. This may be compared to the situation in Lesson 1 where the board texts are generic, complete and essentially independent of the context of the lesson.

Halliday's formulations of the differences between spoken and written language are also instructive in connection with the differing nature of the discourses across the lessons and the semantic orientation of mathematical texts. Halliday summarizes the differing nature of the complexity of written and spoken language as 'density of substance' compared to 'intricacy of movement' (Halliday 1985: 87). Halliday formulates these differing lexicogrammatical strategies in written and spoken discourse as 'lexical density' and 'grammatical intricacy' respectively. I suggest that through the multiple rankshift embedding of nuclear configurations of Operative processes in symbolic mathematics these complexities conflate to give 'grammatical density'. This means the restricted code users are furthermost positioned from the written discourse of mathematics in terms of both semantics and complexity as displayed in Figure 9.8.

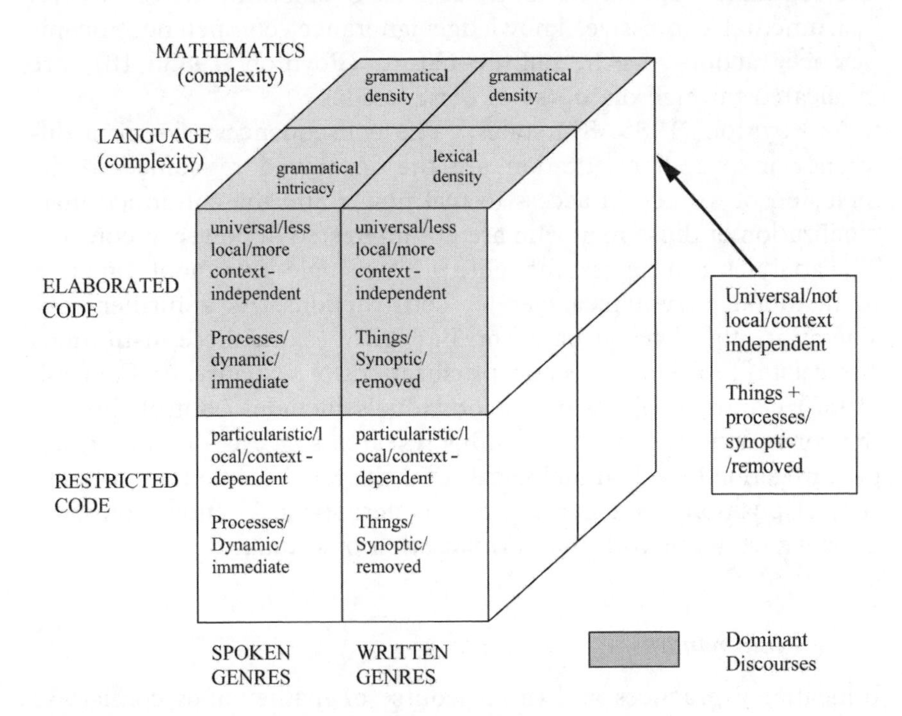

Figure 9.8 Semantic orientation of discourses

9.6.4 Gender implications

The analyses of Lessons 1 and 2 suggest that stereotypical gender constructions are reinforced in single-sex classrooms in elite private schools. Poynton (1985: 87) summarizes the differences in discourse according to gender as follows: 'In terms of gender, let us refer to *the male controlling code* and *the female responding code*, where males aim to control things, events, and most crucially people; and females show much more responsiveness to things, events, and particularly people [my emphasis].' Poynton's formulations accord with my analyses of the differences in interpersonal relations in Lessons 1 and 2. That is, the male students operate from a position of power, the social relations are involved but not intimate, there is minimal expression of affect and few instances of reacting. Interpersonal relations are maintained as formal, constant and steady. In contrast, the female students operate from a more deferential position, express less certainty, utilize politeness strategies, enter into less formal and more intimate relations, express euphemistically a range of attitudes and comments and react with an increased volume of interpersonal meaning. The results of the analysis also suggest that some masculine–feminine oppositions, such as reason–emotion, active–passive, instrumental–expressive, knowledge–ignorance, competence–incompetence, action–speech, culture–nature (Poynton 1985: 18), are inculcated through discourse in these lessons.

As Poynton (1985: 87) states, 'The consequences of such a difference in overall orientation are the continued resistance to the inclusion of women in access to real power and the continued marginalization of those men who are not interested in power or control.' The analyses also suggest that elite private single-sex schools function to maintain stereotypical gender constructions. As a further consideration, the division based on biological sex in these institutions also relates to Foucault's conceptualizations of sexuality. As Foucault (1980) claims, subjugation of individuals includes control through the constructions of sexuality. This research suggests that one result of segregation based on biological sex is the reinforcement of different subject positionings according to the stereotypical gender constructions which occur with the normalisation of sexuality.

9.6.5 Final remarks

Educational practices and the discourse of mathematics conflate in mathematics classrooms which consequently become critical sites for the operation of power. It is here that students are exposed to the discourse that underpins the scientific constructions and the consequent legitimisation of particular views of reality in Western culture. And the analyses presented here suggest that access and participation in mathematical discourse are restricted to particular groups. Further investigation into the nature of mathematical discourse is needed if we are ever to have a level playing field where the 'right to speak' is no longer in the hands of a minority. This would include documenting pedagogical implications of a social semiotic perspective of mathematics as a multisemiotic construction.

Particularly disturbing is the position adopted in political circles in Australia since the 1980s whereby the interests and privileges of the elite private school sector are continually extended to the detriment of the government school sector (Kenway 1987, 1990; O'Halloran 1991, 1996). This situation is unlikely to improve in Australia in the near future with the reinstatement of the right wing Liberal government in 2001.

References

Allen, K. and Burridge, K. (1991) *Euphemism & Dysphemism: Language Used as Shield and Weapon*. New York: Oxford University Press.

Bernstein, B. (1971) *Class, Codes and Control: Volume 1: Theoretical Studies towards a Sociology of Language*. London: Routledge and Kegan Paul.

Bernstein, B. (1973) *Class, Codes and Control: Volume 2: Applied Studies towards a Sociology of Language*. London: Routledge and Kegan Paul.

Bernstein, B. (1977) *Class, Codes and Control: Volume 3: Towards a Theory of Educational Transmission* 2nd edn. London: Routledge and Kegan Paul.

Bernstein, B. (1981) Codes, modalities and the process of cultural reproduction: a model. *Language and Society*, 10: 327–63. (Reprinted in M.W. Apple (ed.), *Cultural and Economic Reproduction in Education: Essays Class, Ideology and the State*. London: Routledge, 1982.)

Bernstein, B. (1990) *The Structuring of Pedagogic Discourse: Volume IV: Class, Codes and Control*. London: Routledge.

Borowski, E.I. and Borwein, I.M. (eds) (1989) *Collins Dictionary of Mathematics*. London: Harper Collins.

Christie, F. (1994) *On Pedagogic Discourse: Final Report of a Research Activity Funded by the ARC 1990–2*. University of Melbourne.

Foucault, M. (1980) *The History of Sexuality: Volume 1*. New York: Random House.

Halliday, M.A.K. (1975) *Learning How to Mean: Explorations in the Development of Language*. London: Edward Arnold.

Halliday, M.A.K. (1978) *Language as Social Semiotic: The Social Interpreta-*

tion of Language and Meaning. London: Edward Arnold.

Halliday, M.A.K. (1985) *Spoken and Written Language*. Geelong, Victoria: Deakin University Press (Republished by Oxford University Press 1989).

Halliday, M.A.K. (1994) *An Introduction to Functional Grammar* 2nd edn. London: Edward Arnold.

Kenway, J. (1987) High status private schooling and the processes of an educational hegemony. PhD thesis, Murdoch University, Perth, Western Australia.

Kenway, J. (1990) Education and the Right's Discursive Politics: Private versus State Schooling. In S.J. Ball (ed.), *Foucault and Education: Disciplines and Knowledge*. London: Routledge, 167–206.

Lemke, J.L. (1990) *Talking Science: Language, Learning and Values*. Norwood, NJ: Ablex Publishing Company.

Martin, J.R. (1992) *English Text: System and Structure*. Amsterdam: John Benjamins.

O'Halloran, K.L. (1991) An evaluation of achievement in algebra under the unit curriculum in the Western Australian lower secondary school. Honours, University of Western Australia.

O'Halloran, K.L. (1996) The discourses of secondary school mathematics. PhD thesis, Murdoch University, Western Australia.

O'Halloran, K.L. (1999) Towards a Systemic Functional Analysis of Multisemiotic Mathematics Texts. *Semiotica*, 124 (1/2): 1–29.

O'Halloran, K.L. (2000) Classroom discourse in mathematics: a multisemiotic analysis. *Linguistics and Education*, 10(3 Special Edition: Language and Other Semiotic Systems in Education): 359–88.

O'Halloran, K.L. (in press(a)) Implications of multisemiotic constructions for mathematics education. In M. Anderson, V. Cifarelli, A. Saenz-Ludlow and A. Vile (eds), *Semiotic Perspectives on Mathematics Education*. New York: Peter Lang.

O'Halloran, K.L. (in press(b)) Intersemiosis in mathematics and science: grammatical metaphor and semiotic metaphor. In L. Ravelli and M. Tavemiers (eds), *Lexicogrammatical Metaphor: Systemic and Functional Perspectives*. Benjamins: Amsterdam.

O'Halloran, K.L. and Judd, K. (2002) *Systemics 1.0*. Singapore: Singapore University Press.

O'Toole, M. (1994) *The Language of Displayed Art*. London: Leicester University Press.

Poynton, C. (1984) Names as Vocatives: Forms and Functions. *Nottingham Linguistic Circular*, 13 (Special Issue on Systemic Linguistics): 1–34.

Poynton, C. (1985) *Language and Gender: Making the Difference*. Geelong, Victoria: Deakin University Press.

Poynton, C. (1990) Address and the semiotics of social relations: a systemic-functional account of the address forms and practices in Australian English. PhD thesis, Department of Linguistics, Sydney University.

Rotman, B. (2000) *Mathematics as Sign: Writing, Imagining, Counting*. Stanford, CA: Stanford University Press.

Notes

1 Rotman (2000: 42) cites this approach as a productive step towards a semiotics of mathematics.

2 For discussion of the problematic nature of oral pedagogical discourse of mathematics arising from the lexicogrammar of mathematical symbolism, see O'Halloran (1996, 2000).

10

Teaching Radha to (Re-)Write: Authority, Positioning, Discourse

Anneliese Kramer-Dahl

10.1 Introduction

'A good child accepts and does what she is told to do.' This is what I was taught from young. To express a view that is different from that of an adult is unacceptable. So I started from an early age to try to be a 'good child' by pleasing everybody. At times I strayed. My first composition was entitled, 'Myself'. Ironically, however, instead of encouraging us to write a personal piece of writing, the teacher had actually structured the ten sentences we had to write. All of us produced ten identical sentences except for our names which appeared in the first sentence. So we began learning to write about ourselves by imitating the teacher's compositions. Such exercises were very boring and I attempted to inject some originality into my work. Once I wrote about my kite. I loved a kite that I had been given as a present and tried very hard to describe it and what made it so special to me. It was very different from the 'teacher's kite'. However, when I got back my work it was all 'chilli-sauced'. Corrections were found all over and the mark I got was 3 out of 10. There was a final remark, 'Untidy work! You have to continue writing in pencil.' No effort had been made to appreciate my effort to be different.

These bewildering moments of pedagogy were related by a student of mine, whom I call Radha, in an autobiographical exploration of her literacy experiences. Other classmates recounted similar anecdotes of sometimes-coercive discipline and regulation in early primary classrooms. Admittedly, in the case of Radha – an Indian student in her mid-thirties who had entered university after a number of years in the workforce as a non-graduate teacher – we might be tempted to brush these off as 'tales of the bad old days' (Morgan 1997: 57), relics of a time before the advent of student-centred learning and personal growth pedagogies in our English classrooms. But similar recollections by her classmates, young second-year Singapore undergraduates who attended primary school as recently as 1985, serve as a useful reminder that despite new conceptions and practices in education, early English lessons in Singaporean schools have changed less in the way they operate pedagogically than we might want to believe.[1]

Both episodes which Radha recalls drive home an important lesson about being a competent writer in primary school: that even allegedly autobiographical writing assignments are not culturally neutral. Even as one writes about oneself, one's own experiences and cherished objects, teachers prefer certain textualizations of the personal over others, expect certain 'standard' possible worlds, experiences and subjectivities, and when students attempt to interject statements of different cultural experiences and backgrounds into the texts of schooling, their 'efforts to be different', to use Radha's words, are, if not punished outright, rendered invisible.

That in Radha's case these early school practices have left particularly powerful traces, 'persist[ing] as a palimpsest' (Morgan 1997: 58), is obvious, as we will see later, from the immediacy with which she recalls and chooses to write about them. Not only that, since these early regimes were continually reinforced during her secondary school years, any overwriting of that palimpsest by her subsequent, more encouraging experiences with writing instruction at university and her successes as a student of English Language and Literature there could not but be faint. Listening to teacher injunctions like 'weak composition students like me should not write anything but narratives, since arguments require students to express their points of view' and reading teacher responses like ' 'good word choice' next to vocabulary and turns of phrases I had memorized from the model compositions, as if my own words were no good', Radha had acquired the *habitus* (Bourdieu 1990) of a weak, alienated student writer and had internalized ways of thinking, knowing and constructing social relations that marked her as lacking words and opinions of her own. As she explains,

> I have found it very difficult to inject personality into my writing because exploring myself is like exploring a dark vacuum, a meaningless exercise. I always have a tendency to accept someone else's views as my own, almost like the pair who rode the donkey to the market in Aesop's tale. If a critic says it is black, I tend to agree

that it is black. If another says, 'white', I tend to say, 'Oh yes, he is right too.'

And this, ironically, despite the fact that by the time she was in my class on Advanced Academic Writing, for which she wrote this, in her final undergraduate year, she had gained a reputation among teachers and classmates as a highly motivated, conscientious and bright student. When, in preparation to a follow-up assignment to the autobiographical task, I asked her to bring in the undergraduate essays with which she felt the sort of dissatisfaction expressed above, I was surprised to see literature essays that displayed knowledge of the appropriate discourse conventions: clear organization, competent use of primary and secondary sources and strict adherence to complex attribution formats. Also, rather than being 'chilli-sauced' all over, her essays had largely positive tutor comments, commending her ability to provide intelligent, coherent textual interpretations and gained consistently B+ or A grades. But then she pulled out one from the bottom of the pile, written for her course on literature and feminism, gesturing towards the C+ and the summative evaluative comment which her tutor had attached: 'You've obviously understood the issues in the literature on Austen, summarized them well, thought deeply, read widely, perhaps too widely, but the presentation of the essay doesn't match the self-evident intellectual work. What is *your* opinion? What are *you* trying to argue here?' 'See,' Radha said, 'he says it right there, my voice doesn't come through in my writing at all.'

Radha's dilemma, her anxiety about her inability to position herself within these texts, may at first glance seem quite easy to make sense of by composition researchers and teachers, especially those familiar with the literature in the recent field of cross-cultural rhetorical studies. This body of work, informed by what I will call here 'cultural shift' theory, focuses on how cultural and linguistic difference interferes with the Western-influenced critical, analytic approach to learning expected of students in academic writing at tertiary institutions. Supporting an essentializing East/West discourse, much of cross-cultural literacy research would construct Radha and her classmates as quintessential Asian learners, hard working and academically motivated but bound by a culture whose 'dominant approach to learning favours strategies of memorisation and rote learning and positively discourages critical questioning of either the teacher or the text' (Ballard and Clanchy 1991: 23). Researchers locate such an attitude towards knowledge at the collectivist-preserving end of an individualism/collectivism continuum. Worse still, more often than not they identify the Western/individualist end of this continuum as the benchmark, the centre or norm from which these Asian learners are judged to deviate (see for instance Osterloh 1986; Matalene 1985; Deckert 1993).

However, as researchers like Spack (1997), Zamel (1997) and Biggs (1996) have recently argued, we need 'a healthy dose of skepticism' (Spack 1997: 772) in regard to such conceptual frames and the sort of static generalizing about Asian rhetoric, wordviews and the learners they mediate, and be aware of their dangers. According to Bourdieu (1991: 223), 'The act of categorization, when it manages to achieve recognition or when it is exercised by a recognized authority, exercises by itself a certain power.' Such categorizing along ethnic or regional criteria ends up instituting Asian or Chinese culture as an objective reality rather than a social construct. To be sure, researchers may find such reductive constructs reassuring in that they provide them with a sense of control when explaining the perplexing and complex behaviour of students like Radha. Yet, unfortunately, such versions of the Asian student have significance beyond the realms of theory and academic research. Most damaging, if academics essentialize learners, they give others (most notably teachers) tacit permission to do so, and thus, very dangerously, severely constrain the kinds of interpretations that teachers make of their students on the basis of their cultural and linguistic background and the kinds of pedagogical interventions that they suggest. A most telling and relevant example is provided through Ritchie's reflections on her study of two students from Singapore and Malaysia (reported in Kirsch and Ritchie 1995), in which she shows how her assumptions about 'Asian women students' led to myopic understandings of these student writers of difference. In one instance she misread the silence of one of the two as a sign of 'Asian acquiescence to authority' rather than 'a form of resistance', and on the whole tended to 'analyse the style, form and rhetorical features of their writing according to [her] own training in [Western] rhetoric' (ibid.: 12–13).

There is evidence, as we shall see later, that in Singapore this essentializing discourse that represents cultural groups in broad sweeps and some of them as normative and others as 'lacking', recirculates through an intertextual universe of school materials, newspapers and ministry statements, informing the ways in which even local teachers and learning institutions make sense of their students. The effect on students can be detrimental:

> In viewing students as fixed by their world views, as less capable of critical thought or analysis, we limit our expectations of [them], misread and underestimate what our students' work represents, underconceptualize the reading and writing we ask students to do, and reduce instructions to ... 'a caricature' of academic work. (Zamel 1997: 343)

Furthermore, by rushing to attribute problems with voice and authority to students' Asian backgrounds, we tend to overlook the wealth of research attesting to similar struggles faced by their Western counterparts when learning the various discourses of the academy. Of course, the bulk of these describe the problems of basic and inexperienced writers, for whom issues of voice and critical analysis pale behind their more obvious difficulties with the command of elementary linguistic and organizational patterns. Radha's dilemma, on the other hand, you will recall, is that her texts adhered to the relevant rules of academic discourse all too well, with the writer constantly deferring to the relevant experts and losing herself in the process. Perhaps the closest parallel I have come across in the literature on composition research is an investigation of an American undergraduate writing classroom undertaken by Bolker (1979). In her article entitled, 'Teaching Griselda to write', Bolker describes the conflict which several of her students – high-achieving (females from non-traditional backgrounds – face. Though seemingly in control of the dominant academic discourse, they fail to see themselves in it and therefore feel silenced by it. When articulating their problems, Bolker's students use words that echo those with which Radha started the autobiographical fragment in the opening of this essay: 'Part of learning to be 'a good girl' means learning what pleases those around you and acting that way.' As a result of having learnt, like Chaucer's Griselda, to speak only what they think the master wants to hear, their papers 'are highly polished, so much that it is hard to catch a human voice in them. And like Griselda, they are dull; competence is all' (Bolker 1979: 907).

Since they are producing academic writing that appears highly competent, these student writers do not usually take centre stage with composition researchers and teachers. Yet, it is precisely their performative fears, their problems with, in Bakhtinian terms, 'populating their writing with their own intentions', that should convince us of the urgency to study this relatively neglected and complex area. What role do our practices of teaching writing play in the emergence of these fears? And why do we as teachers of academic writing face constant difficulties when we try to explain to students who feel powerless like Radha that there are ways of taking active control over their meaning-making even within discursive constraints and institutional protocols? As Brodkey has recently argued:

> I can think of no more important project for teachers and researchers than studying classroom discursive practices in relation to the part they play in alienating students from literacy by failing to articulate their representations of themselves as subjects who are different from their teachers. That would mean, of course, taking the position that literacy begins not in reading but writing, and would in turn mean inviting students to begin writing back and supporting them while they hone critical discursive literacy practices in our classes. Ultimately, taking literacy seriously would constitute a decision to rewrite the subjects of educational discourse. (1996: 22)

The few studies that have followed Brodkey's call and sought to investigate these vital issues of authority and subject-representation in student writing have acknowledged the complexity and delicacy of such an agenda (e.g., Fuller and Lee 1997; Kamler *et al.* 1996; Lillis 1997; Baynham 2000). For one thing, writing-across-the-curriculum and genre pedagogies, currently among the dominant approaches to academic literacy, are text-based in focus. Largely concerned with making explicit the linguistic patternings of disciplinary registers and genres, they view their main purpose to inculcate students into the cultures of the various disciplines. But there are several problems with purely text-based explanations. First, how readily can the registers of particular academic disciplines be delineated? Many of the initiation or apprenticeship-based pedagogies have given rather monolithic and idealized representations of academic discourse communities, and essentialized them, reminiscent of the way much cross-cultural rhetorical work has essentialized cultures. Their tendency to simplify the notion of community has been challenged by a growing body of research in discourse analysis and 'new literacy studies', which sees academic disciplines as heterogeneous, hybrid and conflicting, with competing beliefs and practices overlapping (Harris 1989; Lea and Street 2000). For example, when examining the multiple array of discourses that are mobilized within the one discipline of English Literature, which Radha studies, Elbow concludes almost wearily,

> I can't tell my students whether academic discourse means using lots of structural signposts or leaving them out, bringing in their

> feelings and personal reactions or leaving them out, referring to the class, gender, or school of other interpreters or leaving them out. . . . In short, it's crazy to talk about academic discourse [of Subject English] as one thing. (1991: 139–40)

Second, to what extent can text-based accounts capture the inter-subjective complexities of academic literacy in any realistic detail, especially if we bear in mind the relative marginalization of the non-referential (i.e., interpersonal) ways of meaning in linguistics? Fuller and Lee, in their Bakhtinian-inspired analysis, have argued that

> Within a text, a complex fabric of textuality can be discerned in which students sometimes speak, sometimes echo and sometimes distance themselves from certain propositional meanings. This is part of a process that is not always self-conscious; nevertheless, there is tacit agreement among communities of scholarly writers about where and how a writer can weave herself into this fabric. Moving into literacy is not about writing 'your own' ideas; rather, it is about negotiating a positionality within the heteroglossic terrain of writing. (1997: 414)

Third, even if this complex process of negotiation could be fully explicated, text-based approaches on their own tend to overlook the fact that when students like Radha fail to articulate a position of their own, there is more at stake than their lack of control over relevant linguistic technologies through which to assert authority. For even if students know the relevant linguistic devices, there are often deep affective and ideological conflicts involved when it comes to their deployment. These are the result of students' past literacy practices, of their teachers' ways of teaching and responding to their writing, all of which play a vital part in the construction of certain kinds of subjectivities, in the production of bodies and minds that are shaped and habituated in certain ways. The question, then, which becomes paramount when one works with students who share Radha's anxieties, is, 'How is it possible to assert the authority required of argument when one has been disciplined, from early childhood on, to accept that one is a weak student writer, who does not have experiences, opinions and subjectivities worth hearing?' (Kamler 1997: 395–6). To answer this sort of question requires us to read student writing from a perspective which incorporates text-based accounts 'into a more encompassing understanding of the nature of student writing within institutional practices, power relations and identities' (Lea and Street 2000: 33).

The situation of students like Radha has convinced me of the need to assemble a critical writing pedagogy and to explore what such a pedagogy might look like in an undergraduate classroom. While various extensive critical literacy curricula have been proposed around reading as a sociocultural practice (e.g., Wallace 1992; Freebody *et al.* 1991), less attention has been given to the phenomenon of writing (for exceptions see Kamler *et al.* 1996; Clark and Ivanic 1997), and this despite the wide recognition that it is writing practices that form the substance of the pedagogical transactions between students and teachers that count. Even though a move from a critical reading to a critical writing pedagogy involves the application of similar critical literacy principles, most notably (1) repositioning students as researchers of their literacy practices, and (2) problematizing classroom texts (Comber 1994), in a critical writing class these would have to be applied to the students' own writing rather than that of others. Such a shift in focus would require far more careful scaffolding and reflection. For time and again I have seen the same students who in my course in Critical Discourse Analysis can intelligently point to the construction of power and positioning in the texts of others, particularly if these are non-academic in nature, find it very difficult to recognize the same aspects in their own writing. It would be even more remote for them to grasp how these practices of construction contribute to their formation as particular kinds of schooled subjects/writers and how, if necessary, they can reposition themselves as more authoritative subjects/writers.

In the following narrative, I will sketch two specific ways of working with students like Radha which I developed for a module on Advanced Academic Discourse – a course that sought to help students rewrite their relationship with academic writing. Building on Comber's key critical literacy principles mentioned above, one of the tasks, rather archaeological in nature, would ask the students to research past classroom practices surrounding writing in relation to the part they played in alienating them from writing. The other, present- and future-oriented, would involve a critical reading of specific instances of their present writing within the context of academia and its reception by their teachers, and would explore ways, linguistic and otherwise, of crafting more authoritative positions for themselves within the given pedagogical and textual spaces. Working within such a critical orientation is especially vital for students like mine, all of them future teachers of literacy, as it can offer them a more politicized set of lenses through which to view the literacy practices they will adopt in their own classrooms. More specifically, a critical orientation will enable them to recognize the power that rests with naming and constructing their pupils and to keep their constructions open to questioning and change, as these will shape the tasks they set, the ways they read their pupils' responses and, ultimately, the ways their pupils read themselves.

10.2 Collective literacy autobiographies: the assignment

One of the major writing tasks, adopted from Benson *et al.* (1994), Davies (1992), and Morgan (1997), was a collective literacy autobiography project. It asked the students to 'undertake a case study of three or four students in their class in order to examine the role their literacy experiences [had] played in shaping them as writers and in preparing them for the literacy tasks they [had] to handle in university' (Assignment Prompt). The assignment, which was, in 'process writing' fashion, mostly discussed and drafted in classroom time, was to be carried out in two stages: initially the students were to compose their individual autobiographies, which were then to form the raw data for a comparative study, which required them to pull out of the range of individual accounts some of the patterns of similarity and difference. In earlier versions of the course, when the task had involved merely the writing of their individual literacy narratives, students had usually been so close to their own experience that they read their lives as unique, and, in modernist fashion, unproblematically viewed themselves as the sole cause and origin of actions and difficulties. Any acknowledgement of the work that the ideologies and practices of their institutions and cultures do in shaping their lives had been peripheral or altogether absent. On the other hand, by taking the project up to the collective and comparative level, students could more easily view the construction of their autobiographies 'as something at the same time experienced as personal and their own . . . and yet visibly made out of, even determined by, materials and practices not originating from them' (Davies 1992: 84). In other words, as Morgan (1997: 73) lucidly explains it, 'out of the particulars of a range of narrated lives students may come to trace some of the cultural threads, the discursive threads, out of which unique-seeming lives are woven'. They would be able to see these patterns even more clearly because of their preliminary course readings, which had introduced them to the literacy autobiographies of students from a variety of non-Singaporean backgrounds and thus would allow them to tease out disjunctions and continuities in discourses or literacy practices.

Such collective–comparative work could also be valuable for other reasons. All our undergraduate students are simultaneously being trained to become primary or secondary school teachers. A thorough exploration of the particular social contexts of their literacy practices would foster their professional development as future teachers of literacy, since it would enable them to detect the inherently ideological dimensions of literacy – and to question and challenge the dominant discourses of teaching reading and writing which inform the practices in their own future classrooms. Moreover, by getting the students to carry out their research into the literacy experiences among a group of Singaporeans and asking them to write it up in the form of a case study to be anthologized, I attempted to construct a different set of positionings for them than they normally occupy in their classes. For they are rarely given the chance to work on academic projects,

> projects that allow students to act as though they were colleagues in an academic enterprise. Much of the work students do is test-taking, report or summary – work that places them outside the official discourse of the academic community, where they are expected to admire and report on what *we* do. (Bartholomae 1985: 144)

By crafting a proper study of their own, building on, and in negotiation with the case studies of researchers in non-local contexts, which they had read as background material, the students would no longer simply be consumers but be at least on the way to becoming producers of authoritative knowledge themselves.

10.3 Critical reading of student texts

The first step of the class project required the students to apply critical literacy questions to the individual autobiographies that they had written for class. In groups of three or four in workshop, the students would read each other's pieces and apply the kinds of questions to them that they had previously, for instance in their class on discourse analysis, only asked of the texts of others (see Kamler *et al.* 1996; Wallace 1992):

> What was powerful in the writing? Identify an image, trope, line, or metaphor that was powerful.
> What other ways are there of writing about this?
> What is the text trying to do to you?
> How is the topic written about?

What wasn't said about the topic?
What was absent or marginalized? Why?
Whose voices and positions are being expressed? Whose are left out? What does not fit? What contradictions, if any, emerge?
What common issues, experiences, storylines do the autobiographies in your group have in common? What commonalities do the autobiographies in your group and those you have read by students in non-Singaporean contexts have in common?

Note the difference between these types of questions and those often asked in process and reader-response classrooms, which highlight writing as an individual experience which students are supposed to appreciate and with which they are supposed to identify. Questions like, 'How did you feel when reading the text?', 'What did you like best in it?' 'What persons could you identify most with?' invite the students to surrender themselves to the story as if it were a slice of real life. This act of uncritical involvement is especially difficult to resist with autobiography, generally considered the most personal among the narrative genres. Students are led to treat it as a transparently personal act of 'self-expression', with the key protagonist as an autonomous, unified centre of consciousness, whose development and psychology is of prime concern.

In reading the autobiographies as textual constructions of lives as story, on the other hand, students might well start with co-operatively identifying with the preferred readings constructed by the text but then, through questions that ask for the identification of topics and discourses, writer and reader positioning, as well as strategic silences, would be challenged to move deliberately to resist the text's apparent naturalness. Rather than seeing the subject of autobiography as a single, unified subjectivity, who moves along a clear, straight trajectory towards an end consistent with her beginning, students would learn about the fragmentary, provisional and often contradictory nature of subjectivity. They could also see how any act of narrating their lives, even if deliberately crafted, 'has already been perhaps unconsciously (re)constructed by a selective memory and the discourses that tell us the meaning of such stories' (Morgan 1997: 64). In particular, the students' texts being literacy accounts, they would feature

> stories . . . that foreground language acquisition and literacy. These narratives are structured by learned, internalized 'literacy tropes,' . . . any prefigured ideas and images. Literacy narratives sometimes include explicit images of school and teaching; they include texts

> that both challenge and affirm culturally scripted ideas about literacy. (Eldred and Mortenson 1992: 513)

Perhaps the most obvious of such culturally scripted ideas is the 'progress plot', in which literacy becomes featured as a necessary tool for success, for improved school performance and for enhanced access to jobs. The first task was for the students, in groups of four, to investigate their texts for their overall narrative structure. The students in Radha's group, all of whom but her came from majority-Chinese, middle-class and English speaking, or at least English literacy-supporting, homes, found that most of their autobiographies affirmed the progress script. All except Radha recalled and dwelt on, in the resolution-to-problem stage of their narrative, the literacy practices of one or at most two teachers, usually the only individuated ones in their stories, who lead their students to realize in the end that literacy provides power. The stories highlighted at length the encouraging, supportive environment this teacher typically provided and how this enabled them to develop a positive self-image as writers and, along with it, a change in attitude, ability and grade received. When students went on to reread their texts against the far more episodic, circularly woven text of Radha's, this narrative logic, assumed 'normal' or 'normative' by most students in the class, was suddenly put into question. Issues like the professed meritocracy of a largely elitist education system like Singapore's were raised, and the extent to which it does and does not redress the inequalities caused by pupils' linguistic and socio-economic backgrounds. Also, Radha's story, and her present dilemma as a writer, convincingly delineated for them that while mastery of the relevant disciplinary writing practices may be a necessary condition for academic success, it is hardly sufficient in itself. For as the version of literacy in her story tells us, there is far more to cultural capital than teaching the relevant subject knowledge and discoursal forms can impart. Especially in humanities subjects like English Literature, Radha's major field of study, there is also a certain disposition towards that knowledge and discourse, a 'habitus' characteristic of writers from middle-class, English-speaking backgrounds which has to be displayed. Fuzzily described by such criteria as 'flair', 'maturity', 'ease with the language', its features and devices cannot be taught successfully. According to Radha's story, the harder she struggled to achieve that sophistication with the language that comes effortlessly to those with the 'right' home backgrounds, the 'right' dialects and the 'right' cultural membership, the more it resulted in stilted, laborious performances, and, worse still, an undermining of her confidence as a writer. In her own words:

> Soon teachers began to encourage me to read more story books so that it would improve my writing skills. While earlier I had been imitating the teacher's style of writing from her model compositions, now I began to imitate and follow the style of writing found in books. I began to keep vocabulary books where I copied down words and phrases from the books recommended. I tried to insert these into my writing so that I could get ticks for 'better words' used. Such a practice, meant to improve the 'maturity' of the pieces of work I submitted, resulted in the teacher commenting on the inconsistencies in the language of my stories. More than that, it also undermined my confidence. It seemed as if my own words were no good. My writing, even though intended to be about personal experiences, became more and more depersonalized, less and less mine.

From the analysis of the generic structure of the student autobiographies we moved to an investigation of their relevant lexicogrammatical features. The first set of features the students examined in their texts was vocabulary choices, especially the networks of words which could illuminate the sorts of discourses about literacy that the texts were drawing upon. Most texts are hybrid in nature, drawing on more than one discourse, and the specific hybridity displayed in the student texts would provide evidence of the discourses fluctuating in the educational system at large. What was most noticeable was that, despite the students' avid criticism of the Singapore educational system as one concerned with 'product not process', 'appearance and not meaning', their own narrations nevertheless took up subject positions within the very discourse they criticized. The students were astonished at the overwhelming frequency with which they themselves used such nouns as 'work' and 'piece of work' to describe their writing, 'produce' to describe the activity, accompanied by such choices as 'tidy/untidy', 'neat', 'correct', 'success', 'results' and 'marks' or 'grade'. All these suggested the prevalence of a 'managerial or quality discourse' in which competent literacy teaching is seen as the close monitoring of outward signs of quality in students' products, the physical appearance of their writing, and the obtaining of tangible outcomes (Comber 1997: 393). However unintentionally, the frames of assessment used by their teachers and by the system at large seemed to have clearly affected how the students constructed themselves as literate subjects in their accounts.

Yet they could also see traces of a struggle of alternatives, less apparent in Radha's account than in those of the others. In the latter, the students uncovered obvious discursive shifts, where outcome-driven, managerial discourse was blended with the near-oppositional one of progressivism, and its stress on process-writing and developmental literacy pedagogy – reflecting a pedagogical trend that came into fashion in Singapore with the implementation of the current English Language syllabus and that has been especially pervasive in the language pedagogy courses our students take during their first two years at university.[2] However, in their discussion, students astutely pointed out that in the larger educational system this discourse rests rather uneasily with, and is more often than not undercut by, the reality of an examination culture, to the demands of which even the most process-committed teachers have to bow when selecting the most useful practices for their students (Cheah 1998). Similarly, they could see this uneasy alliance mirrored in their own literacy narratives, which though taking on the vocabularies of both managerial and developmental discourses, in the end tended to distort or substantially revise developmentalism. Many of the students mentioned that, ironically, even at present in their whole-language-professing pedagogy courses at the university, the instructional message of process, non-prescriptivism and pupil development was undermined by the rigorous result-oriented classroom and examination regimes. This line of discussion led to the posing of questions like, 'Could these texts have been produced by students who went through the education system in the early 1980s?', 'Would students outside Singapore have produced texts which show similar discursive conflicts at work?'

Apart from raising questions about the contextual factors affecting the production of the student texts, especially their lexical preferences in some places for a developmental discourse, we also centred group discussion on the possible interests served by this trend. For the students had noticed that it was especially the two in their group from top-ranked schools and high tracks who described their later literacy experiences in terms of 'meaning-making', 'expressing my own point of view', 'ownership', 'developing' and 'encouraging'. Radha and the fourth student in the group, however, who had attended average neighbourhood schools, regarded the impact of progressivist discourse as marginal on, or as excluding, students like themselves, as was evident from passages like the following in their texts:

> Ironically, however, instead of encouraging us to write a personal piece of writing, the teacher had actually structured the ten sen-

> tences we had to write. All of us produced ten identical sentences.
>
> By the time I got to Secondary three weak composition students like me were discouraged from writing anything apart from narratives. We had very few chances of attempting writing where we could express our own points of view.
>
> I realized that writing, which could have been a tool for communicating one's thoughts or to discover oneself (I sadly learnt about this only much later while in university), was during my years of schooling merely an assessment of one's hardwiring, syntax and grammar. (Thank goodness I had few spelling problems.)

Far less visible than lexical selections, yet an equally vital line of analysis the students were asked to pursue when reading their literacy autobiographies, was the range of transitivity choices made. This involved the identification of dominant verb selections, their semantics (whether they encode, for example, material or verbal actions, or mental processes) and the semantic roles of their accompanying subject and object participants. The students were also asked to consider at the same time which selections were not made but could have been made instead. In this grammatical deconstruction exercise our focus was on those clauses with verbs which involved the narratorial 'I' and the teacher(s) as principal participants. By analysing patterns in transitivity selection in a text it is possible to make more general statements about the way that characters view their position in the world and their relation to others. Applied to our literacy autobiographies, this meant that the extent to which the textual 'I' is portrayed as a passive 'victim' of circumstance, or of the actions of others, most notably teachers, or as actively in control, making decisions about and taking action in her writing, could tell us a great deal about the sorts of educational discourses which are available for students to draw upon when describing their literacy events and practices of their past. Not that this was taken to be a deliberate choice on the writers' part; in fact, students were able to see that since transitivity is much more deeply embedded in the syntax than other lexicogrammatical features, it suggests far less conscious control by the writer and, in turn, also demands far more deliberate work on the part of readers to tease it out (Janks 1997).

The first thing that struck the students as they read Radha's text was the relative lack of dynamism on the principal protagonist's, i.e. Radha's, part. Upon analysing her text for its principal verb types and related participant roles, they discovered that this sense of passivity was not achieved through the usual means, i.e. through an avoidance or downplaying of verbs denoting material actions with 'I' as actor. On the contrary, there were quite a high and almost identical number of material and mental verbs with 'I' as actor and senser, with processes like 'writing' and 'thinking' and 'realizing' as the most frequently repeated. Yet, interestingly, upon closer inspection, the students could see that the sense of control and creativity which an action like 'write' often connotes was undermined by the more specific semantic selections of other clauses, which described the act of writing as 'imitate', 'follow the style of writing', 'copy down' and 'produce [10 identical sentences [the teacher had structured for us on the blackboard]]'. More than that, in those cases where the 'I' was linked to verbs that are unambiguously dynamic and suggest some taking of control on the part of the writer, for instance, 'inject some personality into my writing', 'insert some phrases', 'improve my English', these were typically preceded by modifying verbs like 'attempt' and 'try', suggesting intention rather than action, the process as a goal to attain but ultimately outside reach. Similarly, mental verbs of cognition were also often qualified or negated, such as 'Why should I think when adults always do the thinking for me?', 'I never tried to think critically about what I had read', 'I have never valued my own writing', or they are weakened in their force through the choice of cognitive verbs like 'memorize', 'regurgitate' and 'tended to agree'. These disenabling transitivity choices were found to be further reinforced through the striking expressions and images of desperation Radha uses to describe her mind, such as comparing it to 'a dark vacuum' and 'a neutral container of information' and repeatedly characterizing it as 'intellectually obedient' and 'accommodating'.

When turning to an examination of the ways in which the teacher–student dynamic was constructed in their various texts, the group found quite divergent portrayals. While in the narratives of her group mates the autobiographical 'I' was frequently constructed in direct interaction with the teacher, albeit largely at the receiving end of her teachers' often discouraging actions and comments, in Radha's text teachers were discovered to be notably absent; through a large number of agentless passives, the classroom world constructed by Radha was portrayed as one in which she is alone, the goal/target of actions, comments and commands whose initiators are left unclear.

> 'A good child should be seen and not heard.' This is what I was taught from young. When I got back my work it was all chillies-sauced.

> The remark I received was, 'Untidy work.' No effort was made to appreciate my effort to be different.
> By the time I got to Secondary three, weak composition students like me were discouraged from writing anything apart from narratives.
> I was being marked down for my 'bad English.'
> I was asked to write a commentary on a passage.

When asked about the deletions, Radha explained that she had not deliberately chosen these wordings but upon reflection felt that they should stay unrevised. Most of her teachers had not figured in her literacy learning process enough to deserve explicit mention or have responsibility assigned. If anything she had felt their absence:

> They never did anything but assign work and grade it. There was never any real, tangible advice how to improve; they had decided that there were those students who were able to think on their own and express their views and those who were not. I belonged to the second group. That we needed to develop confidence with the language first and learn the kinds of devices in order to express our opinions they couldn't, or were unwilling to see. It's only when I got to university and had one or two lecturers in Literature who took the trouble to explain some of my problems that I realized that teachers could make an impact.

Students also commented on what seemed a contradiction or at least temporary change in the way Radha constructed the scene of academic writing and its principal participant in one of her narrative episodes. It reads as follows:

> My first attempt to inject some personality in my work was my Shakespeare assignment where I was asked to write a commentary on a passage from *A Midsummer Night's Dream* from the point of view of a teacher, pointing out what is most important and interesting to a new student. For days I had cracked my brains for the 'most important and interesting' thing in the extract. Titania, the fairy queen, is infatuated with Bottom, ass-bearded mortal weaver, in this extract. I suddenly realized (as I was thinking about it on the bus) – it is a point where the world of immortals meets the mortals, the supernatural meets the natural, fantasy and illusion meet the world of reality, irrational passion meets reason. A juxtaposition of contrasts! The situation in the extract had just caused an explosion in my mind – an idea had germinated in my brain as the result of the explosion. It was not someone else's idea. It was mine. This

> time I was not going to let it go hiding. I went home and I decided to write an essay based on it. It was the first piece of essay I produced without any reference to secondary texts. I got a B for it just like most of the assignments I had done before but I valued this 'B' more than anything else!

They saw the above segment as standing out from the rest of Radha's text for the high degree of dynamism attributed to the textual 'I', the sudden unqualified verbs of cognition (e.g., 'decided', 'valued'), the high amount of positive attitudinal interpolations and the new, enabling way the process of idea-generation is described. Questions arose about the extent to which this sudden and one-off change in control and affect could be capturing the fact that in the writing situation Radha was recalling she had been able to draw uniquely on her prior experience and authority as a teacher and had felt free of the pressure to negotiate between personal statements and scholarly material. Despite the excitement she expressed about this assignment in her text, in subsequent discussion Radha saw the situation in a far less positive light. She found it unforgivable that schooling had given her so few meaningful tasks to do, let alone any helpful instruction ('More than the sorts of general guidelines we're usually given on the mechanics of referencing') in how to move successfully beyond the rare essays 'without any reference to secondary texts'. After all, what the more common academic tasks required of her, especially in literature, was that she incorporate the texts of others into her own without rendering all authority to them.

The above segment in Radha's text was also seen as standing out against the texts of the other students, who typically described change as a final, resolving move in their narrative, with one or two supportive teachers liberating them and, as principal causers, enabling them to take control of their writing. In Radha's story the above was merely one stage among many, the reversal of agency, the result of her own or, in her own view, the text under study's ('the situation in the extract had caused an explosion in my mind') initiative. Since this was abruptly followed by the clause, 'But something shook my confidence very badly after that', a return to a less dynamic, less positive state of affairs was clearly signalled. Through such cross-textual reading, the normativity of student literacy narratives as linear, goal-directed journeys, with specific heroic teachers propelling students along, could be put into relief through Radha's account, and this allowed the students to explore the cultural and ideological loadings of these generic realizations.

On the whole, our workshop sessions helped the students to go beyond giving an affective response to the texts of each other's literacy experiences and to tease out their, at times, differing constructions of literacy and literacy practices. They also provided an avenue to discuss the possible reasons for and implications of the commonalities and differences they uncovered. What one of Kamler's students says about the experience of doing this critical language awareness work on her own texts echoes strongly the responses of the students in Radha's group at this point as well:

> As each piece of writing was placed on the table to be conferenced it became a 'fiction' in the sense that it was my representation of reality. The divorce of my 'story' from my inner personal self to become a 'text' which, like any other, used language to construct representations and positionings was not always an easy one. (Kamler *et al.* 1996: 8)

It was especially difficult, since for several of the students, including Radha, opening up their literacy lives in writing and then communally reading and critiquing them in my presence was at times discomfiting, if not downright painful. There is clearly the danger, alerted to by a number of critical pedagogy critics, of students' autobiographical writing turning into 'one more avenue for pedagogical, pastoral surveillance' (Morgan 1997: 70). Yet Radha's final textual metaphor, which she added on in a later draft of her autobiography, gives me a sense that, despite its potential dangers, the memory and deconstructive work she had done had yielded some important insights for her. The following passage, ending her autobiography in its final version, shows her increasing awareness not only of the complexities of her writing situation but also of the possibility, albeit difficult to pursue, which she sees now of consciously weaving herself into the fabric of her writing through what she chooses to say and how she says it:

> At present, as a writer in the university, I imagine myself having metaphorized into a tightrope walker with a long pole to balance. On one side is the urgency to conform to the ideas of those who are well established in the discipline I study and on the other hand, there is the need to be critical and think for myself. I also see the need to meet up with the requirements of the lecturers with regard to the style I have to adopt and at the same time I need to find a way of maintaining my identity in the way I write. If I want to do well I have to be careful not to lose my balance.

10.4 Strategic action with and/or against student texts

Since in effective critical literacy lessons textual deconstruction is not considered as an end in itself but as providing the means for socially productive work, the essential follow-up action to our workshop activities should ideally be the students' 'strategic action with and/or against the text' (Luke *et al.* 1994: 144). Hence the questions which emerged and which guided the next segment of the student project of writing the case study were: What difference would the textual deconstruction make to the subsequent writing that students produced? What further research could students do about the institutions mentioned and issues raised by the texts that they had written and critiqued?

As for the first question, a couple of excerpts from Radha's subsequent critical analysis of assignments she was doing for her concurrent literature classes show that the previous deconstructive work could make a difference. In the first segment, Radha shows an ability to assert herself more strongly than before in what she wanted to say in her essay, even if this involved the risk of not saying what her lecturer (and what he viewed as an authoritative critic) wanted to hear:

> In my assignment for my module on feminist readings of literature I chose the question, 'Achebe's view of Igbo culture is male-centred. Emechata, on the other hand, shows a woman's perspective. To what extent do you agree with this statement?' The moment I read the question I felt that I wanted to bring out the fact that it is not necessarily Achebe's view that is male-centred. What I think he could be doing is depicting the views of a male-centred society and of a male protagonist, which are not necessarily his, but which he has a very hard time rewriting. Even though the course had taught me to question the ideological implications, especially gender-related ones, that are found in literary texts, I did not get blindly carried away with the enthusiasm of Emecheta in her critical text. As a matter of fact, I questioned her viewpoint on the Achebe novel, and see her imposing her Westernized feminist views on the female character. When I read her saying, 'The good woman, in Achebe's portrayal, is one who kneels down and drinks dregs after her husband' I told myself, Wait a minute, this is not necessarily what Achebe thinks – this is the male protagonist's view of a good woman. Emecheta has fused the writer and the protagonist into one and can write with the authority required of academic argument.

Even though she had decided to take up an unconventional reading of the text, and was convinced of its validity, there lurked the danger of getting trapped in other sets of conventions. As our course reading by Ivanic and Simpson (1992) had emphasized, since there are simultaneous constraints on 'how we can say what we want to say' and 'who we are allowed to be' in our writing, these could ultimately interfere with her ability to express her own viewpoint. Notice how in the depiction of this dilemma she leaves behind, at least temporarily, the discourses of helplessness and victimization so evident throughout her earlier autobiography. Moreover, as a result of honing her critical reading practices, she developed strategies to take action against her earlier draft of this essay and to rewrite it by fashioning a subject positioning that could negotiate more successfully her own authority against the texts of others:

> When it came to writing down my views I had a difficult time because of the many sources which tended to drown out my own voice. As I read my draft I can see that my own position got lost under what Ivanic and Simpson call 'the academic waffle and pretentiousness'. What I have to do instead is state my own view on Emecheta's critique right at the beginning and use it as the main point of my argument. Why did I not do this? I guess in this assignment the reading of the critics played the role of a litmus paper in the sense that I used them to test whether my ideas are all right. None of them had mentioned what I felt and I started feeling insecure. These secondary readings overshadowed the 'I' in the sense that what I actually had intended to write as my main point went into hiding. It only appeared as an afterthought hidden in an insignificant spot of my essay. I allowed the views of these writers and their construction of knowledge to impose them on me. Beginning my essay with one of the critics, Florence Stratton, was like a shield, a back-up by an authority, which allowed me to hide, and this distorted what I really wanted to say in this draft. There is no focal point and my argument falls apart.

Before myself falling prey here in the telling of my story to the dominant complication-resolution structure of literacy narratives, I need to stress – and Radha herself would have acknowledged this perhaps more readily – that what the above excerpt suggests is not a key moment in Radha's academic life that brought about a permanent transformation or signalled the reaching of a permanent resolution of her difficulties. Instead she had solved a specific problem, and others, perhaps even more complex, would be there for her to solve in the future.

One of these, which would turn out to be far more complex for her and her classmates to struggle with, was related to the issue of constructs of the Asian/Chinese learner. It had repeatedly arisen in the texts we had read by composition specialists working with students from Asian backgrounds and in the students' own autobiographies. Hence it was this issue which we decided to further investigate as a final task in our attempts to take action with/or against the texts of our classroom. We did not have the time to explore in detail the historical continuity of such cultural representations with colonialism (see Pennycook 1998 for an account), but could see how widespread they have become in the Western educational literature and how their continuous reinvocation even in local texts renders their deconstruction and rewriting, by even the most critical students, an uphill task.

When examining some of the literature on the problems which 'Asian learners', or similarly essentializing, 'the Chinese learner' have with Western academic demands, students in their discussions fiercely objected to the kinds of reciprocal constructions found in the work of, among others, Ballard and Clanchy (1991) and Matalene (1985). Despite their benevolent liberal intentions, these articles, in the students' view, clearly advocated a kind of biculturalism, asking teachers of English to respect the students' cultural heritage but only in the end to rationalize the imposition of so-called Western rhetoric and its values in the teaching of English. They took on the work of Ballard and Clanchy for the sweeping generalizations it makes about cultural dispositions in styles of learning, when it labels the Asian way as tending towards the superficial 'conserving/reproductive' and the Western way as tending towards the deep 'extending/speculative'. They critiqued Matalene for its way of exoticizing the Chinese student as one still steeped in traditions like the 'eight-legged essay', who values community over individuality, harmony over conflict, and who writes in, what seem to a Westerner, interestingly poetic and flowery ways.

The students' initial interest was in proving the truth or falsehood of such binary representations. Reading Biggs' (1996) review of stereotypes of Asian learners as a critical counterpoint to Ballard and Clanchy and related studies, they briefly raised such issues as the recency of the questioning, speculative nature of Western academic practices that Ballard and Clanchy describe, as well as the uneasiness with which these often rest within undergraduate curricula, which are, even in the West, largely transmission-oriented (Bartholomae, Lillis). Students also pointed out that most Singaporean students, especially in English Literature, find the texts to which they have to 'personally' respond so far removed from their own cultures and experiences that they feel compelled to regurgitate the views of others. The set literature students have to cover for their Cambridge O- and A-Level examinations – long discarded in this traditional form in Britain but still retained in former colonies like Singapore – are texts as alien as the compulsory Shakespeare play and the Hardy or Austen novel. Hence my students could not help wondering: Is it the case that we are unable to think for ourselves, or could it be that in the context of having to construct academic knowledge about texts in which we are rendered invisible, we have pragmatically decided that reciting the views of others undigested is the path of least resistance?

My main concern, however, in our examination of these East/West constructs was not their truth or falsity but their productive force in the students' own texts and literacy lives (Pennycook 1998). The prior transitivity analysis of the autobiographies in Radha's group had shown up the repeated use of processes like 'memorizing', 'regurgitating', 'copying' and 'imitating', which had been chosen by the students to indicate what they perceived as their stymied thinking and writing practices, and attributes like 'uncritical' and 'intellectually obedient' to describe their passive attitudes towards learning. When re-examining their autobiographies now, against the literature on cross-cultural rhetoric which they had just taken apart, they were surprised at the repetition of such stereotypical representations in their own texts. More than that, despite her objections to Ballard and Clanchy's cultural stereotypes, Radha and her group mates continued to draw on the same essentialist discourse in their subsequent writing of the collective case study, viewing some of their predicaments as writers quite readily in its terms. Here are two brief examples among many:

> Now that we think back in the light of what Ballard and Clanchy (1991) have said about the writing of students of the East, we can see to what extent our own pieces were products of 'the reproductive approach to learning and the discouraging of critical questioning of either the teacher or the text' during our days of schooling.
>
> In reviewing the autobiographies of the three Chinese students in our group, one obvious similarity emerged. All three Chinese females agreed that their Chinese heritage has prevented them

> from becoming the potential they can be and even made them doubt their individual identity. As Mona mentions, 'There was always a fear in me that I was over-emphasizing my views and downplaying the importance of the subject I was writing on. I guess this train of thought can be traced back to Chinese culture.' The Chinese culture greatly emphasizes the idea of preserving harmony and consensus. A person who questions or voices out disagreements therefore spoils the harmony and creates disunity.

Why are these cultural images so fixed, so resilient, echoing, albeit inadvertently, even in the writing and thinking of those that they describe? In which ways could students begin to disrupt these debilitating ways of thinking about themselves and their cultures? This is a task for me to take up in future versions of the course. The task will be all the more difficult since the very same discursive constructions of a binary division between Asia and the West are constantly mobilized in Singapore contemporary public discourse as well, only here 'post-modernized' with 'Asia' as the norm and 'the West' relegated to the realm of the other (Ang and Stratton 1995: 66). And just as in the texts of the Western academics which our class had read, this Asianness, or in other instances, Chineseness, is a thoroughly synthetic, planned construct, conceived essentialistically as a traditional culture encapsulated in Asian or Confucian values. It fails to acknowledge the complexity and hybridity of the cultural and linguistic practices of the various ethnic groups which are so neatly contained in the official Chinese–Malay–Indian–Others racial schema, which is, in turn, subsumed under a larger unitary entity, the Singapore New Asian. Moreover, for pragmatic reasons, as a capitalist culture which is aware of its vital dependence on the outside world and of the need to prepare its future workforce for the challenges of 'new times', the Singapore state has retained the binary divide between the West and Asia with its Orientalist inflections in some areas. In what are considered the more 'neutral' realms of education, business and technology, the historically privileged discourse of the West as normative still prevails. One has only to think about the continuation of externally administered examinations, the need for Western experts to audit Singapore colleges and universities, the tendency to import Western educational practices wholesale without much of an attempt to indigenize them (Cheah 1998) and, most recently, the plan by the Singapore Education Ministry to turn the two local universities into 'the Harvard and MIT of the East'. All these practices clearly suggest the inherent superiority of Western educational institutions and practices, in relation to which local ones are considered 'lacking'.

Similarly, when those with local authority speak about Singapore students, they frequently cast them as 'lacking critical thinking skills' and as 'exam-smart muggers', dismissing their outdated learning practices and ultimately their entire cultural background. In the perennial news reports in the Singaporean daily on 'yet better examination results', we come across local academics deridingly questioning whether more 'A's in public exams mean 'brighter students ... or just students who are more exam-smart' (*Straits Times* 31 March 1996); we hear them laconically maintaining that 'Junior Colleges are doing a good job in producing competent students but they lack an enquiring mind', since Singapore students largely 'learn by rote', 'mug', and 'regurgitate' model answers to standard questions (ibid.); an arts faculty professor laments that 'even Arts students, commonly thought as being more articulate, are deficient in expression and critical thinking skills' (ibid. 19 April 1993). Most recently and perhaps most authoritatively, in the context of urging Singaporeans to nurture much-needed entrepreneurs, the senior minister, Lee Kwan Yew, is quoted as saying, 'It's a whole basic culture of not questioning your teacher. I think we've got to try and amend or modify our educational system. Or more important, the mindset' (ibid. 10 June 1999).

It is most powerfully through these discourses of public and community culture, reinforced through a whole network of related local curricular practices, that Singapore students acquire their understanding of what kinds of schooled subjects and writers they are and can be. Since they are immersed in these discourses and their supporting practices, that is, learning inside rather than about them, they are induced to comply actively with their values and constructions, rather than criticize or change them.

10.5 Final comment

In the previous narrative, I have explored a number of teaching interactions with a group of students which took a first step towards getting them to critique and renegotiate these constructions. However uneven and exploratory, the collective autobiography project described allowed the students to begin to understand the power that lies with existing constructions and the role these play in maintaining their sense of helplessness when it comes to writing from positions of authority. Quite often during the project, the students remained stuck in reproducing the very constructs that limit them but in places they also ventured to challenge existing images and reposition themselves as more authoritative subjects. Being educators of the future, this act of reconfiguring themselves as learners and writers is all the more important as it is in their own image that they will make their future students (Haas-Dyson 1994). That Radha is at least beginning to do this sort of rewriting is perhaps nowhere more obvious than in the following excerpt from her final assignment for my class. Note here how she revisits, and 'talks back to', the same tutor's comments that had caused her so much frustration in the beginning of my class. The authoritative final word is hers:

> In many ways the remarks that Tutor X had made on my Austen assignment influenced the writing of my subsequent assignments. I did disguise my opinions with hedges like 'seems' and 'could have'. But I decided to take him up on his advice 'not to end a paragraph with quotes but to comment on them.' I went to see him armed with some 'ammunition.' I showed him that in quite a bit of Eastern scholarship the pattern of ending the paragraph with a quotation 'constitutes the force' and the essence of one's point. In my opinion the point I was making was perfectly clear from the preceding bit of text. Naturally it could also be a way of saying 'I have someone, an authority to back me up' – another sign of insecurity perhaps. But this is the way I feel like writing and I don't feel comfortable changing it. And I wonder, why should I when my tutor finds this style of writing perfectly acceptable when his most admired critic Raymond Williams uses it? [Here follow two examples from a Raymond Williams essay the students had read for the class].

References

Ang, I. and Stratton, I. (1995) The Singapore way of multiculturalism: Western concepts/Asian cultures. *Sojourn*, 10: 65–83.

Ballard, B. and Clanchy. I. (1991) Assessment by misconception: Cultural influences and intellectual traditions. In L. Hamp-Lyons (ed.), *Assessing Second Language Writing in Academic Contexts*. Norwood, NI: Ablex, 21–35.

Bartholomae, D. (1985) Inventing the university. In M. Rose (ed.), *When a Writer Can't Write*. New York: Guilford, 134–65.

Baynham, M. (2000) Academic writing in new and emergent discipline areas. In M.R. Lea and B. Street (eds), *Student Writing in Higher Education: New Contexts*. Buckingham: Open University Press and SHRE, 17–31.

Benson, N. *et al.* (1994) The place of academic writing in whole life writing. In M. Hamilton, D. Barton and R. Ivanic (eds), *Worlds of Literacy*. Toronto: Multilingual Matters, 52–72.

Biggs, I.R. (1996) Western misperceptions of the Confucian-heritage learning culture. In D.A. Watkins and I.R. Biggs (eds), *The Chinese Learner: Cultural, Psychological and Contextual Influences*. Hong Kong and Melbourne: CERC and ACER, 25–42.

Bolker, I. (1979) Teaching Griselda to write. *College English*, 40: 906–9.

Bourdieu, P. (1990) *The Logic of Practice*. Cambridge: Polity Press.

Bourdieu, P. (1991) *Language and Symbolic Power*. Cambridge, MA: Harvard University Press.

Brodkey, L. (1996) *Writing Permitted in Designated Areas Only*. Minneapolis: University of Minnesota Press.

Cheah, Y.M. (1998) The examination culture and its impact on literacy innovations: The case of Singapore. *Language and Education*, 12: 192–209.

Clark, R. and Ivanic, R. (1997) *The Politics of Writing*. London: Routledge.

Comber, B. (1994) Critical literacy: An introduction to Australian debates and perspectives. *Journal of Curriculum Studies*, 26: 655–68.

Comber, B. (1997) Managerial discourses: Tracking the local effects on teachers' and students' work in literacy lessons. *Discourse: Studies in the Cultural Politics of Education*, 18: 389–408.

Davies, B. (1992) Women's subjectivity and feminist stories. In C. Ellis and M. Flaherty (eds), *Research on Subjectivity: Windows on Lived Experience*. Newbury Park, CA: Sage, 55–76.

Deckert, G. (1993) Perspectives on plagiarism from ESL students in Hong Kong. *Journal of Second Language Writing*, 2: 131–48.

Elbow, P. (1991) Reflections on academic discourse. *College English*, 53: 135–55.

Eldred, J. and Mortensen, P. (1992) Reading literacy narratives. *College English*, 54: 512–39.

Freebody, P., Luke, A. and Gilbert, P. (1991) Reading positions and practices in the classroom. *Curriculum Inquiry*, 21: 435–57.

Fuller, G. and Lee, A. (1997) Textual collusions. *Discourse: Studies in the Cultural Politics of Education*, 18: 409–24.

Haas-Dyson, A. (1994) Confronting the split between 'the child' and children: Toward new curricular visions of the child writer. *English Education*, 26: 12–28.

Harris, J. (1989) The idea of community in the study of writing. *College Composition and Communication*, 40: 11–22.

Ivanic, R. and Simpson, J. (1992) Who's who in academic writing? In N. Fairclough (ed.), *Critical Language Awareness*. London: Longman, 141–73.

Janks, H. (1997) Critical discourse analysis as a research tool. *Discourse: Studies in the Cultural Politics of Education*, 18: 329–68.

Kamler, B. (1997) Toward a critical writing pedagogy in English: Response to Terry Threadgold. In S. Muspratt, A. Luke and P. Freebody (eds), *Constructing Critical Literacies*. Creskill, NJ: Hampton Press, 387–409.

Kamler, B. *et al.* (1996) Developing a critical writing pedagogy: A discontinuous narrative. *English in Australia*, 118: 24–42.

Kirsch, G. and Ritchie, J. (1995) Beyond the personal: Theorizing a politics of location in composition research. *College Composition and Communication*, 46: 7–29.

Lea, M.R. and Street, B. (2000) Student writing and staff feedback in higher education: An academic literacies approach. In M.R. Lea and B. Street (eds), *Student Writing in Higher Education: New Contexts*. Buckingham: Open University Press and SHRE, 32–46.

Lillis, T. (1997) New voices in academia? The regulative nature of academic writing conventions. *Language and Education*, 11: 182–99.

Luke, A., O'Brien, J. and Comber, B. (1994) Making community texts objects of study. *Australian Journal of Language and Literacy*, 17: 139–49.

Matalene, C. (1985) Contrastive rhetoric: An American writing teacher in China. *College English*, 47: 789–807.

Morgan, W. (1997) *Critical Literacy in the Classroom: The Art of the Possible*. London: Routledge.

Osterloh, K.H. (1986) Intercultural differences and communicative approaches to foreign-language teaching in the third world. In J. Valdes (ed.), *Culture Bound*. Cambridge: Cambridge University Press, 70–82.

Pennycook, A. (1998) *English and the Discourses of Colonialism*. London: Routledge.

Spack, R. (1997) The rhetorical construction of multilingual students. *TESOL Quarterly*, 31: 765–74.

Wallace, C. (1992) Critical language awareness in the EFL classroom. In N. Fairclough (ed.), *Critical Language Awareness*. London: Longman, 59–92.

Zamel, V. (1997) Toward a model of transculturation. *TESOL Quarterly*, 31: 341–52.

Notes

1 Over the 30 years since Singapore's independence, English education has replaced vernacular education in all schools (except for a select few which the government has set up to preserve Chinese education). This policy of adopting a non-ethnic and hence 'neutral' language was implemented largely to bond a national mix of Chinese (77 per cent), Malays (14.1 per cent), Indians (7.1 per cent) and others (mostly Eurasians), who all speak their own vernacular. English is the official language, working language, lingua franca, and also the language for the expression of national identity. It is now spoken by 21.4 per cent of Singaporean families compared to half that in 1980; significantly, it is largely the families that fall in the higher income groups which speak English while more of lower

income families use the official ethnic languages (Malay, Tamil, Mandarin) and 'dialects' (as other Chinese, Indian and Malay languages, are derogatorily referred to locally in official discourse). Most young Singaporeans nowadays develop literacy in English first, instead of in their ethnic languages, since it is the medium of instruction from pre-school and kindergarten onward. In fact, English is referred to as the 'first language' in the school context while mother tongues are labelled 'second languages', taught in special second language classes, which take up a minor part of curriculum time (see Cheah 1998).

2 While the old (1982) English Language syllabus was essentially product-oriented, with much emphasis on grammar teaching and test-taking, in line with the British Cambridge examinations which Singapore as a former colony still administers, the 1991 syllabus has been shaped by communicative, process-and-learner-centred approaches to language teaching. However, since it has not been complemented by a change in the number and nature of examinations, which remain more or less the sole mechanism for selection and tracking from as early as Primary four, this innovative syllabus has been implemented highly selectively and superficially.

11

The Evaluation of Causal Discourse and Language as a Resource for Meaning

Bernard Mohan and Tammy Slater

11.1 Introduction

Systemic Functional Linguistics (SFL) has produced a volume of work that has made significant advances in the analysis of discourse, including discourse in education. Halliday's distinctive view of linguistics is concerned with texts in social contexts and is oriented to the description of language as a resource for meaning rather than with language as a system of rules (Halliday and Martin 1993). SFL has major implications for the assessment of discourse, particularly in the important area of assessing learners of English as a second language in tertiary education, an area which test developers have a strong interest in improving. Halliday's rich perspective on discourse sets standards of adequacy for the assessment of discourse in general and of scientific discourse in particular. Do present language evaluation theories and practices meet these standards? To address this question, we examined the evaluation of causal explanations, an essential part of academic literacy, and found disturbing issues in both theory and practice which seriously question the adequacy of present models designed to assess competence in a second language.

We have chosen causal explanations for a variety of reasons. The topic of causal explanations in scientific discourse has been a continuing focus of SFL interest (Halliday and Martin 1993; Martin and Veel 1998), and its analysis illustrates features of the SFL approach in general. Causal discourse is part of the metalanguage of science and an essential part of scientific literacy (Rowell 1997). Causal explanations are not limited to science, however; since they occur across many academic disciplines[1], they are part of academic literacy generally. If language assessment instruments at the university level are not capable of dealing adequately with causal explanations, we have reason to question their value and specifically their relation to scientific literacy in particular and academic literacy in general.

Our research strategy is a benchmark strategy: we elicited discourse of causal explanations, analysed the texts to illustrate relevant contrasts between them, and used the texts and their analysis as benchmarks for the critical examination of models of testing and test procedures. Our aim was to illustrate a test case which illuminates some of the confusion surrounding the assessment of discourse. We have discussed this case with two different groups: those familiar with an SFL approach to discourse and applied linguists who have an interest in second language evaluation. It has been our experience that there are significant mutual misunderstandings between these groups, and for that reason we have written this paper for both audiences.

11.2 The two written explanations of the water cycle

The following two explanations of the water cycle were elicited using a visual prompt – a diagram of the water cycle. Explanation A was written by a secondary school teacher whose first language is English, and Explanation B was written by a university student who speaks English as a second language.

Explanation A:

The water cycle
What are the processes that 'water' goes through?

1) Initially, the water cycle begins as snow melts from the glaciers.
2) The water then meanders through various water sheds until it reaches rivers and lakes. Water eventually reaches the oceans.
3) Water, then, becomes water vapour (it evaporates into the air) and accumulates in what we call clouds.
4) The 'clouds' then distribute water in the form of rain, snow, or sleet back to the mountains where the cycle begins again.

Explanation B:

The water cycle: The sun is the source of our water. The water, or hydrological, cycle begins when the sun heats up the ocean to produce water vapour through evaporation. This water vapour mixes with dust in the atmosphere and forms clouds. Cool air causes condensation of water droplets in the clouds, bringing about precipitation, or rain. This rain then falls into rivers, streams and lakes and eventually returns to the ocean, where the cycle begins again.

To analyse and therefore assess these causal explanations, Halliday's work encourages us to ask three related questions. These questions and the concepts they include are not generally understood in the language assessment literature, yet without them we do not see how it is possible to assess the discourse of causal explanations adequately. We will deal with each question in turn.

11.2.1 How do writers use language as a resource for meaning?

If we contrast Halliday's view of linguistics with that of traditional grammar (see Derewianka 1999) as in Table 11.1, we find very different implications for the evaluation of discourse. Where Halliday deals with discourse, considers functions of language and how they evolve in our culture, and explores how discourse varies with context, traditional grammar deals with the sentence, considers the form and structure of language, and offers a general description of language. Where Halliday sees language as a resource for making meaning in context and language learning as extending resources for making meaning, traditional grammar sees language as a set of rules and language learning as acquiring correct forms. In Halliday's view, meaning and form are intrinsically related. In the traditional view, meaning and form in language are typically not seen as related under

Table 11.1 Assumptions of SFL and traditional grammar

Systemic Functional Linguistics	Traditional Grammar
Discourse	Sentence and below
Functions of language and how they evolve in our culture to enable us to do things	Form and structure of language
How discourse varies with context	General description of language
Language as a resource for making meaning	Language as a set of rules
Language learning as extending resources for making meaning in context	Form unrelated to meaning ('conduit')
Evaluate discourse as making meaning with resources in context	Evaluate correctness. Judge meaning independently from form.

Source: Adapted from Derewianka (1999: 19).

a conduit metaphor: language is a conduit through which meaning flows rather than being inherently associated with meaning. The obvious implication for the evaluation of discourse from traditional grammar and the language as rule perspective is to evaluate the correctness of form to see whether language rules are violated or not. Judgements about the meaning of discourse may be made at the same time, but they are usually holistic, impressionistic and, consistent with the conduit metaphor, made independently of the evaluations of form. The implications for evaluation from Halliday's view are much different. The emphasis shifts from what the learner *cannot* do to what the learner *can* do. This view encourages us to evaluate discourse as making meaning using linguistic resources in context. How does the writer relate form and meaning? How do our writers use language as a resource for causal explanation? How do they express causality? Do they control a wide or narrow range of causal language?

11.2.2 How do writers build causal meanings from a range of different features of language and discourse?

Halliday and Martin (1993) argued that the language of science – discourse that can be challenging and alienating to both children and adults alike – reflects the evolution of scientific knowledge itself. The historical development of scientific English discourse offers more powerful ways of talking, writing and thinking about cause-and-effect relationships. Causal discourse, the authors suggested, has taken the following developmental path:

from A happens; so X happens
because A happens, X happens
that A happens causes X to happen
happening A causes happening X
to happening A is the cause of happening (Halliday and Martin 1993: 66)

Thus, some of the language features that are important for causal explanation will be verbs of doing and happening, causal conjunctions such as *so* and *because*, causal dependent clauses, lexical verbs of causation such as *cause* and nominalizations such as *happening*.

11.2.3 How do writers construct causal (and other) lines of meaning?

Both writers were presented with a visual of the water cycle, a series of events that are linked together causally, and their written explanations each construct an account of the water cycle. Each contains a line of meaning that runs through the discourse. The notion of lines of meaning was put forth by Longacre (1990), who proposed that there exist in discourse lines of meaning which are constructed using various language features. His discussion, which revolved around the storyline in narratives, illustrated how, for example, verbs are used in clauses to distinguish the main storyline from other strands of development. Existential verbs, he claimed, serve to establish the setting whereas verbs in the past continuous refer to actions which are occurring alongside the main storyline. He further suggested that other forms of discourse, such as procedural or hortatory discourse, have similar lines of meaning which can be constructed, visualized and analysed in similar ways. An adequate analysis of a text, therefore, needs to show how grammar and meaning interact intimately to construct the line of meaning in the discourse.

A competent reader of the water cycle texts should be able to reconstruct the line of meaning (i.e., she should be able to draw the cycle of the water cycle), and a competent evaluator should be able to recognize how the line of meaning is constructed by the relevant language features. Clearly the line of meaning need not be the only aspect of discourse that is of interest in causal texts, but it is central for many causal explanations and any evaluation which fails to deal with it is inadequate. The line of meaning provides a natural focus for the evaluator and suggests a holistic view of the discourse.

11.3 Comparison of participants' texts

Table 11.2 compares the language features of the two explanations with respect to time sequence and cause. The writer of Explanation A has constructed a *time* line of events in time sequence; in other words, event A comes before event B. She has constructed a line of meaning with time conjunctions which reflects an explicitly sequential explanation of the water cycle. For example:

1) *Initially*, the water cycle begins as snow melts from the glaciers.
2) The water meanders through various water sheds until it reaches rivers and lakes. Water *eventually* reaches the oceans.

The writer of Explanation B has constructed a *causal* line: a series of actions (and some events) in a cause and effect relation; in other words, A causes B. He has constructed a line of meaning with causal language features which reflects an explicitly causal explanation of the water cycle. For example, consider his use of lexical verbs of causation, closely linked to nominalized processes:

- ... the sun heats up the ocean to *produce* water vapour through evaporation.
- Cool air *causes* condensation of water droplets in the clouds, *bringing about* precipitation, or rain.

Unlike the writer of Explanation A, the writer of Explanation B uses a range of language resources for causal meaning. Where Explanation A uses one explicitly causal feature ('clouds distribute water'), Explanation B uses a number of causal features of different kinds. Actions, causal dependent clauses, lexical verbs such as *cause*, nominalizations, and causal metaphors are all features which play a part in constructing the causal line of Explanation B. Linked together through cohesion, they contribute to the line as a structure of ideational meaning.

Thus our analysis shows how Explanation B, but not Explanation A, draws on causal resources of English to create an explicit causal explanation. Is second language assessment at the university level capable of recognizing such differences and able to deal adequately with causal explanation? If not, we may question how well assessment deals with scientific literacy and academic literacy in general.

It is worth noting here that a language as rule perspective is not able to address these texts as causal explanations at all. The language as rule perspective does not address how meanings are constructed by a discourse; it can only describe the forms occurring in a discourse. For those who see language acquisition as the learning of correct form, there is nothing to be said by comparing our two texts, since neither contains grammatical errors.

11.4 Models for evaluating communicative competence and language as rule

We have now analysed our causal explanation texts, showing a contrast between them. We now move to the next stage of our study and use the texts and their analysis as a benchmark for the critical examination of models of testing and test procedures. In this we have shown how the analysis of these causal explanations relies on the assumptions of SFL (language as resource), and we have noted that a language as rule perspective is not able to address these texts as causal explanations. When we examine the assumptions which underlie current theory and practice in the assessment of discourse in the second language, we find that they are closer to language as rule than they are to language as resource.

Table 11.2 Language features of the two explanations

Language features	Explanation A	Explanation B
Time Sequence		
Events (sequence of happenings)	Water cycle begins, snow melts, water meanders, water reaches lakes and rivers, water reaches oceans, water becomes water vapour, it evaporates, cycle begins again	water cycle begins, rain falls into rivers, returns to ocean, cycle begins again
Time conjunctions	1, 2, 3, 4, initially, as, then, until, eventually	Then, eventually, and
Dependent clauses of time	As snow melts	when the sun . . .
Cause		
Actions	Clouds distribute water	Sun heats up ocean, produces water vapour, evaporation causes condensation, bringing about precipitation
Causal conjunctions	Ø	Ø
Causal dependent clauses	Ø	To produce water vapour
Cause/means as circumstance	Ø	Through evaporation
Cause as process	Ø	Produces, causes, brings about
Causal metaphor	Ø	The sun is the source of our water

At first glance, it would appear that currently accepted models for evaluating communicative competence or communicative language ability would be consistent with a language as resource perspective, since these models were influenced by early work in functional linguistics. According to Canale and Swain (1979, 1980), discourse can be assessed in an integrated manner using their theoretical framework of communicative competence. They defined communicative competence as the relationship and interaction among three main competencies: grammatical competence, or the knowledge a speaker has about the rules of grammar; sociolinguistic competence, or the knowledge of the rules of language use in social situations; and strategic competence, which refers to the knowledge of strategies, both verbal and non-verbal, that a speaker may have which can compensate for deficiencies in the other two areas of competence. Although Canale and Swain stated that each of these competencies can be examined separately, they emphasized that for second language teaching and testing purposes, a communicative approach '*must integrate* aspects of both grammatical competence and sociolinguistic competence' (1980: 6). In their view, an integrative theory of communicative competence

> may be regarded as one in which there is a synthesis of knowledge of basic grammatical principles, knowledge of how language is used in social contexts to perform communicative functions, and knowledge of how utterances and communicative functions can be combined according to the principles of discourse. (ibid.: 20)

However, models for evaluating communicative competence, while appearing to accommodate causal explanation and the systemic analysis of discourse generally, contain deep differences of assumptions that set the stage for mutual misunderstanding. This was brought home to us powerfully by the remark of a language assessment specialist who commented: 'Both Explanations A and B are competent. I don't see why you have to bother to say anything further than that.' In other words, from this specialist's standpoint, there was no need for the analysis of causal explanations or for the discourse analysis that lay behind it. Both writers were 'competent' in the sense that they did not violate the rules of the language. The notion of competence did not extend further than that, and did not need to.

These fundamental differences can be illuminated by a closer analysis of the development of Canale and Swain's theory. Bachman (1990) developed Canale and Swain's work, but he accomplished this primarily by expanding the taxonomy of competencies. From his work we now have grammatical, textual, illocutionary and sociolinguistic competence, plus strategic competence. Interestingly, he included Halliday's work in a number of these taxonomic categories. However, Bachman assumed the standard view of language as rule with its concomitant of language error, and extended it via the notion of convention. Grammatical competence is spoken of in terms of rules, textual competence is stated in terms of 'conventions for organising discourse', illocutionary competence is described as 'the pragmatic conventions for performing acceptable language functions' and sociolinguistic competence is said to encompass 'the sociolinguistic conventions for performing language functions appropriately in a given context' (ibid.: 88, 90). There is no evidence of any consideration given to language as a resource for meaning in Bachman's work. Without the concept of language as resource for meaning, a taxonomy of communicative language ability is too easily interpreted as a series of categories in which a learner can be judged right or wrong. At its most basic, it can be seen as a simple extension of the practice of assessing the language learner's discourse for grammatical errors. Bachman's development now presents us with an extended taxonomy in which the learner can be incorrect in a variety of ways, not only in grammar but also in discourse conventions, sociolinguistic appropriateness, and so on.

Canale and Swain's emphasis on integration of the parts of their taxonomy seems to call precisely for the kind of question that we were pursuing in our systemic analysis of causal explanation: 'How does the speaker/writer create a line of meaning which is causal, using the resources of discourse semantics and lexico-grammar, taken together?' From the standpoint of discourse analysis, it is very hard to see how discourse evaluation could avoid facing questions like this, yet integration, in that sense, has not been developed at all by Bachman. He has interpreted it in quite a different way. Bachman considered his model of strategic competence to provide the notion of integration which Canale and Swain presented. He redesigned strategic competence to provide a model which performs assessment, planning and execution functions in determining communication goals. This model, however, is a psycholinguistic model of the generalized processes involved in communication, which is vastly different from a discourse analysis model of the kind offered through systemic functional linguistics, a model which has the ability to address questions such as how causal lines can be constructed from the resources of language. Questions such as these are ignored, since they become irrelevant when models of communicative competence based on the assumption of language as rule are used as frameworks for the assessment of error, because the assessor does not need to consider how categories of the taxonomy are related to each other. A judgement of error in each category on the checklist is all that is required, as we will see in the next section.

11.5 Using the assessment instruments

In order to see whether assessment tools based on the taxonomic model of communicative competence discussed above could address the question of how causal lines differ in their construction, our water cycle texts were explored using two assessment instruments. The first was a locally developed tool for evaluating the communicative competence of potential second language teachers, and the second was the scoring guide for the Test of Written English (TWE). As can be seen from the discussion below, neither instrument was able to distinguish between the two texts, thereby suggesting that neither can adequately assess causal explanations.

The initial assessment was done by two raters who were experienced in using the scoring criteria of a test locally developed from Canale and Swain's Theoretical Framework of Communicative Competence (1979, 1980). Previous statistical analyses had determined that the overall reliability for this instrument was high. The actual test had ten tasks and, in the assessment of each, errors were classified in one of five categories of competence: linguistic, sociolinguistic, discursive, strategic and receptive. Linguistic competence referred to the knowledge an individual has of the lexis, phonology, morphology and syntax of the language, and included the ability of the individual to use this knowledge to create words and sentences. Within this category, the raters distinguished among vocabulary, mechanics (including spelling and punctuation), and morphology and syntax. Sociolinguistic competence in this instrument was concerned with whether the writer or speaker could carry out linguistic functions in particular social contexts. Having discursive competence meant that the individual was able to demonstrate an ability to connect sentences into cohesive and coherent discourse using devices such as transitional phrases and conjunctions or, in the raters' words, whether the text made sense or not. The definition of strategic competence for these raters was whether or not the writer got the message across, but the category primarily referred to the use of survival strategies such as paraphrasing and guessing to compensate for a lack of other competencies. Finally, receptive competence was the ability to understand what was being asked or said. An error in any of the above competencies could be assigned only to one category, determined by the raters. The scoring was binary within the categories for each of the ten tasks; in other words, the raters could give one point to a category if there were no problems exhibited and zero if there were one or more examples of errors.

Our writing task paralleled one from their test that the raters could identify with to some extent, yet there were still important differences to consider. Our water cycle task did not assign a specific role to the writer, and nor did it give the writer a context or an audience. Their test stated these explicitly for the writers. These differences prevented the raters from addressing the category of sociolinguistic competence because they could not judge whether the writer was communicating appropriately for the assigned context, role and audience. This comment was brought up very quickly in the assessment discussion.

Instead of noticing a difference in the two texts and crediting Explanation B as being the better of the two, these raters judged them as equal, assigning both a score of five out of six. The writer of Explanation A was faulted in the area of mechanics because she spelled *watersheds* as two words. A supposed mechanics problem was the reason for an imperfect score for Explanation B: the raters felt that it was wrong to use an upper case letter after a colon. Although the assessment focused on the negative aspects of the writing, the raters had good things to say as well. One rater, for example, appreciated the writer's use of *meanders*, commenting that it was 'a nice word'. Explanation B, both raters agreed, made sense:

> This one is textbook, unless no I don't see anything wrong unless ah but I'm not a scientist. But as far as the English and the you know like the sequence, it makes sense.

Unfortunately, there was nothing in the assessment instrument that allowed the raters to add points for what they considered exceptional because it was assessing the errors made rather than the resources each writer was exhibiting.

Intuitively, however, these raters judged Explanation B as definitely 'more advanced', 'scientific' and at a 'higher calibre than' Explanation A, yet they admitted that the assessment instrument would not account for this discrepancy:

Researcher:	So [Explanation A] and [Explanation B] you consider to be equal?
Rater 2:	Yeah, I would say. Yeah. Yeah.
Researcher:	But intuitively?
Rater 1:	To me [Explanation B] is a higher calibre than
Rater 2:	Yeah, yeah, yeah.
Researcher:	It's more sophisticated or?
Rater 2:	Yeah, yeah.

Researcher: But there is nothing in your instrument that would make that difference?
Rater 1: No.
Rater 2: No.

They stated that the only way they could distinguish levels with this assessment instrument was when there were errors, and because these two explanations did not contain a great number of errors, they were difficult texts to assess.

Because the instrument above was developed to assess general communicative competence in a second language rather than the ability to write academically, we decided to see if a difference between the explanations could be detected by using a more appropriate instrument, the scoring guide for the Test of Written English. This guide breaks competency into six levels, with a score of six being the highest. At each level there is a brief general description of what the rater can expect at that level, followed by a somewhat more detailed list of points to look for in the writing. Although these details are in point form, our exploration revealed that the points can be addressed quickly by the rater by turning them into yes/no questions, and the score which is arrived at will probably be the score which contains the greatest number of positive responses to these questions. A paper which is rated at a level five, for example, suggests in the general description that it should demonstrate that the writer has a good level of competence in syntax and rhetoric regardless of occasional errors. Among the list of points to consider for a level five paper is that it should be quite well developed, although not as well developed as a level six paper and with fewer details. It will also be likely to contain more errors than a level six paper. On the other end of the scale, a level one paper demonstrates incompetence, may be severely underdeveloped and will contain serious and persistent errors.

Our initial step was to find individuals who had been trained to use this assessment tool. As our interest was primarily exploratory, we asked the one trained individual we knew to hold a training session for eight volunteers from our university's language and literacy department. Two of the volunteers had undergone the training session two years previously. After the trainer held the session, the participants were asked to score various samples of writing to establish whether they were using the scoring guide correctly. After examining the results of the training, we asked the participants, in pairs, to work together to assess the two water cycle explanations using the TWE scoring guide, and these interactions were audio-taped. The individual who had conducted the training session was also asked to rate the two explanations. The results of the nine raters paralleled that of the two raters who used the communicative competence instrument above; in other words, all eleven raters judged the two explanations to be more or less equal regardless of the instrument they were using. Whereas the previous raters had assigned scores of five out of six to each of the two explanations using their locally developed tool, the raters using the TWE scoring guide gave Explanation A an average score of 5.67 and Explanation B a score of 5.89, the difference being non-significant. According to the TWE raters, the reasons for the lower score given to Explanation A was that it resembled an outline more than a written explanation and that it overused the word *then*.

As with the raters who used the locally developed instrument, these raters had an intuitive judgement of the explanations that did not always match the TWE score they assigned. Moreover, just as with the previous raters, there was general agreement among the TWE raters that when two texts are relatively well-written and contain few or no errors, they are difficult to assess because both can receive only the highest grade despite any apparent differences between them. A good example of this difficulty surfaced in the discussion between two raters who had just finished discussing Explanation A and had assigned a level six to it, justifying their decision by discussing each point on the scoring guide. When they read Explanation B, they began to laugh. Compared to Explanation A, they claimed, Explanation B was a much better piece of writing, yet they had confidently given Explanation A the maximum score based on the scoring guide. Laughing, one of the raters concluded, 'So much for criteria-referenced marking!' In general, all raters agreed that intuitively Explanation B was a better example of academic writing. It was judged as sounding more scientific and academic than the 'more elementary school' writing of Explanation A, and was credited as being able to show 'how it's all working'. In Explanation A, one rater claimed, 'the phrases are there but not the process' and, according to the intuitive judgements of these raters, the process was explained much more clearly in Explanation B.

The results of these exploratory assessments can be related to the traditional view of language as rule. Using both instruments, a broken rule – an error, in other words – suggests that the writer is lacking the necessary knowledge to complete the task successfully. In these two explanations, however, the writers were successful and no rules were seriously broken, so the resulting scores were similar. Both instruments encouraged the raters to adopt a binary-style checklist method of assessing categories of error. Once the raters narrowed a text down to a particular category, they asked themselves the questions listed in the scoring guide. Are there mechanical errors? Does it contain some serious errors which occasionally obscure meaning? Yes or no? There were also questions which solicited vague impressions of the meanings of the text as a whole, but which did not ask the rater to consider the specifics of the text, which presumably was considered to be a mere conduit for these meanings: Did the writer understand the task? Is the paper adequately organized? The answers to all the above and other questions provided the rationale for scoring the paper at a particular level or moving the score up or down. The weakness of this taxonomic checklist approach can be seen by contrasting it with the description which Halliday and Martin offered regarding the integration of features in scientific writing:

> Whenever we interpret a text as 'scientific English', we are responding to clusters of features ... But it is the combined effect of a number of such related features, and the relations they contract throughout the text as a whole, rather than the obligatory presence of any particular ones, that tell us what is being constructed is the discourse of science. (1993: 56)

Although this binary, taxonomic and error-based approach may be used to record in some sense whether the writer has or does not have the linguistic knowledge to complete the writing task, it is not able to show *how well* he uses that knowledge to construct the text as a whole, and therefore it is not able to record a difference between these two explanations. Furthermore, there was considerable evidence during both assessments that raters were intuitively able to recognize that Explanation B was superior to Explanation A, strongly suggesting that the assumptions built into these testing procedures actually suppress the reporting of differences easily noticed by the raters.

11.6 Conclusion

Our examination of the evaluation of written causal explanations seriously questions the adequacy of present models and practices which purport to assess competence in the second language. These models, and the testing practices which are associated with them, reflect underlying rule-based assumptions about the nature of language and the role of evaluation, which at their worst degrade the evaluation of discourse to a reductive exercise in the detection of errors. If these underlying theoretical assumptions are not recognized and changed, it is hard to see how the major implications of the SFL analysis of discourse can be incorporated so as to change present practices. What is most likely to happen is that present practices will grind remorselessly on within their present goals.

This chapter has demonstrated that it is possible to assess causal explanations with due regard to the three important questions posed earlier and repeated here: How do speakers and writers use language as a resource for meaning? How do they construct causal (and other) lines of meaning? How do they build meanings such as causality with a variety of features from different components of language? It is imperative at this time that we extend this work to move towards more acceptable practices in the assessment of scientific and academic literacy.

References

Bachman, L. (1990) *Fundamental Considerations in Language Testing.* Oxford: Oxford University Press.

Canale, M. and Swain, M. (1979) *Communicative Approaches to Second Language Teaching and Testing.* Ontario: Ministry of Education.

Canale, M. and Swain, M. (1980) Theoretical bases of communicative approaches to second language teaching and testing. *Applied Linguistics*, 1(1): 1–47.

Derewianka, B. (1999) *Introduction to systemic functional linguistics: Institute readings.* Singapore: Department of English Language and Literature, National University of Singapore.

Halliday, M.A.K. and Martin, J.R. (1993) *Writing Science: Literacy and Discursive Power.* Washington DC: The Falmer Press.

Longacre, R.E. (1990) *Storyline Concerns and Word Order Typology in East and West Africa.* Los Angeles, CA: The James S. Coleman African Studies Center and the Department of Linguistics, UCLA.

Martin, J.R. and Veel, R. (1998) *Reading Science.* New York: Routledge.

Rowell, P.M. (1997) Learning in school science: The promises and practices of writing. *Studies in Science Education*, 30: 19–56.

Tang. G.M. (in press) Knowledge framework and classroom action. In B. Mohan, C. Leung and C. Davison (eds), *English as a Second Language in the Mainstream.* Harlow: Pearson Education Ltd.

Notes

1 Tang (in press) offers an example of ESL students in the elementary school writing causal explanations of the Fall of the Roman Empire.

12

Sense and Sensibility: Texturing Evaluation

J.R. Martin

12.1 Evaluation, metaphor and image

In this paper I will consider aspects of the role played by evaluation in texturing discourse. Although the analysis of evaluation has tended to be marginalized in linguistics (Poynton 1990, 2000; Martin 1992a), it plays a powerful role in organizing texts – a role which is perhaps most transparent in texts relating to highly charged political issues. 'The stolen generations' issue in Australia, as presented by Manne (1998), is one such arena.

Bringing Them Home (1997) – the report of the National Inquiry into the Separation of Aboriginal and Torres Strait Islander Children from their families – suggests that between one in three and one in ten Aboriginal children were separated from their mothers. All one can say for certain is that in the seventy or so years in question tens of thousands of babies and children were removed. Yet there is an even more extraordinary fact than this. Until the last year or so most non-Aboriginal Australians either did not know or were at best only dimly aware that for some seventy years Australian governments had been involved in a more or less routine practice of part-Aboriginal child removal. This was something almost every Aborigine understood (Manne 1998: 53).

Sir William Deane, governor-general of Australia, has commented on the issue as follows:

> It should, I think, be apparent to all well-meaning people that true reconciliation between the Australian nation and its indigenous people is not achievable in the absence of acknowledgement of the wrongfulness of the past dispossession, oppression and degradation of the Aboriginal peoples. That is not to say that individual Australians who had no part in what was done in the past should feel or

acknowledge personal guilt. It is simply to assert our identity as a nation and the basic fact that national shame, as well as national pride, can and should exist in relation to past acts and omissions, at least when done or made in the name of the community or with the authority of government...

The present plight, in terms of health, employment, education, living conditions and self-esteem, of so many Aborigines must be acknowledged as largely flowing from what happened in the past. The dispossession, the destruction of hunting fields and the devastation of lives were all related. The new diseases, the alcohol and the new pressures of living were all introduced. True acknowledgement cannot stop short of recognition of the extent to which present disadvantage flows from past injustice and oppression...

Theoretically, there could be national reconciliation without any redress at all of the dispossession and other wrongs sustained by the Aborigines. As a practical matter, however, it is apparent that recognition of the need for appropriate redress for present disadvantage flowing from past injustice and oppression is a prerequisite of reconciliation. There is, I believe, widespread acceptance of such a need. (Deane 1966 quoted in *Bringing Them Home* 1997: 3–4)

These comments were included as part of the Introduction to Australia's remarkable *Bringing Them Home*. It includes a number of explicit ethical evaluations:

well-meaning people; the wrongfulness of the past dispossession, oppression and degradation; personal guilt; national shame; national pride; past injustice and oppression; other wrongs; past injustice and oppression

In addition, Deane deploys metaphorical language to amplify the plight of indigenous Australians – the 'river of disadvantage' motif:

The present plight ... flowing from what happened in the past; present disadvantage from past injustice; present disadvantage flowing from past injustice

Bringing Them Home also includes a large number of quotations from Aboriginal people; the voice of the stolen generations is foregrounded throughout the report. And there are numerous photographs, generally positioned at the beginning of parts, chapters and sections of chapters.

In considering the texture of evaluation, we need to take the role of all three of these resources into account (appraisal, imagery and images) – since they co-articulate the stance that multimodal texts naturalize for viewer/readers. For further consideration of verbiage/image relations in this regard, see Martin (in press a and b).

12.2 APPRAISAL resources

In order to deal with the texture of evaluation we need a framework for interpersonal resources in English that moves beyond traditional concerns with speech function and exchange structure (e.g., NEGOTIATION in Martin 1992b). Following Halliday's work on the grammar of MOOD (e.g., Halliday 1994), early work on interpersonal discourse analysis leaned towards the interactive dimension – the ways in which interacts give and demand goods-and-services and information. Paul Kelly, in his famous land rights narrative 'From Little Things Big Things Grow', reports on the negotiation of propositions and proposals as follows:

negotiating propositions (probabilities at risk)
Vestey man and Vestey man thundered
You don't stand a chance of a cinder in snow
Vincent said if we fall others are rising
From little things big things grow.
negotiating proposals (inclinations at risk)
Let us sort it out, your people are hungry
Vincent said no thanks, we know how to wait (Kelly 1999: 107–8)

Our work on secondary school and workplace discourse in the 1990s (e.g., Christie and Martin 1997; Martin and Veel 1998) convinced us that this essentially grammatical perspective on interactivity needs to be complemented with a more lexically based focus on 'personal' meanings. So alongside NEGOTIATION we tried to develop systems for evaluative meaning, which we referred to as APPRAISAL (Martin 2000a). In doing so we concentrated on gradable resources, which meant setting aside regions of meaning with clear interpersonal implications as far as communing are concerned. For example, we set aside the solidarity function of technical and specialized vocabulary (including slang; for anti-languages see Halliday 1976), swearing (Veltman 1998), terms of address (Poynton 1996) and so on as a Pandora's box called INVOLVEMENT (as yet unopened):

> In a few days we were in the Granites, and there we saw all those Europeans who were working in the mines; we didn't say 'Kardiya' then, that word comes from the Gurinji language. (*Stories from Lajamanu* 1985: 6)

> 'In the Kimberleys they shoot bastards like you!' . . . 'you blood*** mongrel half-breed', he muttered, 'I can't trust you!' (Morgan 1989: 45)

> Where are you headed young fella? . . . You've walked a long way son. (Morgan 1989: 34)

The box we did open was regionalized as three systems: ATTITUDE, ENGAGEMENT and GRADUATION. ATTITUDE focused on gradable resources for construing evaluation, comprising three regions of its own: AFFECT, JUDGEMENT and APPRECIATION (emotion, ethics and aesthetics if you will). AFFECT deals with resources for construing emotional reactions: for example, the mental process of affection and attitudinal adjective underlined below:

> Mrs Sullivan taught me how to love and what was right and what was wrong. I'm glad she taught me values because I now know what was wrong. [*Bringing Them Home* 1997: 8]

JUDGEMENT is concerned with resources for assessing behaviour according to various normative principles:

> It was wrong the way my natural mother was treated. Mrs Sullivan told my mother she should lock herself away. The Sullivan family told people my mother was *** and the court gave us to the Sullivan family. My mother was not crazy she was only nineteen. She was the right one and she shouldn't have killed herself but she knew no better and there was no-one to help her keep the children. (*Bringing Them Home* 1997: 8)

APPRECIATION looks at resources for construing the value of things, including natural phenomena and semiosis (as either product or process):

> Muecke's book provides more proof that the most interesting work in cultural studies is being done in Australia. Operating in the space between discourse theory and textual analysis, Muecke examines an extraordinarily wide range of material with unequalled sympathy and sophistication. (Muecke 1992: back cover)

As interpersonal meanings, attitudes have a tendency to colour phases of discourse. Splashes of stance for emotion, ethics and aesthetics are illustrated below (prosodic realizations, to put this in technical terms; Martin 2000b).

AFFECT (emotions; reacting to behaviour, text/process, phenomena)

> Another wrote of having to leave her younger siblings behind in an orphanage when she was sent to work elsewhere at the age of 14: 'So this meant the grieving took place again. The grief came for my younger sister and two brothers whom I thought I would never see again. The day I left the Orphanage – that was a very sad day for me. I was very unhappy and the memories came back. There was nowhere to turn. You was on your own. I was again in a different environment ... I had no choice but to stick it out. With the hardships going and thinking of my sister and brothers which I left at the Orphanage. My heart full of sorrows for them. (*Bringing Them Home* 1997: 12)

JUDGEMENT (ethics; evaluating behaviour)

> Worse, this is a mean administration; a miserly, mingy, minatory bunch if ever there was one. It has a head but no heart, a brain but no soul. Without generosity of spirit, devoid of compassion, absorbed in narrow self-interest the Howard Government has no concept of any over-arching duty to articulate the aspirations of the governed and to lead them, with some hope, to a happier and more complete nationhood. If the polls slump, how easy it is to play the Hansonite politics of greed and to send in the bovver brigade: Herron to cosh the boongs, Tony Abbott to drop-kick the unemployed, Jocelyn Newman to savage those on social welfare. This is not government, it is mere management, a very different thing, and it is what will do for them in the end. A cold and bloodless lot, their veins run with piss and vinegar. (Carleton 2000: 38)

APPRECIATION (aesthetics; evaluating text/process, phenomena)

> In 1983, the new school headmaster (Mr Terry Lewis) brought considerable excitement to the Yuendumu community by his interest in and support of traditional Warlpiri culture and language. One of his more modest suggestions was to make the school look less 'European' by commissioning senior men to paint the school doors with traditional designs. The results were more spectacular

> that anyone envisaged. Both European and Aboriginal residents of Yuendumu took considerable pleasure and pride in the achievement. Visitors to the community were equally enthusiastic, and word about these remarkable paintings began to spread. My own response was to see this accomplishment as a major one for contemporary international art as well as an achievement in indigenous culture. For me, these doors seemed to strike a chord with issues and images that were being negotiated in the art galleries of Sydney, Paris and New York. (Michaels 1987: 135)

As attitudinal systems, AFFECT, JUDGEMENT and APPRECIATION are all concerned with feeling. AFFECT is the embodied system we are born with, which we develop into culturally specific emotional repertoires. JUDGEMENT and APPRECIATION on the other hand might be viewed as uncommon sense feeling: JUDGEMENT as the institutionalization of feeling with a view to prescribing behaviour, APPRECIATION as the institutionalization of feeling with a view to assessing the value and social significance of things. An outline of this genetic perspective is presented in Figure 12.1.

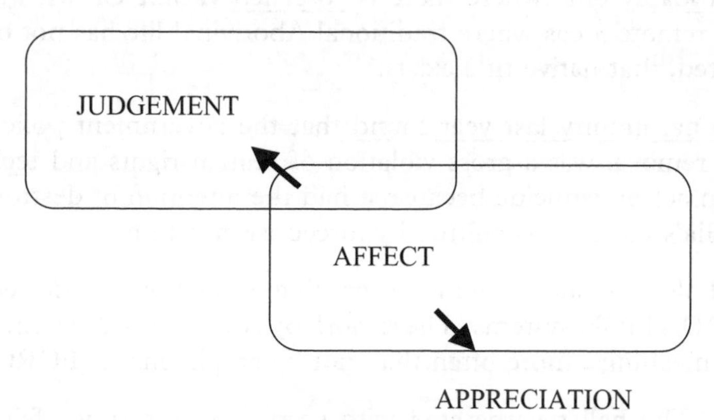

Figure 12.1 JUDGEMENT and APPRECIATION as institutionalized feeling

Alongside these attitudinal resources, APPRAISAL includes systems for adjusting a speaker's commitment to what they are saying – referred to as ENGAGEMENT systems. ENGAGEMENT includes options for both eliding and referencing dialogism in discourse (Fuller 1998, 2000; Fuller and Lee 1997; White 1997). The option monogloss construes a proposition or proposal baldly, with no referencing to sources or alternative positions:

monogloss (elide dialogism) – The Lord Mayor handed Aunty Iris the key to the city and a Sorry Book signed by the Melbourne town councillors.

Heteroglossing opens things up in various ways – modalization (*I bet, would*), projection and negation (*Aunty Iris never thought, Jeff Kennet has said*), counter-expectation (*ever, even*) and restricted provenance (*so-called, technically*):

heterogloss (reference dialogism) – I bet Aunty Iris never thought when she was living on the mission listening to the wailing of mothers mourning their stolen children, that she would ever be guest of honour at the Melbourne Town Hall.

Even the Thacherite premier of Victoria, Jeff Kennet, has said, 'We're sorry for what happened and we're sorry for the hurt and pain.'

It is probably only where there is so-called vacant Crown Land, and in remote areas where traditional Aboriginal life has not been disrupted, that native title exists.

A national inquiry last year found that the government policy of forced removal was a gross violation of human rights and technically an act of genocide because it had the intention of destroying Australia's indigenous culture by forced assimilation.

Appraisal also includes systems for grading evaluations – referred to as GRADUATION systems. These work by adjusting the 'volume' of gradable meanings, more often than not by amplifying it (FORCE):

high – The hall reverberated with sorry business as we felt the anguish of people such as Margaret Harrison, once confined to Ebenezer Mission in Victoria, who pleaded with the Board of protection: 'Please would you allow me to have my two girls here as [another] one of them died and I have not seen her before she died and I should like the other two to be with me to comfort me.'

low – We could just catch its amplified strains above the racket of construction work and the rattle of trams.

Even if the charge of genocide remains contentious between people of good will, as I suspect it might...

GRADUATION also includes resources for fine-tuning the value of experiential meanings – either to strengthen or weaken categorizations (FOCUS):

sharpen – Unexpected evidence of the rapport between Aborigines and Irish can also be found in the history of that quintessential Irish-Australian – rapparee – bushranger, Ned Kelly.

true reconciliation between the Australian nation and its indigenous people is not achievable in the absence of acknowledgement of the wrongfulness...

soften – and, just for a minute ... I could feel something of the spirit of Wurundjei land before the concrete and trams took over.

Until the last year or so most non-Aboriginal Australians either did not know or were at best dimly aware that for some seventy years Australian governments had been involved in a more or less routine practice of part-Aboriginal child removal.

An overview of these and related interpersonal systems across strata is presented as Table 12.1. As far as APPRAISAL is concerned, realizations tend to foreground lexis over grammar; phonologically speaking appraisal draws a number of features which have been traditionally relegated to paralinguistics back into the system.[1]

An alternative representation of interpersonal discourse semantics is outlined in Figure 12.2. Looking upwards to context, APPRAISAL, NEGOTIATION and INVOLVEMENT construe tenor relations – including both status and contact. APPRAISAL plays a key in construing communities, and so should play a key role in developing better understandings of solidarity; for groundbreaking work in this area see Eggins (2000) and Eggins and Slade (1997).

A typological overview of APPRAISAL resources is presented in Figure 12.3. For discussion of the relation of APPRAISAL to NEGOTIATION see Martin (2000b), where Halliday's MOOD grammar is reconsidered from a lexical perspective as grammaticalized stance.

Table 12.1 Interpersonal resources across strata

REGISTER	DISCOURSE SEMANTICS	LEXICO-GRAMMAR	PHONOLOGY
	NEGOTIATION		
TENOR (voice)	• speech function		
	• exchange		
	APPRAISAL		
	• engagement	• 'evaluative' lexis	• loudness
	• affect	• modal verbs	• pitch movement
	• judgement	• modal adjuncts	• voice quality
power (status)	• appreciation	• polarity	• (formatting)
	• graduation	• pre/numeration	
		• intensification	
		• repetition	
		• manner; extent	
		• logico-semantics	
	INVOLVEMENT		
solidarity (contact)	• naming	• vocation/names	• 'accent'
	• technicality	• technical lexis	• whisper
	• anti-language	• specialized lexis	• acronyms
	• swearing	• slang	• 'pig latins'
		• taboo lexis	• secret scripts

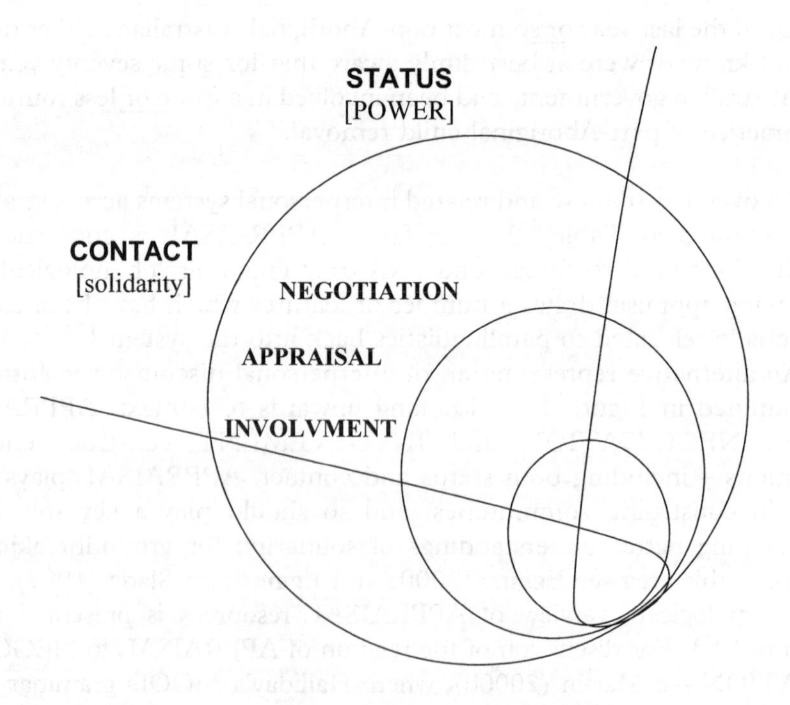

Figure 12.2 Interpersonal discourse semantics in relation tenor

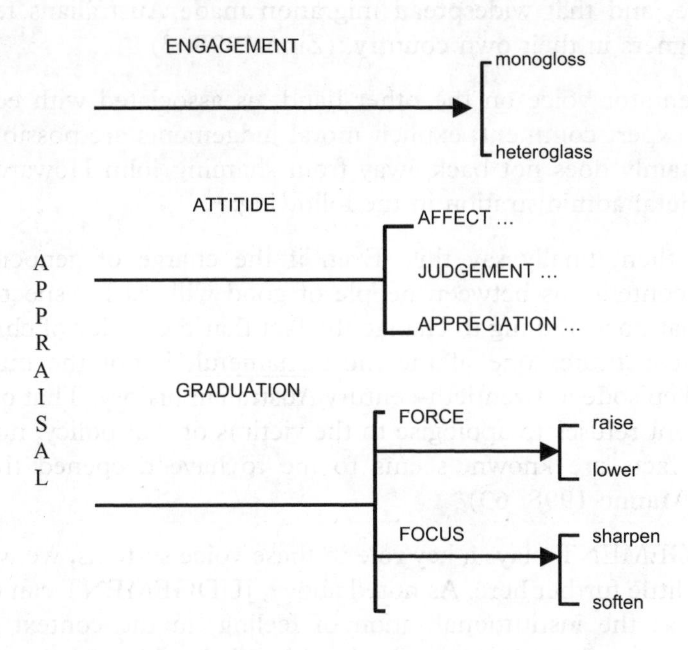

Figure 12.3 APPRAISAL systems: ENGAGEMENT, ATTITUDE and GRADUATION

12.3 Voice

The prosodic colouring of phases of discourse according to one kind of stance or another raises the issue of appraisal keys – the rhetorical voices through which we speak. Work on media discourse (Iedema *et al.* 1994; Iedema 1997; White 1997) and history (Coffin 1997) has identified some relevant keys, referred to as authorial voice. For the media, reporter voice, for example, was contrasted with commentator voice. Reporter voice is the more 'objective' key; for this voice, all explicit moral judgements have to be projected since the reporter cannot be the source of these. Note that the charge of racism in the following text is in fact doubly projected – as something the reporter says that Hanson says that someone else has said:

> Aboriginal and ethnic groups warned last weekend that Pauline Hanson's One Nation party ... could set back race relations in Australia for decades ... Ms Hanson responded that although she was branded a **racist**, no one could point to any **racist** comment she had made. But she said many Asians were not prepared to

> assimilate, and that widespread migration made Australians feel like foreigners in their own country. (Zinn 1998: 3)

For commentator voice on the other hand, as associated with editorials and expert comment, explicit moral judgements are possible. Manne certainly does not back away from shaming John Howard's churlish federal administration in the following:

> Let me, then, finally say this. Even if the charge of genocide remains contentious between people of good will, as I suspect it might, that does nothing to change the fact that the policy of child removal constitutes one of the most shameful, if not the most shameful episode in twentieth-century Australian history. That our government refuses to apologise to the victims of that policy, now that the facts are known, seems to me to have deepened that shame. (Manne 1998: 63)

Since JUDGEMENT plays a key role in these voice systems, we will explore it a little further here. As noted above, JUDGEMENT can be thought of as the institutionalization of feeling, in the context of proposals (norms about how people should and should not behave). Like AFFECT, it has a positive and negative dimension – corresponding to positive and negative judgements about behaviour. Iedema *et al.* (1994) suggest dividing judgements into two major groups, social esteem and social sanction. Social esteem involves admiration and criticism, typically without legal implications: if you have difficulties in this area you may need a therapist. Social sanction, on the other hand, involves praise and condemnation, often with legal implications: if you have problems in this area you may need a lawyer. Judgements of esteem have to do with normality (how unusual someone is), capacity (how capable they are) and tenacity (how resolute they are); judgements of sanction have to do with veracity (how truthful someone is) and propriety (how ethical someone is).

At this level of delicacy the types of JUDGEMENT are related to MODALITY (Halliday 1994), in the following proportions:

	normality	is to	usuality
as	capacity	is to	ability
as	tenacity	is to	inclination
as	veracity	is to	probability
as	propriety	is to	obligation

With this system in mind we can be more explicit about media keys, including reporter, correspondent and commentator voice as outlined

Table 12.2 Types of JUDGEMENT

SOCIAL ESTEEM 'venial'	POSITIVE (admire)	NEGATIVE (criticize)
normality (fate)	lucky, fortunate, charmed ...	unfortunate, pitiful, tragic ...
	normal, average, everyday ...	odd, peculiar, eccentric ...
	in, fashionable, avant garde ...	dated, daggy, retrograde ...
capacity	powerful, vigorous, robust ...	mild, weak, wimpy ...
	insightful, clever, gifted ...	slow, stupid, thick ...
'is s/he capable?'	balanced, together, same ...	flaky, neurotic, insane ...
tenancity (resolve)	plucky, brave, heroic ...	rash, cowardly, despondent ...
	reliable, dependable ...	unreliable, undependable ...
'is s/he capable?'	tireless, persevering, resolute	weak, distracted, dissolute ...

SOCIAL SANCTION 'mortal'	POSITIVE (praise)	NEGATIVE (condemn)
veracity (truth)	truthful, honest, credible ...	dishonest, deceitful ...
	real, authentic, genuine ...	glitzy, bogus, fake ...
'is s/he honest?'	frank, direct ...	deceptive, manipulative ...
propriety (ethics)	good, moral, ethical ...	bad, immoral, evil ...
	law abiding, fair, just ...	corrupt, unfair, unjust ...
'is s/he beyond reproach?'	sensitive, kind, caring ...	insensitive, mean, cruel ...

in Figure 12.4. Specifically, reporter voice makes use of graduation (force) to call attention to its news, but proscribes explicit judgement (unless projected); correspondent voice allows explicit judgements of social esteem; and commentator voice allows explicit judgements of both social esteem and social sanction, explicit causality and commands. Related keys were established for history discourse by Coffin (1997), labelled recorder, interpreter and adjudicator voice respectively.

The possibility of voiceless writing is an interesting issue. Hunston (e.g., 1993, 1994, 2000) and Myers (1989) have done important work on evaluation in scientific writing, a register we might initially think of as purely objective. *Star Trek*'s Mr Spock and Data aside, the only site I know of which regularly features faceless discourse is recount writing in the early school years, where the labour of scribing seems to have the effect of turning evaluation off:

> 'The Journey of Healing'
> Yesterday I went into the library and we talked about Aboriginal people. When they were little someone took them to another place.

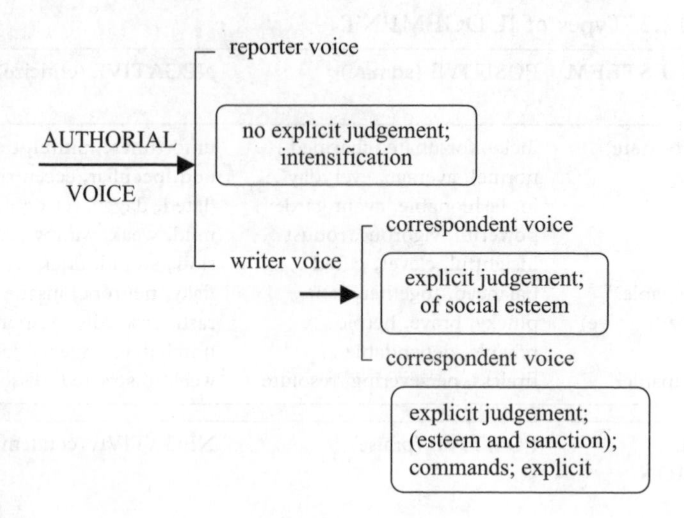

Figure 12.4 Appraisal keys for media discourse

> When they grew up they couldn't find their families. (Year 1, Vietnamese student)

In mature writing, perhaps the closest we get to facelessness is reporter or recorder voice; even there, the objective stance tends to be just one phase, and in any case allows for engagement and graduation of various kinds. Robert Manne, reporting on the case of Nellie Bliss, whose son was taken near the beginning of the Australian government's policy of systematic child removal, begins as follows:

> The story begins with a letter sent on February 17, 1903, to the police in Townsville. It was written by the Northern Protector of Aboriginals in Queensland, the notable anthropologist, Dr Walter E. Roth, who was shortly to become Chief Protector in Queensland, and later the sole royal commissioner looking into the conditions of Aborigines in the north of Western Australia. Historians may eventually come to see him as the architect of the policy of Aboriginal child removal in Australia. (Manne 1999: 11)

Manne soon follows up this stance with interpretation, commenting explicitly on the social esteem (capacity) of William Craig, who was opposed to the policy and tried to intervene on Nellie Bliss's behalf:

> Craig followed his telegram with a letter. He had listened to Nellie Bliss with genuine attentiveness. He was able to put to the Home Secretary, in a morally and legally persuasive language, the kind of

case he now knew Nellie herself would have put before the court if she had been able to speak English or . . . pay for a barrister.

Further on, Manne culminates his history with some adjudication, commenting on the morality of separating Aboriginal children from their families and the truthfulness of Prime Minister John Howard's spin doctors on this theme.

(finally) adjudicating [social sanction – propriety, veracity]:

> We have, in recent times, been told flatly that this policy was driven by a concern for the best interests of the children. We have been told, too, that the policy accorded with the moral standards of the time. No-one, however, who follows this story – who witnesses the grief of Nellie Bliss, the terror of Walter, the arrogance of Dr Walter E. Roth and the astonished indignation of William Craig – could seriously come out believing that what we have been told is true. (Manne 1999: 11)

12.4 Voice dynamics

Manne's rhetoric raises the more general issue of how voices unfold in discourse – the texture of evaluation. Hunston and Thompson (2000a: 11), citing Sinclair, make the point that evaluation tends to occur at boundary points in discourse. Read in relation to Martin (1992b, 1993) this might be explored in relation to layers of Theme and New in discourse. Drawing on Fries' (1981/1983) work on patterns of Theme (method of development) and New (point), Martin unpacks Halliday's notion of hierarchy of periodicity in terms of layers of prediction and accumulation – suggesting that method of development may be predicted by higher-order Hyper-Themes, a pattern of which may in turn be predicted by Macro-Themes and so on, just as point may be consolidated in higher-order Hyper-New, a pattern of which may in turn be further consolidated in Macro-new and so on (see Figure 12.5). The more planned and edited the writing, the more layers of Theme and New we find – ultimately resolving as Tables of Contents and Indexes in published work.

In my experience, across many registers, evaluation is strongly associated with higher-order Themes and News. Fries' classic exemplar, 'The English Constitution', nicely illustrates the point. Its method of development, as realized through clause Themes, is the opposition of wisdom and chance; and this pattern of Themes is predicted by the Hyper-Theme *It is the child of wisdom and chance.*

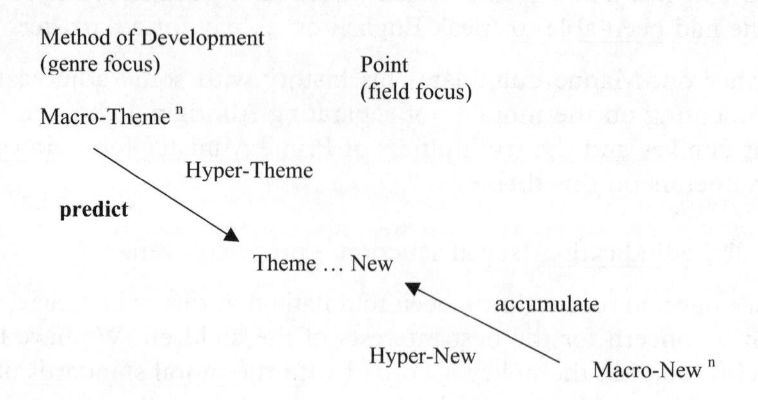

Figure 12.5 Layers of Theme and New

This involves two judgements of social esteem along the dimension of normality (*chance*) and capacity (*wisdom*):

> [1] The English Constitution – that indescribable entity – is a living thing, growing with the growth of men, and assuming ever-varying forms in accordance with the subtle and complex laws of human character. **It is the child of wisdom and chance**.
>
> The wise men of 1688 moulded it into the shape we know, but the chance that George I could not speak English gave it one of its essential peculiarities – the system of a cabinet independent of the crown and subordinate to the Prime Minister. The wisdom of Lord Grey saved it from petrification, and set it upon the path of democracy. Then chance intervened once more. A female sovereign happened to marry an able and pertinacious man, and it seemed that an element which had been quiescent within it for years – the element of irresponsible administrative power – was about to become its predominate characteristic and change completely the direction of its growth. But what chance gave chance took away. The Consort perished in his prime, and the English Constitution, dropping the dead limb with hardly a tremor, continued its mysterious life as if he had never been. (Fries 1983:123–4)

The introduction to text 2 below operates along similar lines, focusing in this case on the social esteem variable capacity (diplomatic skills and bravery):

> [2] This most successful phase of the Long March owes a great

deal to **the diplomatic skills of Zhou Enlai** and to **the bravery of the rearguard**.

> Knowing that the south-west sector of the encircling army was manned by troops from Guangdong province, Zhou began negotiations with the Guangdong warlord, Chen Jitang. Chen was concerned that a Guomindang victory over the Communists would enable Chiang Kaishek to threaten his own independence. Chen agreed to help the Communists with communications equipment and medical supplies and to allow the Red Army to pass through his lines.
>
> Between 21 October and 13 November the Long Marchers slipped quietly through the first, second and third lines of the encircling enemy. Meanwhile the effective resistance of the tiny rearguard lulled the Guomindang army into thinking that they had trapped the entire Communist army. By the time the Guomindang leaders realised what was happening, the Red Army had three weeks' start on them. The marching columns, which often stretched over 80 kilometres, were made up of young peasant boys from south-eastern China. Fifty-four per cent were under the age of 24. (Buggy 1988: 224)

Appraising forecasts of this kind can be used to construct the momentum of adventure in 'ripping good yarns'. In *Nathaniel's Nutmeg* (Milton 1999) the reader is at times left gasping as one complication resolves into another, with Hyper-Themes predicting worse to come:

[3] This was only the beginning of his misfortune.
=/x
When all the Englishmen in the town had been captured, including Nathaniel Courthope, they were herded together and clapped in irons; 'my selfe and seven more were chained by the neckes all together: others by their feete, others by their hands.' When this was done, the soldiers left them in the company of two heavily armed guards who 'had compassion for us and eased us of our bonds, for the most of us had our hands so straite bound behind us that the blood was readie to burst out at our fingers' end, with pain unsufferable'.

Middleton still had no idea why he had been attacked, but he was soon to learn the scale of the Aga's treachery.
=/x
Not only had eight of his men been killed in the 'bloudie massacre'

and fourteen severely injured, he now heard that a band of one hundred and fifty Turks had put to sea 'in three great boats' with the intention of taking the *Darling* – now anchored off Mocha – by force.

The attack caught the *Darling*'s crew completely unawares.
=/x
Knowing nothing of the treachery ashore they first realised something was amiss when dozens of Turks were seen boarding the ship, their swords unsheathed. The situation quickly became desperate; three Englishmen were killed outright while the rest of the company rushed below deck to gather their weapons. By the time they had armed themselves the ship was almost lost. 'The Turkes were standing very thicken in the waist [of the ship], hollowing and clanging their swords upon the decke.'

It was a quick thinking crew member who saved the day.
=/ix
Realising their plight was helpless he gathered his strength and rolled a huge barrel of gunpowder towards the Turkish attackers, then hurled a firebrand in the same direction. The effect was as dramatic as it was devastating. A large number of Turks were killed instantly while the rest retired to the half-deck in order to regroup. This hesitation cost them their lives for the English had by now loaded their weapons which they 'set off with musket shot, and entertayned [the Turks] with another trayne of powder which put them in such feare that they leaped into the sea, hanging by the ship's side, desiring mercy, which was not there to be found, for that our men killed all they could finde, and the rest were drowned, only one man who was saved who hid himselfe till the furie was passed, who yielded and was received to mercie'.

The *Darling* had been saved but Middleton's situation was now even more precarious ... (Milton 1999: 206–7)

The association of evaluation with Hyper-Themes is revealing as far as logico-semantic relations between Hyper-Themes and ensuing text are concerned. Over the years I have often felt torn as to whether to analyse the relations marked '=*ix*' in text 3 as elaborations or enhancements. In the first paragraph for example, is Milton specifying the details of Nathaniel's misfortune (elaboration) or explaining why he is saying Nathaniel was unfortunate (enhancement)? In the present context we could resolve this conundrum by arguing 'both' – since the paragraph elaborates the sense of its Hyper-Theme (its ideational meaning) at the same time as it justifies its sensibility (its evaluative meaning):

SENSE	elaboration (=)	'what I'm saying...'
and		
SENSIBILITY	justification (x)	'why I'm feeling...'

Examples of evaluation associating with Hyper-New are well-known from narrative analysis (e.g., Martin 1997; Martin and Plum 1997). In text 4 a dog breeder constructs an exemplum illustrating how mad dog people can get – as forecast in the story's Abstract (*how mad*) and consolidated in its Interpretation (*real absolute lunacy*).

> [4] [Abstract] GP: You got a favourite story concerning your dogs? HF: Well, yes, another story which will show you **how mad** dog people can get.
>
> [Orientation] I think we set some sort of record in that with two friends of ours we went to Queensland for a big speciality show and between us took twenty-three dogs.
>
> [Incident] Arrived in Queensland on the Friday morning, right, with caravan and dog trailer in tow, set up caravan and tents and things like that in the yards of friends in Queensland, hired a grooming salon for the Friday afternoon, Friday evening, Friday night, Saturday morning, started bathing the first one at four o'clock Friday afternoon and we finished the twenty-third at three o'clock Saturday morning. Piled them all into dog trailers and cars and things, took them back to the caravan and left at six o'clock that morning for the show. Showed them all...
>
> [Interpretation] You know, and I'd think that was some sort of record. And that was real absolute lunacy, doing that. We wouldn't do it again, but my God we had a ball doing it though, didn't we? [addressed to partner] We really had a good time. You know, but there was so much work. (Plum 1988: 222)

Similarly, Kelly's land rights narrative cited earlier (1999: 107–8) makes its point explicit in its Orientation, referring to an eight year story of power and pride and returns in its Coda reference to a story of power and privilege.

12.5 Imagery and evaluation

Although not touched on above, ATTITUDE may be inscribed,

using evaluative lexis, or evoked by experiential meaning that invites evaluation. For example, Archie Roach, in his anthem for the Stolen Generations, describes his own experience of being taken from his family as a series of events in which his father's feelings are mentioned (fighting mad) and also those of his mother (tears were falling down), but in which his own feelings at being taken are not explicitly noted at all. It goes without saying, of course, that his story evokes a reaction simply by being told, and that his music and singing co-articulate his grief.

Chris Sitka (1998), on the other hand, reacting to one of Roach's performances of the song, does explicitly inscribe Roach's feelings (as *anguish*):

> [7] As Archie Roach got up to sing the words of the song Uncle Ernie had played on his gum leaf, he also indicated his **anguish** at being taken from his parents, and how he had gone on, not to the better life promised at the time by the white authorities, but to face discrimination and destitution. 'I've often lived on the streets and gone without a feed for days and no one ever said sorry to me.'

Beyond this, as Joan Rothery has suggested to me (cf. Rothery and Stenglin 2000), lexical metaphor can be used to provoke a reaction where ideational selections alone might not naturalize the appropriate response. For example, early in his anthem Archie Roach draws on metaphor to describe the effect of driving indigenous people from their lands and herding them together on missions prior to taking their children away, singing of his people being fenced in like sheep.

Bob Ellis deploys imagery along these lines below, to construct what it feels like to live as a victim of economic rationalism:

> [9] John Howard says he knows how vulnerable people are feeling in these times of economic change. He does not. For they are feeling as **vulnerable** as a man who has already had his arm torn off by a lion, and sits in the corner holding his stump and waiting for the lion to finish eating and come for him again. This is something more than vulnerability. It is injury and shock and fear and rage. And he does not know the carnage that is waiting for him if he calls an election. And he will be surprised.

This stance-provoking function of metaphor lies behind its association with the Evaluation stage of thematic narrative (Rothery 1994), and beyond this its prestige in creative writing. Note how the Evaluation in one of Rothery's key exemplars uses an array of imagery to amplify the effect of the dead girl on Jenny's mind:

[10] Jenny decided to check out the accident during the commercial. She could probably get back in time before the show started again. She went out into the hallway and walked down the stairs until she got to the top of the stairs outside the block of flats. From there, she saw the girl.

The white body and red blood were **like fresh paint splotches** against the black footpath. **The image froze into Jenny's mind**. The girl's face was horrible and beautiful at the same time. It seemed more real than anything Jenny had ever seen. Looking at it, Jenny felt **as though she was coming out of a long dream**. It seemed to **cut through the cloud in her mind like lightning**.

Suddenly Jenny was aware of everything around her. Police cars were pulling up. Ambulance lights were flashing around. People sobbed and covered their faces.

A summary of these strategies for construing attitude is presented in Figure 12.6. The inscribe option is realized through explicitly evaluative lexis; the evoke option draws on ideational meaning to 'connote' evaluation, either by selecting meanings which invite a reaction or deploying imagery to provoke a stance:

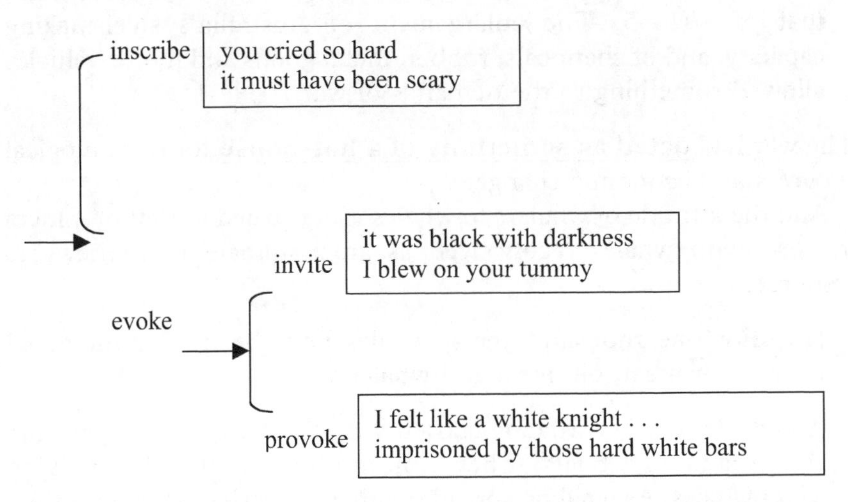

Figure 12.6 Strategies for encoding attitude – inscribe, invite, provoke

In popular culture, a gifted lyricist like Bruce Springsteen may deploy imagery in Hyper-Theme (Orientation) and Hyper-New (Coda) to provoke the appropriate reaction in a receptive audience. In his famous exemplum, the protest song 'Born in the USA', he evokes the feelings of a Vietnam veteran.

Springsteen's vet begins life feeling like a dog that's been kicked around from the moment it was born, and ends up feeling like a prisoner or unemployed refinery worker desperately running nowhere. It is useful to compare these lyrics with the effect of Cold Chisel's Vietnam veteran's recount, 'Khe Sanh', where Don Walker uses more conventional imagery in the Orientation (with the vet selling his soul to a black market man) but none at all in the Coda to construe a closely related message (Martin 1997).

In history discourse, my impression is that imagery is associated with Hyper-New and tends to offer as relatively concrete a reconstrual of one field as another. The effect is to transfer a naturalized reaction from one field to another. Thus the effect of war on Australian manufacturing is construed as nurturing:

> [13] The Second World War further encouraged the restructuring of the Australian economy towards a manufacturing basis.
>
> Between 1937 and 1945 the value of industrial production almost doubled. This increase was faster than otherwise would have occurred. The momentum was maintained in the post-war years and by 1954–5 the value of manufacturing output was three times that of 1944–5. The enlargement of Australia's steel-making capacity, and of chemicals, rubber, metal goods and motor vehicles allowed something to the demands of war.

The war had **acted as something of a hot-house** for technological progress and economic change.

And the attitude of whalers to whales is construed as that of miners to coal, with whales reconceived as an inanimate non-renewable resource:

> [14] For one thousand years, whales have been of commercial interest for meat, oil, meal and whalebone.
>
> About 1000 A.D., whaling started with the Basques using sailing vessels and row boats. They concentrated on the slow-moving Right whales. As whaling spread to other countries, whaling shifted to Humpbacks, Grays, Sperms and Bowheads. By 1500, they were whaling off Greenland; by the 1700s, off Atlantic America; and by the 1800s, in the south Pacific, Antarctic and Bering Sea. Early in this century, the Norwegians introduced explosive harpoons, fired from guns on catcher boats, and whaling shifted to the larger and faster Baleen whales. The introduction of factory ships by Japan and the USSR intensified whaling still further.

The global picture, then, **was a mining operation** moving progressively with increasing efficiency to new species and new areas. Whaling reached a peak during the present century.

12.6 Imagery and image

The use of imagery to provoke the evaluation outlined above suggests a comparable role for images in multimodal text (explored in more detail in Martin in press a). Consider, for example, the following autobiographical recount used by Mandela (1995) as a high-order New to sum up the meaning of his life:

Orientation

[15] I was not born with a hunger to be free. I was born free – free in every way that I could know. Free to run in the fields near my mother's hut, free to swim in the clear stream that ran through my village, free to roast mealies under the stars and ride the broad backs of slow-moving bulls. As long as I obeyed my father and abided by the customs of my tribe, I was not troubled by the laws of man or God.

Record of Events

It was only when I began to learn that my boyhood freedom was an illusion, when I discovered as a young man that my freedom had already been taken from me, that I began to hunger for it. At first, as a student, I wanted freedom only for myself, the transitory freedoms of being able to stay out at night, read what I pleased and go where I chose. Later, as a young man in Johannesburg, I yearned for the basic and honourable freedoms of achieving my potential, of earning my keep, of marrying and having a family – the freedom not to be obstructed in a lawful life.

But then I slowly saw that not only was I not free, but my brothers and sisters were not free. I saw that it was not just my freedom that was curtailed, but the freedom of everyone who looked like I did. That is when I joined the African National Congress, and that is when the hunger for my own freedom became the greater hunger for the freedom of my people. It was this desire for the freedom of my people to live their lives with dignity and self-respect that animated my life, that transformed a frightened young man into a bold one, that drove a law-abiding attorney to become a criminal, that turned a family-loving husband into a man without a home, that forced a life-loving man to live like a monk. I am no more virtuous or self-sacrificing than the next man, but I found that I could not even enjoy the poor and limited freedoms I was allowed when I knew my people were not free. Freedom is indivisible; the chains on anyone of my people were the chains on all of them, the chains on all of my people were the chains on me.

It was during those long and lonely years that my hunger for the freedom of my own people became a hunger for the freedom of all people, white and black. I knew as well as I knew anything that the oppressor must be liberated just as surely as the oppressed. A man who takes away another man's freedom is a prisoner of hatred, he is locked behind the bars of prejudice and narrow-mindedness. I am not truly free if I am taking away someone else's freedom, just as surely as I am not free when my freedom is taken from me. The oppressed and the oppressor alike are robbed of their humanity.

When I walked out of prison, that was my mission, to liberate the oppressed and the oppressor both. Some say that has now been achieved. But I know that this is not the case. The truth is that we are not yet free; we have merely achieved the freedom to be free, the right not to be oppressed. We have not taken the final step of our journey, but the first step on a longer and even more difficult road. For to be free is not merely to cast off one's chains, but to live in a way that respects and enhances the freedom of others. The true test of our devotion to freedom is just beginning.

Reorientation
I have walked that long road to freedom. I have tried not to falter; I have made missteps along the way. But I have discovered the secret that after climbing a great hill, one only finds that there are many more hills to climb. I have taken a moment here to rest, to steal a view of the glorious vista that surrounds me, to look back on the distance I have come. But I can only rest for a moment, for with freedom come responsibilities, and I dare not linger, for my long walk is not yet ended. (Mandela 1995: 750–1)

Evaluation plays a critical role in the hierarchy of periodicity of this text. Each of the first five paragraphs begins with a Hyper-Theme taking up a stance on freedom (judgement – capacity, propriety):

i. I was not born with a hunger to be free I was born free – free in every way that I could know.
=. . .

ii. It was only when I began to learn that my boyhood freedom was an illusion, when I discovered as a young man that my freedom had

already been taken from me that I began to hunger for it.
=...

iii. But then I slowly saw that not only was I not free, but my brothers and sisters were not free.
=...

iv. It was during those long and lonely years that my hunger for the freedom of my own people became a hunger for the freedom of all people, white and black.
=...

v. When I walked out of prison, that was my mission, to liberate the oppressed and the oppressor both. Some say that has now been achieved. But I know that this is not the case.
=...

At the same time, paragraphs three, four and five make use of metaphor to consolidate the changing evaluation of the meanings of freedom for Mandela at different stages of his 'enlightenment' (Martin 1999):

iii. I saw that it was not just my freedom that was curtailed, but the freedom of everyone who looked like I did. That is when I joined the African National Congress, and that is when the hunger for my own freedom became the greater hunger for the freedom of my people. It was this desire for the freedom of my people to live their lives with dignity and self-respect that animated my life, that transformed a frightened young man into a bold one, that drove a law-abiding attorney to become a criminal, that turned a family-loving husband into a man without a home, that forced a life-loving man to **live like a monk**. I am no more virtuous or self-sacrificing than the next man, but I found that I could not even enjoy the poor and limited freedoms I was allowed when I knew my people were not free. Freedom is indivisible; **the chains on any one of my people were the chains on all of them, the chains on all of my people were the chains on me**.

iv. I knew as well as I knew anything that the oppressor must be liberated just as surely as the oppressed. A man who takes away another man's freedom is a prisoner of hatred, he is locked behind the bars of prejudice and narrow-mindedness. I am not truly free if I am taking away someone else's freedom, just as surely as I am not free when my freedom is taken from me. The oppressed and the oppressor alike are **robbed of their humanity**.

v. The truth is that we are not yet free; we have merely achieved the freedom to be free, the right not to be oppressed. We have not taken **the final step of our journey but the first step on a longer and even more difficult road**. For to be free is not merely **to cast off one's chains**, but to live in away that respects and enhances the freedom of others. **The true test** of our devotion to freedom is just beginning.

And the recount itself concludes with a Macro-New, which further develops the journey metaphor begun in paragraph five:

vi. I have **walked that long road to freedom**. I have **tried not to falter**; I have made **missteps along the way**. But I have discovered the secret that after **climbing a great hill**, one only finds that there are **many more hills to climb. I have taken a moment here to rest**, to steal **a view of the glorious vista that surrounds me, to look back on the distance I have come**. But **I can only rest for a moment**, for with freedom come responsibilities, and **I dare not linger, for my long walk is not yet ended**.

The metaphors evoke how it feels to live like a monk, to be in chains, to be robbed, to take a long journey and to be tested – all by way of provoking in readers some sense of how it felt to live Mandela's life.

I don't have an image to hand of Mandela or other South Africans in chains. But I do have one of Aboriginal Australians. The effect of this image seems to me similar to that of the imagery. The concrete image demands evaluation, which stance is then transferred to the meaning of freedom. Here are the relevant metaphors again, and the image below.

Freedom is indivisible; **the chains on any one of my people were the chains on all of them, the chains on all of my people were the chains on me**.

For to be free is not merely **to cast off one's chains**, but to live in a way that respects and enhances the freedom of others.

The remarkable Australian government report *Bringing Them Home* (1997) deploys both images and imagery in tandem to co-articulate evaluative orientations to ensuing text. On page 186, for example, at the beginning of a major section on the effects of institutionalization, we have a photograph of Sir Charles and Lady Gairdner with Abbot Gomez inspecting the children of St Joseph's Orphanage in Western Australia; dozens of stolen children are lined up in rows on either side of the inspecting dignitaries. For me, the sight of so many children, so

Figure 12.7 Aboriginal Australians in chains

young, aligned like soldiers on parade is an extremely poignant one.

> I remember all we children being herded up, like a mob of cattle, and feeling the humiliation of being graded by the colour of our skins for the government records
> *Confidential submission 332, Queensland: woman removed in the 1950s to Cootamundra Girls' Home*

Reinforcing the point is the Aboriginal voice inscribed below the photograph, with imagery reinforcing the point of the image:

> [16] I remember all we children being herded up, **like a mob of cattle**, and feeling our humiliation of being graded by the colour of our skins for the government records.

In the verbiage which follows, bureaucratic discourse is intermingled with quotations from members of the Stolen Generations – the evaluation established by image and imagery on this section's first page develops prosodically over the following text.

On page 90 we find a similar pattern. The photograph this time is

Figure 12.8 The Governor Sir Charles and Lady Gairdner with Abbot Gomez inspecting the children of St Joseph's Orphanage, New Norcia, Western Australia

from a newspaper and features six young stolen children under the Heading 'Homes Are Sought For These Children'. One of the children (the lightest skinned) has been marked with an 'x' by someone wishing to adopt the child.

> We was bought like a market. We was all lined up in white dresses, and they'd come round and pick you out like you was for sale.
> *Confidential submission 695, New South Wales: woman fostered at 10 years in the 1970s; one of a family of 13 siblings all removed; raped by foster father and forced to have an abortion.*

> I clearly remember being put in line-ups every fortnight, where prospective foster parents would view all the children. I wasn't quite the child they were looking for.
> *Confidential evidence 133, Victoria: man removed at six months in the 1960s; institutionalized for three years before being fostered by a succession of white families.*

Below, imagery is used to reinforce the image as follows:

> [17] We was all bought **like a market**. We was all lined up in white dresses, and they'd come round and pick you out **like you was for sale**.

Figure 12.9 Newspaper photograph of six young stolen children waiting to be adopted

This by way of orientation to the report on the stolen generations of Tasmania.

These are powerful images and the report is full of them. They typically precede the verbiage they are orienting readers to. From the perspective of discourse structure they work as higher-level Themes; if we make an analogy to clause grammar, the appropriate connection as far as I can see is to interpersonal Theme – to comment Adjuncts encoding a speaker's disposition towards the message:

[18] **Unfortunately**:, there was little we could do.

Summing up then, we can argue that both imagery and image play an important role in provoking appraisal; and like explicit inscribed evaluation they are associated with boundaries in texts – with higher-level Themes and News. Metaphor has the function of provoking a reappraisal of one field with respect to the evaluation of another; images provoke a reaction which co-articulates, in tandem with verbiage, the appraisal of a field. Both imagery and images appear to take advantage of strong bonding between relatively concrete experience and reactions to provoke appraisal in less concrete, or even relatively abstract discourse.

12.7 Texture and evaluation

In this paper we have considered the function of evaluation in texturing discourse, suggesting that evaluation has an important orienting and consolidating function associated with higher-level Themes and News. A range of resources for construing sensibility have been reviewed, including explicit lexicalization, ideational selection, metaphor and image – as summarized in Figure 12.10.

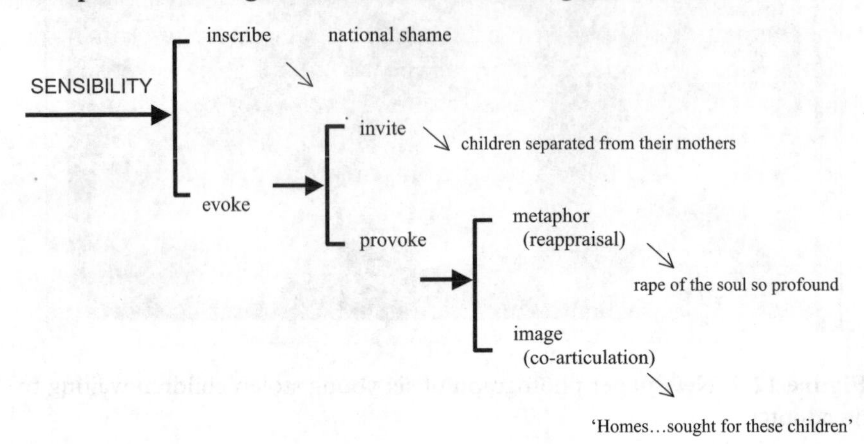

Figure 12.10 Images, imagery and the construal of evaluation

Taken together, these resources have the effect of amplifying one another – of multiplying meaning as Jay Lemke puts it (1998b). Peter Read's (1999) book on the Stolen Generations, for example, has a front cover involving the title *A Rape of the Soul so Profound* (imagery) and a comment by Henry Reynolds on the book ('Powerful and passionate: a major contribution to understanding what the Stolen Generations means.') over a bleak image of the remains of a former Aboriginal reserve – inscription x metaphor x image.

Similarly Bird's (1998) edition of extracts from *Bringing them Home*, uses the title *The Stolen Generations: their stories* (imagery) and the sub-title *Including extracts from the Report of the National Inquiry into the separation of Aboriginal and Torres Strait Islander children from their families* (inviting appraisal) on the 'Homes are sought for these children' image presented above – metaphor x ideational selection x image.

The back covers of both books multiply meaning in similar ways. One might suggest that marketing pressures are at work here; appraisal has been amplified to grab the attention of prospective readers. And from a retailing perspective, this is probably true.

Reading deeper, however, we might ask how this marketing works. And the appropriate answer here would be one that considers the ways in which appraisal resources are deployed to negotiate solidarity – to construct a community of readers with shared values around the Stolen Generations issue. Exploring evaluation from this solidarity perspective is beyond the scope of this paper; for glimpses of this rich arena see Eggins and Slade (1997) and Martin (2000a).

Before closing, a note of caution. By way of somewhat balancing the ledgers, in this paper we have focused on the texture of evaluation, dealing with ideational meaning simply as a backdrop to sensibility. But it is the bonding of classification with feeling that shapes discourse and moves the world. And as the possibility of inviting appraisal shows, classification is intrinsically charged with evaluation. Contests over classification underscore this point. Was Australia discovered, settled or invaded? Was there a hundred years war between Europeans and indigenous Australians? Or, most recently, was there really a stolen generation (since, as Howard's government has argued, only one in ten children were taken, the separations were legal, and the intentions of past governments benign)? Passions run wild over namings such as these. As Clive Hamilton has commented:

> On taking office the Howard government mounted a cynical and sustained campaign to discredit the institutions of Aboriginal welfare and the processes of self-determination and reconciliation, culminating in Howard's shameful refusal to apologise on behalf of the nation for the policies of forced removal of Aboriginal children from their parents. The prime minister invited the outpouring of racial hatred through the calculated persecution of the 'Aboriginal industry' and his attacks on the 'black arm-band view' of Australian history. (Hamilton 1998: 12)

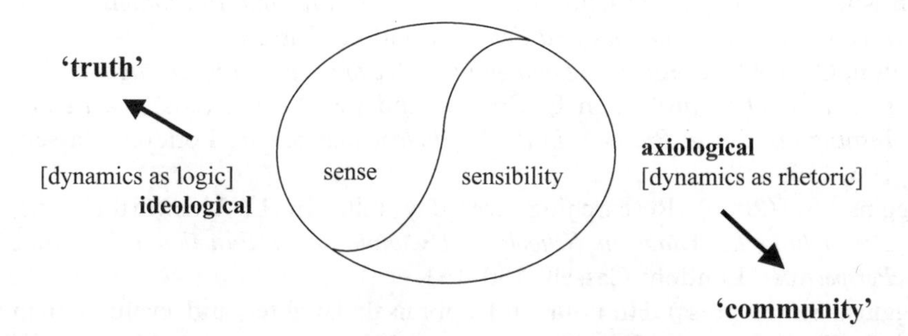

Figure 12.11 Sense and sensibility as complementarities

Howard's *Aboriginal industry* does not inscribe evaluation; but his attitude is just as clear as when he provokes *metaphor (black arm-band history)* or Hamilton inscribes *(shameful refusal)*. Sense and sensibility are the yin and yang of discourse; texts unfold logically as truth as the same time as they develop as community. In every instance, Bakhtin's ideological and axiological always already intertwine.

In closing, let me flag two pressing sites for the development of our appreciation of the texture of evaluation. One is the extension of appraisal analysis to the study of humour and its role in negotiating social relations, as previewed by Eggins (in press). The other is work across modalities, beyond verbiage and image to the 'embodiment' of sensibility in sound (van Leeuwen 1999) and action (Martinec 1998). Challenges aplenty, to wind this chapter down.

References

Arnheim, R. (1982) *The Power of the Centre: a study of composition in the visual arts*. Berkeley: University of California Press.

Bakhtin, M. M. (1981) *The Dialogic Imagination* (translated by C. Emerson & M. Holquist). Austin: University of Texas Press.

Baldry, A. (ed.) (1999) *Multimodality and Multimediality in the distance learning age*. Campo Basso: Lampo.

Barthes, R. (1977) *Image Music Text*. London: Fontana.

Bird, C. (ed.) (1998) *The Stolen Children: Their Stories*. Sydney: Random House.

Bringing Them Home: National Inquiry into the Separation of Aboriginal and Torres Strait Islander Children from Their Families. (1997) Sydney: Human Rights and Equal Opportunity Commission.

Buggy, T. (1988) *The Long Revolution: A History of Modern China*. Sydney: Shakespeare Head Press.

Carleton, M. (2000) Thin edge of wedge politics. *Sydney Morning Herald*, 8 April: 38.

Christie, F. and J.R. Martin (eds.) (1997) *Genre and Institutions: Social Processes in the Workplace and School*. London: Cassell.

Coffin, C. (1997) *Constructing and giving value to the past: an investigation into secondary school history*. In F. Christie and J.R. Martin (eds), *Genre and Institutions: Social Processes in the Workplace and School*. London: Cassell, 196–230.

Eggins, S. (2000) Researching everyday talk. In L. Unsworth, (ed.), *Researching Language in Schools and Communities: Functional Linguistic Perspectives*. London: Cassell, 130–151.

Eggins, S. (in press) Humour and appraisal: laughter and evaluation in casual conversation. *Text* (Special issue – Negotiating heteroglossia: social perspectives on evaluation.)

Eggins, S. and Slade, D. (1997) *Analysing Casual Conversation*. London: Cassell.

Fries, P.H. (1981) On the status of theme in English: arguments from discourse. *Forum Linguisticum*, 6(1): 1–38. (Republished in J. S. Petofi and E. Sozer (eds.) (1983) *Micro and Macro Connexity of Texts*. Hamburg: Helmut Buske Verlag (Papers in Textlinguistics 45): 116–52.

Fuller, G. (1998) Cultivating science: negotiating discourse in the popular texts of Stephen Jay Gould. In J.R. Martin and R. Veel (eds), *Reading Science: Critical and Functional Perspectives on Discourses of Science*. London: Routledge, 35–62.

Fuller, G. (2000) The textual politics of good intentions. A. Lee and C. Poynton (eds), *Culture and Text: Discourse and Methodology in Social Research and Cultural Studies*. Sydney: Allen & Unwin, 81–98.

Fuller, G. and Lee, A. (1997) *Textual Collusions Discourse: studies in the cultural politics of education* 18(2): 409–23.

Halliday, M.A.K. (1976) Anti-languages. *American Anthropologist*, 78(3): 570–84. (Reprinted in Halliday, M.A.K. (1978) *Language as a Social Semiotic: The Social Interpretation of Language and Meaning*. London: Edward Arnold, 164–82)

Halliday, M.A.K. (1994) *An Introduction to Functional Grammar*. London: Edward Arnold.

Hamilton, C. (1998) Australia's populist political earthquake. *Guardian Weekly*, June 21: 12.

Hasan, R. and G. Williams (eds) (1996) *Literacy in Society*. London: Longman (Language and Social Life).

Hunston, S. (1993) Evaluation and ideology in scientific writing. In M. Ghadessy (ed.), *Register Analysis: Theory and Practice*. London: Pinter, 57–73.

Hunston, S. (1994) Evaluation and organisation in a sample of written academic discourse. In M. Coulthard (ed.), *Advances in Written Text Analysis*. London: Routledge, 191–218.

Hunston, S. (2000) Evaluation and the planes of discourse: status and value in persuasive texts. In S. Hunston and G. Thompson (eds), *Evaluation in Text: Authorial Stance and the Construction of discourse*. Oxford: OUP, 176–207.

Hunston, S. and Thompson, G. (2000a) Evaluation: an introduction. In S. Hunston and G. Thompson (eds), *Evaluation in Text: Authorial Stance and the Construction of discourse*. Oxford: OUP, 1–27.

Iedema, R. (1997) The history of the accident news story. *Australian Review of Applied Linguistics*, 20(2): 95–119.

Iedema, R., Feez, S. and White, P. (1994) *Media Literacy*. Sydney: State Equity Centre (Bridge and Swanson St., Erskineville, NSW).

Johnston, T. (1992) The realisation of the linguistic metafunctions in a sign language. *Language Sciences*, 14(4): 317–53. (Republished as Function and medium in the forms of linguistic expression found in a sign language. In W.H. Edmondson and R.B. Wilbur (eds), *International Review of Sign Linguistics. Vol. 1.* Mahwah, NJ: Lawrence Erlbaum, 1996: 57–94)

Kelly, P. (1999) *Don't Start me Talking: Lyrics 1984–1999.* Sydney: Allen & Unwin.

Kress, G. (1997) *Before Writing: rethinking the paths to literacy.* London: Routledge.

Kress, G. and T. van Leeuwen (1996) *Reading Images: the grammar of visual design.* London: Routledge.

Lemke, J. (1998a) Resources for attitudinal meaning: evaluative orientations in text semantics. *Functions of Language,* 5(1): 33–56.

Lemke, J. (1998b) Multiplying meaning: visual and verbal semiotics in scientific text. In J.R. Martin and R. Veel (eds), *Reading Science: Critical and Functional Perspectives on Discourses of Science.* London: Routledge: 87–113.

Mandela, N. (1995) *Long Walk to Freedom: The Autobiography of Nelson Mandela.* London: Abacus.

Manne, R. (1998) *The stolen generations.* Quadrant No.343. Volume XLII. Numbers 1–2. 53–63.

Manne, R. (1999) No mercy for Nellie Bliss. *Sydney Morning Herald,* 26 April: 11.

Martin, J.R. (1992a) Macro-proposals: meaning by degree. In W.C. Mann and S. Thompson (eds), *Discourse Description: Diverse Analyses of a Fund Raising Text.* Amsterdam: Benjamins, 359–95.

Martin, J.R. (1992b) *English Text: System and Structure.* Amsterdam: Benjamins.

Martin, J.R. (1993) Life as a noun. In M.A.K. Halliday and J.R. Martin (eds), *Writing Science: Literacy as Discursive Power.* London: Falmer, 221–67.

Martin, J.R. (1995a) *Text and Clause: Fractal Resonance.* Text 15.1. 5–42.

Martin, J.R. (1995b) Interpersonal meaning, persuasion and public discourse: packing semiotic punch. *Australian Journal of Linguistics* 15.1. 33–67.

Martin, J.R. (1997) Register and genre: modelling social context in functional linguistics-narrative genres. In E.R. Pedro (ed.), *Discourse Analysis: Proceedings of First International Conference on Discourse Analysis.* Lisbon: Colibri/Portuguese Linguistics Association, 305–44.

Martin, J.R. (1999) Grace: the logogenesis of freedom. *Discourse Studies,* 1(1): 31–58.

Martin, J.R. (2000a) Beyond exchange: appraisal systems in English. In S. Hunston and G. Thompson (eds), *Evaluation in Text: Authorial Stance and the Construction of Discourse.* Oxford: Oxford University Press, 142–75.

Martin, J.R. (2000b) Factoring out exchange: types of structure. In M. Coulthard (ed.), *Working with Dialogue.* Tubingen: Niemeyer.

Martin, J.R. (in press a) Fair trade: negotiating meaning in multimodal texts.

In Patrick Coppock (ed.), *The Semiotics of Writing: Transdisciplinary Perspectives on the Technology of Writing*. Turnhout: Brepols.

Martin, J.R. (in press b) Positive discourse analysis: power, solidarity and change. *Social Semiotics* (Special Issue – 'Critical Semiotics').

Martin, J.R. and Plum, G. (1997) Construing experience: some story genres. *Journal of Narrative and Life History*, 7(1–4): 299–308.

Martin, J.R. and Veel, R. (1998) *Reading Science: Critical and Functional Perspectives on Discourses of Science*. London: Routledge.

Martinec, R. (1998) Cohesion in action. *Semiotica*, 120(1/2): 161–80.

McGregor, W. (1991) Photographs of Aborigines and police. *Social Semiotics* 1.2. 123–58.

Michaels, E. (1987) *Afterword. Yuendumu Doors*. Canberra: Australian Institute of Aboriginal Studies, 135–43.

Milton, G. (1999) *Nathaniel's Nutmeg: How One Man's Courage Changed the Course of History*. London: Hodder & Stoughton.

Morgan, S. (1989) *Wanamurraganya: The Story of Jack McPhee*. Freemantle: Freemantle Arts Centre Press.

Muecke, S. (1992) *Textual Spaces: Aboriginality and Cultural Studies*. Sydney: New South Wales University Press (Communication and Culture).

Myers, G. (1989) The pragmatics of politeness in scientific articles. *Applied Linguistics*, 10: 1–35.

O'Halloran, K. (1999) Interdependence, interaction and metaphor in multisemiotic texts. *Social Semiotics* 9.3. 317–54.

O'Toole, M. (1994) *The Language of Displayed Art*. London: Leicester University Press (a division of Pinter).

Plum, G. (1988) *Textual and Contextual Conditioning in Spoken English: a genre-based approach*. PhD Thesis. Department of Linguistics, University of Sydney.

Poynton, C. (1990) The privileging of representation and the marginalising of the interpersonal: a metaphor (and more) for contemporary gender relations. In T. Threadgold and A. Cranny-Francis (eds), *Feminine/Masculine and Representation*. Sydney: Allen & Unwin, 231–55.

Poynton, C. (1996) Amplification as a grammatical prosody: attitudinal modification in the nominal group. In M. Berry, C. Butler, R. Fawcett and G. Huang (eds), *Meaning and Form: Systemic Functional Interpretations*. Norwood, NJ: Ablex (Meaning and Choice in Language: studies for Michael Halliday), 211–27.

Poynton, C (2000) *Linguistics and discourse analysis*. Lee and Poynton (eds) 19–39.

Read, P. (1999) *A Rape of the Soul so Profound: The Return of the Stolen Generations*. Sydney: Allen & Unwin.

Reynolds, H. (1999) *Why weren't we Told: a personal search for the truth about our history*. Melbourne: Viking.

Rothery, J. (1994) *Exploring Literacy in School English (Write it Right Resources for Literacy and Learning)*. Sydney: State Equity Centre.

Rothery, J. and Stenglin, M. (2000) Interpreting literature: the role of appraisal. In L. Unsworth (ed.), *Researching Language in Schools and Communities: Functional Linguistic Perspectives*. London: Cassell, 222–44.

Sitka, C. (1998) Letter from Melbourne. *Guardian Weekly*, 7 June: 25.

Stories from Lajamanu (1985) Darwin: Northern Territory Department of Education.

Van Leeuwen, T. (1999) *Speech, Music, Sound*. London: Macmillan.

Van Leeuwen, T. (2000) It was just like magic – a multimodal analysis of children's writing. *Linguistics and Education* 10. 273–305.

Veel, R. and Coffin C. (1996) Learning to think like an historian: the language of secondary school history. Hasan and Williams (eds) 191–231.

Veltman, R. (1998) Lars Porsena and my bonk manager: a systemic-functional study in the semogenesis of the language of swearing. In A. Sanchez-Macarro and R. Carter (eds), *Linguistic Choices across Genres*. Amsterdam: Benjamins [CIL T 158]. 301–16.

Ventola, E. (1998) *Interpersonal Choices in Academic Work*. Sanchez-Macarro and Carter (eds) 117–36.

White, P. (1997) Death, disruption and the moral order: the narrative impulse in mass 'hard news' reporting. In F. Christie and J.R. Martin (eds), *Genre and Institution: Social Processes in the Workplace and School*. London: Cassell, 101–33.

Zinn, C. (1998) One nation gains divide Australia. *Guardian Weekly*, 21 June: 3.

Note

1 Similarly for graphology, appraisal renders formatting of all kinds 'emic'; for sign language, the distinction between 'etic' and 'emic' on the expression plane has in any case already been blurred (Johnston 1992).

13

On the Preferential Co-occurrence of Processes and Circumstantial Adjuncts: Some Corpus Evidence

Fiona C. Ball and Gordon Tucker

13.1 Introduction

In this paper we explore the relations that hold between Processes and Circumstantial elements in English clauses, as evidenced by co-occurrence patterns elicited through corpus linguistic investigation. In particular, we set out to explore any potential preferential co-occurrence patterns that may throw light on the nature of the relations between Processes and attendant Circumstances. The data were elicited from the 339 million word COBUILD Bank of English Corpus at the University of Birmingham.

Process, Participants and Circumstances are the defining functions in the system of Transitivity and are conflated with or 'mapped onto' the Main Verb, Subject and Complement, and Adjunct respectively.[1] Thus the transitivity configuration of a clause may be characterized as below:

The conference organizers	*greeted*	*the guest speakers*	*at Hyderabad airport*
Subject	Main Verb	Complement	Adjunct
Participant Role	Process	Participant Role	Circumstantial Role

The relations that hold between these three functions have been described in terms of nuclearity (Martin 1992; Matthiessen 1995). Nuclearity captures both the semantic distance expressed in the relations between them and the semantic continuity between them. Thus for Martin, Circumstances are located at the periphery of this semantic space, with the Participant of Medium and that of Agent being located at the nucleus and margin respectively in respect of the Process at the centre (Martin 1992: 319).

The peripherality of Circumstances/Adjuncts is observable in a number of ways. In particular, they are wholly optional elements. A Main Verb is typically accompanied by a Subject and one or more Complements. And even in those cases where a Participant is not expressed, a given Process is **inherently associated** with one or more Participants.[2] Thus, for example, the Process *hit* is inherently associated with the Participant Roles of Agent and Affected, irrespective of whether the Affected is expressed or not, as illustrated by (1).[3]

(1) he hits very hard

The Main Verb is accompanied by one or more Adjuncts just in case the Circumstances expressed are required for communicative ends by the speaker in a given discourse context. Thus, the speaker may provide circumstantial information, e.g. about the time, place, manner, frequency, etc. which, in Halliday's terms, are 'attendant on the Process'. But 'attendant on the Process' is not the same as 'inherent to the Process'. Halliday again states that 'typically they [Circumstances] occur freely in all types of process, and with essentially the same significance wherever they occur' (1994: 150). This is unsurprising, given that events take place in time and space and that a speaker could specify such circumstances for practically every event. And as circumstances are likely to remain constant over a stretch of discourse (e.g., the location at which an event takes place), they are unlikely to have to be repeated if they remain unchanged.

The inherence of Participant Roles is another matter, however. Although they may be expressed by different referring expressions (e.g., by anaphoric pronouns referring to previous more specific reference), and, as discourse 'topics', the referents concerned may appear again, with different Processes, they are typically required by the lexicogrammar of each of the Processes in question.

In specifying the lexico-grammar of Processes, then, it would appear to be redundant to include attendant circumstantial Adjuncts, as if in some sense they were arguments of the verb itself. The 'true' arguments of each verb, however, do need to be specified. For each Process or Process type the lexico-grammar must at least specify the number of Participant Roles associated with it, the particular Participant Roles (e.g., Agent, Sensor, Phenomenon, etc.) and the extent to which the expression of each Role is obligatory. Even in strictly formal theoretical approaches to grammar (e.g., Chomskyan generative grammar), the Participant Roles (Theta Roles) for individual verbs need to be specified in the lexicon entry for the verb in terms of a Theta Grid (see, for example, Haegeman 1994).

The assumption of the optionality and relative freedom of Circumstantial Adjuncts is, however, a broad generalization. Qualifying his statement on the freedom of their co-occurrence with Processes, Halliday adds that '[t]here are of course, some combinations which are less likely, and some special interpretations' (1994: 150). He gives the example of the fairly unusual occurrence of Circumstances of Manner with attributive clauses. This can be illustrated by the oddness of (4), a relational, attributive clause, compared to (2) and (3) which are material and mental clauses respectively:

(2) he struck the ball perfectly
(3) he knew his lines perfectly
(4) ?he is perfectly a poet

Another example that comes readily to mind is the Process/Verb *behave*. Apart from the unmarked case, where the Manner Circumstance is understood, e.g. *the children behaved all evening*, the Process requires Manner to be expressed, as (5)–(7) illustrate.[4]

(5) they behaved badly
(6) you're behaving like a spoilt child
(7) never behave like that again

The more precise nature of Process-Circumstance co-occurrence remains, therefore, to be investigated. Although it is unlikely to be the case that, as a result of an in-depth investigation, the general principles underlying the relationship between Processes and Circumstances will need substantial revision, our understanding of preferential co-occurrence and its correlation with the semantics of Processes may be significantly increased.

13.2 A corpus linguistic approach

Justification for this kind of investigation is to be found in the constant quest for greater delicacy in lexico-grammatical description. Grammatical description can, and indeed must, develop in two opposite directions. On the one hand, the grammarian seeks to generalize, to uncover the general organizational principles of language. On the other hand, she seeks to incorporate as much of the apparently 'exceptional' behaviour of lexico-grammatical systems and items into the overall model. Many grammarians will adopt a unidirectional approach, dependent on their individual goals or those established by theoretical paradigms. Yet a focus and personal preference for one direction does not and should not invalidate a focus on the other. It seems to us that there are inherent dangers in prioritizing either direction at the expense of the other.

Another compelling reason is that we are now able to investigate such aspects of language using extremely large language corpora and databases. If much of previous linguistic enquiry has been based on the grammarian's intuition and introspection, on the informant's judgements and on the use of invented examples, we are now in a position to observe the patterning in linguistic utterances on the basis of many hundreds of millions of words of running text. Two large contemporary language corpora, the Bank of English at Birmingham University (Sinclair 1987) and the British National Corpus (Aston and Burnard 1998) total between them a resource approaching 0.5 billion words. Evidence of forms of significant co-occurrence need no longer be gleaned from introspection or a handful of examples. And statistically significant co-occurrence phenomena can hardly be simply dismissed as peripheral to grammar.

Furthermore, the kinds of significant co-occurrence patterning that corpus investigation reveals go well beyond the general phenomena that tend to suggest a neat 'grammatical versus ungrammatical' distinction. If we assume that most patterning in a large corpus, especially when found in significant quantities, is grammatical – apart from the occasional 'performance' errors – then we are dealing with probabilistic grammar, or the probability of certain lexicogrammatical patterns occurring rather than others. Indeed, we are even in a much better position, given the quantity of data, to observe that certain structures deemed grammatical on formal grounds do not in fact occur. In many cases, the argument that they are acceptable grammatical structures in the language, but simply will not necessarily turn up in a limited amount of data, is no longer totally convincing.

It can also be argued that probabilistic differences found in respect of co-occurrence phenomena, especially when all are deemed to be equally grammatical, are simply a question of semantic or contextual differentiation. Yet this same argument can be equally used against a strict 'grammatical *versus* ungrammatical' distinction. It is reasonable to postulate that certain strings are ungrammatical because they do not correspond to any conceivable meaning that speakers might need to make.

The observation that probabilistic co-occurrence is a semantic rather than a grammatical phenomenon is furthermore not one that should carry much weight for a theory of language that sees lexico-grammar as a resource for meaning. As such a theory of language, systemic functional grammar is primarily concerned with what meanings can be made through the lexico-grammatical resource and also what meanings are made. Any co-occurrence evidence that suggests that a speaker's meaning potential is constrained in a particular way is of significance both for modelling the nature of semantic choice and for the lexicogrammar through which it is expressed.

13.3 The preferential co-occurrence hypothesis

We now set out the hypothesis on which this investigation is based. It is primarily that some degree of co-occurrence between Process types and Adjunct types will be found, at least in probabilistic terms. The hypothesis is not based on any previous partial findings, nor motivated by any preconceptions. In experimental terms, we might even suggest that we are exploring the null hypothesis that corresponds with Halliday's 1994 statement on a general adjunctival freedom of co-occurrence with all Process types, in other words, either (a) no circumstantial Adjunct type has a significantly greater probability of co-occurrence with any Process type, or (b) no Process type is statistically more likely to presuppose any circumstantial Adjunct type. Besides the question of potential probabilistic difference, there is also the potential finding that certain Adjunct types never occur with certain Process types.

We take as the basis for different Process types the classification that is generally agreed upon within systemic functional linguistics. This consists of a broad distinction between **Material**, **Mental** and **Relational** Processes. At this broad degree of systemic generality, there is agreement across existing models within Systemic Functional Linguistics (SFL), although beyond this some degree of alternative classification is found. For example, Halliday (1994) distinguishes Verbal Processes from strictly Mental Processes, and recognizes **Behavioural** and **Existential** Processes as separate categories. Fawcett, on the other hand, includes Verbal Process as a subcategory of Mental Processes; Behavioural as a subcategory of Material and Existential Processes as a subcategory of Relational processes (Fawcett in press a and b).

This broad distinction is not to be seen as a semantically determined working hypothesis. The systemic categories are recognized on the basis of their transitivity configurations in the lexico-grammar and by the organization of Participant Roles associated with each of the three types (see Halliday (1994: 106ff) for a discussion of distinguishing lexico-grammatical correlates of the three).

Given the maximum systemic distinction between these three types, it was decided to explore Adjunctival co-occurrence initially across two of the types, namely Material and Mental Processes. At the same time, three semantically related Processes from each type were selected. This opened a second line of enquiry, namely that at the most delicate degree of distinction (e.g., between the Material Processes *assassinate, execute, murder*) some degree of Adjunct co-occurrence distinction might possibly be found.

For each Process type, three closely related verbs were selected using Levin's classification of verbs, which she arrives at on the basis of shared meaning and grammatical behaviour (Levin 1993). Levin claims that 'a verb's meaning influences its syntactic behaviour', taking a 'semantic motivation' position shared by Wierzbicka (1988). One could, of course, take an 'expression' motivation, following Halliday (1991), which sees linguistic expression as realizing the difference in meaning (for a detailed discussion of these two positions in linguistic theory see Davidse 1996). From either perspective, the present preferential co-occurrence hypothesis, if valid, would add further weight to the relationship between semantics and lexico-grammatical expression. The two sets of three verbs selected were *assassinate, execute* and *murder* for Material Processes and *detest, hate* and *loathe* for Mental Processes.

The decision to investigate the co-occurrence of Adjuncts with Processes, rather than the co-occurrence of Processes with individual classes of Adjunct, was made on purely corpus linguistic methodological grounds. Whilst the specification of Processes in a corpus query is straightforward, in the sense that one can search either simple items or lemmata (either *murder* or *murder/murdering/murders/murdered)*, Adjuncts are expressed with a whole range of lexico-grammatical devices. As the Bank of English corpus is not tagged for the functional category 'Adjunct', it would have been difficult to construct a set of queries that elicited anything near the range of possible expressions of a particular Adjunct. Furthermore, many Adjuncts use a similar range of lexico-grammatical realizations, which make eliciting any single one in other than a typical realization far too complex and difficult. By selecting a number of verb lemmata, we were able to produce concordances through which to identify any circumstantial Adjunct that occurred.

13.4 Adjunct classification

Although we are concerned specifically here with circumstantial Adjuncts, which express experiential meaning, Adjuncts also express meanings associated with the other metafunctions. Thus there are interpersonally oriented Adjuncts, such as those expressing modality (Validity Adjuncts in the framework used here), e.g., *probably, possibly, certainly*, or expressive Adjuncts, such as *frankly, personally, surely*, and textually oriented Adjuncts such as *however, in that case, nevertheless*. The distinction of these elements based on their metafunctional orientation allows their classification to subsume what Quirk *et al.* (1985) and Downing and Lock (1992: 58–64) treat distinctively as 'Adjuncts', 'Conjuncts', 'Disjuncts' and 'Subjuncts'.

There are naturally a good number of Adjunct classifications (e.g., Jacobson 1964; Quirk *et al.* 1985; Halliday 1994; etc.), but given that the Cardiff Grammar (Fawcett, *et al.* 1993; Tucker 1998) currently recognises 54 different Adjuncts, we consider this classification more than adequate for the present purposes. The central criterion for distinguishing one Adjunct from another is itself co-occurrence. By this criterion, if two Adjuncts co-occur, they are considered to be different, and will be assigned a different label. Each Adjunct is distinguished in analysis and description by the symbol A (as an element of clause structure) accompanied by two or more letters indicating its type, e.g., TPA (Time Position Adjunct), DuA (Duration Adjunct) etc. A list of Cardiff Grammar experiential Adjunct types is found in Appendix 1.

Besides classificatory differences there is one important difference between Halliday's (1994) analysis and the Cardiff Grammar framework. For Halliday, clauses such as *when the clock struck five*, in the sentence *they finished work when the clock struck five*, is treated as a hypotactic clause in a clause complex, fulfilling the general function of expansion. For Fawcett and the Cardiff Grammar, this hypotactic clause is considered to be the lexico-grammatical unit that fills the Adjunct element of structure and expresses time position. It is therefore analysed – as *at five o'clock* – as a TPA in the main clause.

In the Cardiff Grammar classification, the primary division of Adjuncts is in terms of eight strands of meaning in the clause (Fawcett in press a and b). Five of these strands of meaning have Adjuncts realizing them with many Adjunct types being Experiential, others expressing Interpersonal, Logical Relations, Validity and Affective meanings. Each class of Adjuncts is further divided into up to nine specific Adjunct types, there being, as we noted, 54 different types in all. The largest group of Adjuncts is Experiential and includes temporal and many other types. Note that with experiential Adjuncts, Fawcett's classification (see Appendix 1) is already based on general patterns of co-occurrence with Process types. This classificatory device is, however, purely indicative and is not criterial or definitional in any strict sense. To some extent, the findings of this present study may throw light on the validity or otherwise of this type of sub-classification. As with any study of this type, the findings are therefore dependent on the analytical categories recognized by a given model. This we do not feel to be a shortcoming of the investigation itself. It is open to the reader to compare the findings here, on the basis of other ways of classifying Adjuncts. On the whole, there are unlikely to be wildly differing interpretations of the function of a given Adjunct.

13.5 Corpus interrogation and data analysis

13.5.1 Method

The corpus resource queried for this study is the full COBUILD Bank of English Corpus (Sinclair 1987) based at the University of Birmingham. The corpus currently contains 339 million words of running text, of both spoken and written language, across a range of genres (e.g., books, magazines, newspapers, miscellany). Given the general nature of the inquiry, the whole corpus sample was included, rather than restricting the range to one or several sub-genres. The ratio of written to spoken material of 80:20 would suggest that findings are potentially more reliable for written text.

The Bank of English is tagged for word classes, but is otherwise not marked up for grammatical information, either of a formal or a functional nature. For this investigation, word class specification is of relatively little importance, given that we are investigating specific lexical items, although it does allow the items *kill*, *murder*, and *hate* to be restricted to the verb class, thereby excluding the equivalent nouns. The search software's lemmatization facility is, however, useful, since it allows citations of a given verb to be retrieved with all its morphological variants. Thus for example, specifying all the forms of the lemma *murder* in a query, elicits *murder, murders, murdering* and *murdered.*

The corpus was initially queried for all citations of each of the six verbs including each of the morphological forms. The number of citations retrieved clearly differed from lexeme to lexeme. The fewest number of citations elicited for any verb was 1670 for *loathe.* Given the difference in sample sizes, no attempt was made to adopt precise, numerically equivalent sample sizes for comparison. Wherever sample sizes for a given lexeme were extremely high, they were reduced to a figure of 1000 by random selection. In order to lessen any effect that might arise from unequal samples, percentages alone have been used in comparisons between the lexemes.

Each concordance was subjected to triage in order to remove citations involving senses other than the primary sense for each verb. Thus, for example, extended and metaphorical senses, such as those in (8) and (9) were removed at the outset:

(8) I could murder a cup of tea
(9) They brutally assassinated her character

This post-editing of the concordance clearly further reduced the number of the citations. Wherever the number fell below 1000 further random citations were added to achieve some rough equivalence.

Each of the concordance lines was examined and hand-coded for Adjuncts and Adjunct type. Both pre- and post-Main Verb positions were included, although in this initial study the variable of Adjunct Place in the clause was not considered.

13.5.2 Problems in analysis

Although a sufficiently large line-length in terms of characters per line was used in order to include as much of any relevant clause as possible, there were, of course, a number of clauses which did not reach completion within the boundary of the concordance line. All clauses for which the presence or absence of an Adjunctival element could not be safely ascertained were excluded from the analysis.

Other difficulties arose concerning Adjunct classification within the classification system adopted. All problematic Adjuncts were discussed individually until consensus on their classification was obtained.

13.6 Results of the analysis

13.6.1 Frequency of Circumstantial Adjuncts in the data

Of the total clauses analysed, 29 per cent had some type of circumstantiation, in the form of one or more associated Adjunct(s), as shown in Table 13.1.

Table 13.1 Frequency of circumstantial Adjuncts with Material and Mental processes

Process Type	**Process**	**Percentage Circumstances**	**Average Circumstantiation**
Material	assassinate	46	
	execute	39	
	murder	14	33
Mental	detest	31	
	loathe	26	
	hate	17	25
Overall per cent Circumstantiation			29

The average frequency of co-occurrence suggests that Material processes have a higher proportion of circumstantiation than Mental processes, although both process types have a fairly low frequency of circumstantiation overall. A recent parallel study by Matthiessen found that Material and Mental processes had circumstantiation in 30 per cent of clauses, a finding commensurate with our general observations from the data (Matthiessen 1999).

Of the Material processes, *assassinate* had accompanying circumstances in 46 per cent of cases, whereas *execute* had nearly 40 per cent and *murder* the least circumstantiation of all six verbs, with only 14 per cent. Of the Mental processes, *detest* had the highest amount of circumstantiation at 31 per cent, followed by *loathe* (26 per cent) and *hate* the lowest of the set (17 per cent).

There are interesting similarities in the general degree of circumstantiation between the two process types. In each type, one process had substantially fewer Adjuncts co-occurring with it than the other two, which have a similar percentage of circumstantiation. In the case of Material processes, *murder* had significantly less circumstantiation than *assassinate* and *execute*. In the case of Mental processes, *hate* had less than *detest* and *loathe*. These differences within and between the Process types support the hypothesis that some degree of co-occurrence between Process types and Adjunct types will be found in probabilistic terms and suggests, furthermore, that substantial, in-depth analysis is necessary with this type of data.

13.6.2 Adjunct Types co-occurring with each Process

The detailed analysis of the data revealed a more complex pattern of circumstantiation than could be shown by frequency count alone.

The number of Adjunct types co-occurring with each process is shown in Table 13.2.

Table 13.2 Number of Adjunct types co-occurring with each process

	Material			Mental		
	Assassinate	Execute	Murder	Detest	Hate	Loathe
No. of Adjunct Types	18	19	11	16	12	16
Average number	16			14		

Each of the six processes occurred with an average of 15 Adjunct types out of the 39 experiential types recognized in the Cardiff Grammar framework. This suggests that the potential range of circumstantiation may well be substantially restricted in the case of particular processes and that certain circumstances occur much more rarely than others.

Of the Material processes, *murder* had 11 types of circumstantiation, almost half that of *assassinate* or *execute*, which suggests that a different pattern of co-occurrence is found with this process. The Mental processes as a group had fewer associated Adjunct types, with an average of 14. The least variety was exhibited by *detest*, with only 14 types co-occurring with it.

Tables 3a and 3b show the relative frequency of co-occurrence between Adjunct type and process.

Table 13.3a Most frequent Adjunct types (> 1 per cent occurrence) co-occurring with Material Processes

assassinate		**execute**		**murder**		**most frequent adjuncts**	
Time	62	Time	43	Time	46	Time	50
Place	30	Place	18	Place	28	Place	26
Manner	2	Manner	17	Manner	13	Manner	8
Reason	1	Reason	9	Reason	4	Reason	7
Instrument	1	Instrument	6	Instrument	4	Purpose	4
		Accomp't	1	Accomp't	2	Instrument	3
		Duration	1	Duration	1	Duration	1
						Accomp't	1
TOTAL	96		95		98		100

Several Adjunct types, other than the commonest Adjuncts of Time, Manner and Place, co-occurred with all six processes, the most prominent of these being Reason. Many Adjunct types occurred

Table 13.3b Most frequent Adjunct types (> 1 per cent occurrence) co-occurring with Mental processes

detest		hate		loathe		most frequent adjuncts	
Degree	30	Degree	30	Degree	31	Degree	33
Manner	17	Reason	34	Time	22	Reason	17
Time	13	Usuality	17	Manner	15	Manner	12
Usuality	8	Time	6	Reason	10	Time	13
Place	8	Comparison	3	Usuality	6	Usuality	7
Duration	7	Duration	2	Place	5	Place	5
Reason	7	Manner	2	Duration	4	Duration	5
Parallel sit'n	3	Condition	1	Comparison	3	Comparison	3
Comparison	3	Place	1			Part Spec	3
Periodic freq	1					Condition	1
Condition	1					Period freq	1
TOTAL	98		96		96		100

rarely in the data and some did not occur at all. Of the 18 types which occurred with *assassinate*, for example, 13 account for 4 per cent of its circumstantiation.

Most importantly, it appears to be the case that two or three Adjunct types are extremely prominent with each process and process type, which suggests that the probabilistic nature of co-occurrence is a highly relevant phenomenon.

There also seems to be an inverse relationship between the number of Adjunct types co-occurring with a particular process and their relative frequency. The process *detest*, for example, has fewer types of Adjunct co-occurring with it in a more evenly spread distribution than *assassinate*, which has 18 types in an uneven distribution.

It is clear that the Material processes have fewer of the frequently occurring Adjunct types co-occurring with them than the Mental processes: namely eight types as opposed to eleven. Furthermore, these patterns of Circumstantiation differ in several other respects.

With Material processes, a Time Position Adjunct (e.g., *at three o'clock)* occurs in half of the clauses on average, whereas a Place Adjunct is half as likely, and Manner and Reason each make up 8 per cent of the total circumstantiation. The other Adjuncts co-occurring with Material processes are not particularly noteworthy, although the lack of variety in Temporal Adjuncts, for example, does seem surprising, with only two out of the nine types available being found.

The Adjunct type which occurred most frequently with Mental processes was Degree, with Reason and Manner occurring more often than Time Adjuncts. This latter observation suggests an important difference between the Material and Mental processes in respect of placing them in time. Interestingly, however, the Mental Processes exhibited a greater range of Time Adjunct types than did the Material processes, with Usuality, Duration and Periodic Frequency additionally being found.

13.6.3 Frequency of Adjuncts by Cardiff Grammar classification

As was discussed in section 4 earlier, Fawcett's Cardiff Grammar classification of experiential Adjuncts is based both on type (e.g., Manner, Role, Duration, etc.) and on general co-occurrence phenomena (e.g., 'Adjuncts that occur with processes with an Agent', 'Adjuncts that occur with many process types: temporal Adjuncts' etc.). We now discuss the Adjuncts found in the data according to the general co-occurrence patterns suggested by the Cardiff Grammar classification. Indeed, the substantial amount of data that is presented here may well give rise to a revision of the Cardiff Grammar classification as it currently stands.

Tables 13.4a and 13.4b show the relative frequency of Adjunct types in each Adjunct subclass co-occurring with each Process, therefore providing the most detailed view yet of which Adjunct types were found most frequently in the data and, by omission from the tables below, which did not occur at all.

When the Adjuncts are analysed by subclass in this way, and compared to Tables 13.3a and 13.3b, a number of significant tendencies emerge. For example, the centrality of Temporal circumstances for both sets of processes can be seen. Interestingly, 48 per cent of Adjuncts with *murder* are temporal; of these, 96 per cent are the straightforward Time Position Adjuncts and only 4 per cent are another temporal type, namely Duration (e.g., *for twelve hours*).

Overall, Mental processes are found with a greater range of Adjunct types from each subclass than are Material processes. In an extreme case, *murder* has only two types of Temporal Adjunct, whereas *assassinate* has six of the possible nine types in this subclass. There are also some processes which have only one Adjunct type from a particular subclass co-occurring with them, and others which co-occur with a number of types from a single subclass. In the following sections, some of the key findings on the distribution of Adjunct types in each subclass will be presented.

13.6.3.1 Temporal Adjuncts Co-occurrence

Both Material and Mental processes have Time, Repetition, Duration, Periodic Frequency and Usuality Adjuncts from the Temporal

Table 13.4a Percentage of Adjunct types by subclass co-occurring with Material processes.

Adjunct subclass	assassinate		execute		murder	
Temporal	Time	98	Time	96	Time	96
	Reduplication	1	Duration	2	Duration	4
	Repetition	0.4	Usuality	1		
	Duration	0.2	Periodic freq	0.7		
	Periodic freq	0.2	Repetition	0.3		
	Usuality	0.2				
Processes with an Agent	Manner	52	Manner	95	Manner	100
	Replacement	28	Method	3		
	Method	20	Replacement	2		
Many Process Types:	Reason	69	Reason	90	Reason	46
Quasi-Logical Relations	Purpose	25	Condition	5	Purpose	46
	Parallel sit'n	6	Purpose	2	Condition	8
			Concession	1		
			Parallel sit'n	1		
			Result	1		
Many Process Types:	Place	94	Place	69	Place	95
Others	Instrument	4	Instrument	22	Instrument	4
	Accompaniment	2	Accompaniment	5	Accompaniment	1
	Comparison	<1	Comparison	3		
			Participant spec	1		
Few Process Types	Degree	50			Exchange	100
	Exchange	50				

Adjunct subclass, whereas only Mental processes have the Ordinative Adjunct (an example would be *for the first time*).

13.6.3.2 Adjuncts that occur with Processes with an Agent Co-occurrence

In this second subclass, Manner is the only Adjunct accompanying *murder* and *detest*. It has a high co-occurrence frequency with *execute, hate* and *loathe* but occurs less frequently with *assassinate*. Replacement and Method Adjuncts are found with *assassinate* and *execute*, but not with *murder*. The Mental processes co-occur with Role Adjuncts, which are not found with the Material processes, whereas Replacement Adjuncts co-occur with this latter process type, but not with the Mental processes.

13.6.3.3 Quasi-Logical Relations Adjunct Co-occurrence

Reason Adjuncts co-occur commonly with all six processes, although with varying frequency. Within this subclass, they account for >90 per cent of Adjuncts with *execute, hate* and *loathe*, a considerably higher frequency than with the other two Material processes (69 per cent and 46 per cent respectively) and the other Mental process *detest*

Table 13.4b Percentage of Adjunct types by subclass co-occurring with Mental processes

Adjunct Subclass	Detest		Hate		Loathe	
Temporal	Time	43	Usuality	48	Time	67
	Usuality	27	Time	35	Usuality	17
	Duration	25	Duration	3	Duration	13
	Periodic freq	4	Periodic freq	4	Repetition	1.5
					Usuality	1.5
Process with an Agent	Manner	100	Manner	75	Manner	97
			Role	25	Method	3
Many Process Types: Quasi-Logical Relations	Reason	57	Reason	93	Reason	91
	Parallel sit'n	28	Condition	4	Condition	4
	Condition	10	Concession	1.5	Addition	4
	Addition	5	Parallel sit'n	1.5		
Many Process Types: Others	Place	66	Comparison	57	Place	50
	Comparison	28	Place	29	Comparison	35
	Result	5	Concurrent state	14	Accompaniment	5
					Participant spec	5
					Alternative sit'n	5
Few Process Types	Degree	100	Degree	100	Degree	100

(57 per cent). The relatively low co-occurrence in the case of *murder* might suggest that this form of killing has a lesser requirement for a reason to be provided.

Adjuncts of Purpose occur with all of the Material processes, but not with the Mental processes. Condition Adjuncts occur with all processes except *assassinate*. The Parallel situation Adjunct (*also*) occurs with *detest*, but with no other Mental process. Finally, the Addition Adjunct type (*as well as*) occurs with *detest* and *loathe*.

13.6.3.4 Adjuncts which occur with many process types Co-occurrence

In the fourth subclass, Place was the most frequent Adjunct type in the data, although, as already noted for Time, it was less in evidence with Mental processes. Instrument Adjuncts were as unsurprisingly found with the Material processes as they were absent with Mental processes. Clearly, agentive processes of killing can involve some form of instrument, whereas Mental processes, which are not physical actions, cannot. Comparison abounded with both sets of processes – an indication perhaps of the use of figurative language in texts surrounding negatively charged processes. Accompaniment Adjuncts occurred with all three Material processes and with *loathe*.

13.6.3.5 Adjuncts which occur with few process types Co-occurrence

In this final subclass, Exchange Adjuncts (e.g., *for* £100), classified in the Cardiff Grammar as occurring solely with Relational: Possession processes (e.g., *he bought it for* £100), appear to co-occur with both *assassinate* and *murder* (e.g., *assassinate the president for* $100,000). This raises the question of either the validity of the Exchange Adjunct and its Cardiff Grammar specification or, alternatively, of the classification of *for* $100,000, in the example above, as an Exchange Adjunct.

What is clear from these findings is that there are differences in the circumstantiation of Processes between, as well as within, process types and that there is a lot more which could be said about these findings. The question which arises at this point is, therefore: Why is there this variety in circumstantiation between verbs which at first glance seem to have a similar meaning?

13.7 Concluding remarks

To draw solid conclusions from these findings is a difficult task, given the fairly narrow constraints of the data. What can be clearly stated, however, are the following observations on the nature of co-occurrence between processes and their circumstances which this study has begun to reveal:

- Circumstantial Adjuncts neither occur freely with all process types nor with all members of a specific process type, even when they are closely related semantically, as in this study (i.e., *assassinate, execute, murder*, and *detest, hate, loathe*).
- There is considerable variation in the frequency of co-occurrence amongst Circumstantial Adjuncts in relation to a given process or process type. Thus given a process or process type, we may begin to predict the likelihood of the co-occurrence of one Adjunct or another.
- Certain Adjunct types appear to be uniquely or very strongly associated with either Material or Mental process types, whilst others are associated with both types.

These general findings support our hypothesis that co-occurrence between Process Types and Adjunct Types exists and, as we suggested earlier, this range of phenomena may be modelled in terms of probabilities associated with options in the lexico-grammar.

This study, we believe, as a model for further studies, based upon corpus data, has important implications for several fields to which the findings can be applied.

(a) *Language description*
The delicacy of description to which modern large-scale descriptive grammars aspire can only be achieved with the help of corpus-based data of the kind presented here. Without such data, statements on the co-occurrence relations between processes and circumstances, for example, would either have to remain at a high level of generality, or would be dangerously speculative. We have already observed that a number of statements in the current Cardiff Grammar classification of Adjuncts may well require revision on the basis of the data elicited and analysed.

Furthermore, the kinds of co-occurrence phenomena that can be observed may throw considerable light on the semantics of a language. Thus, beyond simply observing that a given process co-occurs with given circumstances rather than others, we need to ask ourselves what this may indicate in terms of the semantics of that process or the circumstances that co-occur with it.

(b) *Language teaching*
The accuracy and delicacy of description of English and any other language is clearly important in language learning and teaching. Co-occurrence phenomena, in terms of colligation and collocation, are important aspects of the development of linguistic competence, yet have received less attention than they deserved in the past, principally because of a lack of reliable information. The kind of linguistic information that corpus-based studies such as this provide must be considered an invaluable resource in language teaching.

(c) *Natural language processing*
Wherever natural language processing (generation and understanding) incorporates probabilities (as with the computationally implemented Cardiff Grammar itself), the evidence of corpus-derived frequency data is clearly fundamental in establishing the validity of probabilistic lexicogrammatical statements.

References

Aston, G. and Burnard, L. (1998) *The BNC Handbook: Exploring the British National Corpus with SARA*. Edinburgh: Edinburgh University Press.
Davidse, K. (1996) Turning grammar on itself. In M. Berry, C. Butler, R.

Fawcett and G. Huang (eds), *Meaning and Form: Systemic Functional Interpretations*. Norwood, NJ: Ablex, 367–93.

Downing, A. and Locke, P. (1992) *A University Course in English Grammar*. New York: Prentice Hall.

Fawcett, R. (in press a) *Functional Syntax Handbook: Analysing English at the Level of Form*. London: Continuum.

Fawcett, R. (in press b) *Functional Semantics Handbook: Analysing English at the Level of Meaning*. London: Continuum

Fawcett, R.P., Tucker, G.H. and Lin, Y. (1993) How a systemic functional grammar works: the role of realization in realization. In H. Horacek and M. Zock (eds), *New Concepts in Natural Language Generation: Planning Realization and Systems*. London: Pinter, 114–86.

Haegeman, L. (1994) *Introduction to Government and Binding Theory* 2nd edn. Oxford: Blackwell.

Halliday, M.A.K. (1991) Towards probabilistic interpretations. In J. Benson, M. Cummings and W. Greaves (eds), *Linguistics in a Systemic Perspective*. Amsterdam: John Benjamins, 27–51.

Halliday, M.A.K. (1994) *An Introduction to Functional Grammar* 2nd edn. London: Arnold.

Jacobson, S. (1964). *Adverbial Positions in English*. Stockholm: AB Studentbok.

Levin, B. (1993) *English Verb Classes and Alternations: A Preliminary Investigation*. Chicago and London: University of Chicago Press.

Martin, J.R. (1992) *English Text: System and Structure*. Philadelphia and Amsterdam: John Benjamins.

Matthiessen, C.M.I.M. (1995) *Lexicogrammatical Cartography: English Systems*. Tokyo: International Language Sciences Publishers.

Matthiessen, C.M.I.M. (1999) Ideational patterns in grammar and lexis: transitivity and collocations. Plenary paper presented at the 1st International Congress on English Grammar, CIEFL, Hyderabad, India.

Quirk, R., Greenbaum, S., Leech, G. and Svartvik, J. (1985) *A Comprehensive Grammar of the English language*. London: Longman.

Sinclair, J. (1987) *Looking Up: An Account of the COBUILD Project in Lexical Computing*. London and Glasgow: Collins.

Tucker G.H. (1998) *The Lexicogrammar of Adjectives: A Systemic Functional Approach to Lexis*. London: Cassell Academic.

Wierzbicka, A. (1988) *The Semantics of Grammar*. Amsterdam: John Benjamins.

Notes

1 There are some differences in terminology between the Hallidayan Framework (e.g., Halliday 1994) and the Cardiff Grammar framework. In the latter, 'Participant/Circumstantial Role' is preferred to 'Participant/Circumstance' and 'Main Verb' is taken as the element of structure at Clause level which expresses the Process.

2 Exceptionally, processes have no inherent participants (e.g., 'meteorological verbs' such as *rain*)).
3 Note that there is more of a generic 'behavioural' or 'activity' sense about such processes used in this way. Other examples would be *she cooks well, she paints all day long.*
4 An alternative analysis of processes like *behave* and *act*, as adopted by Fawcett, is to treat the obligatory Manner element as a Participant Role, precisely on the grounds that it is required by the process (Fawcett in press).

Appendix 1: The Cardiff Grammar Classification of Experiential Adjuncts

Adjunct subclass	Label	Example
1.1 ADJUNCTS THAT OCCUR WITH MANY PROCESS TYPES: TEMPORAL ADJUNCTS		
1.1.1 Time Position	**TPA**[5]	six were assassinated yesterday[6]
1.1.2 Duration	**DuA**	clerics assassinated by Islamic militants since May last year
1.1.3 Repetition	**RpA**	trying to assassinate him on a number of occasions
1.1.4 Reduplication	**RdA**	they have been assassinated one by one
1.1.5 Periodic Frequency	**PFA**	targeting and assassinating every day 27 labour leaders
1.1.6 Regularly Repeated Time Position	**RRTPA**	He read it each night last year
1.1.7 Regularly Repeated Duration	**RRDuA**	He read it for an hour each night
1.1.8 Usuality.	**UA**	and sometimes assassinated Government officials
1.1.9 Ordinative	**OA**	for the first/second/last time
1.2 ADJUNCTS THAT OCCUR WITH PROCESSES WITH AN AGENT		
1.2.1 Manner	**MaA**	promptly/vengefully/callously/mysteriously/brutally/selectively
1.2.2 Method	**MeA**	Goldman verbally assassinated both Elvis and John Lennon
1.2.3 Role	**RoA**	He gave it to us as a first instalment/ using it as a lever
1.2.4 Client	**CliA**	Ivy knitted Fred a jersey./ He bought a desk for his study
1.2.5 Please	**PleA**	Fred played Ivy a tune./Ivy played a tune for Fred
1.2.6 Replacement	**RepIA**	he was assassinated 'on behalf of the IRA' by Dutch members
1.3 ADJUNCTS THAT OCCUR WITH MANY PROCESS TYPES: QUASI-LOGICAL RELATIONSHIPS		
1.3.1 Condition	**CnA**	If/Unless/Provided (that) he goes/went there ... If so/not
1.3.2 Reason	**RsA**	**group assassinated Dr Mahgoub in revenge for more than**
1.3.3 Purpose	**PuA**	**assassinated to keep his memory savoury**
1.3.4 Result	**ResA**	they went to his house, only to find
1.3.5 Concession	**CcA**	although he's poor/in spite of his poverty/this
1.3.6 Addition	**AddA**	as well as/besides being rich/besides this
1.3.7 Parallel Situation	**PSA**	**He was also assassinated**
1.4 ADJUNCTS THAT OCCUR WITH MANY PROCESS TYPES: OTHERS		
1.4.1 Place	**PIA**	he was murdered outside his home in Amman
1.4.2 Accompaniment	**AccA**	assassinated with his wife
1.4.3 Respect	**ResA**	She helped him with the washing up. /He beats me at tennis.
1.4.4 Instrument	**InsA**	assassinate the general with a pistol
1.4.5 Comparison	**CompA**	assassinated as a 'collaborator' in 1989
1.4.6 Concurrent State	**CoStA**	(Feeling) proud of his achievement, he sat down.
1.4.7 Subsequent State	**SuSRtA**	He went home, (feeling) very much happier.
1.4.8 Participant Specification	**PtSpA**	besides/in addition to/except for Mary
1.4.9 Alternative Situation	**ASA**	instead of using a spade, he ... y
1.5 ADJUNCTS THAT OCCUR WITH FEW PROCESS TYPES: MATERIAL PROCESSES		
1.5.1 Body Part	**BPtA**	He kissed her on the nose.
1.5.2 Material	**MatA**	He made it from/out of leather.
1.5.3 Physical Cause	**PhCaA**	She died of/from cancer.
MENTAL PROCESSES		
1.5.4 Degree	**DegA**	He loves her a lot.
RELATIONAL: POSSESSION PROCESSES		
1.5.5 Exchange	ExchA	You were prepared to assassinate the President for 100k $
RELATIONAL: DIRECTIONAL PROCESSES		
1.5.6 Direction	DirA	He drove north(wards) through Watford.
1.5.7 Distance	DisA	He walked northwards (for) five miles.
1.5.8 Process Manner	PrMA	He came strolling lazily into the room.

[5] Only the highlighted Adjunct types were found in the data

[6] Bold example are from the data

Index

Entries in **bold** refer to figures/diagrams

Aboriginal children, separation from families 270, 271, 273, 274, 294, 298
abstract thinking skills 5, 47, 102
abstraction 47, 175
adjuncts 305, 306, 310, **314–316**, 317–20, **318**
circumstantial **111**–12
classification 311–12
mood 199, **110, 201**
types **109**
affect (evaluation discourse) 273, 274, 275, 280
alienation
effects on children of scientific language 258
from writing 231, 233
Allen, K. 200
appraisal
analysis of humour 300
children's history text 10, 136–40
evaluation discourse 272, 276, 277, **279, 282**
resources 13, 14, 272, 276–7, **279, 282**
appreciation (evaluation discourse) 273, 274, **275**
assessment of causal discourse *see* causal discourse
Aston, G. 308
attitude (evaluation discourse) 273, **279**, 287, **289**
Australia 7, 10
approach to KAL 151
see also Aboriginal children; Melbourne; Perth
authority *see* power

baby *see* child
Bachman, L. 262, 263
background knowledge, assumptions 9, 125–31
Bakhtin, M.M. 300
Ball, F.C. 14, 305–24
Ballard, B. 228, 247
Barnes, D. 148
Barthes, R. 134, 300
Bartholomae, D. 235, 248
Barton, D. 2
Bateson, G. 50, 56
Bateson, M.C. 20
Baugh, A.C. 175
Baynes, K. 181
Baynham, M. 231
Benson, N. 234
Bernstein, B. 5, 9, 12, 46, 49, 56, 62, 63, 67, 68, 69, 70, 89, 100, 121, 122, 191, 216–19
bias, children's history text 121–2
Biggs, I.R. 229, 247
bilingual competence 7, 13, 77, 78, 97
Bird, C. 298
Birmingham University COBUILD Bank of English Corpus 305, 308, 310, 312
Blisse, Nellie 281, 282, 283
Bloomfield, L. 175
body language, young child 20
Bohm, D. 188
Bokhorst-Heng, W. 78
Bolinger, D. 175, 186
Bolker, I. 230*g*
bonding, infant 19
Borowski, E.I. 207
Borwein, I.M. 207
Bourdieu, P. 227, 229
brain development 3, 4, 30, 33, 40, 41
discontinuity 30, 32
neurolinguistic studies 69
Bringing Them Home National Inquiry into the Separation of Aboriginal...Children from Their Families 270, 271, 273, 274, 294, 298
British National Corpus 308

Brodkey, L. 231
Bruner, J. 77
Buggy, T. 285
Bullock Report 150
Burnard, L. 308
Burridge, K. 200

Canale, M. 261, 262, 263, 264
Cardiff Grammar framework 311, 317–20, **324**
Carleton, M. 274
Carter, R. 7, 97, 146
causal discourse 13, 14, 255–69
  alienation 258
  assessment instruments, limitations 264–8, 269
  conduit metaphor 258
  communicative competence, theoretical framework 262–6
  evaluative models 260–3, **261**
  meaning construction 258–9
  SFL analysis 255, 256, **257**, 260, 263, 269
  taxonomy of competence 262–3
  Test of Written English (TWE) 264, 266, 267
  traditional grammar analysis **257**
  water cycle example 256–7, 258, 259–60
Cheah, Y.M. 239, 249
child as semiotic being 3, 4, 19–42
  birth to 18 months 21, 22
  body language 20
  material development 19, 22, 23
  mother tongue development *see* speech development; *see also* protolanguage
  and movement 4, **22**, 23, 32, 33, 34
  perspectives, changing 23, 24, 33
  semiotic development 3, 4, 19, 20, **22**, 23, 24, 29, 30, 34
  signifiers 21, 33
  signifying body 34, 35, 36, 40
  symbolic expressions 20, 22, 23
  system networks analysis 21
  young child 20
children's literature, moral/socializing function 88, 89
choice, linguistic 2
Chomsky, A.N. 307
Christie, F. 10, 49, 98, 100, 121, 145–73, 193
Christopher Columbus: The Discovery of the New World 9, 122–5
  field 122–3
  mode 124–5
  tenor 124
  visual design 134–6
Chua, B.H. 78
circumstances (corpus linguistic studies) 305, 306, 307, 310, 320
Clammer, J. 79
Clanchy, I. 228, 247
Clark, R. 233
class issues in teaching *see* mathematics discourse
classroom discourse analysis, infant primary 1, 5, 6, 47–71
  data collection 47–8
  deutero learning 50, 56 (learning to learn)
  meaning interpretation 64
  meaning orientation 62, 66, 69, 70
  mood tags, reversed polarity 61
  object of teaching 48–51
  picture reading examples 51–3, 54–5, 57–65
  power/control issues 65, 70
  production of pedagogic subject 51–7
  variant readings/interpretation 53, 54, 56
see also inference; perspective; social background; thinking
clause (KAL study) 160
Cloran, C. 48, 69
COBUILD Bank of English Corpus, Birmingham University 305, 308, 310, 312
Coffin, C. 121, 279, 281
cognitive development *see* brain development
colloquialisms 202
Columbus, Christopher (history icon) *see* Christopher Columbus: The Discovery of the New World
Comber, B. 12, 233, 238
communicative competence
  evaluative models 260–3, **261**

theoretical framework 262–6
taxonomy of competence 262–3
conjunction use
analysis 115–16
development 8
KAL study 166
teaching 166
consciousness
developing 30
higher level/higher order 4, 23, 24. 30, 33, 34, 40 *see also* speech development
primary 4, 23, 24, 30, 33, 34 *see also* protolanguage
of self 4, 35
shaping by teaching 5, 6, 47–51, 53, 55, 56, 66 *see also* thinking
control discourse *see* power
corpus linguistic studies 13, 14, 15, 305–24
adjuncts 305, 306, 310–12, **314–316**, 317–20, **318**
analysis results 313–17, **314–316**
British National Corpus 308
Cardiff Grammar framework 311, 317–20, **324**
circumstances 305, 306, 307, 310, 320
COBUILD Bank of English Corpus 305, 308, 310, 312
corpus interrogation 312–13
corpus linguistic approach, reasons 307–9
language teaching 321
manner 307
material processes 309, 310, **314**, **317**
mental processes 309, 310, **314**, **316**, **319**
natural language processing 321
nuclearity 305
participants/participant roles 305–7, 310
preferential co-occurrence hypothesis 309–10, **314**, **316**, **317**, **319**
processes 305, 306, 307, 320
relational processes 309
significant co-occurrence 308
and systemic functional linguistics 309
theta grid 307
transivity configuration 305
Coulthard, M. 48, 53
Cox Report 151
Craig, William 282, 283
crawling, infant *see* movement
critical discourse analysis 233
cultural background *see* social background
cultural development, psychological/social plane 88
culture
change 50
as false consciousness 89
learning in Singapore 76–96
maintenance 50
one language one culture policy 78
transmission through rhymes 77, 80, 88, 93
transivity system 92–3

Davidse, K. 310
Davies, B. 234
Davies, N. 9, 121, 122
Deacon, T. 69
Deakin University 151
Deane, Sir William (governor-general of Australia) 270, 271
Deckert, G. 229
declarative meaning 4, 35
deduction, logical 45, 46 *see also* inference
Derewianka, B. 98, 121, 122, 141, 257
Desired Outcomes of Education 79
deutero learning (learning to learn) 50, 56 *see also* thinking
development
material, infant 19, 22, 23
meaning *see* child as semiotic being
see also brain development; speech development
discourse, definition 1
discursive practices theory 217–19
of mathematics 219–21
semantic orientation **221**
Dixon, J. 148, 150
Donaldson, M. 46
Doughty, P. 1, 146, 147, 148, 149, 152
Downing, A. 311

Edelman, G. 30
educational
  achievement and language 12, 191, 216
  ideology 69
Edwards, A.D. 49
Eggins, S. 87, 299, 300
Einstein, Albert 177
Elbow, P. 231
Eldred, J. 237
elitism/privilege, and teaching/learning 223 *see also* mathematics discourse
Ellis, Bob 288
engagement (evaluation discourse) 273, 276
English, teaching 7, 8
  LINC programme 98
  Melbourne 146, 153–71
  Singapore **99**–101
  see also grammar; knowledge about language (KAL)
'The English Constitution,' textural evaluation 283, 284
evaluation in texturing discourse 14, 270–304
  appraisal resources 272, 276, **279**, **282**
  'The English Constitution' text 283, 284
  historical 290
  imagery and evaluation 287–90, **298**
  imagery and image 291–7, **295**
  interpersonal resources 272–7, **278**, **279**, 280, **281**
  'Khe Sanh' 289–90
  'Long March' text 284–5
  Mandela, N. autobiography 291–4
  metaphorical language 271, 288, 297, 300
  Nathaniel's Nutmeg 285–6
  news 283, **284**, 290, 291, 294, 297
  sense/sensibility 286, 298, 299
  stolen generations discourse 270, 271, 273, 274, 276, 281, 282, **295–7**, 298, 299
  texture and evaluation 283, 298–300
  themes 283, **284**, 285, 286, 289, 297
  voice dynamics 283–7
  voice/media discourse 277–83, **282**
Evans, J. 45
examinations culture 239, 250
experiential meaning, mathematics discourse 204–9, **209**

failure, educational 6, 70, 121
  and intelligence 121
  mastery of technical knowledge phase of language development 120, 121
  and motivation 121
  resistance from dominated groups 69
  under-funding 121
Fairclough, N. 1
Fawcett, R. 311
Feez, S. 154
Firth, J.R. 68
Foley, J.A. 1–15, 97–119
Foucault, M. 222
four race model 78, 79
Freebody, P. 233
Freedman, A. 151, 155
Fries, P.H. 'The English Constitution' 283, 284
Fuller, G. 231, 232, 276

Gee, J.P. 89
gender issues in teaching 12, 222 *see also* mathematics discourse
generalization, thinking skill 5, 47
generic structures, development in writing 97
genre-based approaches 97, 98, 146, 151, 155, 160, 166
genres
  lesson/curriculum, mathematics 193, **194**, 195, 196, **197**, 199, 205, 212, 217
  use of different 98
Goh, Li Wah 97
Goh Chuk Tong, Prime Minister, Singapore 78
Goom, B. 8, 9, 10, 120–42
Gopinathan, S. 79
graduation (evaluation discourse) 273, 276, 277, **279**
grammar
  analysis 107, **257**
  ideational 36
  interpersonal 36
  mood systems 37

sentence grammar/structure 169
teaching 3, 10, 11, 151, 152, 163, 168
see also knowledge about language (KAL)
grammatical metaphor 153
mathematics discourse **207**, **208**, **209**
Greenfield, S. 68, 69
Growth through English 148

Haas-Dyson, A. 251
Hacker, D. 185
Haegeman, L. 307
Halliday, M.A.K. 1, 3, 4, 14, 19–42, 56, 61, 68, 80, 88, 89, 90, 91, 92, 120, 121, 122, 140, 147, 148, 149, 153, 167, 175, 176, 177, 178, 179, 180, 186, 187, 188, 191, 192, 255, 257, 258, 262, 268, 272, 280, 283, 306, 307, 309, 310, 311
Hamilton, C. 299
Harré, R. 66
Harris, J. 100, 231
Hartnett, C.G. 11, 174–90
Hasan, R. 5, 6, 43–75, 76, 80, 89, 92, 140, 151
heterogloss (reference dialogism) 276
Hickman, M. 46
history teaching analysis 8, 120–42
appraisal in text 10, 136–40
background knowledge assumptions 9, 125–31
conclusions 140–2
density of text 125, 129, 130
hagiography 123
history specialists 122
implicit assumptions in text 121, 122, 136
implicit learning 141
incoherences/dislocations 121
national bias 121–2
national consciousness 122–3
recontextualization 123
social positioning of reader 9, 131–4
text: *Christopher Columbus: The Discovery of the New World* 9, 122–5, 134–6
writer's perspective 132–4
Ho, W.K. 78
Holland, J. 62
Hollindale, P. 89
Howard, John (Australian Prime Minister) 282, 288, 299, 300
Huber, M.B. 76
humour
appraisal analysis 300
as control mechanism 200
Hunston, S. 281, 283
Hunt, P. 88

ideational meaning, mathematics discourse 203–12
blackboard texts **207**, **208**
experiential meaning 204–9, **209**
grammatical metaphor **207**, **208**, **209**
mathematical register items **205**
operative processes 203–4
ideology 4
of education 69
and inference 43–75
Iedema, R. 279, 280
imperative meaning 4, 35
implicit
assumptions, children's history text 121, 122, 136
information 5, 69
learning 141 *see also* invisible learning
teaching 56, 58, 71
infant *see* child
inference 4, 5, 43–7
and deduction 45, 46
disembedded information 46
and experience 46
explicit/implicit teaching 56, 58, 71
given information 43–4, 46
instructional discourse/official pedagogy 46, 47, 56, 57
and intelligence 45, 46
logical 45, 46
shaping by teaching 47, 50, 51
and social perspective/ideology 5, 44, 45–7, 55, 56
survival value 43, 44
see also classroom discourse analysis; thinking
information
domain 20, 30 *see also* meaning
explicit 5
implicit 69

perception/interpretation 5, 19, 64
recognition 5
transmission 49, 50, 57
see also knowledge
institutional roles 2
instructional discourse 5, 49, 56 *see also* classroom discourse analysis
intelligence
and inference 45, 46
pupil 121
interpersonal
component 90, 107–10
distance 92
meaning 192, 198–203, **199**, **201**, **203**, 217–19
metaphor 199, 200
invisible learning 6, 7, 76–96 *see also* implicit learning
involvement (evaluation discourse) 272, 277
Ivani, R. 187
Ivanic, R. 2, 233, 246

Jacobson, S. 311
James, C.L.R. 123
Janks, H. 240
Jesperson, O. 175
Joyce, H. 154
Judd, K. 191
judgment (evaluation discourse) 273, 274, **275**, 280, **281**

KAL *see* knowledge about language
Kamler, B. 231, 232, 233, 235, 244
Kelly, P. 272, 287
'Khe Sanh,' textural evaluation 289–90
Khoo Kim Choo 76
kindergarten teaching *see* classroom discourse analysis
Kingman Report 151
Kirsch, G. 229
knowledge
acquisition 80
background knowledge assumptions 9, 125–31
nature of 50
production/interrogation 51, 56
reproduction 49, 50, 57
technical 120, 121, 128
see also information
knowledge about language (KAL) 10, 145–73
Australian approach 151
Bullock Report 150
clause 160
conjunction 166
controversy/debate 149–50, 151
Cox Report 151
curriculum design 146–7
functional elements 169
genre-based approaches 146, 151, 155, 160, 166
grammar teaching 151, 152, 163, 168
grammatical metaphor 153
historical antecedents 147–50
holistic/integrated approach 146, 163, 164
intervention 150, 151, 152
Kingman Report 151
linguistics application/role 148, 149, 150
literacy issues 152–3, 170
metalanguage/terminology 153, 154, 158, 161, 166, 167, 168
modality 158, 160
mood systems 158, 160, 164, 165
national curriculum 151
number 164, 165
ordered approach 146–7
person 164, 165
recent developments (1980s to present) 150–2
register model 151
sentence grammar/structure 169
student improvements 160
study 152–71
teachers' ignorance 153–4, 155, 157, 158, 161–2
tense 157, 159, 160, 164, 167
textbooks production/content 156–7, 163–7
theme recognition 158, 160
training for teachers 156, 157, 158, 159, 160
transition into secondary school 152
UK/Australian parallels 149
Kramer-Dahl, A. 12, 226–54
Kress, G. 92, 134, 151

Kuo, E.C.Y. 77
language
corpus studies 321
and cultural transmission 78, 87–9
development *see* speech development
evaluating use 100 *see also* evaluation in texturing discourse
evolution 40, 41
invisible learning through 7, 88
knowledge about *see* knowledge about language (KAL)
learning in Singapore 76–96
problems 120, 121
and reality construction 87, 88
spoken (dynamic view) 80
text-type teaching approach 8
written (synoptic view) 80

Language Development Project (LDP) 149
Language and Meaning textbooks 163
Lavoisier, A.-L. chemist 176, 177
Laxmi, J. 97
Lea, M.R. 232
learning
deutero 50, 56 *see also* thinking
invisible learning 6, 76–96 *see also* implicit learning
resistance to, and power relations 69
and social background *see* social background
Leckie-Tarrie, H. 179
Lee, A. 231, 232, 276
Lee, C. 7, 97–119
Lemke, J.L. 49, 121, 196, 298
Levin, B. 310
Lillis, T. 231, 248
LINC programme of English teaching 98
Linguistics and Education on Entering the Twenty-First Century. International Systemic Functional Congress (1999) 3
linguistic/s
application/role 148, 149, 150
choices 2
metalanguage 153, 154, 158, 161, 166, 167, 168
sign 33
see also language
literacy
Breakthrough to Literacy 148
critical 12
demands, Singapore 99–100
ideology 2, 3
issues 152–3, 170
multimodal approach 8
and power 237
reflection 71
literature, children's, moral/socializing function 88, 89
Lock, P. 311
logical inference *see* inference
logical meaning, mathematics discourse 209–12
'Long March,' textural evaluation 284–5
Longacre, R. 175, 185, 259, 269
Luke, A. 49, 245
Luria, A.R. 5, 45, 46, 47, 56, 57, 66, 69

McCarthy, M. 7, 97
MacNamara, J. 187
Macquarie University 47
Mandela, N. autobiography 291–4
Manne, R. 271, 279, 280, 281, 282, 283, 283
manner (corpus linguistic studies) 307
Martin, N. 148
Martin, J.R. 14, **90**, 91, 92, 98, 101, 102, 121, 124, 136, 150, 151, 154, 175, 177, 178, 179, 186, 187, 198, 200, 209, 214, 255, 258, 268, 270–304, 305, 306
Martinec, R. 300
Matalene, C. 229, 247
material domain 20, 30, 33
material processes (corpus linguistic studies) 309, 310, **314**, **317**
mathematics discourse 11, 12, 191–225
analysis implications 216–23
blackboard texts **207**, **208**
contextualization of lessons 193–8
covert lexis 199, 200, 202
discursive practices theory 217–21
elitism/privilege 223
exchange structure **199**
experiential meaning 204–9, **209**
formality 198, 201, 202

gender implications 222
genres, lesson/curriculum 193, **194**, 195, 196, **197**, 199, 205, 212, 217
grammatical metaphor **207**, **208**, **209**
ideational meaning 203–12, **205**, **207**, **208**, **209**
interpersonal meaning 192, 198–203, **199**, **201**, **203**, 217–19
lesson/curriculum genres 193, **194**, 195, 196, **197**, 199, 205, 212, 217
logical meaning 209–12
logico-semantic relations 209, **210**, 211
mathematical register items **205**
mode 215–16, 217, 219
mood adjuncts/choices 199, **201**
operative processes 203–4
pedagogical practices theory 191, 216—17
power relations/teacher status 192, 198, 199, 200, 201, 202, 203
semantic orientation **221**
systemic linguistic analysis 191, **192**
tenor of lessons 198, 202, **203**, 217, 219
Tertiary Entrance Examination results 216, 217
textual meaning 212–16
theme 212, **213**
variation in lesson structure 195–8
Matthews, C.M. 175
Matthiessen, C.M.I.M. 305, 314
meaning 19–42
causal *see* causal discourse
declarative 4, 35
development *see* child as semiotic being
experiential 204–9, **209**
ideational meaning 203–12, **205**, **207**, **208**, **209**
imperative 4, 35
instance 19
interpersonal 192, 198–203, **199**, **201**, **203**, 217–19
interpretation 5, 19, 64
language as carrier of 89
moment/momentum 19
and movement 4, **22**, 23, 32, 33, 34
orientation 62, 66, 69, 70
potential 30, 40, 41
study of 89
media discourse 277–83, **282**
Medway, P. 149, 151
Mehan, H. 49
Melbourne, Australia
English teaching study 146, 153–71
University students 162
Mencken, H.L. 175
mental processes (corpus linguistic studies) 309, 310, **314**, **316**, **319**
Mertz, E. 46
metalanguage
linguistic 153, 154, 158, 161, 166, 167, 168
scientific *see* causal discourse
metaphor
grammatical 153, **207**, **208**, **209**
interpersonal 199, 200
textual 214
Michaels, E. 275
Milton, G. *Nathaniel's Nutmeg* text 285–6
Mr Frog rhyme 6, 7, 80
children's interpretation 94
as object regulation 88
SFL analysis **81**, **82**, **83**, **84**, **85**, **86**, 87
textual features 80
transmission of cultural values/ socialization 77, 80, 88, 93
modality (evaluation discourse) 280
Mohan, B. 13, 255–69
monogloss (elide dialogism) 276
mood
adjuncts/choices 199, **110**, **201**
analysis **107**, 108, **110**, 116
evaluation discourse 272, 277
grammar of 14
socio-semiotic perspective 91
systems 37, 158, 160, 164, 165
Morgan, S. 273
Morgan, W. 227, 234, 236, 244
Mortensen, P. 237
mother tongue, transition from protolanguage 28, 29, 30, **31–2**, 35, **38**
content 40
expression 40
functional factors 33, 34
mathetic/pragmatic domain 38, **39**

proto-mood development 35, 37
proto-transivity 35
stratal factors 33–4
see also protolanguage; speech development
movement, and language development 4, **22**, 23, 32, 33, 34 *see also* child as semiotic being
Muecke, S. 273
multilingual competence 7, 13, 77, 78, 97
Myers, G. 281

Narandran, N. 97
narrative, writing 98, 101, 102, 104–7
Nathaniel's Nutmeg textural evaluation 285–6
negotiation (evaluation discourse) 272, 277
Newton, Isaac 176
nominalizations, verb-change 11, 174–90
and abstractions 175
effects 183–6
English 179–80
future trends 186–8
research analysis 180, **181, 182,** 183
scientific 176–8
Thai 11, 178–9
NTUC (National Trade Union Council) Childcare Co-operative, Singapore 6, 77, 91, 93
bilingual pre-school education 77
Nuffield/Schools Council Programme in Linguistics and Language Teaching 147, 149
Breakthrough to Literacy 148
Language and Communication 148
Language in Use 148
number 164, 165
nursery rhymes 76
and cultural values 77, 80, 88, 89, 91, 93
educational role 88
socio-semiotic perspective 89–92, **90**
see also invisible learning; *Mr Frog* rhyme

Obernstein, K.L. 88
O'Halloran, K.L. 11, 191–225
Opie, P. and I. 76
Orwell, G. 60
Osterloh, K.H. 229

Painter, C. 29, 35, 102, 141
Parmentier, R.J. 46
participants/participant roles (corpus linguistic studies) 305–7, 310
pedagogical practices theory 191, 216–17
Pennycook, A. 248
People's Association Party (PAP) 77
Perera, K. 100
person (grammar) 164, 165
perspective, individual 2, 5, 44, 45–8, 56, 57, 61–71
effect of teaching on 61–3
semantic distance **63**, 70
socio-semiotic 89–92, **90**
symbol interpretation 57–65
Perth, Australia 193 *see also* mathematics discourse
phases of language development 120, 121, 128
Phillips, J. 30
picture reading 51–3, 54–5, 57–65
Plum, G. 287
Popper, K. 50
positioning theory 66, 67
power
control issues 65, 70
explicit 69
invisibility 5, 65, 70 *see also* invisible learning
of language 2
relations/teacher status 69, 192, 198, 199, 200, 201, 202, 203
Poynton, C. 91, 198, 222, 271, 272
Prasithrathsint, A. 178
preferential co-occurrence hypothesis 309–10, **314, 316, 317, 319**
Primary School Leaving Examination (PSLE), Singapore 8
primary consciousness 4, 23, 24, 30, 33, 34 *see also* protolanguage
problem solving 5, 47 *see also* thinking skills

process writing 49
processes (corpus linguistic studies) 305, 306, 307, 320
progressive education 49
protolanguage 4, 20, 22, 23, 24
  and crawling/movement 23
  imitation 24
  intonation, use 22, 37
  limitations 29
  material to semiotic transformation **22**, 24, 29, 30
  microfunctions/domains 24
  relevant models 29
  representation 24, 28, 29, 40, 41
  signifiers 24
  stages **25–7**
  transition to mother tongue *see* mother tongue
  universal 40

Quah, J.S.T. 78
Quirk, R. 311

Read, P. 298
reading, teaching 6 *see also* Mr Frog rhyme; nursery rhymes
reasoning through language 176, 177 *see also* thinking skills
re-entrant mapping 35
reflection literacy 71
Regional Training and Resource Centre in Early Childhood Care and Education for Asia 76
regulative discourse 5, 49, 56 *see also* classroom discourse analysis
Reid, I. 151
relational processes 309
representation 24, 28, 41
  phonetic 28
  prosodic 28, 40
  stages 28, 29
Reynolds, H. 298
Rhada, teaching to write 226–54 *see also* writing pedagogy
rhetorical organization 8
rhymes, for teaching reading *see* Mr Frog rhyme; nursery rhymes
Ritchie, J. 229
Roach, Archie 287, 288
Roth, Dr Walter E. 282, 283
Rothery, J. 90, 98, 100, 101, 151, 154, 288
Rowell, P.M. 255

Saffia bte Mohammed Amin 97
Samraj, B. 97
Sawyer, W. 155
scientific
  metalanguage *see* causal discourse
  nominalization 176–8
second language competence 7, 13, 77, 78, 97
semantic distance (of differing perspectives) **63**, 70
semantic interfaces 4, 33, 34, 35, 36
semantic orientation **221**
semiotic
  development *see* child as semiotic being; *see also* brain development; speech development
  domain 20, 30 *see also* meaning
semogenic vectors 29
sense/sensibility, evaluation discourse 286, 298, 299, 300
sexuality, constructions 222
Shared Values 78
Simpson, J. 246
Sinclair, J. 308, 312
Sinclair, McH.J. 48, 53, 283
Singapore 6, 7, 76—96
  bilingual policy 78
  collective identity 77, 79, 81, 82, 83, 85, 86, 87, 93–4
  core values 78, 84
  Desired Outcomes of Education 79
  educational system 79, 80
  Housing Development Board (HDB) 79
  literacy 99–100
  Ministry of Education guidelines 98
  multiracial policy (four race model) 78, 79
  nation building 77, 79
  People's Association Party (PAP) 77, 79
  writing analysis *see* writing framework for analysis

single-sex education, gender
  stereotyping 12
Sitka, C. 288
Skeat, W.W. 175
Slade, D. 299
Slater, T. 13, 255–69
Slonim, M.B. 80
social background 48, 62, 64, 65, 71
  code 67, 68, 69, 70, 71, 89
  experience and systematic instruction
    66–70
  internalization 67, 68, 69, 94
  issues in teaching *see* mathematics
    discourse
  language community 68
  overcoming effects 69, 70, 71
  positioning theory 66, 67
  speech fellowship 68, 69
  writing pedagogy 238, 239, 240, 247,
    248, 249, 250
social distance 92, 198
social perspective *see* perspective
social roles 1, 2
  and speech systems 89
socialization, role of language learning
  77, 80, 88, 89, 93
sociogenic theory of cognitive
  development 46
sociological theory of pedagogical
  practice 191, 216–17
socio-semiotic perspective 89–92, **90**
Soosai, A. 146, 153, 154, 155, 156, 159,
  161, 163, 167
Spack, R. 229
speech functions 199
speech development 3, 4, 20, 35, 40
  grammar 21, 24, 29, 33
  and movement 4, 32, 33
  phases 120, 121, 128
  phonology 21, 33
  semantics 33
  signification levels 33
  see also mother tongue; protolanguage
speech fellowship 68, 69
speech therapy 120
spoken language, dynamic view 80 *see
  also* speech
Springsteen, Bruce 289
status *see* power
Stenglin, M. 288
Stephens, J. 88, 89, 91
Stevenson, M. 154
stolen generations discourse, textural
  evaluation 270, 271, 273, 274, 276,
  281, 282, **295–7**, 298, 299
story telling 101
Strauss, E. 181
Street, B.V. 2, 12, 231, 232
Swain, M. 261, 262, 263, 264
Sydney Metropolitan East
  Disadvantaged Schools Programme
  98
symbols, social 4
systemic functional linguistics (SFL) 13,
  77, 151, 167
  causal discourse evaluation 255, 256,
    257, 260, 263, 269
  corpus linguistic studies 309
  language learning, Singapore
    77–87
  mathematics discourse 191, **192**
  Mr Frog rhyme **81**, **82**, **83**, **84**, **85**, **86**,
    87
Systemics analysis software 191

Taylor, E.B. 80
teacher training 12
  knowledge about language (KAL)
    156, 157, 158, 159, 160
teaching
  discourse 46, 47, 56, 57
  grammar 3, 10, 11, 151, 152, 163,
    166, 168
  implicit/explicit 56, 58
  inference 47, 50, 51
  languages 321
  and perspective 61–3
  reading 6 *see also* Mr Frog rhyme;
    nursery rhymes
  Rhada 226–54 *see also* writing
    pedagogy
  text-type approach 8
  thinking skills 5, 6, 47–51, 53, 55, 56,
    66
  see also classroom discourse; English
    teaching; history teaching;
    mathematics discourse; writing
  pedagogy

tenor
  lessons 198, 202, **203**, 217, 219
  socio-semiotic perspective 90, 91
tense 157, 159, 160, 164, 167
  analysis 116
Test of Written English (TWE) 264, 266, 267
texts 1, 7
  density 125, 129, 130
  evaluation *see* evaluation in texturing discourse
Thai language 11, 178–9
Theta Grid (corpus linguistic studies) 307
Thibault, P. 21, 34
thinking skills 5, 47, 56, 58, 102
  argumentation 54, 55, 56
  deutero learning 50, 56
  logical inference *see* inference
  natural 5, 46, 47
  problem-solving 5, 47
  social perspective 45–7
  teaching 5, 6, 47–51, 53, 55, 56, 66
  see also classroom discourse; consciousness
Thompson, G. 283
Thompson, L. 6, 76–96
Threadgold, T. 151
Torbe, M. 149
Torr, J. 29, 35
transition into secondary school 152
transivity analysis **110**–11
Trevarthen, C. 19
truth 2, 44, 45, 46
Tucker, G. 14, 305–24
United Kingdom 7, 10, 149
values
  cultural 77, 88, 89, 91, 93
  individualism 78
  national, Singaporean 78, 79, 84
  transmission through literature 77, 80, 88, 89, 91, 93
  Western 78, 83
van Langenhoven, L. 66
van Leeuwen, T. 134, 300
Varghese, S.A. 97
Veel, R. 121, 255
Veltman, R. 272
Ventola, E. 180
voice 36
  dynamics 283–7
  /media discourse 279–83, **282**
  prosidic features 36, 37, 38
Vygotsky, L.S. 46, 56, 88
Wallace, C. 233, 235
Watson, K. 155
Wee Bee Geok 97
Wee Kim Wee, President 78
Weinberg, S. 177
Wells, G. 54
Wertsch, J.V. 46, 88
Westgate, D.P.G. 49
White, P. 14, 124, 276, 279
Whorf, B.L. 188
Wierzbicka, A. 310
Williams, G.C. 20, 70, 169, 170
Wong, R. 97
writing, framework for analysis, Primary Schools, Singapore 7, 8, 97–119
  abstraction, use 102
  adjunct type **109**, **110**, **111**–12
  bi/multilingual 7, 97
  conjunction analysis 115–16
  data collection 101, **102**
  genres based 97, 98
  ideational component 110–12
  interpersonal component 107–10
  lexico-grammatical anaysis 107
  logical relations analysis 112–14, **113**
  macro-level anaysis 101–2, 107
  micro-level anaysis 103, 107–16
  mood analysis **107**, 108, **110**, 116
  narrative 98, 101, 102, 104–7
  network system components **108**
  recount 98, 101, 102, 103
  schematic structure 103
  story telling 101
  syllabus 98
  tense analysis 116
  text-based approach **98**
  theme analysis **114**–15
  transivity analysis **110**–11
writing pedagogy, Singapore 12, 226–54
  advanced academic discourse 233
  alienation, from writing 231, 233
  assessment frames 238
  authority/voice 228–34, 240, 241, 242, 243, 244, 250

collective literacy autobiography assignment 234–5, 238
critical discourse analysis 233
critical reading 235–45
cultural/social background 237–40, 247–50
lexico-grammatical features 238–40
strategic action 245–50
transivity choices 240
Yee, P. 76, 97
Yew, Lee Kwan 250
Zamel, V. 229, 230
zero level learning 50, 51
Zinn, C. 279